Education
As and For
Legitimacy

Developments in
West Indian Education
Between
1846 and 1895

Education

As and For

Legitimacy

Developments in
West Indian Education
Between
1846 and 1895

M. Kazim Bacchus

Canadian Cataloguing in Publication Data

Bacchus, M. K.
  Education as and for legitimacy : developments in
West Indian education between 1846 and 1895

Includes bibliographical references and index.
ISBN 0-88920-231-1

1. Education – West Indies, British – History – 19th
century.   2. Education and state – West Indies,
British – History – 19th century.   I. Title.

LA476.B33 1994   370′.9729   C94-930417-4

Copyright © 1994

Wilfrid Laurier University Press
Waterloo, Ontario, Canada
N2L 3C5

Cover design by Leslie Macredie

Printed in Canada

Education as and for Legitimacy: Developments in West Indian Education Between 1846 and 1895 has been produced from a manuscript supplied in camera-ready form by the author.

This book is dedicated to all children in the West Indies, including my own children (Nari, Zeeda, and Fahiem) and my grandchildren (Zoie, Kostas, Maria, and George), and to the teachers in the region who made such valiant efforts over the years to provide an education to individuals from all levels of these societies.

TABLE OF CONTENTS

LIST OF FIGURES AND TABLES

LIST OF FIGURES

LIST OF TABLES

> They err who count it glorious to subdue
> By conquest far and wide, to overrun
> Large countries, and in field great battles win,
> Great cities by assault. What do these worthies
> But rob and spoil, burn, slaughter, and enslave
> Peaceable nations, neighbouring or remote,
> Made captive, yet deserving freedom more
> Than those their conquerors, who leave behind
> Nothing but ruin wheresoe'er they rove,
> And all the flourishing works of peace destroy.
> —Milton, *Paradise Regained*

Introduction

This is a study of the development of education in the British West Indian[1] colonies during the second half of the nineteenth century — from 1846 to 1895. It looks at the educational policies and the curriculum of schools during the half century following the emancipation of slaves — against the changing economic, political, and social structures of these societies. In addition, the study examines, on one side, the role education played in the social and political changes in these colonies and, on the other, analyzes the role of the state, in the development and implementation of educational policies and programmes for the region.

Contents

This book can be divided into the following three sub-sections: (1) Chapters 1-8 which deal with the provision of basic primary or elementary education throughout the region; (2) Chapters 9-11, which examine the development of secondary and tertiary education; and (3) Chapter 12, the final chapter, which provides a theoretical explanation of the main developments in education during the entire period.

This is the second volume in a proposed three-volume series on education and development of the Caribbean, from the earliest times to the mid-1940s. The first volume, entitled *The Utilization, Misuse and Development of Human Resources in the Early West Indian Colonies*,[2] traced the emergence of formal educational institutions from pre-colonial times until 1845. The present study takes off from this point and examines the factors which contributed to educational expansion between 1846 and 1895, and the contribution education made to the overall development of these societies.

The Introduction describes the changing social, economic, and political structure of British West Indian societies from 1846 to 1896, focussing on those features which affected educational developments during this period.

Chapter 1 examines the role of the elites in supporting and opposing educational expansion in the region.

Chapter 2 comments on the growing demand for education by the masses, as reflected in primary school enrollment and attendance figures, while chapter 3 identifies the major factors which affected primary school attendance, including the levy of school fees and the introduction of compulsory education. It also reviews the development of education for the children of the new immigrants, mainly East Indians, who came in as indentured workers for the sugar estates.

Chapter 4 examines the role of religious education in schools and the dominant position which it occupied in their instructional programmes.

Chapter 5 deals with the efforts made to introduce an industrial education at the primary level. It reviews and assesses the outcomes of the *Kay Shuttleworth Report* and examines the reasons why its proposals were not really implemented, despite the extensive support which existed for this type of education among the elites.

Chapter 6 deals with other issues in the curriculum, such as the teaching of the English language and the contribution of education to the political socialization of the young. It also reviews other efforts at broadening the curriculum of the primary schools — beyond the 3Rs — and examines the effect of the system of inspection on the quality of the instruction provided. Finally, it draws attention to the condition of the primary school buildings and the adequacy of the educational materials available to teachers.

Chapter 7 is concerned with the supply of primary school teachers and their status and remuneration, especially as compared to other occupational groups in these societies at the time.

Chapter 8 concludes this section by reviewing the various developments in primary education during the period. It also attempts to examine the impact which schooling had on both the pupils' cognitive development and improvements in the quality of life in the local communities.

Section 2 includes chapters 9, 10 and 11, which deal with the development of "higher" education.[3]

Chapter 9 traces the increasing provisions being made for secondary and tertiary education, while chapter 10 examines the curriculum of the two main types of secondary educational institutions which emerged in the British West Indies — the model or senior primary schools and the secondary grammar schools. Chapter 11 concludes the section by discussing the role which these higher levels of education played in aiding the upward social mobility of the coloured and the black population.

Chapter 12, which is the final section, presents a theoretical interpretation of the overall developments in education in the region during the period under review.

Limitations

One of the major limitations of the study is that it attempts to cover educational developments in the various West Indian colonies over half a century which in part caused the book to focus on their similarities rather than on their differences. To supplement the present effort, studies which deal with the development of education in each of these colonies are needed. One example is Professor Carl Campbell's work,[4] now in press, which examines the expansion of educational services in Trinidad.

The second limitation is that the study draws heavily from official publications, although these were supplemented by information from primary source materials, documents, reports, and research done by various historians and educators on specific aspects of education in the West Indies. The continuing work of the missionaries and the education of girls are topics which could have been given more attention in a study of this nature. But since it covers so many colonies over such a long period, it could not have dealt fully with every aspect of their educational development.

When an initial study of such a wide-ranging topic as this is undertaken, the researcher has to be selective about materials that are to be examined in some detail. The hope is simply that these proposed three volumes will be a stimulus for scholars to engage in more specialist studies of education in particular fields in the different countries of the region.

Finally, as indicated above, this is the first book of its kind which has attempted to give an overall picture of educational developments in the British West Indies between 1846 and 1895. It was therefore necessary to include much data which could have otherwise been referred to, if there were other published materials dealing with some of the topics covered in the individual chapters.

Notes

1   The "British West Indies" often refers to the former British-owned islands in the Caribbean — Jamaica, Barbados, Trinidad, the Windward and the Leeward Islands. To these are sometimes added the former colonies on the mainland — British Guiana (now Guyana) and British Honduras (now Belize) and occasionally the Bahamas and Bermuda. In this study, the term "British West Indies" is used to include all these countries.

2   M. Kazim Bacchus, *The Utilization, Misuse and Development of Human Resources in the Early West Indian Colonies* (Waterloo, ON.: Wilfrid Laurier University Press, 1990).

3   The term "higher education" was often used in early West Indian societies to refer to any education beyond the basic primary schooling.

4   Carl Campbell, *The Young Colonials: A Social History of Education in Trinidad and Tobago 1834-1939* (Mona, Jamaica: Institute of Social and Economic Research, in press).

ACKNOWLEDGEMENTS

This study benefited tremendously from the assistance of many organizations and individuals. I would like to thank all of them, even though I can mention only a few. First, I would like to express my gratitude to the University of Alberta, in particular to the Faculty of Education and its former Dean, Dr. R. S. Patterson, for the moral support and the leave granted to me at various times which made it possible for the research work for this study to be undertaken.

In addition, my thanks go out to Dr. Carl Campbell, Professor of History at the University of the West Indies (UWI) Mona, Jamaica, one of the foremost authorities on the history of education in the region. He read an earlier draft of the manuscript and made constructive suggestions for its improvement, where this was found to be necessary. Dr. Bridget Brereton, Senior Lecturer in West Indian history at the St. Augustine campus, UWI, and Dr. Hilary Beckles of the Cave Hill campus, UWI, also kindly read and commented on the manuscript. Dr. Ruby King, Senior Lecturer in Education at the Mona campus of the University of the West Indies, who is also a specialist in the history of education in the region, did a thorough job reviewing and editing the manuscript for me. She also made many valuable suggestions for its improvement.

Among others who contributed, in one way or another, to the book were Dr. Carlos Torres, Dr. Nick Kach, Kelly Murphy, Linda Schulz and Dr. Robert Carney of the University of Alberta and Dr. R. Cowen of the Institute of Education, London. Dr. Torres, now at UCLA, was a former colleague of mine, and in our frequent discussions on education in the developing countries continually emphasized the importance of the changing role of the state in influencing the formulation and selective implementation of educational policies and programmes. Our discussions also centred on the conflicting demands which every state must face in trying to establish or reaffirm its legitimacy, and at the same time foster capital accumulation for further economic growth.

Dr. Kach, of the Department of Educational Foundations, Faculty of Education, University of Alberta, edited an early draft of the manuscript as did Kelly Murphy and Linda Schulz, my research assistants.

My wife also assisted me not only by putting up with my frequent absences from home to collect data for the project, but also by gathering materials, especially from the British Museum in London, and by doing some basic calculations required for the various figures presented in the book.

Last, but not least, I must thank the Social Science and Humanities Research Council of Canada for the financial support which it provided for the research work, the University of the West Indies for nominating me for the T.H.B Symons Senior Fellowship in Commonwealth Studies and to the Association of Commonwealth Universities for granting me the award. This made it possible for me to spend some months in the West Indies discussing the manuscript with scholars in the region. In addition to their help I would like to record my thanks to the many students who wrote theses on issues dealt with in this book, and to whose work I have tried to make appropriate references. While these individuals contributed in various ways to this study, the analysis and conclusions are entirely the responsibility of the author.

This book has been published with the help of a grant from the Social Science Federation of Canada, using funds provided by the Social Sciences and Humanities Research Council of Canada.

M. K. Bacchus,
Professor, Faculty of Education, and
Director, Centre for International Education and Development,
University of Alberta, Edmonton, Alberta, CANADA

SOCIO-ECONOMIC AND POLITICAL CHANGES AFFECTING EDUCATIONAL DEVELOPMENTS IN THE BRITISH WEST INDIES, 1846-95

That your petitioners are deeply impressed with the conviction that the colonial policy of England has for many centuries been fraught with tyranny and injustice towards the mass of the people. That by far the greater number of our colonies have been originated by means, in no way justifiable on principles of morality; and to establish and secure which, have millions of pounds been wasted, and millions of our brethren been doomed to an untimely end. That when by their sacrifices they have been secured, instead of regarding them as auxiliaries to the progress of civilization, and teaching them the most efficient means of developing their natural resources so as to promote the general welfare of humanity, we seem to have considered them as legitimate objects of our prey, or as places where the shoots and underlings of despotism might practise their oppression, shameless and regardless of consequences.

—An Address "To The Peoples Of Canada" from the
London Working Men's Association, 1837, U.K.
William Lovett

Introduction
The social structure of the British West Indian societies resulted from a number of forces and events which in turn influenced the development of their educational systems. These included their colonization by different European powers, their experience of slavery, the domination of their economies by a single export crop, i.e., sugar, the introduction of indentured labourers following the abolition of slavery, and the development of a stratification system based on race, colour, and caste. There were major economic, political and social changes which occurred between 1846 and 1895 which also affected the nature of the education that was provided in the region. Some of these are identified below.

Economic Changes Following the Decline of the Sugar Industry
Probably the most important economic change to occur during this period was the decline in the prosperity of the sugar industry, then the main economic activity of the region. This was due to a marked drop in sugar prices and in the demand for West Indian sugar following the decision of the British government to withdraw its preferential treatment of the commodity. In addition, the production of subsidized beet sugar by Europe increased, and West Indian sugar was unable to compete in price with either slave-grown sugar from Brazil and Cuba or bounty-fed beet sugar from Germany.

The industry therefore experienced a fairly steady decline during this half-century. Between 1850 and 1895, the share of Caribbean sugar imported into Britain, as a percentage of all sugar imports (cane and beet) dropped from 85% to 10%.[1] Further, during the last 30 years of the century the amount of West Indian sugar shipped to Britain dropped from 3.7m. cwt. to 0.8m. cwt. — a decrease of about 73%. Sugar exports as a percentage of the total agricultural production of the British West Indies also declined from about 60% to 14.7%.

In addition, the price of West Indian sugar dropped by about 47% — from 22s. 6d per cwt. to 12s. per cwt. from 1834 to 1890. These related factors — a fall in sugar prices and a marked decline in sugar production — reduced the number of sugar plantations from 2,000 to 800 between 1834 and 1890, leading to a substantial drop in the revenues collected by the governments of the region, which obviously affected their ability to meet the increasing popular demand for such services as education. However, a valuable new market was eventually found in the USA during the 1870s, and Canada, too, began to purchase cane sugar from the Caribbean in fluctuating though steadily increasing quantities.

British policies towards West Indian sugar gave the impression that the metropole had abandoned these colonies because, with its focus on "free trade," some new decisions were taken which adversely affected the prosperity of the region. As Waddell pointed out, "the British sugar islands were no longer assured of privileged treatment [from Britain] and from being an important element in a commercial empire they became an almost superfluous adjunct to the workshop of the world."[2]

In a letter to the *Times* in 1848, one J. M. Higgins commented on the hypocrisy of the British government in its policy towards the West Indies by noting that, "We ruin our colonies because slavery is so horrible, and buy our sugar from Brazil because slave produce is so cheap."[3]

But while sugar production did not expand after the 1840s, it nevertheless remained the most important economic activity of these colonies, and exports of sugar and rum still far outweighed the value of other exports from the region. For example, in 1841 sugar and rum together made up about 85% of the value of all agricultural products exported from Jamaica. However, by 1865 these two items were responsible for over half of the export earnings of the region. Thus while the fortunes of some West Indian planters were declining, those who remained in operation still played a key role in the economic life of these societies.

Among the changes which accompanied the decline in sugar production were the following:

1. The sugar crisis bankrupted many of the London merchants on whose credit West Indian planters depended. To ensure the safety of their capital investment and credit, the remaining merchants often set up partnerships with the local planters, which gave them a more direct interest in the production and marketing of sugar. These London financiers were usually in a position to exert a direct influence on the British government's policies towards the region.

2. The fluctuations in sugar prices resulted in a decline in the standard of living of West Indians. During the half-century covered by this study, the planters tried various means to restore the profitability of sugar, but they met with little success. As a result the wages of the black workers

were often slashed by half to reduce the cost of production;[4] for example, in 1846-47 planters lowered the wages of their estate workers by 50% in Antigua, 60% in Trinidad, and 25% in Barbados and British Guiana.[5] In 1847, Cox wrote to the governor of Antigua about the "effect of the diminution of wages on the labouring classes" and suggested that while workers had so far been able to "sustain the pressure of this calamity [i.e., the declining wages] without much physical injury . . . it is impossible for it to continue without serious evils of every description."[6] In 1860 many inhabitants of the region were becoming poorer, except possibly, some of the small-scale farmers.

3. Declining sugar prices also reduced the amount of revenues collected by the West Indian governments. For example, in 1848 the Trinidad treasury was reported to have been empty, making it more difficult for Harris to implement his proposed educational reforms. The revenues received by the government of the Bahamas were reduced by two-thirds between 1864 and 1872. After the American Civil War, St. Vincent and Tobago also faced a deep financial crisis. Jamaica, too, was confronted with financial difficulties, though it was later in a better position economically, due to its export earnings from bananas and coffee. However, while colonial revenues were below expenditures in the 1860s, this situation began to change somewhat between the 1880s and 1890s.

In a review of the impact of the worldwide economic situation on the economy of the Caribbean, it was noted that "the period 1873 to 1896 was characterized by a deep structural crisis in the development of modern capitalism." In addition to "short-term fluctuations, prices of industrial and agricultural goods moved consistently downwards, and were actually lower at the end of the nineteenth century than they were at mid-century."[7] As a result, the West Indian economies suffered heavily because the prices of the local exports fell more steeply than the prices of their principal imports.

4. Some of these colonies also experienced problems with the supply of labour because of the substantial exodus of the ex-slaves from the sugar estates. Many of these labourers sought the opportunity to earn a livelihood outside the plantations, partly due to their detestable experiences with estate work during the days of slavery and the poor wages often offered by the sugar planters. Some became small-scale farmers, thereby securing an alternative source of livelihood and a certain degree of economic independence.

One outcome was a substantial increase in the number of peasant holdings. Those in Jamaica rose by over 88% between 1845 and 1861, while in British Guiana, the number of ex-slaves who owned land almost tripled between 1842 and 1848. When W. G. Sewell of the *New York Times* visited the British West Indies in 1859, he observed that a considerable number of ex-slaves were owners of land. In Jamaica alone there were 50,000 small proprietors, while in Barbados, the number of freed slaves owning five acres of land or less had more than tripled between 1844 and 1859. New villages were also established in Trinidad, though in the Lesser Antilles and Barbados there was little arable land available for peasant settlements.

In 1847 the Poor Law Commission noted that only a small number of locally born blacks were living in villages, but by 1881 there "were comparatively few living on the estates. The village lands are cultivated now to a great extent, and a great many people are engaged in growing provisions."[8] However, despite their low wages, many of the ex-slaves kept on working part-time on the plantations to earn the cash needed to purchase other commodities and to pay the high rents for the land they cultivated.

The decline in the sugar industry also encouraged attempts at crop diversification. This resulted in the production of bananas, cocoa, spices, arrowroot, ginger, coffee, limes, pimento, rice, coconuts, honey, fustic, arrowroot and logwood. External markets for these commodities began to develop, with banana production affording new economic opportunities for the peasantry in many of these islands. After the first banana export from Jamaica in 1869, the cultivation of this crop rapidly spread throughout the region because of the use of refrigeration, which allowed a trans-Atlantic banana trade to emerge. Between 1884 and 1901 the number of stems of bananas exported from the region increased by more than six times.

Rice production also began to assume increasing importance in British Guiana after 1853. Cotton production in the Bahamas, Grenada and St. Vincent was revived between 1860 and 1875 but it began to decline afterward, reducing to almost a trickle during the remainder of the century. Even coffee production started to fall around this period, especially after 1895, although there was again some small-scale tobacco production. Fruit exports improved somewhat after the mid-1880s, as did the production of pimento, arrowroot, sisal, cocoa and spices.

The diversification of agricultural production brought about relative prosperity for some of these farmers. In addition, interest in more progressive farming began to develop as various West Indian governments made extension services available to the small-scale farmers through the establishment of local departments of Agriculture.

However, these peasant farmers made up a relatively small percentage of the black labour force because the local planters sought every means, especially during the early post-emancipation period, to prevent the ex-slaves from withdrawing their services from the sugar estates. To this end, the occupancy of estate house plots was often made dependent on the tenants' willingness to provide labour on a regular basis for the plantations. In addition, the estate owners usually charged high rents for plantation houses and provision grounds from those who no longer worked for them and quickly evicted individuals who were unable to pay their rents. They destroyed hogpens, provision grounds and fruit trees, killed and maimed animals belonging to the ex-slaves, forbade fishing in the canals of the sugar estates, and in other ways attempted to restrict opportunities for occupational mobility among the black population. Some planters even refused permission to the freed Negroes to cultivate the arable lands, nearly all of which were under their ownership and control. In British Guiana, they demanded exorbitant prices from the ex-slaves who tried to purchase land.[9] But these measures were not always very effective, especially in those colonies such as Jamaica, Trinidad and British Guiana, where the workers had access to some other cultivable land.

It was sometimes argued that the ready availability of land in some colonies contributed to the idleness of the ex-slaves, to their indifference to working for wages, and to the extortionate prices which they were said to have been charging for their labour. This added to the indignation of the employers, who decried the increasingly independent attitude of the black population which some of them saw as an outcome of formal education. They therefore suggested that, if the ex-slaves wanted education for their children, they should meet its full cost by working for wages.

There were many problems created by the emergence of this new group of peasant farmers. The conflict of interest which developed between them and the plantation owners over the appropriate use of available land continued without resolution and this, according to Beckford, resulted in the persistent poverty which has characterized life among the West Indian peasantry ever since.[10] Other ex-slaves who left the sugar estates sought alternative employment. Some men became small-scale traders, and those who had received craft training set themselves up as skilled artisans, earning a larger income than workers on the sugar estates. The women were employed as domestics or did sewing, made handicrafts, or sometimes even became petty shop-keepers.

The rise of this independent group of workers often meant that their children could help with the new economic enterprises, such as the cultivation of the family farm. This obviously increased the opportunity cost to the families of sending their older children to school on a regular basis, because it meant that school attendance reduced the economic contribution that they could make to the family. But this was a challenge which the parents faced, since jobs, including part-time and seasonal jobs, were usually available for their children on the sugar estates. The independence which those working as private entrepreneurs enjoyed possibly helped to develop in them a greater desire for social and economic advancement of their children. This had an effect both on the level of enrollment and the regularity with which their children attended school.

5. In some colonies there was a substantial exodus of workers from the sugar estates which was later followed by the emigration of labourers from the region to Panama. This began in the 1850s and was revived in the 1880s with the construction of the Panama Canal. Around the same time, others left for Costa Rica and Cuba. Whites from the region were also leaving in large numbers. For example, their number in Montserrat had dropped by about 85% between 1805 and 1851. A similar decline occurred in most of the smaller islands. This usually meant a loss of managerial and supervisory skills for the sugar industry.

The resulting drain on the estate labour force brought about a tremendous push for the importation of indentured workers. This was considered necessary, not only to replenish the sugar estate labour force, but also to keep the wages of estate labourers low. As K.O. Laurence has pointed out,

> Initially the planters sought immigrants in Europe and the Portuguese Atlantic islands. Many believed that white immigrants might supply a middle class for the West Indies and set an example of industry to the Negroes; some thought that with the removal of the social pressures of a slave society it would be possible to create a white labouring population. In Jamaica it was thought that white settlers and labourers might be used to occupy the higher, cooler areas of the interior, thus forcing the

Negroes into the lower, sugar growing regions and generally reducing the area of land available for them to occupy.[11]

The initial attempts to import European immigrant labourers were not very successful. While some Africans were also brought in, the major thrust was to obtain Asian indentured labourers, especially from India and China. A system of assisted immigration, which was started soon after emancipation, continued until 1917, and the largest group of indentured labourers came from the Indian sub-continent. Chinese immigration to British Guiana and other West Indian colonies reached its peak in the early 1860s and ceased in 1866, while the number of Portuguese labourers brought in was numerically insignificant. But, in the case of East Indians, Eric Williams noted that, "no fewer than 238,000 Indians were introduced into British Guiana, 145,000 into Trinidad, 21,500 into Jamaica, . . . 1,550 into St. Lucia, 1,820 into St. Vincent, 2,570 into Grenada."[12] This immigration was terminated in St. Vincent in 1880, in Grenada in 1885, and in St. Lucia in 1893, but continued elsewhere, especially in Trinidad and British Guiana, until 1917.

The cost of immigration was largely borne by the colonial governments, which in fact meant that the local legislatures were subsidizing the labour on the sugar estates. Some colonies were even spending much more on immigration than on education. For example, in 1896, Trinidad spent £51,798 on its Immigration Department and only £38,248 on education for the entire population. Similarly, British Guiana spent £41,728 on immigration in 1895-96 and only £26,509 on education.

The arrival of such large numbers of East Indians, especially in British Guiana and Trinidad, brought into the West Indies a markedly different ethnic group who attempted to maintain their cultural distinctiveness. They were fairly successful in doing so, particularly in the two colonies where their numbers were quite substantial. However, in the other colonies they became almost totally integrated in the Creole culture. Since the new immigrants were non-Christians, their presence in these colonies changed the religious composition of the West Indian population, especially in Trinidad and British Guiana.

Little or no provision was initially made for the education of the children of these indentured labourers. But, when such provisions became available toward the end of this period, the suitability of the education offered to the educational and cultural needs of their children sometimes came in for criticism. This education was often aimed at deculturalizing and Christianizing the East Indians who were mainly Hindus and Muslims.

Conflicts often developed between these indentured labourers and the emancipated Negroes, who were placed in a weaker position in bargaining for wages with the estate authorities due to the competition they faced from the new immigrants. However, in some islands like Barbados where, due to the unavailability of additional arable land, the freed slaves had to continue in their role as estate labourers, no Asian immigration took place.

The economic difficulties which these colonies faced also had a direct effect on the provision of educational facilities in the region. With the termination of the Negro Education Grant in 1845 and the reduction in the financial assistance formerly provided by the missionary societies abroad for education in the region, the local legislatures were increasingly approached to help meet the cost of operating schools. However, with the deteriorating economic situation, the legislatures were often unable to provide the level of aid being requested. By the 1880s, the financial resources of the West Indies were so limited that the 1882-83 Royal Commission on the financial conditions in these colonies recommended that the various governments undertake a substantial reduction in their expenditures.

In addition, parents were expected to absorb an increasing share of the cost of their children's education. But with the substantial decline in their wages, many could not afford the school fees, not to mention the purchase of school clothes, or the opportunity cost of keeping their older children in school. Low school enrollments and average attendance resulted from this situation. Further, the emigration of whites from the region adversely affected the ability of the smaller islands to sustain any educational institution other than the public primary schools. They could not afford to provide support for secondary schools or even a regional post-secondary institution. When attempts were made to establish secondary schools in the smaller islands, the number of parents who could afford to pay for this level of education was so limited that the institutions were often not economically viable and could only be sustained by a substantial injection of public funds — which had, in any case, become scarce. The outcome of the difficult economic situation which these colonies faced was partly reflected in the almost annual fluctuations in their education budgets, although there was a tendency for these to rise during the last decade of the nineteenth century.

The Continued Dominance of Planters in West Indian Societies
The changes which took place in the distribution of political power also had an impact on the provision of educational services in these colonies. The plantation owners originally exerted almost total economic and political control over these societies and, while there was some change in this situation after emancipation, the planters and the merchant class continued to form a closely knit oligarchy that directed nearly all the activities of the West Indian state in their own interest. Writing about this situation in Jamaica, Ryall noted that the pattern of legislation on that island, at least up to the time of the Morant Bay Rebellion in 1865, "was an attempt to maintain the supremacy of the old planter class."[13] Because of this, the local legislatures which they controlled were at times in conflict with the governor and the Colonial Office over the enactment of legislation, especially those geared to improving the educational and social conditions of the masses.

However, some non-whites gradually began to share political power with the traditional white ruling groups. For example, in Dominica, coloured individuals came to dominate the local legislatures after 1845. Montserrat returned 12 members to the legislative assembly in 1850, six of whom were white and six coloured. In some cases, the coloureds were in a position to elect a majority of the members in the local legislative assemblies but so entrenched was the idea that the whites were superior, especially at governing the country, that voters usually exercised the franchise in their favour. Writing on this issue as late as the 1890s, Stark pointed out that, with the "property and educational qualifications" needed for enfranchisement, "the whites would continue to be the governing race; for, as a rule, the coloured people and Negroes who possessed property would vote with the whites, in the interest of law and order."[14]

With an emergent black and coloured middle class, there was a mounting fear that if the existing representative systems of government remained in place political power in these colonies would eventually fall into the hands of the blacks. This was viewed as a threat to the supremacy of the whites, who therefore continued to oppose the advancement of non-whites. This was particularly marked in islands with a larger resident white population such as the Bahamas, Bermuda, Barbados and Jamaica. For example, in 1855 the white residents of Marsh Harbour in the Bahamas refused to send their children to school because the person appointed as teacher was a black man.

The white minority retained much of their dominance over these colonies, still controlling the "commanding heights" of the local economies, even though a few coloured groups began to vie with them for representation in the local assemblies. Most local legislative assemblies, therefore, represented the interests of a small disgruntled oligarchy, bitter at the betrayal by the British government for abolishing slavery. Some whites became almost disloyal to Britain and were "indisposed to take an interest in the welfare of any class but their own and utterly unwilling to permit taxation to the benefit of the Negroes,"[15] including taxation to provide education for the masses. As Thomas pointed out, "the ruling groups were, by-and-large, single-minded in the use of the state machinery to buttress their authority and consolidate the dominance of the plantation-based cash crop economy. The state actively opposed the rise of both the free labour system and the peasantry."[16]

The negative attitude of the planters to the masses was generally seen in the indifference of the local legislatures to measures aimed at helping to improve the general welfare of the population. Earl Grey, the secretary of state for the colonies, writing in 1853, observed that over the preceding six years in the West Indies, there were no laws enacted which were "calculated to improve the condition of the population and to raise them in the scale of civilization."[17] In 1861 Sewell suggested that the people in Jamaica were not adequately instructed,

> since the planters' policy has been to keep the people uninstructed, and the government has never even encouraged education, much less insisted upon it, as one of the most important of reciprocal duties between a free state and its citizens. . . . It is estimated that there are 65,000 children in Jamaica between the ages of five and fifteen, and for their education the Legislature voted last year the sum of £2,950 — less than a shilling for the instruction of each child during a space of twelve months. About 7,000 scholars were benefited by this grant.[18]

Further, even though they acquired their wealth from the region, the white planters were usually unwilling to leave any of it for the improvement of the local black population. As late as 1877, when the principal proprietor in St. Vincent died, he left £200,000 for distribution among London charities and hospitals and only a paltry £10,000 to endow a ward in a local hospital. Commenting on this incident, Root observed, "This was all that was considered necessary to leave to the place whence all his wealth was derived. Yet this is one of the most generous benefactions in which the black population can claim any share."[19]

Constitutional Changes

However, the direct interventions by the Colonial Office sometimes helped to modify the situation. The British government, intent on protecting its own long-term interest in the region, became increasingly unhappy with the representative form of government in most of these colonies. Key officials at the Colonial Office generally accepted the view of Henry Taylor, who argued that elected assemblies were unsuitable in societies where "property and knowledge were not widely diffused" because this was likely "to lead to government by an irresponsible oligarchy of either black or white."[20] The British government's solution to this problem was to propose the adoption of the Canadian pattern of government as set out in the *Durham Report*, which meant local assemblies giving up some of their powers, especially those dealing with finance. In general, the Crown wanted to become the controlling authority "until education and property were sufficiently diffused to ensure that a representative system [of government] would be reasonably responsible and democratic."[21]

The Colonial Office seized every opportunity, following the Morant Bay Rebellion of 1865, to have the constitution of these colonies changed and replaced by Crown colony government. Under this system the ultimate authority rested with a British minister of the Crown, whose will was to be implemented by the colonial governor. The surrender of financial control of a colony was sometimes extracted in exchange for the British government's guarantee of a loan. After 1865, the Colonial Office was able to persuade Jamaica's legislature to abolish itself and hand over its powers to the British government, in order that political power would not fall into the hands of the rising black and coloured middle class.

Similar constitutional changes occurred in the other British West Indian colonies, and the year 1865 was often seen as marking the end of the full and almost unlimited exercise of constitutional power by the planters. By the 1870s the change to Crown colony government had occurred in most of these colonies, though, again, political power was not shared with the rising coloured and black middle class. Instead, control rested in the hands of the governor, over whose decisions the planters still had considerable influence. Even in Barbados, which was allowed to keep an all-elected Assembly, a compromise constitutional change occurred in 1881.

It was the rise to prominence by the local blacks and the possibility that they might want to manage the affairs of these colonies which prompted the imperial government to reduce the constitutional status of these colonies. Both legislative and executive powers were transferred to the governor, who nominated individuals to serve in the local legislative assemblies. The "chosen few" were those most likely to protect and preserve British, and to a large extent planter, interest. The change in the constitution of these colonies, therefore, gave the Colonial Office and the governor a more direct responsibility for all local legislation, including those dealing with education. The white planters, on the other hand, through their influence on the power structure in Whitehall and on the local administrative elite, continued to exert strong influence on policy decisions made, either locally by the governors, or externally by the Colonial Office.

On the other hand blacks often had little direct influence on the new legislative process. Under the representative form of government and with the weakening economic position of the planters, it was becoming easier for the better-educated non-whites to challenge effectively some of the actions of the plantocracy. But with the Crown colony system, their ability to influence the ruling authorities was seen as minimal. As a result, Crown colony government was accompanied by some degree of resentment on the part of the upwardly aspiring coloureds and blacks. This growing dissatisfaction with the political decision-making process was an underlying factor in the unrest which occurred simultaneously in the 1880s in Jamaica, Trinidad and British Guiana.

Disendowment of the Church of England

Another development in most of the region was the disendowment and the disestablishment of the Church of England in all territories, except Barbados. A step in this direction was probably made easier because the British Parliament had, in 1868, terminated the provision of stipends from the UK Consolidated Fund for any clergyman, catechist or schoolmaster appointed to the West Indian colonies. In Jamaica the money saved by disestablishing the Church of England was said to have been used to pay for a "better education" through the "new system" of grants to schools, that was introduced — one based on the "efficiency rather than the religious doctrine of the school master."[22] Nevertheless, the money that became available was still "hopelessly inadequate"[23] for the task at hand.

The disestablishment of the Church was carried out in most of the other colonies, and by 1874 Dominica and the Virgin Islands abolished the payment of salaries to Anglican clergymen. There was also growing concern for equality in the distribution of government funds among the various denominational groups providing elementary education, and the disestablishment of the Church of England paved the way for a change in this area also.

Changes in Social Structure: Social Mobility among Coloureds and Blacks

While the white planters and merchants continued to occupy the topmost rungs of the social and economic ladder, an increasing number of coloureds and blacks filled white-collar and skilled jobs as teachers, catechists, postmasters, policemen, and artisans. Some even became clergymen, merchants, barristers, magistrates, merchants, and members of the local legislative assemblies. In 1847 Governor Higginson noted that in Dominica, the "former invidious distinctions founded on colour or descent are fast disappearing everywhere, and that the justice of measuring men of all origins by the true standard of moral worth and propriety of conduct is almost universally recognized."[24]

In that year it was also reported that members of the black population in Nevis were occasionally seen riding "their own horses" to work, while a few years later, Governor Grey of Jamaica declared that

> There is no place in the world perhaps, where there is now
> less tenacity than in Jamaica of those distinctions which

are so marked elsewhere, to keep the African, the Mixed and the European races separate; to a considerable extent the amalgamation of all the races, which to the citizens of the United States appears to be impossible, may gradually and slowly come to pass.[25]

In British Guiana, "very few of the mixed or coloured races . . . were still engaged in field work by the 1850s, and many of them were pursuing trades such as coopers, carpenters, tailors, wood-cutters, sailors etc."[26]

The non-whites who had moved into some of these lower level "white-collar" jobs developed even higher occupational and educational aspirations for their children, especially since they were in a better position to contribute to the cost of this education. Below them were the masses of black workers who usually held unskilled jobs or cultivated small agricultural plots, growing crops, partly for their own consumption and to meet their need for cash. Finally, there were the new, indentured immigrant labourers who were brought in to work on the sugar estates and who tended to occupy the lowest rung of the social and occupational hierarchy.

The planters made every effort to maintain the traditional hierarchical structures of these societies but, increasingly, factors other than race, such as wealth, education, political influence, speech, and culture gradually became important in social differentiation in the West Indies. As a result, the total domination by the whites of the white-collar occupations came to be modified in these changing economic circumstances. This led to an erosion of some of the barriers that traditionally separated them from the non-whites.

In colonies like Dominica, Montserrat and Nevis, for example, coloured men began to play an important part in public affairs and, as indicated earlier, even assumed control over the local legislatures. In Jamaica, the coloureds were becoming a "powerful political" element and in St. Kitts and Antigua their increasing influence caused some anxiety among the white elite. The coloureds began to acquire property, held most of the clerkships that were available, and were also occupying an important place in the professions. The whites still held supervisory positions on the sugar estates, but by 1865, the coloureds dominated the lower and middle-level jobs in the public service of some of these colonies. The rise in their social and economic influence often encouraged the steady departure of white doctors, lawyers, clerks, and craftsmen, whose positions the coloureds eventually filled.

Some blacks also made substantial economic progress, and it was even alleged that many of them were even enjoying a standard of living higher than English workers in a comparable position. Harvey and Brevin, writing around 1866 about the situation in Jamaica, observed that there were certain districts where the advance made by some blacks, "in property, education, morals and intelligence . . . [was] so marked, as to excite wonder and admiration in those who . . . [could] recall the moral and physical aspects of an enslaved community." Further, of the 400,000 blacks in the colony, 60,000 had become freeholders, and "had accumulated property to a large aggregate amount." There were also "able black men in the Legislature. . . . There . . . [were] many who, as lay members . . . [were] at once the ornament and support of their respective churches."[27]

But the majority of the blacks remained poor, and their situation worsened as the prosperity of these colonies declined. The conditions in some districts, particularly in the sugar parishes, where the "stamp of degradation" and "a low type of intelligence" (i.e., education) were marked, led to the conclusion that "thirty years of freedom have done less than might reasonably have been expected for the true elevation of the masses."[28]

The Attitude of the Elites to Black Mobility

While some blacks were also moving up the social ladder, the hope of the elite was that the great majority of them would continue to remain as agricultural wage labourers on the sugar estates. Efforts were often made to keep the poorer black labourers in their "proper" place. For example, Earl Grey advocated the introduction of heavy taxes, in order to force those who could not afford to pay them to hire themselves out as wage labourers on the plantations.[29]

These attempts to restrict mobility opportunities among the black population often dampened their occupational and educational aspirations. Many of them therefore sought to remove themselves from their low status jobs as plantation labourers and set themselves up in free villages. This happened especially in the colonies where Asian workers had been brought in to fill the unskilled jobs on the sugar estates.

In reviewing the relationships between the races in the region Green noted that

> In the West Indies, race, wealth, social status, and religious and cultural connections were mutually reinforcing. Wealth and high social standing tended to belong to those who were either white or who had white progenitors. . . . The colour line between the two groups [white and coloureds] had been relaxed. . . . Blacks were not excluded from this intercourse . . . but *comparatively few people of pure African origin could be numbered among the so-called "respectable" classes.* In the West Indies respectability implied a European cultural affinity, a level of education, a manner of speech and a certain approach to religious or spiritual concerns [emphasis added].[30]

An important early development in these societies was the virtual genocide of the native population. The new inhabitants of the region, therefore, came to be constituted almost entirely of immigrants or their descendants. There were very few, if any, native cultural traditions which the colonizers felt that they must preserve or even take into consideration when introducing such institutions as schools. Those which were established were largely replicas, and often pale replicas of similar institutions in the metropolis.

The more successful coloureds often identified themselves with their white forbears, considering European cultural patterns as uplifting and their African inheritance as debasing. The respectable elements of the culture of the region therefore came to be European. The Africans who formed the major ethnic group were largely deculturalized as a result of their enslavement. Even those lower down the socio-economic scale eventually came to accept the culture of their colonizers as superior, especially since it was the one which carried prestige and conferred status in these societies. Henriques, in commenting on the white bias among black West Indians noted that, "in their minds," Black became "associated with the backward, primitive and undesirable qualities in man." White became "associated with everything [that was] desirable."[31] However, it was suggested that significant elements of their African cultural heritage were merged with the local European culture to form a Creole culture which became the popular culture of the West Indies.

The Plural Nature of West Indian Societies

The inhabitants of those colonies which were earlier occupied by Spain, Holland, and France continued to speak the language of their previous colonizers. Often, their loyalties were with the original colonial power, and even their Roman Catholic faith was often seen as the religion of a foreign group. This population, along with the other ethnic groups who arrived from China, India, and the Middle East, came to form what M. G. Smith[32] has referred to as the plural societies of the West Indies.

Social scientists are still sharply divided about the degree of socio-cultural integration that took place among these different ethnic groups in the region. Some have suggested that over the years they increasingly came to share a common set of values and beliefs and as a result there emerged a marked degree of social cohesion among the population. Others, who have placed greater emphasis on such incidents as the frequent racial riots that occurred after 1850, have argued that the West Indies are characterized by marked cultural cleavages between the various ethnic groups. While there might have been some overstatement about the degree of consensus that developed among the different groups in these societies and the extent to which they came to share common values, interests, and orientations, there is no doubt that the degree of cultural separateness which earlier existed between them came to be less pronounced over time. Their education undoubtedly made an important contribution to this development.

Nevertheless, with the poor and declining economic conditions of the 1860s, there continued to be marked differences among the ethnic groups as to what they felt they could achieve in these societies. For example, it was noted that

> the idea of the white man was to maintain the status quo, at least for another generation. The idea of the coloured man was progress, — political and social, — provided such progress was not extended to those of darker skins than himself. The idea of the black man was to catch up with the coloureds for a start. The coolie, [East Indians] at this stage, had no ideas other than survival.[33]

Religious differences also contributed to the divisions among these ethnic groups. The denominational bodies tended to contribute to the maintenance of these distinctions by providing schools mainly for the children of their members. The role of education in reducing the degree of cultural separateness in these societies was a matter of great concern to individuals like Governors McLeod and Harris of Trinidad, and to overcome this problem they advocated a state system of education. But, in order to maintain their distinctiveness from other groups, the religious bodies strongly opposed the establishment of an educational system that would have brought together, in common schools, children of all ethnic and denominational groups. As a result of their opposition, denominational control of education became firmly established in the West Indies. Nevertheless, despite the religious differences, most schools tried to inculcate among their students similar sets of values and orientation to life.

Education to Establish Legitimacy of the State and the Governing Elites

During the immediate post-emancipation period, especially prior to 1846, the major focus of the primary education provided by West Indian schools was to develop in the young the values, beliefs, attitudes and dispositions considered necessary for the maintenance and reproduction of the social order that existed in pre-emancipation times. The aim of this education was to help achieve the above goals by creating in students a particular consciousness of reality — one that prepared them to accept the rigidly hierarchical relations that characterized these societies and willingly comply with the dictates of the dominant groups. This was to ensure the continued hegemonic dominance of the white elites over the black masses in the West Indies. In other words, schools were to produce among the masses the kind of individuals who would (1) accept the general structure of the social relationships, including their subservient role in these societies. This involved their continuing to acknowledge the superiority of the whites — particularly the British; and (2) be willing to pursue their traditional roles as agricultural labourers, especially after they were introduced to the industrial training provided in the schools.

In these efforts the content of the formal curriculum and the lessons learnt from the hidden curriculum were to play a key role. Social order was no longer to be exerted primarily by the use of physical force against the masses as was permitted under slavery. The ruling groups were to exert their influence on the general population through the ideological hegemony which they were to have established over them, partly with the help of such cultural institutions as schools.

But the education provided in the immediate post-emancipation was only partly successful in helping to achieve these objectives. As previously indicated, some blacks were fairly successful in improving their economic and social status, rising to fairly prominent positions such as legislators, school teachers, catechists, and priests. In Tobago, for example, by the 1850s the non-white population owned a considerable amount of property and some of them had even become lessees of sugar estates.

Because of the numerical decline of the white population, particularly in the smaller islands, some opportunities for occupational mobility through education became increasingly available to the blacks, who were needed to fill some of the positions which became vacant at the higher levels of the occupational and social hierarchy.

But the issue of securing legitimacy for the state and developing in the general population a greater respect for those who controlled it was still a major challenge facing the elites, especially since they opposed the extension of the franchise to the masses and the concomitant popular participation in the election of their political rulers. An increasing number of members of the ruling group therefore began to see schools playing an important role in helping to overcome this challenge or creating popular support for the colonial state.

Economic depression and rising education costs also contributed to the growing desire to ensure that education for the masses made a greater contribution to the economic recovery of the region. Thus, although religious/moral education still occupied a dominant place in the curriculum, practical or industrial subjects were increasingly emphasized in schools. This was also seen as a means of developing desirable work habits among the young, who were said to be growing up in idleness and with little respect for their superiors because they were not exposed to the discipline of work under the rigid social order that existed during slavery. There were other goals of education during this period: developing a sense of loyalty to the new colonial rulers among the population in those islands which were more recently ceded to Britain by other European nations, and raising the moral standards of the new immigrants from the East by also trying to Christianize them.

However, the main concern continued to be to use education to legitimize the highly unequal social and economic structures of these societies by getting the masses to accept their subordinate role and thereby modify their occupational and social aspirations. This was one reason why West Indian legislatures became increasingly involved in the financing, administration, and supervision of education, despite the initial reluctance to make a financial contribution to these areas.

Another strategy was to attempt to develop in the public a belief in the openness of these societies. This was done partly by efforts to prevent schools financed from government funds from discriminating against coloured and black students in their admission policies. In addition, many of these colonies established intermediate or model schools to which some coloureds and blacks were admitted. These institutions provided a higher type of elementary education and helped to make it possible for some students from the ordinary primary schools to secure white-collar jobs, thereby further reaffirming the belief in the increasing openness of West Indian societies.

These developments, however, made the ruling class anxious to maintain the social distance between the white population and the black masses. This was to be done partly through providing the former with a different type of education — a classical secondary grammar school education. In some islands, private segregated schools also continued to flourish, and in Bermuda, government subsidies were still given to so-called private but racially segregated schools.

However, the local legislatures provided a few scholarships for primary school students to attend these grammar schools. Although only a limited number of black children were given this opportunity, the chances of their securing this type of education — and hence even higher level jobs — helped to strengthen the belief that these societies were becoming more open to talent and hard work. Later, an even more limited number of awards were provided for students to continue their education in a British university. But even though the winners were mainly children of whites and other high-status groups, it further helped to develop the myth of achievement-based mobility.

The classical education was also meant to reaffirm the view that the knowledge which the colonizers had and which they attempted to pass on through the local school system marked them off as a superior race. An education in the classics, said to have produced "the leaders of the world" was considered a necessary preparation for the comprador elite group of locals emerging in these societies.

Continued Resistance by Whites to the Mobility of Blacks

These limited opportunities for some blacks and coloureds to rise up the educational and occupational ladder resulted in some degree of resistance by the local whites. This can partly be seen in the fact that illegitimate children were excluded from admission to these secondary grammar schools. Such a measure acted as an effective barrier to the admission of black children to these schools, since it was estimated that the great majority of them were illegitimate.

Another step taken to maintain the social division based on race was the increasing reluctance of some plantation owners to employ even coloured overseers. A similar situation developed in connection with recruitment to the public service in Trinidad. There, the introduction of a system of recruitment on the basis of candidates' performance at competitive examinations had allowed a number of coloureds and blacks to move into the better jobs in the civil service. The result was an outcry from the white population, who wanted the examination system dropped and the governor to be given absolute discretion in choosing recruits.

Nevertheless, while blacks and coloureds were gradually moving up the social and economic ladder, many exaggerated statements were being made about the level of economic improvement which they had achieved and the amount of changes which had occurred in their relationships with the whites. Although the number of educated coloureds and blacks was increasing, the number of white-collar jobs to which they could aspire remained quite limited, as can be seen in the occupational structure of these societies. For example, in Grenada, about 81% of the work force in 1884 was still made up of unskilled manual workers, 15% were skilled workers (including seamstresses), 1.9% were lower-middle class positions (such as clerks and hucksters) and 2.2% were somewhat higher-level occupations such as civil servants, managers and overseers, shopkeepers, attorneys of estates, clergy, lawyers, and doctors. Therefore, there were not many white-collar jobs to which blacks and coloureds could aspire.

This situation was exacerbated by the continued existence in the region of a quite rigidly segmented labour market in which occupational stratification was still based mainly on colour. Thus, while some blacks and coloureds were gradually improving their social and economic position, the incomes of most others were declining. In commenting on the growing economic disparity in one of the parishes of Jamaica, the Reverend Campbell, rector of St. Thomas, remarked, "I think that the number of poor persons had been becoming greater for the last few years; but the aggregate wealth of the labouring class has been, and still is, increasing."[34]

These income and rigid status differentials led to much discontent and social unrest among major sections of the population, and it was obvious that the elementary education which attempted to teach the blacks to accept their lowly position in the highly unequal social and economic structures in the West Indies as inevitable, even divinely sanctioned, was not entirely successful. This often resulted in open social conflicts between the colonial authorities and the masses, as can be seen in the number of disturbances which occurred in these colonies, such as the Morant Bay Rebellion in Jamaica in 1865. The ruling groups probably realized that, while education was making a contribution to social stability, there was no assurance that this would happen in all cases. Therefore, even though expenditures on education were gradually rising, the ruling groups still heavily depended on the repressive state apparatus (RSA) to maintain social order. This can be seen in the fact that, although the local legislatures were allocating more funds to education, the amount spent on the RSA remained substantial and considerably higher than the total educational expenditure in these colonies.

Summary and Overview

One of the more important outcomes of the abolition of slavery in the British Caribbean colonies was the release it provided for the pent-up energies and growing desire on the part of the formerly enslaved population to free themselves from the economic, social, legal, and political shackles that had kept them in an exploitative relationship with a small minority of whites. In an effort to respond to this challenge and to use their freedom in a more constructive way, the black population began, where possible, to diversify their economic production. They also saw education as one of the main instruments by which their children could achieve the goal of economic and social advancement and change the dominant/submissive relationship that they had with the white ruling groups. As a result, the popular demand for education continued to increase during the half-century under review.

But important economic, social, and political developments occurred in these societies which, along with certain structural and psychological constraints largely inherited from slave society, made it difficult for most of the population of freedmen and women to achieve substantial improvement in their economic and social position through popular education. Foremost among these were:

1. The decline in the economic prosperity of the sugar industry. This largely affected the ability and willingness of the local legislatures to provide additional funds to support the expansion of popular education, especially since assistance from external sources was declining. It also resulted in lower incomes for many families, which made it difficult for them to meet the cost of educating their children, including allowing them to attend schools regularly and to complete the full course of instruction offered at the elementary level.

2. The sugar planters still remained the dominant economic group in the West Indies, continuing to own and/or control most of the local resources, including nearly all the arable lands. They therefore effectively blocked any rapid increase in opportunities for upward mobility among the black population and created major barriers to the emergence of an independent and vibrant peasantry. However, the blacks who were able to break through some of these barriers attached great importance to the provision of a better education for their children.

3. Political power was still concentrated in the hands of the sugar planters. Even when these colonies were given Crown colony status, the change did not substantially improve the participation of blacks and coloureds in the political decision-making process. As a result, the educational policies and programmes that were later developed were still those which reflected the interests of the planter class.

4. The plural nature of British West Indian societies also posed many difficulties and challenges for their educational systems. The number of ethnic and religious groups that were present made it almost impossible for a common educational system to emerge. The fact that education was provided by various denominational groups, rather than by the state, militated against the establishment of common schools which would have helped in the process of socio-cultural integration in these societies. As late as 1882 the Royal Commission appointed to examine the financial position of the region noted the "regrettable absence . . . of those factors and traditions which make for social cohesiveness and a sense of membership of a community among these groups."[35]

5. During this period there was an increasing social differentiation between the blacks and the coloureds and among the blacks themselves. Many coloureds often regarded themselves as the natural successors to the position of power and influence that was being vacated by the whites. A non-white West Indian middle class was emerging, comprising many elements of the coloured population and, to a more limited extent, some blacks, who had succeeded, either by their wealth or by their education, in moving into somewhat higher economic and social levels. This had an impact on the amount and kind of education they began to demand for their own children. The outcome was that social differentiation, based largely on colour and ownership of property, and to a lesser extent on education, remained fairly firmly in place throughout the region. Although tolerance was increasing toward some of the more successful upwardly mobile coloureds and blacks, in general, each group was expected to know its place within the social order.

Therefore, while the West Indian masses continued to place great faith in education as an instrument of their social and economic upliftment, the elites generally continued to view it as a tool of social control. They regarded education as a means of reproducing the main structural features of slave society, rather than as an instrument for social mobility among the blacks. One of their main objectives was to keep the ex-slaves and their children in their proper place, performing traditional roles as plantation labourers, by limiting their opportunities for education, especially beyond the basic primary or elementary level. Because of the political power which they continued to exert, the elites were in a better position to have their own perceived educational goals for the masses pursued by the schools.

However, the demands of the black and coloured population could not have been entirely ignored, if social stability was to be maintained. Hence opportunities were made available for a limited number of them to obtain an education which would improve their chances for upward social and occupational mobility. Nevertheless, there continued to be an increasing number of planters who saw education as performing a cooling off function among the masses. The two conflicting functions of education, i.e., as an instrument of social mobility and a means of social reproduction and social control, were nearly always apparent in the debates about the provision of educational facilities and programmes during the next half-century.

But, despite the expansion of educational services, discontent nevertheless increased in these societies and was apparent in the number of disturbances which occurred during this period. As a result, the planters never gave up their faith in the importance of the repressive state apparatus in maintaining social order and, though government expenditures on education were rising, they remained far below those spent on the physical and institutional instruments of state control — the police, the militia, the courts and the prisons.

Notes

1   Manning Marable, *African and Caribbean Politics* (Norfolk, UK: Verso Publishers, 1987), 13.

2   D. A. G. Waddell, *The West Indies and the Guianas* (New Jersey: Prentice-Hall, 1967), 71.

3   *The Times*, 17 January 1848; William A. Green, *British Slave Emancipation: The Sugar Colonies and the Great Experiment, 1830-65* (Oxford: Clarendon Press, 1976), 233.

4   Marable, *African and Caribbean Politics*, 14.

5   W. L. Burn, The British West Indies (London: Hutchinson's University Press, 1951), 134.

6   Report of the Government of Antigua, *British Parliamentary Papers*, Vol. 46: *1847-48* (London: Government of Great Britain), 113.

7   Walter Rodney, *A History of the Guyanese Working People, 1881- 1905*, 19.

8   *The Colonist*, 6 July 1881; Rodney, *History of the Guyanese*, 76.

9   See Alan H. Adamson, *Sugar Without Slaves* (New Haven: Yale University Press, 1972).

10   George L. Beckford, *Persistent Poverty* (New York: Oxford University Press, 1972).

11   K. O. Laurence, *Immigration into the West Indies in the Nineteenth Century* (Kingston, Jamaica: Caribbean Universities Press, 1976), 9.

12   Eric Williams, *From Columbus to Castro, The History of the Caribbean, 1492- 1969* (London: Andre Deutsch, 1970).

13   Dorothy Ann Ryall, "The Organization of Missionary Societies and the Recruitment of Missionaries in Britain and the Role of the Missionaries in the Diffusion of British Culture in Jamaica, During the Period 1834-1865" (Ph.D. diss., Univ. of London, 1959), 14.

14   J. H. Stark, *Stark's History and Guide to Barbados and the Caribee Islands* (Boston: n.p., 1893), 196-97.

15   Morley Ayearst, *The British West Indies* (London, Ruskin House: George Allen and Unwin, Ltd., 1960), 21.

16   C. Y. Thomas, *The Rise of the Authoritarian State in Peripheral Societies* (New York: Monthly Review Press, Heinemann, 1984), 21.

17   Earl Grey, *The Colonial Policy of Lord Russell's Administration*, Vol. 1 (London: Richard Bentley, 1853), 173.

18   Wm. G. Sewell, *The Ordeal of Free Labour in the West Indies* (New York: Harper and Bros., 1861), 255.

19   J. W. Root, *The British West Indies and The Sugar Industry* (Liverpool: J. W. Root, 1899), 6.

20   H. A. Will, *Constitutional Change in the British West Indies, 1880-1903* (Oxford: Clarendon Press, 1970), 2.

21   Waddell, *The West Indies*, 101.

22   C. Nicole, *The West Indies: Their People and History* (London: Hutchinson, 1965), 226.

23   Ibid.

24   Government of Dominica, *Annual Report of the Government of Dominica, British Parliamentary Papers*, Vol. 37: *1847* (London: Government of Great Britain), 43.

25   Governor Grey of Jamaica to Earl Grey, *British Parliamentary Papers*, Vol. 62: *1852-53* (London: Government of Great Britain), 31.

26   Report of the Government of British Guiana, *British Parliamentary Papers*, Vol. 31:*1852* (London: Government of Great Britain).

27   Thomas Harvey and William Brewin, *Jamaica in 1866* (London: A. W. Bennett, n.d.), 68.

28   Ibid.

29   CO 295/160, Harris to Grey, 21 February 1848 (London: PRO).

30   Green, *British Slave Emancipation*, 392-93.

31   F. M. Henriques, *Family and Colour in Jamaica* (London: Eyre and Spottiswoode, 1953), 62.

32   M. G. Smith, *The Plural Society in the British West Indies* (Berkeley and Los Angeles: University of California Press, 1959).

33   Nicole, *The West Indies: Their People and History*, 218.

34   CO 137/390, Reverend J. Campbell to the Bishop of Jamaica, April 1865; in Douglas Hall, *Free Jamaica, 1838-1865: An Economic History* (New Haven: Yale University Press, 1959), 194.

35   Government of Great Britain, *West Indian Royal Commission Report on Public Expenditure* (London: HMSO, 1885).

CHAPTER 1

CONSENSUS AND CONFLICT OVER THE PROVISION OF ELEMENTARY EDUCATION

The Provision of Elementary Education

While the provision of elementary education obviously depended on both supply and demand, the forces that influenced the former were far more crucial in determining the rate at which this level of education expanded during the period under review. The masses, who were anxious for their children to receive an education, did not have the economic resources to meet its full cost, nor the political power to ensure that the state took on the entire financial responsibility for providing it. The resources that the state made available to meet the cost of education therefore became a key element in its expansion and improvement.

Therefore, the support for popular education among the groups who controlled or had some influence over government expenditures was crucial. There were a number of key groups in this position, though they had differential amounts of power to influence the provision of government funds provided for elementary education. Among them were the imperial authorities and their local representatives, i.e., the colonial governors, the planters, the missionaries, and the local legislators.

Efforts to formally educate the ex-slaves began after the abolition of slavery in 1834 and the termination of the apprenticeship period in 1838.[1] The British government made a grant for negro education in 1834 and also allowed the Mico Trust funds to be used for this purpose. This provided additional impetus to the missionary societies and other voluntary agencies to increase their contribution to education. There was thus a substantial expansion of elementary education in the region in the years immediately following emancipation, and, by the time the Negro Education Grant was terminated in 1845, day primary schools were available in all these colonies and "the idea of popular education was established for good in the West Indies."[2]

The withdrawal of imperial funds and the declining financial support for education among the parent organizations of the denominational bodies operating locally led to the desire to see the local legislatures step in to help bridge the financial gap. The governments of the region had earlier revealed a reluctance to offer financial assistance to education for the masses, and since the colonies were experiencing severe economic difficulties due to the decline of the sugar industry, a major challenge facing the groups providing education was to win the support of the planters for their work.

To do so, they needed to define, or re-define, the role of education to make its objectives more acceptable to the ruling groups. Therefore, it was suggested that the education offered to the ex-slaves should teach them to accept their new reality by modifying their occupational aspirations and their behaviours. In commenting on the type of education that was needed, the editor of the *Colonist* suggested that it should be directed at motivating the Africans to work and respect authority. . . . [It] should *teach the Negroes not to disregard the diversities of rank and the condition of life imposed [on them] for wise purpose.* They should be brought practically to love honesty, sobriety, reverence to authority and a *Christian respect for all whom Providence has placed in a superior condition* [emphasis added].[3]

Providers of educational services were informed that William Wilberforce, one of the foremost champions of abolition, supported this view and did not want the ex-slaves to aspire "beyond their station in life." In his *Practical Views of Christianity*, Wilberforce suggested of the lower classes that, "their more lowly path has been allotted to them by the hand of God," and that it was "their obligation faithfully to discharge their duties" in their given station in life and "contentedly to bear its inconveniences."[4] These views were seen as applying equally to the children of the ex-slaves as to the working class in England, and were likely to win the support of the local legislatures for popular education.

As a result of the educational goals which were being advocated, a number of influential groups became increasingly willing to support its expansion. They brought pressures to bear on the West Indian legislatures to raise their grants to education and to play a more active role in its general administration and regulation. But while these efforts were commendable, they also represented an attempt by those who had greatly benefited from the inhumane exploitation of the enslaved Africans to salve publicly their uneasy consciences by supporting the education of the children of the ex-slaves.

Nevertheless, a point of view that became increasingly popular in some quarters was that parents should be expected to make a greater contribution to the cost of their children's education. This was to be done by increasing school fees, encouraging local communities to raise additional funds, and persuading parents to pay their children's fees punctually.

Moral Support from the Imperial Government

Even though the British government did not have a consistent educational policy for these colonies and after the termination of its Negro Education Grant took "direct action [only] . . . in exceptional cases,"[5] it nevertheless maintained an interest in the long-term economic rehabilitation of the region. The colonial authorities wanted to ensure a peaceful transition from slavery to a free labour market situation and saw that the "right" type of education for the ex-slaves was needed to achieve this goal. It was one reason why, around 1847, the colonial secretary again expressed the view that the agricultural and commercial prosperity, as well as the moral and spiritual well-being of West Indian communities, depended on the education of their population. He also suggested that the parents should not be allowed to refuse to send their children to school, even if this meant introducing compulsory school attendance in the region.

The British government's positive attitude to the education of the blacks was reflected in the support by a number of colonial governors for education in these colonies. Many of them played an important role in trying to convince the local ruling groups, particularly the legislators, of the need for popular education, and some of them even led the way in proposing new educational policies and programmes.

The Support Provided by West Indian Governors

Many West Indian governors expressed strong support for popular education and recognized that missionary bodies faced great difficulties in providing it with such limited financial support from the local legislatures. They therefore tried to change this situation. For example, Governor Reid of Barbados was appalled at the low character of the schools on the island and, despite the economic difficulties which the government faced, called upon the legislators not to reduce the already limited amount of the education grant. Instead, he suggested that the education vote should be increased, especially since some of the rural areas were not yet provided with schools. He also urged that more efforts be made to improve the quality of instruction offered. His eventual hope was that popular pressure for education would be stimulated to a point where it would compel the legislature to make publicly aided schools free to the masses.

Colebrooke, who succeeded Reid as governor of Barbados, also put forward the case for more government assistance to education, suggesting that parochial schools be placed on a better financial footing to make them less dependent on voluntary support. He refused to accept the argument that government expenditure on education could not be increased because of the island's economic position, since in 1848 the legislature was spending 34% of its budget on the police, 7.2% on jails and only 2.5% on education. Instead, he felt that a substantial reduction could be effected in the current expenditure on the repressive state apparatus (RSA) — the police, the courts, the prisons — without impairing public security. Such a step would release additional funds for schools and this in turn would contribute to the educational and moral advancement of the people. His views probably had some effect on the members of the Barbadian legislature because by 1852 there was a slight change in the structure of government expenditures, with 3.8% of the total budget earmarked for education, as compared with 2.5% in 1848.

In Jamaica, Governor Grey also recognized that the failure of the legislature to provide funds for education during 1848-49, due to depressed economic conditions, was creating many problems for the voluntary agencies which operated schools on the island. He therefore called upon the legislators to recognize the value of education for the masses and urged that above all, they should try to educate the people. As a result, this item of expenditure which was dropped from the budget was reintroduced in the following year.

Many governors went beyond simply requesting more state aid for education; some even put up their own proposals for educational reform in the different colonies. For example, when Grey was governor of Barbados, he developed an outline of a new educational policy for that island in which he proposed that, (1) a basic education should be provided, free of charge, for all children between four and seven years of age, and that the curriculum should place a heavy emphasis on the inculcation of moral and religious values; and (2) that higher elementary education, for which a fee was to be charged, should be made available to those between 7 and 10 years of age. This education was to be entirely secular, though the pupils were to be given religious instruction without charge on weekends.

Governor Grey felt that because of the social benefits expected to accrue from the lower primary education, it was a worthwhile investment for the state. The proposed emphasis on moral development of the students was considered important for the colonies' social stability, since it would help working-class blacks to accept their ordained place within the existing social order. The private returns from the "higher" level of primary education were considered to be substantial enough to induce parents to contribute to its cost.

Governor Reid expressed the hope that the exclusionary admission policy that allowed some schools to bar students because of their colour would soon be replaced by one that admitted all children on the basis of their abilities — on the "qualities of their mind," as he put it. In addition, he advanced the argument, later put forward by the advocates of the human capital theory, that, because education was important to increase economic productivity, a basic course of instruction should be made available to all members of the society. He advocated that the state should play a more active role in producing an intelligent and educated labour force and pleaded with the legislators that, "whilst we strive to encourage religion and morality, let us strive to increase the general stock of intelligence (i.e., level of education) throughout the whole body of the community."[6] Governor Grey of Jamaica made a similar point about the economic benefits of popular education when he suggested that important spin-off benefits would accrue from an educated workforce because it was likely to attract more European capital and machinery that could put the island on the first step toward becoming a happy and prosperous colony.

Reid also drew attention to the importance of continuing education because, as he pointed out, the education provided in schools for the young simply "lays the foundation . . . necessary to enable all men to continue their self-education after they have entered the business of life." As a result, he suggested that facilities such as a public library and a museum should be provided, so that those who had been to school could continue to educate themselves by their own efforts.[7] His proposals met with some success, and the first public library in Barbados was established in 1848.

Around this time Governor Barkly of British Guiana expressed his regret at the "little progress" that had "hitherto been made in the education of the labouring classes," especially since he too considered that "the prosperity of all classes in the colony" was "entirely dependent" on the efforts made "in the cause of education."[8] To ensure that the government took a more active role in education, he established a board of education that was to prepare a plan of public instruction suitable to the requirements of the colony. In addition, he proposed that the central and the local government authorities work together to meet the future cost of education. The governor also tried to get more financial support from the legislature to improve the amount and quality of elementary education offered, again using the economic argument that education was necessary to produce the steady and industrious workforce that was a prerequisite for improved agricultural production.

In his efforts to increase the spread of education in Grenada, the lieutenant-governor tried to dissuade the legislature from making grants to schools conditional upon the levy of school fees because, as he argued, this was likely to reduce overall school attendance. Instead, he favoured a general education tax or levy that would create less financial hardship on the poorer sections of society. In 1853 he too recommended the creation of a board of education, which was eventually established by the Education Act of 1857-58. To secure the co-operation of all sections of society, both Protestants and Catholics were to be represented on this board. The Act even provided for the establishment of a model school, a normal school for the training of teachers, and a grammar school. In that year also, partly due to the influence of Governor Keate, all schools became eligible for government grants.

With the arrival of Governor Sendall in 1886, education was again placed on the front burner. He considered the financial allocation to education inadequate — a view shared by the 1882 Royal Commission enquiring into public expenditure in the colony — and made some attempts to improve the situation. In 1889 he called for the establishment of government-owned and operated schools, though the colony was to continue its financial support for the existing denominational schools.

Noting that during the year 1848, "the education of the working classes has . . . greatly fallen off . . . owing to the [limited] financial resources of the government and the people," the administrator of Montserrat urged the legislature to provide some financial assistance to schools, adding that

> a grant from you, however small, voted with the view of retrieving lost ground and making further progress, [in education] would be of unspeakable use by affording a praiseworthy example, and showing every member of the community that you participate and sympathize with the universal yearning of the wise and good for the extension [of education] to those who so much need it, of a blessing so essential to the advance and amelioration of the human race. . . . A small grant from you would resemble the widow's mite; it would be like a flower in the desert, the more beautiful, the more grateful, the more acceptable, from our knowledge of the poverty of the soil which has produced it. [9]

Despite the reluctance of the legislators to provide funds for education, the administrator continued to ask them to make some provision for the maintenance of the schools. He even suggested to the legislature that it was the first duty of every civilized community to foster and encourage education. Eventually some success was achieved in 1868, when the first grant of £50 for schools was voted.

The governor of St. Lucia tried to impress on the legislature the view that education was "a subject, the importance of which it is impossible to over-rate, as upon its spread and encouragement will mainly depend the social, moral and physical well-being of a people."[10] The governor of the Bahamas also tried to convince the members of the legislative assembly that "the demand for education is the most sacred of any that can be made on the public purse, and that any sacrifice should be made [for it] rather than that the laudable disposition of the rising generation for the acquirement of knowledge should be discouraged."[11]

The administrator of Dominica expressed his hopes that education would continue to expand on that island. He saw it as being "essential to the future well being of the Colony" because it would ensure an ultimate improvement in the moral and intellectual culture of the labouring classes.[12] However, in 1852 he pointed out that after four years of urging the House of Assembly for an augmentation of the grant for education, the programmes continued to be sadly hampered due to lack of funds.

The importance of education in helping to establish social stability was particularly stressed by individuals like Governor Barkly of British Guiana, who expressed the view that, without a sound education, it would be impossible to answer for the peace and safety of society. Governor Grey of Jamaica had emphasized the contribution which education could make to the moral and cultural development of the population. He argued that without the mental and moral culture which religious education provided, the population was likely to become discontented and restless and dissatisfied with the existing institutions of society. This could result in social unrest.

Other colonial administrators shared similar sentiments which became common throughout the region after the Morant Bay Rebellion of Jamaica in 1865. This incident was seen as a rude reminder to the Jamaican government and the elite groups in the other West Indian colonies that there was a need to provide a proper education for the masses if political stability in the region was to be maintained. Therefore, when Jamaica was reduced to a Crown colony in 1867, the governor, Sir John Peter Grant, began to give greater priority to education than his predecessor, partly because he was in a stronger constitutional position to do so. Under him, the education system was reorganized, elementary education placed on a more systematic basis, and higher per capita grants paid for students as they moved up from one grade to another.

In Bermuda, the governor noted that the legislative assembly was in "a state of . . . deplorable apathy" on the subject of education. He argued that if there was no improvement in the education of the youths born around the 1850s, there was "every reason to fear" that they would "relapse into a semi-barbarous condition before the end of the century." To him, the governing elites and the proprietors of large estates stood at a critical point in the history of the colony. They were "between the progress of civilization and a steady improvement" of the population on one hand and, "unhappily, on the other," the "serious risk" of increasing "ignorance, idleness and prejudice" if they failed to adopt the right policies.[13] He suggested that it was only through an effective educational programme for the masses that they could succeed in guiding the development of the society along the proper path.

Governors McLeod and Harris were also strong advocates of the view that government should assume greater responsibility for providing popular education. They argued that in Trinidad there was a need to bring about a greater degree of social cohesion among the culturally diverse elements of the population. Since the colony had only recently been ceded to Britain from France, most of its inhabitants were still considered by the British authorities to be foreign. Therefore, it was necessary to make a special effort to develop in the schoolchildren an allegiance to the British Crown and a sense of loyalty to the new imperial authority. Another concern was that most of the population did not speak the language of their new colonizers. As McLeod noted, "two-thirds of the natives still speak exclusively either Spanish or French" — a situation that was regarded as unacceptable, since it was considered "absolutely necessary that people living under British rule and claiming the benefit of British subjects should be able to read the laws by which they are governed."[14] Schools were to transmit a knowledge of English to all their students as part of an effort to develop in them a strong psychological attachment to the mother country.

McLeod felt that this could only be achieved through a vigorous policy of Anglicization and proposed that the state should assume full responsibility for public education, thereby ending the denominational system of schooling. This would give the state a role in deciding upon, or at least strongly influencing, the content of the curriculum offered in schools. He saw the Irish system of education as an ideal model for Trinidad to copy, and in 1846 he put forward a proposal to reform education in the colony which would achieve the above objectives. His resolution to the Trinidad legislature also provided for the establishment of a board of education and a salaried inspector of schools to oversee educational developments in the colony. The government was to pay the salaries of teachers and meet half the cost of new school buildings. In addition, students were expected to pay fees.

When Lord Harris became governor around April 1846 he also observed that education in Trinidad had been neglected and that those attending school were receiving poor instruction. He reiterated the need for greater social cohesion among the population, pointing out that although "liberty has been given to a heterogeneous mass" and "a race has been freed, a society has not [yet] been formed."[15] Another factor contributing to the social divisiveness among the local population was its religious composition and the inequality of the educational facilities available to children of these different denominational groups. He was convinced, therefore, of the need for common schools, not only to help increase the extent of understanding and tolerance among the population, but also to ensure to a greater degree equality of educational opportunity among them. This, he felt, could only be brought about if the state played a more active role in the provision of education. Although he was of an aristocratic background and accepted the view that people had certain given positions to occupy and duties to perform, he nevertheless believed in providing opportunities for upward social mobility among the lower orders through education.

However, the dilemma which Harris faced and to which he drew attention was the scanty means of instruction available in the colony. He recognized the need for more financial resources to extend educational facilities to all groups and was not convinced that the government could not afford to provide those additional funds. In fact, he felt that the subject was not given enough priority in the colony's budget.

To overcome some of these problems, Harris directed his efforts to developing a state-operated decentralized ward system of secular education which would provide fairly equal access to children from all sections of society. He also wanted to ensure that there was an improvement in the quantity and the quality of education offered in the primary schools. To help achieve the latter goal, he offered "encouragement" to the poorer classes by providing Governor's Prizes varying in value from $50 to $3.[16] These awards were to be made on the basis of students' performance at the annual public examinations. His 1851 Education Ordinance provided for the purchase of textbooks from England. In 1852 the governor also hired an experienced teacher trainer from Britain to take charge of the normal school in Port-of-Spain and to open a model school on the Woodbrook estate for student-teachers to undertake their practice teaching. He tried to help the legislature develop a greater appreciation for the value of education.

Many of Harris's ideas were ahead of his time, and he initially made little progress with them. He had to modify some of them partly because of the prevailing poor economic conditions, and partly because of Catholic opposition to the secularization of education. However, by the time Harris's term of office ended in 1854, the government of Trinidad was much more heavily involved than a decade before in providing elementary education.

There were other West Indian governors, public officials, and policy-makers who tried to persuade the local legislatures to become more actively involved in providing education for the masses. The above provides only a sample of the individuals and the kind of arguments they were advancing in support of public education. It also suggests that, overall, the Colonial Office and its local representatives were willing to exert pressure on the local legislatures to make more government funds available for primary education. Some individuals even began to advocate the introduction of compulsory education throughout the region.

Pressures for Increasing Support of Popular Education
In addition to the positive attitudes to popular education shared by most West Indian governors, there was also growing support for it among other influential groups in these societies. Many church officials were concerned about the declining moral standards among the youth as evidenced by the rising incidence of unruly behaviour and delinquency. In 1850 the Presbyterian Synod of Jamaica put forward a plan for a comprehensive *state* system of education to be administered by local boards as a means of checking the downward progress of society.

Schomburgk, the historian, along with other prominent individuals, argued that, since moral and religious education would result in an improvement of the human mind, educating a larger section of the population should eventually result in a diminution in crime and a concurrent reduction in public expenditure on the physical control mechanisms of the state. This would compensate for the additional expenses incurred on education. Around the late 1840s, James Maxwell also urged that responsibility for education should be taken over by the state, and that "the advantages of an elementary education should be *extended to every creed and colour, without money and without price.*"[17]

Many individuals in Barbados supported Governor Grey's proposal for an extension of education in the colony, with some even advocating that it be provided on a universal rather than a parochial basis, and be under public, not sectarian control. The *Barbadian* newspaper also considered government expenditure on education highly inadequate. While it recognized that the poor economy was partly responsible for this, it pointed out that when the first education grant of £750 was made by the legislature in 1846, the colony could have afforded a much larger sum. It also drew attention to the fact that, while the total government grant for popular education during that year was only £750, the island's upper class willingly diverted £1,000 per annum from the Codrington estate to educate 12 of their children in England.

One Dr. Bascom argued that the local legislature had a special duty to help shoulder the responsibility for the education of the masses, since there was no question of greater importance which could occupy its attention. Reverend Richard Rawle, the principal of Codrington College, pointed out that education was necessary in preventing mischief and promoting good in the society. He, too, advanced the view that money spent on schools and teachers would eventually result in substantial savings in expenditures on the police.

Resistance to Increasing the Supply of Elementary Education

But while such support for popular education had an influence on the various West Indian legislatures, all planters were not convinced of the need to extend educational facilities to the masses. Many of them did not want the colonial governments to increase their financial commitment to include any item that might become a regular part of the recurrent budget. They de-emphasized the social returns to education, and many of them subscribed to the views of the Trinidadian legislator, P.N. Aumaitre, who argued that the common man had no right to look to government to help raise himself to a more elevated sphere of life, as education was likely to do. This was one of the main reasons why the bills which sought to tax the propertied class to provide funds for education, such as the one put forward by Lyons in the Jamaican legislature in 1854, and the Compulsory Education bill which was part of a House Tax bill proposed in 1856, never found enough support to be made law.

Possibly even more important, many planters still believed that education not only alienated the labouring classes from their ordained role as agricultural labourers, but was likely to make them a threat to social stability. In St. Kitts, there was "a large and influential portion of the proprietary" class, who, in the late 1850s, continued to suggest that "the worst labourers in their employment, the most deceitful, unruly, disrespectful, and impatient of direction and control were invariably those who had been to school."[18] Therefore, some of the planters continued to oppose the extension of education to the masses, claiming that it only made the newly emancipated averse to estate work and gave them strange ideas of their social status.

In 1857 the inspector of schools for Grenada continued to draw attention to the lack of support for popular education from the elites on that island and observed that

> it is to be lamented that the efforts to educate the lower classes should be regarded by some persons here with a certain degree of jealousy and coldness as likely to impair their usefulness as labourers, they cannot and will not believe that the more general education becomes, the less likely it is to have the effects they anticipate. They judge from the fact of the few who have acquired a little knowledge, having thereby raised themselves above the level of their more ignorant companions.[19]

Up to the late 1860s, many members of the local upper class on the island continued to regard it as a "positive evil, calculated to induce the educated portion of the poor to regard their fellow labourers as beneath them and to withdraw themselves from the class to which they properly belonged."[20] In 1875 the *Chronicle* of Trinidad was still highly critical of the primary schools, where "you will find . . . the children of our labouring poor . . . becoming rapidly ruined by so-called education, puffed up with vanity and conceit, . . . ashamed of their parentage."[21] In general, the evidence from this colony indicated that "most of the 'respectable' classes, . . . regarded the education of the working class as at best a necessary evil, at worst, positively harmful to themselves and to the society."[22]

As late as 1876 the inspector of schools for Antigua also observed that, "even in the present day there are too many people to be found who regard an education given to the peasantry as serving only to unfit them for the labours which fall to their lot."[23] In the same year the Education Commission for Barbados made similar observations, noting that some local planters and estate managers still had misgivings about popular education, fearing that to teach the agricultural labourers' children was to unfit them for such duties which must necessarily be their lot in life.

Finally, some members of the elite blamed the slow educational progress in the region not on the reluctance of the legislatures to provide additional funds for schools but on the attitudes of the blacks themselves. It was even suggested that instead of depending on more financial support from the state they ought to make a greater contribution to the education of their own children, eventually meeting the full cost of their schooling. Others expressed the view that any increase in the provision of education should only take place gradually, since, as the administrator of the British Virgin Islands contended, the local population was not yet fully appreciative of its value. However, he saw that this would eventually come about as education became more available to them, arguing that

> an appreciation of the value of education sufficient to induce the Negro to make a sacrifice of his means, for the education of his children, cannot be expected from the present generation of the emancipated classes in these colonies; it must be the *gradual result* of full experience by the people themselves of *the practical benefits arising from the acquisition of knowledge*; it must be the result of a better educated state of the mass of the population, and this must be a work of time [emphasis added].[24]

Support from Local Legislators

With the conflicting pressures resulting from the increasing support for popular education by some members of the plantocracy and opposition to it by others, legislators were caught in a dilemma. For example, Schomburgk, writing about Barbados during the mid-1840s, reported that, by then, "a more liberal system [of education had] . . . spread over the Colonies; it . . . [was] no longer the wish of the great proprietors of the land to keep the labouring classes in the darkness of ignorance."[25] But around 1858 the governor of the island, while deploring the inadequate provision that the local legislature was making for education, noted that many influential members of the community were unimpressed by this failing. However, they later began to show an increasing appreciation for the value of education, and by 1876, the Mitchinson Commission observed that many planters were "far-sighted enough to recognize the superior value of labourers who had been under teaching and discipline to the entirely untaught child."[26]

West Indian legislators, therefore, though sometimes with great reluctance, began to give greater financial support to the missionary societies to help them continue their educational activities. The financial commitments made to the voluntary agencies were often on an annual or even an ad hoc basis, and the sums voted could be, and on many occasions were, reduced or withdrawn without much prior notice. Sometimes when new schools were built there were insufficient funds to meet their regular operating costs, even after the economy of the region had somewhat improved. In 1851 the Crown colony government in Trinidad itself assumed the major responsibility for directly funding elementary education. But, despite the colonies' financial problems, their expenditure on state-control mechanisms continued to be substantially higher than their allocations to education.

The Barbadian Legislature

The attitude of the Barbadian assembly to the provision of popular education was influenced somewhat by the 1846 *Circular of the Education Department of Upper Canada*, which stipulated that every member of a society must contribute to the support of its public institutions and that every child has a right to education "which will fit him for the duties of a useful citizen of the country." Further, he should "not be deprived of such education on account of the inability of the parents or guardians to provide it."[27] Therefore, the local legislators made an initial grant of £750 for education in 1846 and doubled this amount four years later. In addition, most of them indicated some support for Governor Reid's proposal for a comprehensive system of education based on the assumption that "instruction to all classes of the community . . . would confer benefits eminently advantageous, both from the moral and economic point of view."[28] However, they suggested that the time to implement such proposals was inopportune because of the prevailing economic circumstances. In fact, the government was then considering a reduction in the salaries of public officers, and while this did not take place, the wages of agricultural workers on the sugar estates were cut by 20-30%. In such circumstances, it was felt that the colony could not afford the additional costs that would have been incurred if Governor Reid's proposals were fully implemented.

Nevertheless, the legislature appointed a Joint Committee on Education in 1850 to examine the best mode of promoting the more extensive and general education of the people. These recommendations, which were approved by both Houses of the Legislature, resulted in an Education Act that provided for an increase in the range of educational activities eligible for government assistance. This included the establishment of "dame" or infant schools in the rural districts, an extension of primary education for the masses, the development of secondary education for children of the middle class, and the provision of scholarships for tertiary level education. Financial assistance was also provided to schools operated not only by the Anglicans but also by other denominational bodies, and the grants for education steadily improved, reaching £3,000 by the late 1850s and £9,000 by 1875. The *Mitchinson Report* of 1876 even attempted to widen the involvement of the government of Barbados in education by stressing the importance of establishing nursery schools, an issue which came under consideration again in the 1890s.

Despite the economic hardship which it faced, the government of Barbados was said to have been spending more per capita on education than the British government by 1850 — 5s.2d per head as opposed to 1s.6d per head in Britain, where most of the education costs were then being met by voluntary agencies. The establishment of an Education Committee, comprising members of the two legislative houses, was recommended so that the government could exercise some control over the ways in which public funds voted for education were spent. The appointment of an inspector of schools was also proposed, and his responsibility was to monitor the quality of education offered in schools and to evaluate pupil performance. These recommendations were approved by the legislature, and a part-time inspector was appointed. This provided the government with some mechanism to keep it informed about the activities of schools.

The 1850 Education Act was the first real indication that the legislature felt the need to provide education for all sectors of the population. The Education Committee, however, continued to place the main responsibility for the instructional programme of schools on the missionary societies and other voluntary agencies, arguing that the business of government was simply to stimulate, encourage, and strengthen the educational work of these bodies, not to be totally responsible for it. Such involvement by the various denominational groups in the provision of education was considered particularly important, since the island was unable to afford a free and extensive system of general education.

Finally, the view that the government should be financially supportive of, rather than be fully responsible for, education represented an improvement in the attitude of some members of the legislature who, in 1837, had argued that it was the responsibility of the imperial government rather than the colonial legislatures to provide funds for the religious and moral education of the West Indian masses. The policies established by the Barbadian legislature not only laid the foundation of the island's educational system but, in some ways, also served as a model for the educational services later provided by most other West Indian colonies.

By 1857, when there was a slight improvement in the finances of the island, the Education Committee requested more liberal support for education, and in the following year there was a positive response to this request. Public funds were made available for infant schools and a full-time inspector of schools was appointed. By then the Barbadian government was providing financial assistance for education from the infant to the tertiary level, and the percentage of the island's budget allocated to education rose from 2.4 % in 1849 to 4.4% in 1856. By the 1860s, when about 50% of the population 4-15 years of age were enrolled in schools, the inspector observed that there was no locality on the island which was "not within a reasonable distance from a school." He added, probably with some exaggeration, that education on the island was "progressing at a pace equal to that of any other country" including the metropole.[29] In 1878 another Education Act resulted in the establishment of a new board of education, composed mainly of members of the legislative assemblies. This resulted in a substantial increase in government expenditure on elementary education.

The Jamaican Legislature

The Jamaican legislature started to make an allocation for elementary education by the end of 1843. By 1845 it had appointed its first board of education to take over the responsibility for making grants to schools, though it initially had no system of inspection in place to ensure that the funds provided were properly spent. In 1849 an Education Act to establish a board of education on a more permanent basis was introduced. The legislature soon began to increase its educational grants and liberalize its funding policy to provide financial support for schools operated not only by the Anglicans but by other denominational bodies as well. Therefore, from 1844 onwards, the education vote rose substantially, and by 1847-48 the island was spending about 3.5% of its total budget on education.

However, as the economic position of the island declined, the education vote not only fluctuated annually but was often reduced or even terminated quite abruptly. In 1852 the allocations for operating the Normal School of Industry and for paying the salary of the inspector of schools were deleted from the budget, and in the following year the financial situation was so tight that the Jamaican government made no grant whatsoever to its board of education. However, by 1855 the situation had improved, with the government providing an education grant of £6,000 p.a.

One measure that was proposed to ensure a reliable source of financial support for education was the imposition of an education tax on houses. While this bill failed to win the approval of the majority of members of the legislature, the governor was able to secure a 50% increase in the education vote, even though the amount provided remained at this level for the next nine years. Between 1864-65 and 1867-68, a remarkable impulse was given to elementary education, when government grants rose by 18% over the three-year period, and subsequently there was a relatively large increase again of about 50%.

After 1867 the "payment by results" scheme was introduced, and this too contributed to an improvement in the quality of education as reflected in the rising number of schools which were rated as first and second class institutions. These rankings entitled them to higher grants which increased the level of expenditure on education. The government introduced a system of opening grants in order to encourage and aid trustworthy managers or teachers to establish new schools in the more remote areas. In addition, funds were provided for the increased number of schoolmasters who were annually becoming available, and who were to help establish these additional schools.

In 1885 the Education Commission for Jamaica recommended an improvement in the conditions of employment for teachers by providing them with suitable residences and a superannuation allowance. It was also proposed that compulsory education for children between 7 and 13 years be introduced, that school fees be abolished, and that a Central Board of Education and local education boards be established. As a result of these proposals, in 1893 education was made free, a house tax was introduced to help recover some of the funds lost through the abolition of school fees, and a new board of education was established. One outcome of these developments was the steady increase in the annual budget for education in the colony. Figure 1 shows the increasing amounts allocated to education between 1862 and 1881 and Figure 2, the rising per capita expenditure on students on the island between 1868 and 1896.

The Government of Trinidad

The Crown colony status of Trinidad generally gave the governor a greater degree of authority and responsibility for initiating legislation. In 1845 the island granted a subsidy of £1,418 for elementary education, and the various denominational bodies were at liberty to establish schools wherever they pleased and to offer whatever curriculum they liked. Public funds were used for the salaries of teachers and the maintenance of schools, though the government had no control over the quality of the education offered or the qualifications of the teachers. Incidentally, this practice whereby the government funded education without having any control over it was common throughout the region at this time.

Later, the legislature also supported Harris's new Education Ordinance of 1851 which provided for the establishment of a board of education and a system of ward schools. This introduced a state system of education with the government almost fully responsible for financing its elementary schools. The administrators of the wards — wardens — were responsible for establishing schools wherever they were most needed, and many immediately set upon this task. The costs of erecting such schools, of providing suitable accommodation for teachers, and of paying teachers' salaries were to be defrayed from funds made available to the wards by the central government and supplemented by an education rate levied on local landowners. The 1851 Education Act also approved the appointment of an inspector of schools and provided funds for the establishment of a teachers' training institution. But, despite these new provisions, the central government expenditure on education was still only about 1.2% of its total budget in 1869, as compared with the 15.8% allocated to its state-control mechanisms — a figure which had fallen from 18.6% the previous year. As a result, at no time were all of the wards able to provide enough facilities for educating the total eligible population.

FIGURE 1

The Increasing Allocation for Education in Jamaica, 1862-81 (£)

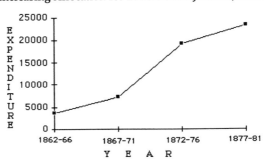

Source: *Annual Reports of Jamaica.*

FIGURE 2
The Increasing Per Capita Expenditure on Elementary Education for Jamaica, 1868-96 (in shillings)

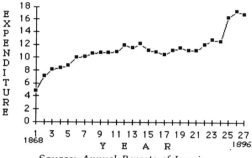

Source: *Annual Reports of Jamaica.*

By the late 1860s, as a result of Catholic opposition to the state-funded secular schools, Governor Gordon made a request to the Colonial Office for someone to review the educational situation on the island. Patrick Keenan, the young chief inspector of the Board of National Education in Ireland, was appointed in 1869 to undertake this task. Keenan recommended a dual system of education, with state-aided church and government ward schools, a policy that was accepted and introduced after 1870. An 1888 Education Ordinance provided for even greater government involvement in education since it allowed the board of education to exercise complete control over most of the instructional activities of the elementary schools. It also made available liberal grants for schoolhouses and teachers' residences, along with a new and somewhat more generous formula for the remuneration of schoolmasters. In addition, the government was to meet three-quarters of the expenses incurred by the denominational schools, which had to accept all children, irrespective of their religious affiliation.

The Legislatures of Other West Indian Colonies
In British Guiana, where the legislature allocated only 1% of its annual budget to education in 1846, the number of schools available was simply insufficient to meet the growing popular demand for education. The Combined Court had withdrawn all salary payments for teachers in the late 1840s, which resulted in a substantial drop in school enrollment, and the situation was made worse by the uncertainty as to whether the grant for education would be resumed. Around the late 1840s, consideration was given to the establishment of an educational fund, the money for which was to be raised by the vestry of each parish through an assessment on every house. The sums collected were to help all schools which were operated by licensed teachers, irrespective of their denominational affiliation. However, this proposal, like others of its kind in the West Indies, did not find enough support among the legislators.

In 1850 a board of education was established in British Guiana by the governor at the request of the Combined Court, and the first inspector of schools for the colony, George Dennis, was appointed in 1851. Dennis tried to secure increased government support for education, arguing, like others of his time, that money laid out for the "encouragement of virtue" and the "removal of ignorance" was a far more profitable investment than that expended on the repression and punishment of crime. Partly as a result of such arguments, the legislature gradually became more supportive of popular education. A local commission appointed to examine the state of education in the colony drew attention to the serious problems arising from the lack of national cohesion among the variety of races in the colony. This was particularly marked with the arrival of a large number of Asian immigrants, who were described as being immersed in the "grossest paganism."

Because of the ethnic diversity of the society, it was considered necessary to encourage the children of all groups to attend the same schools. To achieve this goal the commission recommended the introduction of a secular system of education – a recommendation which received the support of the Combined Court. However, this measure was strongly opposed by the various denominational bodies and was eventually overturned by the Colonial Office. Therefore, church control of schools continued, and educational opportunities for the population were extended along denominational lines. This explains why so little was done locally during this period for the education of East Indian children.

The economic situation continued to pose a problem for the legislators, and while they provided financial assistance for the schools, this support failed to keep pace with increasing enrollments. For example, between 1880 and 1896 the average attendance in elementary schools rose by almost 50%, while the grant provided by the legislature was only increased by about 7% at current prices. As a result, the number of pupils who were presented for annual examination rose while the expenditure per student examined fell. This can be seen in Figure 3, below.

FIGURE 3
Rise in Number of Students Examined in the Primary Schools of British Guiana, 1880-95, and the Declining Per Capita Expenditure per Pupil Examined

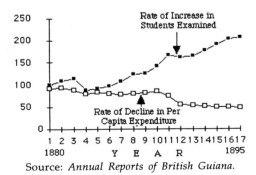

Source: *Annual Reports of British Guiana.*

The government of Grenada not only reversed its 1842 decision to withhold funding from schools but also increased its grant to help with the costs which the denominational bodies bore on their own, when no state assistance was being provided. At the time, there were schools operating in the capital city of St. George's and at least one in each parish, to which the legislature granted aid. However, after 1845 the sum voted for education remained virtually fixed for a number of years and was used to support only Anglican (£230) and Methodist (£117) schools, despite the fact that the majority of the population on the island was Catholic. In 1846 this policy was changed and government grants to education were extended to the Roman Catholic schools. In 1848, there was a marginal increase in the education allocation, which rose from £347 to £390, and then to £500 by 1851. The island was also spending a relatively small percentage of its budget on education — 2.3% in 1845 — as compared with 25% on its repressive state apparatus (RSA). However, this situation gradually changed, and by 1852 these percentages were respectively 5% for education and 15.9% for the RSA.

Despite the financial difficulties which the various religious bodies faced, the Catholics continued to establish new schools on the island. This resulted in even greater pressure on the legislature to improve its funding for education. Consequently, in 1855 the government allocation for education was increased to almost double the 1851 figure, at current prices. In 1862 the legislature again decided to discontinue its education vote, and financial hardships were once more imposed on the schools and on those church bodies that had decided to establish new ones. The result was an increasing demand for a return of the education subsidy, which occurred in the late 1860s.

In 1882 the Grenadian legislature, following the steps taken by Trinidad, enacted a new Education Ordinance which (1) made grants-in-aid available to assist schools that reached certain standards in terms of their enrollment and academic results; (2) provided for the establishment of schools in areas where no assisted schools existed; (3) doubled the education vote between 1881 and 1882; (4) allowed funds to be voted for the appointment of an inspector of schools; and (5) permitted the Roman Catholics to have a 50% representation on the board of education.

The governments of most member states which formed the Leeward Islands had accepted the importance of education for the masses. In 1846, for example, the St. Kitts legislature made a liberal three-year grant for the purpose of "promoting the education of the industrial classes." Yet in 1849 the grant of £600 p.a. was withdrawn, and for some years after, no further subsidy to education was provided. In 1856 a new Act came into force which increased funds for education by means of a tax on provision grounds. In the 1860s there was again an improvement in the amount of school accommodation available on the island, after the government began to provide one-third of the cost of building proper schoolhouses and made education grants available on the basis of school enrollment.

While Nevis had schools which were creditably constructed, the number of children admitted to them had to be limited, due to lack of financial support from the legislature for recurrent expenditures. Up to the end of the 1850s, the government had not yet made any funds available for education, despite the obvious desire of the population to have schooling available for their children. The levy of an educational tax had been proposed, but no successful action was taken on the issue. The legislature did, however, make an annual grant of £50 for education, which was increased to £150 in 1866 and continued to rise after this date. In the neighbouring island of Anguilla, it was noted that money was not circulating in 1847, which meant that the government was unable to provide funds for the support of schools.

The continuing apathy of the Montserrat legislature toward the issue of education was a matter of constant complaint by the administrator. The island's poverty, he asserted, was no excuse for the legislature's neglect of this need, especially considering "how small the grant was necessary to effect a vast amount of good and what large sums are constantly voted for objects comparatively trivial. They feel it is the duty of the people to provide education for their own families."[30] It was, therefore, not until 1868 that the government made its first grant to assist the various bodies operating schools on the island. Although the initial sum was small, it represented almost 1% of the total government budget. The authorities, however, required a certain minimum attendance before schools could qualify for aid.

The Dominican legislature also initially made little financial contribution to the operation of schools, though during the 1850s its involvement in the provision of popular education substantially increased. For example, in 1849 it passed an Act which raised its grants for schools from £300 to £800. In Antigua, although overseas aid to the missionary bodies was declining, the colonial legislature nevertheless refused to make up the growing financial shortfall needed to operate the primary schools. As a result, many of them were forced to close, and the total dissolution of the school system on the island was seen as a possibility. However, in 1857 the government began to provide additional funds for education.

In St. Vincent also there was a general reluctance on the part of the legislature to vote money for education after the withdrawal of the Negro Education Grant. A proposal was put forward for a small rate of tax to be levied to support the common school and, with some reluctance, the legislature began to make a contribution to the operational cost of schools. But it was so indifferent to this activity that not only was there a substantial reduction in school grants between 1854 and 1855, but in the latter year the legislators allowed the Education Act to expire, without introducing a new one. This led the lieutenant-governor to enter an urgent plea to "the honourable House" to make "the largest provision possible . . . for ensuring the systematic and *permanent* establishment of schools."[31] While funding was restored, in 1856, the education grant was again drastically reduced — from £903 to £152. However, by the end of the decade the situation began to improve and the education vote eventually reached £1,000 p.a. In addition, many schools were re-established and put on a better footing and a regional inspector of schools appointed.

In 1845 the government of St. Lucia provided its first grant of £450 for education and raised it to £500 the following year. At the time the only public schools on the island were those operated by the Mico Trust. In 1848 the government established a board of education and agriculture with the responsibility of apportioning government grants to existing schools and extending educational facilities to districts where schools did not yet exist. In 1852, the government began to open its own schools while still providing financial assistance for the denominational schools. Incidentally, two infant schools received a grant of £1,000 in 1851 from the Society of Friends, which occasionally gave limited financial assistance to schools in the region. By the 1860s, government support for education was provided from the fines levied in the inferior courts, hawkers' and boat licences, an export duty on coffee, cocoa, charcoal, firewood, logwood, hides, and farine manioc, plus an annual grant of £500 from general revenue.

Because of the absence of schools in the more remote rural areas in the Leeward Islands, the inspector of schools recommended that the grant not be withdrawn when a school was the only one in a district, even if it did not have the minimum enrollment, or if the students failed to attain the prescribed levels of academic performance. According to the inspector, the closure of such schools would mean that "the little flickering light" which they provided "will be extinguished and the children living in that neighbourhood will be left to grow up in utter darkness and ignorance."[32] To some extent this advice was heeded, when funds were available.

For a number of years after the withdrawal of the Negro Education Grant, the legislature of the British Virgin Islands also provided no aid for education and schools continued to depend on church or other private sources for support. The government later began to provide an occasional subsidy for education, but by 1853 there was still no regular annual government grant available to schools. The situation began to improve some years later, when the legislature granted aid to the Anglican schools. The hope was expressed that such assistance would be extended to other bodies, when "the state of the public finances" permitted it. In the early 1860s an Education Ordinance was introduced to provide funds for education from the annual budget.

A problem which the island faced was the emigration to St. Thomas of a number of youngsters who, having received an education locally, moved to this neighbouring island to fill clerical positions. This led the administrator to observe that he did not think that it was fair for the colony "to educate lads here at public expense so as to fit them for clerks at St. Thomas; if they desire this, they must educate themselves at their own expense."[33] This point of view continued to influence the attitude of the local legislature toward the provision of additional funds for education and thus government grants to education were often subject to considerable fluctuations.

Overall, while the total expenditures incurred jointly by the Leeward Islands (Antigua, St. Kitts/Nevis, Montserrat, the British Virgin Islands, and Dominica) during the two decades between 1869 and 1889 increased by 21.5%, the portion of the budget spent on education had risen by 36.3%. During the latter year, education was taking 3.73% of the budget, instead of the 3.32% which it did in 1869. While care must be taken in interpreting data pertaining to increases in educational expenditures because of their variability from one year to another, one can observe certain trends in the following graphs. Figures 4 and 5 indicate that while there were almost annual fluctuations in funds voted for education in the Windward and the Leeward Islands between 1867-1881, there was an overall tendency for these to rise. Further, increases in educational expenditure in the Leeward Islands, as a group, matched overall expenditure fairly closely (Figure 6), though this did not seem to happen in the Windward Islands (Figure 7).

However, an interesting picture emerges if the data for individual islands in these regions are examined separately, as is done in Figures 8, 9,

10 and 11. One can see that, over these years, such islands as Grenada (Figure 8) and St. Kitts (Figure 9), which were making higher grants to education at the beginning of this period, gradually reduced the percentages of their budget spent on this service. On the other hand, the islands which originally made smaller contributions maintained or gradually improved their position. These included St. Vincent and St. Lucia (Figure 8), Dominica (Figure 9), Montserrat and Nevis (Figure 10) and Antigua (Figure 11). The marked fluctuation in allocations to education in the British Virgin Islands (Figure 11) reflected the marked instability of the economy of this colony.

FIGURE 4
Increase in Educational Expenditure in Three Windward Islands (St. Lucia, St. Vincent, and Grenada, combined), 1867-81 (£)

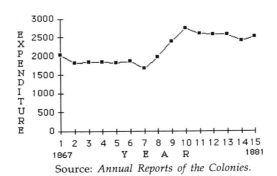

Source: *Annual Reports of the Colonies.*

FIGURE 5
Increases in Expenditure in the Leeward Islands (Antigua, St. Kitts, Nevis, Montserrat, British Virgin Islands, and Dominica, combined), 1867-81 (£)

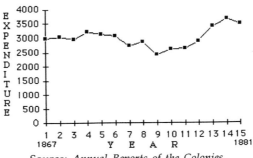

Source: *Annual Reports of the Colonies.*

FIGURE 6

Rate of Increase in Overall Expenditure in the Leeward Islands (Antigua, Nevis, British Virgin Islands and Dominica, combined) Compared with Rate of Increase in Expenditure on Education , 1868-81 (£)

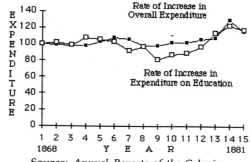

Source: *Annual Reports of the Colonies.*

FIGURE 7

Rate of Increase in Total Government Expenditure as Compared with Increases in Educational Expenditures Alone in Three Windward Islands (St. Lucia, St. Vincent, and Grenada, combined), 1867-81 (£)

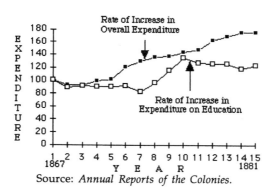

Source: *Annual Reports of the Colonies.*

FIGURE 8

Percentage of Annual Budget Spent on Education in St. Lucia, St. Vincent, and Grenada, 1867-81

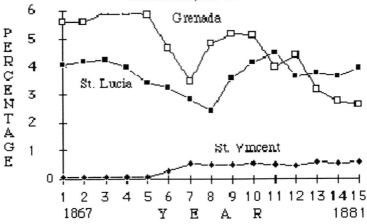

Source: *Annual Reports of the Colonies.*

FIGURE 9

Percentage of Annual Budget Spent on Education in Dominica and St. Kitts, 1867-81

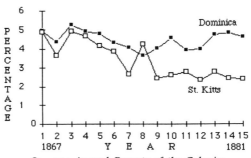

Source: *Annual Reports of the Colonies.*

FIGURE 10

**Percentage of Annual Budget Spent on Education in Montserrat
and Nevis, 1867-81**

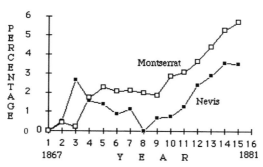

Source: *Annual Reports of the Colonies of Montserrat and Nevis.*

FIGURE 11

**Percentage of Annual Budget Spent on Education in the British Virgin
Islands and Antigua, 1867-81**

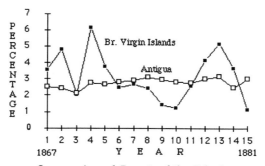

Source: *Annual Reports of the Colonies.*

During the latter half of the 1860s the government of the Turks and Caicos Islands began to provide financial assistance for education, increasing its funding between 1868 and 1869 by slightly over 50%. By then, the colony was spending about 7.2% of its limited government budget on education. Here, too, while the actual figure was quite small, the percentage of the budget allocated to education was the highest in the region. Commenting on this point, the governor observed in 1866 that, "for the size of the colony and the number of children under tuition" the vote which the colony allocated to education was quite liberal and would "stand a favourable comparison with that in other portions of Her Majesty's dominions."[34] However, after the colony began to experience a tighter economic squeeze, the legislature abolished the public schools with the 1872 Act and reduced its £700 p.a. education grant to £200 p.a. This amount was then given as a subsidy to those teachers who continued to operate schools. By 1873 the government had further reduced this allocation to under £105.

In 1850 the government of British Honduras voted only £100 for education. One outcome was that up to the mid-1850s, about one-sixth of the pupils were attending schools that were unsupported by the legislature, even though the inadequacy of financial resources was recognized as one of the major obstacles to improving the local education system. However, in 1850 an Act was passed to provide educational assistance for the benefit of every denomination of Christians and to establish a board of education. By 1856 the legislature made funds available for the board to grant £30 p.a. to every school with no less than 50 children, to provide books and stationery for each school, and to erect "new and spacious" central schools. The board was also charged with the responsibility of supervising these schools and providing improved salaries for teachers, in order to facilitate the engagement of superior trained and certificated individuals. It also made financial assistance available for the "proper" supervision of schools by competent headmasters.

While the legislature recognized that there was still a major imbalance in the distribution in educational funds between town and country in favour of the former, it could do little to overcome the problem, partly because of the difficulty in finding qualified teachers for the rural areas. Due to the financial situation which the colony faced, the government gradually let the responsibility for providing education shift almost entirely to the religious bodies. In the 1890s, it closed its one remaining school because it was too expensive to operate and finally decided that the money might be more effectively spent to assist religious agencies in their educational efforts. As the governor stated at the time, "the religious bodies are now to be recognized as the popular educators."[35]

In 1845 the government of the Bahamas was allocating about 5.5% of its recurrent budget to education. Large though this percentage was, it was inadequate to meet the demand for schools in the "Out Islands," especially in such areas as Marsh Harbour, Abaco, Governor's Harbour, Grand Bahama, Deadman's Cay, and Long Island. The reluctance of the legislators to provide additional funding for schools was again seen in 1851, when the education vote was exceeded and the governor sought an increase in the allocation to cover the deficit. His request was not only turned down, but legislators argued that there needed to be an overall reduction in the amount voted for education. Another effort at reducing expenditure in the Bahamas and other islands with a scattered population was to consolidate existing school facilities, and one of the steps taken was the closure of schools with limited enrollment. However, despite these efforts, in 1860 the Bahamian legislature approved the continuation of grants for the "education of our poorer classes."

In 1873 the allocation for education in this colony was again reduced by almost half, thereby adversely affecting the level of enrollment and the level of remuneration received by teachers. By the mid-1870s the legislature discontinued its funding of schools in the more remote areas, which often resulted in the closure of these schools. It was suggested that the steps taken by the legislature partly reflected the fact that, up to the 1870s, there were still influential individuals in these islands — most of whom were white — who continued to regard an education given to the black masses as serving only to unfit them "for a life of steady labour such as falls to the lot of a similar class in other countries."[36]

In Bermuda, an Act was passed in the late 1840s to promote general education in the colony. The aim was to assist and encourage education along whatever lines those who established schools might choose, while the government was to assume the responsibility for impartial but vigilant inspection. As a result, an initial sum of £300 was provided for schools in 1847. The amount was then increased to £600 for two years and an inspector of schools appointed in 1858. However this grant later fell to £400. Between 1868 and 1869, the colony experienced a drop of 13% in total government revenues, which resulted in a further substantial reduction of the education vote. The per capita expenditure on pupils declined by just under half, adversely affecting school enrollment and attendance, teachers' salaries, and the overall quality of education. These various cost-cutting measures particularly affected the education of the black population, toward whom it was noted that the Bermudan legislature displayed deplorable apathy.

In 1874 another Ordinance was passed by the legislators in Bermuda which approved the payment of grants to private institutions, thereby resulting in the establishment of additional primary schools. This payment was subject to the schools maintaining certain standards, to be verified by inspection. As a result, the education grant rose to £700 in 1876 and then to £1,200 by 1879 when a new Education Act was passed by the legislature. This Act levied a school tax of 6s. per quarter on all parents with children 6-13 years of age, except on those whose children were attending private schools. This made more funds available for education, and school attendance doubled in two years.

But the nature of the provision was such that schools remained racially segregated. All schools in the colony, even aided ones, therefore were regarded as private schools and were conducted "how and where" the "master or mistress pleases." This enabled the predominantly white legislature to free itself from the responsibility of having to prevent racial segregation in schools, including those receiving government funds. However, the schools were still subject to inspection as a condition of receiving aid. Thus, while there was a substantial increase in the education grant provided by the government, this proved of benefit mainly to the "poor whites," as it compelled them "to extend the blessings of education to their children, instead of allowing them to grow up in ignorance and barbarism."[37] The benefits to the black population were much more limited.

Summary and Conclusions

An important factor that affected the supply of educational facilities for the masses was the support provided for their education by influential groups within and outside these societies. In response to mounting pressure, the legislators became more involved, though often reluctantly, in increasing their allocation for popular education. However, as a percentage of the total annual budgets of these colonies, the financial support was still modest, often subject to marked annual variations, and even a reduction and suspension during some years. In Jamaica, the data indicate that during the latter part of this period the total education vote and the per student allocation for education rose steadily, while for British Guiana the situation was one of decline.

The British government continued to give moral support to efforts at providing education for the black masses, even after it had terminated its Negro Education Grant in 1845. The colonial governors also played an important role in securing the financial support of the local legislatures, as did many other groups, such as the missionaries and the journalists. However, some planters were still not convinced that the provision of education for all was a sound policy and did not support the idea of extending educational facilities to the children of the labouring classes.

Only a few years earlier it had been a common assumption that education would produce a discontented labouring population and lead to social and economic unrest. Some planters therefore experienced difficulty in reversing their attitude towards education for the black population over this short period of time. It was also suggested that those blacks who had received some education tended to look down on their fellow labourers, and to seek higher status jobs away from the sugar estates. This gave the planters another reason to oppose education for the masses.

However, despite such opposition, some West Indian legislatures began to make a gradually increasing commitment to the provision of popular education by voting additional sums for it and by assuming a greater responsibility for its administration and monitoring. Especially in the smaller colonies, however, these efforts were not always consistent, and in many cases, the local legislatures repeatedly withdrew their financial support for schools, placing a heavy burden on the denominational bodies which were providing education in the region.

There were many other constraints on the expansion of elementary education, including the reduction of funds available to the local missionary societies from overseas and the colonies' difficult economic conditions, especially after 1845. With the fluctuating and declining prices of sugar, legislators were unwilling for the state to make any long-term financial commitment to fund education. Thus even though various West Indian governments were gradually increasing their financial contribution to primary education, as yet there was no definitive picture of a firm commitment by the local legislatures to provide funds for it on a permanent basis. Commenting on this situation in Grenada, the governor observed that in the provision of funds for education the island's legislature was guided by no clear principle. The subsequent uncertainty for those involved in operating schools had an adverse effect on the amount and quality of elementary education provided in these colonies.

And yet there was a growing recognition in the West Indies that education for the masses had come to stay and that its expanded provision was necessary for social stability and economic growth in these colonies. The challenge therefore was to increase the efficiency and effectiveness of the education in order to justify the additional expenditures required to expand the service and improve its quality. Within this context, considerable controversy developed over the nature of the instructional programme that schools should offer. Financial difficulties also led to the increasing acceptance of the idea that parents should make a larger contribution toward their children's education, to the strengthening of the denominational system of education, and to the provision of more private schools in these colonies.

Notes

1   See M. K. Bacchus, *The Utilization, Misuse and Development of Human Resources in the Early West-Indian Colonies* (Waterloo, ON: Wilfrid Laurier University Press, 1990.)

2   Shirley Gordon, *A Century of West Indian Education: A Source Book* (London: Longmans, 1963), 43.

3   Vere T. A. Daly, *A Short History of the Guyanese People* (Georgetown, Guyana: The Daily Chronicle, 1966), 264.

4   Nicholas Hans, *Yearbook of Education, 1938* (London: Evans Bros., 1938), 779.

5   F. A. J. Johnston, "Education in Jamaica and Trinidad in the Generation After Emancipation" (Ph.D. diss., Univ. of Oxford, 1971), 266.

6   Gordon, *A Century*, 43.

7   Ibid.

8   CO 111/259, John McSwiney, *Report of The Inspector of Schools for British Guiana, The State of Public Schools in the Colony*, 20 October 1848 (London: PRO, 1848).

9   Report of the Government of Montserrat, *British Parliamentary Papers*, Vol. 46: *1847-48* (London: Government of Great Britain), 135.

10   Report of the Government of St. Lucia, *British Parliamentary Papers*, Vol. 62: *1852-53* (London: Government of Great Britain), 84.

11   Report of the Government of the Bahamas, *British Parliamentary Papers*, Vol. 34: *1851* (London: Government of Great Britain, 1851), 41.

12   Report of the Government of Dominica, *British Parliamentary Papers*, Vol. 62: *1852-53* (London: Government of Great Britain), 107.

13   Report of the Government of Bermuda, *British Parliamentary Papers*, Vol. 34: *1851* (London: Government of Great Britain), 28.

14   CO 295/134, McLeod to Secretary of State for the Colonies, 13 October 1841 (London: PRO).

15   Governor Harris to Earl Grey, 19 June 1848: 71 (London: PRO).

16   *Royal Gazette* [Trinidad], 8 October 1851.

17   James Maxwell, *Remarks on the Present State of Jamaica* (London: Smith Elder, 1848), 36.

18   Report of the Government of St. Kitts, *British Parliamentary Papers*, Vol. 10: *1857* (London: Government of Great Britain), 195.

19   Report of the Government of Grenada, *British Parliamentary Papers*, Vol. 40: *1857-58* (London: Government of Great Britain), 84.

20   George Brizan, *Grenada, Island of Conflict, From Amerindians to People's Revolution 1498-1979* (London: Zed Books, 1984), 157.

21   *Chronicle*, 12 March 1874. Cited in B. Brereton, *Race Relations in Colonial Trinidad, 1870-1900* (Cambridge: Cambridge University Press, 1979), 78.

22   Ibid.

23   Report of the Government of Antigua, *British Parliamentary Papers*, Vol. 51: *1876* (London: Government of Great Britain), 100.

24   Report of the Government of the British Virgin Islands, *British Parliamentary Papers*, Vol. 37: *1847* (London: Government of Great Britain), 56.

25   Sir Robert Schomburgk, *The History of Barbados* (London: Longmans, 1848), 108.

26   *Report of the Commission on Education in Barbados (The Mitchinson Report), 1875-76* (Bridgetown, Barbados: Barclay and Fraser, Printers to the Legislature, 1876), 6.

27   Schomburgk, *History of Barbados*, 109.

28   CO 31/56, Governor Reid's Address to the Legislature, 29 December 1847.

29   Report of the Government of Barbados, *British Parliamentary Papers*, Vol. 36: *1862* (London: Government of Great Britain), 45.

30   Report of the Government of Montserrat, *British Parliamentary Papers*, Vol. 39: *1846* (London: Government of Great Britain), 109.

31   Report of the Government of St. Vincent, *British Parliamentary Papers*, Vol. 42: *1856* (London: Government of Great Britain), 90.

32   Report of the Inspector General of Schools in the Leeward Islands, *British Parliamentary Papers*, Vol. 44: *1882* (London: Government of Great Britain), 188.

33   Report of the Government of the British Virgin Islands, *British Parliamentary Papers*, Vol. 37: *1865* (London: Government of Great Britain), 93.

34   Report of the Government of Turks and Caicos Islands, *British Parliamentary Papers*, Vol. 49: *1866* (London: Government of Great Britain), 68.

35   Report of the Government of British Honduras, *British Parliamentary Papers*, Vol. 55: *1892* (London: Government of Great Britain), 9.

36   Report of the Government of the Bahamas, *British Parliamentary Papers*, Vol. 51: *1876* (London: Government of Great Britain), 80.

37   Report of the Government of Bermuda, *British Parliamentary Papers*, Vol. 44: *1881* (London: Government of Great Britain), 143.

CHAPTER 2

PRIMARY SCHOOL ENROLLMENT AND ATTENDANCE

Introduction

Elementary school enrollment and attendance between 1846 and 1895 was characterized by the following features: (a) substantial differences between the colonies in the percentage of their child population attending schools; (b) a marked drop in school attendance during the early years of this period, following a rapid increase in enrollments during the immediate post-emancipation years, i.e., after 1838; and (c) great fluctuations in enrollment and attendance, with a high degree of irregularity in attendance. This occurred even though enrollments were rising after 1870.

Differences in Percentage of Population Attending School

Evidence of the wide differences in the percentage of school-age children attending schools in the different West Indian colonies can be seen in the graph in Figure 12, which shows the number of students in school per 100 population in the region. The figures were calculated on the basis of the total population rather than the population at risk, i.e., those in the 5-15 age group, because the latter data were not available. However, there is no reason to believe that the age structure of the population in these colonies was different, so that for purposes of comparison the data are still useful. A number of factors were responsible for these differences.

In some colonies, proportionately fewer schools existed due to their slower start in providing elementary education for the masses. In addition, some local legislatures were initially reluctant to grant aid to Roman Catholic schools and hence the pace at which they were being established was slow. Moreover, the fact that instruction was provided only in English deterred the non-English-speaking parents in some islands from sending their children to school.

Decline in Enrollment and Attendance in the 1840s

A number of events combined to bring about a marked drop both in school enrollments and in attendance in the 1840s. These included the withdrawal of the Negro Education Grant, the reluctance of local legislators to bridge the financial gap it created, the difficulties in securing alternative sources of funding, the economic hardships which the population faced due to fluctuations in the price of sugar and the higher school fees levied on nearly all children attending schools.

These factors resulted in a severe setback for education, as evidenced by the closure of the Mico schools (although some of these schools were taken over by the missionary societies). The educational efforts of the Church of England in these colonies also suffered. Only the Wesleyans maintained and even increased the number of their schools largely because the grant which the parent Methodist Society provided was increased by about 12%. In addition, this denominational group made a concerted effort to collect more school fees and also established a number of minor schools in which the teachers were paid very low salaries, to be supplemented by the school fees collected.

FIGURE 12
Number of Students in School per 100 Population in Various Colonies in the West Indies

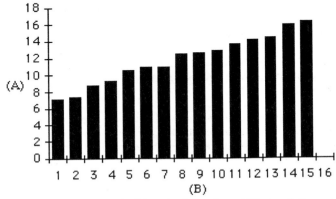

(A)   No. of Children in School per 100 population

(B)   The Various West Indian Colonies

Key: 1. St. Kitts 2. Montserrat 3. Nevis 4. Antigua 5. Turks Islands 6. St. Vincent 7. Virgin Islands 8. Barbados 9. Bahamas 10. British Guiana. 11. St. Lucia 12. Jamaica 13. Dominica 14. Grenada 15. Honduras
Source: *British Parliamentary Papers*, Vol. 49: *1877* (London: Government of Great Britain), 13.

Fluctuations in School Enrollment and Attendance from 1846 to the late 1860s

Not only did the number of schools operating in the region decline from about the mid-1840s, but pupil enrollment and attendance fluctuated considerably. For example, during the period from 1845 to 1870, the number of schools in Jamaica was increasing, though at a much slower rate than during the decade prior to 1845. The government discontinued its grants for schools with less than 30 pupils, causing an overall drop of about 26% in the number of schools and teachers on the island between 1844-45. In addition, the failure of the legislatures to vote funds for education in 1848-49 also further reduced school enrollments. Over the next few years even the Wesleyans had to close 19 day schools. The number of their schools in Jamaica was almost halved, having been reduced from 46 with a total enrollment of 3,045 in 1844-45, to 24 with an enrollment of about 1,832 in 1848-49.

But the situation gradually improved and the number of day schools rose from 209 in 1845 to 291 in 1858, excluding those operated by the Moravians. The increase in enrollments by between 2-3,000 pupils in 1858 was "attributable" to the restoration of government funding for education. By 1861 the number of pupils in the elementary schools rose again, reaching a figure that was about 7.7% of the total population.

Later, enrollments began to decline again. In 1864, the superintendent of the Wesleyan Mission found it necessary to discharge a large number of teachers for lack of funds. Nevertheless, enrollments again increased gradually, and for the period between 1861 and 1870, the overall numbers rose by an average of just under 2.5% p.a., although attendance was sometimes more irregular than in previous years. The number of schools conducted by all religious denominations had risen to 361, and the inspector of schools even reported that he had counted 490 schools when he toured Jamaica in 1864. This pattern of gradual increase in school enrollment and considerable fluctuation in attendance continued almost to the end of the period. This, as Campbell[1] pointed out, was a period of crisis for education in Jamaica, especially since there was a net loss of 23 day schools during these years.

In 1849 Bishop Parry noted that, in Barbados, enrollments in the Church of England schools were also fluctuating considerably, though over the years there was an increase both in the number of schools and their enrollments. In 1857 there were three times as many government-aided schools as there had been in 1851 and in 1860 about one of every two children in the 5-12 age group was said to have been enrolled in a public elementary school.

In Trinidad, elementary education virtually stagnated during the years immediately following 1845. In 1846 there were 54 day schools in the colony, with an enrollment of 2,518 pupils and a daily average attendance of 1,772, or 70.4% of those enrolled. At the time it was estimated that only 4% of the population was receiving any form of instruction. Between 1845 and 1848, the number of schools decreased by about 20%, though it later rose slightly until about the early 1850s. From then on there was no marked improvement in enrollments. After the first three years following the introduction of the ward system in 1851, only 11 government schools were in operation. According to the 1851 census only about 10% of the population were then able to read and write, with another 5% who could only read. However, enrollments had begun to improve from about 1852, and by 1855 the numbers who could read and write had more than doubled, reaching 23% and climbing to 31% by 1869. But average attendance as a percentage of enrollment fell, from 57.5% in 1851 to 52.8% in 1860, after which, as can be seen in Figure 13 it declined further, to 47.8% by 1868.

After nearly 20 years of operation, the ward schools had made little progress in increasing their numbers and enrollments. The percentage of pupils attending these schools was low, and the quality of the instruction poor. The wardens tended to neglect the school buildings and at times even failed to pay teachers' salaries. Some of them were even opposed to primary education for the masses. One of the overall outcomes was that enrollment in the ward schools "failed to keep pace with the natural increase in the population;" still less did they extend "the benefits of education to an ever increasing proportion of the young."[2]

FIGURE 13
(A) Rate of Increase in Average Attendance (B) Percentage Decline in Attendance in Trinidad, 1859-69

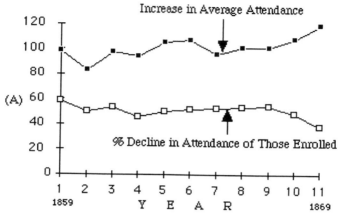

(A): ENROLMENT AND ATTENDANCE

Source: C. C. Campbell's *The Young Colonials*, p. 24 (in press).

After nearly 20 years of operation, the ward schools had made little progress in increasing their numbers and enrollments. The percentage of pupils attending these schools was low, and the quality of the instruction poor. The wardens tended to neglect the school buildings and at times even failed to pay teachers' salaries. Some of them were even opposed to primary education for the masses. One of the overall outcomes was that enrollment in the ward schools "failed to keep pace with the natural increase in the population"; still less did they extend "the benefits of education to an ever increasing proportion of the young."[3]

In addition, only about 57% of students in ward schools were attending for an average of more than 50 of the 182 days in the school year, and the average time spent by pupils in school in the late 1850s was about 14 months. Nor were they punctual, so that, at nine o'clock when school started, the buildings were usually empty. As late as 1870 Keenan observed that barely more than a quarter of the children of school age were attending schools, and enrollments in that year were still lower than in 1846.

In most of the other British Caribbean colonies, especially those still poorly supplied with schools, enrollments were also rising only slightly or fluctuating around the same level. In Antigua, it was estimated that there were about 2,403 pupils enrolled in schools in 1848. This number gradually increased, but levelled off during the years immediately prior to 1853, though there was a slight increase in the numbers attending the United

Brethren schools. Nevertheless, by 1852 there were 52 day schools on the island with 4,467 students and 37 Sunday schools with an enrollment of 6,418. By then, it was observed that a substantial number of the 8,000 youths between 5-15 years of age in the colony were already receiving some education.[4] However, from 1863 to 1868, enrollments dropped by about 22%, or 4.4% p.a., with average attendance falling by about 3.75% p.a. between 1864 and 1868. On the other hand it was noticed that there was still a growing desire for education, and by 1870 the educational levels of the island's black population compared favourably with those of other West Indian colonies.

In St. Lucia the Roman Catholic bishop made some efforts from about 1838 to establish new schools, but ten years later there were still no Roman Catholic schools on the island. The Mico authorities remained the chief provider of primary education and continued its work there, even after the termination of the Negro Education Grant. But despite the efforts to support education, only a relatively small percentage of the children under 16 years of age were attending schools in St. Lucia during the early 1840s. In 1847 the Mico schools had a total enrollment of just over 500 pupils and about half that number in schools operated by other agencies. Enrollments began to increase somewhat during the latter part of the decade, and between 1846 and 1849 the numbers in attendance doubled, due to the establishment of new schools, some of which depended entirely upon fees for their existence.

In 1850 a boarding school was opened in the capital city of Castries by the Order of St. Joseph of Cluny, and in 1852 the first government schools on the island were established. By 1855, there were four government schools, eight Mico schools, two infant schools, and a convent free school. In 1859 the government schools were handed over to the Mico Charity, which continued its operations in St. Lucia until 1891. These developments helped to ensure that overall school attendance and enrollment were maintained and improved, rising, on the average, by 5% p.a. between 1852 and 1871.

In St. Vincent school attendance fell between 1846 and 1848, but during the period 1849-60 the number of schools increased from 38 to 68 and attendance rose slightly, at an average of about 1.2% p.a.. Over the next decade enrollment increases were more substantial, averaging nearly 4.9% per annum until 1870. The number of schools in Montserrat and the level of school enrollment had "greatly decreased" with the withdrawal of the support of the Mico Charity, and education in the colony suffered greatly as a result. During the remainder of the 1840s enrollments remained fairly static, but by the 1850s an increase in attendance was again reported. A decline set in once more during the 1860s, however, and by 1870 enrollments were no higher than they had been in the mid-1840s.

In British Guiana, too, schools were closed due to poor financial support, resulting in a reduction of the number of children receiving an education. Between 1847 and 1848 alone, the numbers attending schools aided by the colonial treasury declined by about 20%. From then on, until the 1850s, there was a gradual increase in overall average attendance. Increases and/or fluctuations in school enrollment occurred in Montserrat, Dominica, Antigua, Grenada, St. Vincent, and the British Virgin Islands (BVI) during the same period. But while enrollments rose quite noticeably between 1840 and 1870, there was, on the other hand, a marked decline in their average attendance. In BVI, due to inadequate financial resources, the number of schools gradually declined until they eventually ceased to operate by August 1853.

In 1847 those attending regular schools in the Bahamas made up somewhat slightly less than half the children "fit to attend school" although, as happened in other West Indian colonies, some of those not enrolled in regular schools were attending Sunday schools. There seems to have been a low, if somewhat erratic, increase in enrollment and attendance, and by 1865 the colony had 30 government-aided schools, with an enrollment of just over 2,000 and an average attendance of about 60%. But over the next four years the numbers in school increased by almost 50%.

In the mid-1840s an Education Act was passed in Bermuda for the promotion of general education, and individuals and organizations were encouraged to establish new schools. As a result, the number of schools, along with their enrollments, increased substantially during the school year 1847-48. Most of these schools, however, were racially exclusive. In 1850, soon after the expiry of the Act which had provided funds to assist these schools, there was said to have been a "universal apathy of the population" toward 'the subject of education," and the rate of increase in school facilities and pupil enrollment dropped considerably.

In reviewing the overall picture it is obvious that during the period 1846-70 school attendance in the British West Indies was very irregular, and the pattern of increase in enrollments inconsistent. Due to the closure of a number of schools and the merging of others, educational facilities became less accessible to children in the rural and more isolated districts. This also contributed to a drop in school enrollment.

However, as the years went by, fluctuations continued in the levels of school enrollment, with a drop in the percentage of school attendance. In addition, there was always an insufficient number of day schools to accommodate all those who were eligible to receive an education. The situation in Jamaica was probably quite typical of that in most of the other colonies, and there, as Campbell pointed out, "what emerges from this see-saw as indicated by the school returns is that during the period, 1845-1865, the increase of day schools continued but at a slower rate than in the decade of the parliamentary grants." [5]

However, putting the issue within a broader perspective, the educational situation in some of the West Indian colonies was probably not much worse than that in other countries at a similar level of development. For example, in 1851 it was suggested that, in British Guiana, "the supply of the means of instruction equals in regard to quantity that afforded by most European countries," even if "it was woefully defective in quality." [6]

Fluctuations in School Enrollment and Attendance 1870-96

From about the early 1870s to 1896, there continued to be an overall increase in the enrollment and average attendance in primary schools in most of these colonies, though, as Capper, the inspector of schools for Jamaica noted, "irregularity of attendance" still remained "one of the greatest evils" with which the educational authorities in almost all the West Indian colonies were forced to contend.[7] While the overall enrollment in schools was rising, the percentage of attendance among those enrolled began to decline somewhat from around the early 1870s or the late 1860s. Figure 13 illustrates this point in relation to Trinidad.

Further, there continued to be wide variations, both in the enrollment and in the percentage of attendance, among the school-age population from island to island, from district to district, from year to year and from month to month, though these annual variations became less marked after the 1870s. Figures 15 A to E show the monthly variations in total average attendance for the islands of Jamaica, Grenada, Barbados, Bahamas, and British Guiana during the years from about 1870 to 1897. However, while the average number of days on which school was held every year in the region was low, it compared quite favourably with such areas as the southern USA. For example, around 1892 the figure for Jamaica was 109, for Trinidad and Barbados it was 98, and for Grenada 93, while states like Alabama registered only 62 days, and Mississippi 59 days, though in Massachusetts it was 164 days.

Jamaica

In Jamaica, the establishment of new schools helped enrollments in the elementary schools to continue to increase. For example, between 1868 and 1884, the number of schools in Jamaica increased by about 145%, school enrollment improved by about 190%, and the average attendance by 163%. In 1872 alone, 29 schools were opened in the more remote areas with the assistance of the starting-up grants provided by the government. Even though a cyclone struck the island in 1880, causing a 20% drop in average attendance, within three years enrollments returned to their 1880 levels.

Other evidence of a rise in the numbers receiving an education could be seen in the fact that in 1871 only an estimated one-third of the children between 5-15 years of age were attending school, but by 1882 this figure had risen to about 43%. In the following year it was again reported that "the number on the school registers increases steadily."[8] This was an improvement over the previous years, when the average length of stay in school was estimated to have been about two years. However, irregularity of attendance continued to be a great obstacle to the proper working of the schools.

After 1892, when school fees were abolished, there was a continuing rise in enrollment and attendance figures. By 1895 the number of schools on the island had nearly doubled since 1866, increasing from 490 to 900. Average attendance reached about 66.4% of enrollment. This figure was as high, if not higher, than any other colony in the British West Indies and only 11% below the average for England and Wales.

Barbados

The educational situation in Barbados continued, as in Jamaica, to progress favourably in the post-1870 years. Until the mid-1880s the number of schools and their enrollments increased almost annually. The latter rose by about 36%, or an average of 3.6% p.a., between 1871 and 1881, and by an average of 4.8% p.a. from 1881 to 1896. In addition to the government-aided primary schools, there were many private fee-paying ones which were invariably located in the urban and more populated districts and were said to have been among the best schools on the island. Their numbers indicated the growing desire for education, especially among the urban population. However, children in the more remote communities continued to face difficulties in finding schools within easy reach of home. Up to 1895 the board of education was still expressing regret that the educational opportunities for small and isolated communities continued to be limited.

By 1894 the Bree Commission expressed satisfaction with the overall level of school enrollment and attendance. Nevertheless, it proposed that there should be, on average, one school per square mile. By then, however, Barbados was already considered well supplied with schools, and from the available data, which was sometimes not very specific, it appears that the island had already exceeded the Commission's recommendation for the populated areas by about 12%.

Trinidad

In 1870 Keenan recommended that church schools in Trinidad should be granted state aid on the condition that they admit children of every faith and that a conscience clause be included which allowed parents to withdraw their children from religious instruction, if they wished. These recommendations were accepted, and government aid became available to them, providing a great impetus to the religious bodies to establish new schools.

However, the church schools, which were "crippled by poverty" and not in a position to improve their academic standards, were initially unable to qualify for government financial assistance. Therefore, while the island had 37 denominational schools by the early 1870s, none were state-aided. Years after the 1870 Act was passed, only three schools were receiving government assistance. The 37 ward schools, along with two model schools and the three borough schools, remained the major beneficiaries of government financial support. The situation later improved for the denominational schools when the only condition for them to receive government aid was that they should have an average attendance of no less than 25 pupils and be open to government inspection. This eventually resulted in a considerable increase in aided denominational schools.

The total enrollment in the government and unaided denominational schools in the early 1870s was about 4,000, with an average attendance of about 60%. It was then estimated that 40% of the children of school age on the island were enrolled in a school. Between 1870 and 1875, the number of government schools increased from 35 to 49 (by about 40%) and by 1879 there were also 39 assisted schools. Their numbers continued to rise — to 55 government and 61 denominational schools by 1885, while the number of denominational schools rose by over 20% between 1857 and 1868 — from 27 to 32. This increase in the number of schools, especially those provided by the denominational bodies, increased from 1878 to 1895, and the average number of students in attendance rose by about 6.2% p.a. between 1878 and 1889. Nevertheless, in 1886 about one-quarter of the population of school age in Trinidad was not enrolled in any school, another 25% "attended for only a few days each term, and the average daily attendance in government and assisted schools was only 8,282 out of a school-age population of about 22,500" (36.8%).[9]

In his desire to improve school attendance, Governor Robinson strongly supported the view that more assisted schools — which cost the government much less than state schools — were needed. He therefore introduced a new Educational Ordinance in 1890 by which schools were granted aid on a uniform basis, depending on enrollment, rather than on the results of the annual examination conducted by the inspector of schools. The new grants covered three-quarters of the cost of school buildings, furniture and teachers' salaries. The result was that the number of assisted schools increased rapidly — usually at the expense of government schools. However, as Brereton noted, while school enrollments on the island increased between 1870 and 1910, the population was growing quite rapidly through immigration from India, the Eastern Caribbean and Venezuela, and school attendance barely kept pace with the increase in the school age population.

Other British West Indian Colonies
The rate of expansion of educational services was somewhat more limited in the smaller British West Indian colonies. Efforts were made to reduce government expenditure by closing smaller schools, and school consolidation often meant that access became increasingly difficult for some children, especially those who lived in the very rural areas. As a result, despite the overall improvement in attendance, in the Leeward islands, "large numbers of little children" were growing up in "idleness and ignorance" for lack of a school within easy reach of their communities.

The closure of some schools usually meant that more funds were available to improve the quality of the instructional programmes offered in the others. This sometimes resulted in an increase in the enrollment of the remaining schools and as a result, it was suggested that one of the outcomes of the closure of the smaller schools was that a better quality of education became available to a larger number of students.

In these smaller West Indian colonies, the growth in school facilities continued to proceed rather slowly. Between 1875 and 1880, the total number of schools in the Leeward islands actually fell from 125 to 119 as a result of the policy of closing schools with very limited enrollments. But between 1888 and 1896, enrollments nearly doubled, even though average attendance had increased only about 83%. In other words, regularity of attendance was declining — it fell from about 55% in 1888 to about 50% in 1896 — while the numbers enrolled continued to rise. But in St. Kitts not only enrollments but also average attendance improved, despite the large number of children who were still kept out of school to work on the "fourpenny" gangs that were organized on almost every estate in the sub-region.

In 1890 the restrictions placed on the employment of children under nine years old also contributed to increased attendance. Between 1865 and 1875, enrollment in schools in Grenada rose by about 4.2% p.a., which was substantially higher than the increase between 1853 and 1876. In the early 1880s, popular education on the island was somewhat neglected, and only one of every six children of school age was attending school. But by 1882, a new Education Ordinance was enacted along the lines of one previously introduced in Trinidad, and its various provisions helped to increase popular interest in education, resulting in further improvements in school enrollment and attendance.

In St. Lucia, the average school attendance fell from 62% of enrollment to 51% between 1870 and 1876 and, by the latter year, only about one-third of the children of school age were receiving an education. In 1891, following the introduction of the 1889 Compulsory Education Act, the island had 24 assisted and four government-owned schools which together could provide sufficient accommodation for students should compulsory school attendance ever be enforced. However, during that year, the island suffered a significant educational loss with the withdrawal of the operations of the Mico Trust, which had conducted seven "excellent" schools. This proved a setback to the colony's efforts at improving the quantity and quality of its educational services.

Between 1870 and 1879 the number of children in schools in St. Vincent increased by about 22%, or by an average of approximately 2.4% p.a.. In Antigua, the rate of increase between 1869 and 1892 was less than 1% p.a., while in British Honduras, new schools were said to be springing up in various localities during the late 1870s.

In the Bahamas, enrollments hardly increased in the 1870s, but by the 1880s the situation had improved somewhat, with the numbers in school rising by about 20% between 1886 and 1895 — an average of 2.2% p.a.. This was due to the expansion of education into the more isolated areas of the Out Islands. By 1875 the board of education found itself unable to continue financing the extension or maintenance of schools to the less accessible districts, partly because of the poor attendance of the children. Therefore, by 1890 it was reported that only about one-quarter of the children of school age in these areas were not enrolled in any school.

School attendance in the Turks and Caicos islands remained unsatisfactory, even though in the early 1870s the government remitted to parents all the school fees that they had paid. By 1872 the economy had deteriorated so badly that public schools were abolished and the education vote was severely reduced.

In Bermuda, up to the 1870s, about 58% of the population between 5-15 years of age were attending schools. However, between 1873 and 1874, school enrollment fell by 8% and average attendance by about 10%. In the latter year, the payment of grants to private institutions was approved. This facilitated the establishment of additional primary schools, thereby increasing enrollments. In addition, the 1879 Education Act levied a school tax on all parents with children between 6-13 years of age. More funds thus became available for education, and school attendance doubled in two years. But these grants mainly benefited the children of the poor whites.

Compulsory Attendance

The general picture which emerges during the period under review is that while an increased number of school places were made available and enrollments rose, irregularity of attendance remained a major problem, and a considerable number of children were not enrolled in any school. In an attempt to improve school attendance, some individuals became attracted to the idea of introducing compulsory education in the region. The introduction of such a measure began to gain some support, especially after the 1870s, from a wider group, including the Baptists, who had traditionally opposed it. In an 1860 letter to the Student Missionary Society of Edinburgh University, a Presbyterian minister from Jamaica pointed out that

> many children in the neighbourhood, and in all parts of the island are growing up in ignorance, being often sent out to work when they should be at school; and the general complaint is, that things are worse in this respect than they were a number of years ago. A compulsory education bill which would be rather indigestible perhaps with you, would be more easily swallowed by our missionaries here. [10]

Others, such as senior officials in the Colonial Office, local government officials, missionaries, and even a few planters were either becoming more supportive of, or at least less strongly opposed to, the idea. For example, as early as 1835, Lord Glenelg, the colonial secretary, had despatched a circular to the various West Indian governors calling attention to the need for compulsory education in these colonies. In 1847 he emphasized again that

> ignorance should not be permitted to perpetuate itself [among the blacks]. . . . The present generation are insensible to the blessings of education (but) they *are not therefore to be allowed to refuse education to their offspring*. When they have ample means to do it [i.e., educate their children] they may be, as justly and fairly *compelled* to provide them with education, as to provide them with food and clothing. . . . Such compulsion in education is not incompatible with perfect liberty of conscience and freedom of choice as regards doctrinal differences in the religious portion of it [i.e., such education] [emphasis added]. [11]

This more positive attitude toward compulsory education continued over the years, especially after its introduction in Britain in 1870. Six years later the inspector of schools for Antigua suggested that it was

> never more strongly recognized that, while the education of children is one of the primary duties of parents, a function proper to government is to *enforce* the performance of this duty, and where necessary to *aid in providing*, or even itself *actually provide*, the means for acquiring what, in any community aspiring to be called civilized, may be considered the essential rights of every rational being, viz., the power of reading with facility, of writing legibly and with sufficient correctness to be intelligible, and of making arithmetical calculations sufficient for the everyday purposes of ordinary life [emphasis added]. [12]

In Trinidad, Lord Harris had contemplated the introduction of compulsory primary education, but with the poor financial state of the colony the idea was temporarily dropped. But in the late 1860s, the introduction of free and compulsory education was again strongly advocated by the inspector of schools, R.L. Guppy.

Another influential public figure, L. de Verteuil, argued that when education was offered to only a few, those who received it were likely to feel "superior" and despise agricultural work, while if it was compulsory and therefore universal, this situation would not arise. The issue was again revived in 1895 when a commission was set up to study and report on it. The teachers' association supported the measure, and the commission recommended, along with the abolition of school fees, that education be made compulsory for children between 6-10 years of age. But the recommendation was not implemented because it was felt that the cost would have been excessive.

In the Bahamas, it was pointed out that, while in 1845 about 45% of the children of primary school age were enrolled in schools, a quarter of a century later this percentage had not improved. In view of this, the board of education suggested that a compulsory education law should be enacted "as soon as [and] wherever practicable." However, this proposal was not very popular with the local legislators, as in the same year that it was put forward, the government per capita grant for education was considerably reduced. This seems to indicate that, while there was some public concern for increasing school enrollments, the legislators were either unable or unwilling to provide the funds necessary to support such a measure.

In 1871 the board of education again claimed that the only solution to the problem of poor attendance was to make education compulsory. A few years later, compulsory education was introduced in New Providence for children 6-12 years of age living within one and a half miles of a school. After a temporary increase in attendance, however, it was reported that the measure did not produce the expected results, partly because no officer had been appointed to see that the provisions of the Act were being enforced. Yet, in 1879 when a constable was appointed to make house visits and warn the parents about their "dereliction of duties," and even to take some to court for their children's non-attendance at school, the magistrates, who were generally not supportive of the measure, tended to be very lenient with the offenders. For example, one newly appointed constable took 40 individuals before the courts, but the magistrate excused them all on the basis of their poverty, their illness, or their inability to provide "proper" school clothes for their children. Despite the reported high enrollment in schools in the 1880s, only 50% of those enrolled attended regularly. In 1886, the Act was extended to include the Out Islands. It abolished school fees and reduced to one mile the distance which a child could live from a school and still be legally required to attend.

In 1852 the inspector of schools for British Guiana also proposed the introduction of compulsory education, but his recommendation was not acted upon by the legislature. The number of children enrolled in schools locally then made up about 38% of the 5-15 age group, with an average attendance of 70% of enrollment — a figure which the inspector considered far from satisfactory. Therefore, in 1856 he again advocated the introduction of compulsory education, arguing that planters who still opposed this measure were short-sighted. He advanced a number of reasons to support his recommendation, including the following:

1. Education would help the masses acquire a greater respect for "life and property, the law and the law giver, . . . their family and community,"

and "not the least, the blessedness of industry," which he considered was a precondition for their material prosperity. The masses should be "elevated to civilization," if necessary, by legally compelling them to attend school, "despite themselves."

2. Universalizing education was one of the surest ways to counter the feeling of superiority among those who were fortunate enough to attend schools. This would also help to overcome the unwillingness of those who had received an education to do agricultural work.

3. Finally, compulsory education was necessary to counter the "threat" posed by the "large additions of the semi-barbarian element" (the recent immigrants from Asia) in the population.[13]

But this proposal still did not find much support. However, by the early 1870s, it was noted that there was no longer the same objection to compulsory education as in previous years, primarily because the principle had been accepted in Britain. Therefore, when the Snagg Commission recommended the introduction of compulsory education, the proposal was accepted and the measure introduced in 1876. For financial reasons, however, the law was never rigidly enforced. Consequently, in 1877 irregularity of school attendance in British Guiana was still high, even in the capital city of Georgetown, where there were two district attendance officers. The same problem of irregularity of attendance was reported in 1880. One explanation of why the law was never rigidly enforced was that it was "not unlikely that too stringent a measure of compulsion would defeat its own object."[14] In 1882 a new law forbidding the employment of children under nine years as domestic servants or agricultural labourers helped to increase attendance.

However, up to the mid-1890s, many members of the elite continued to opposed mass education, particularly education for the children of East Indian labourers. The inspector of schools observed that many influential individuals still thought that it was a mistake to teach these children to read and write because, by doing so, the school was "spoiling a good shovelman."[15]

In Barbados, where a substantial number of children were still employed on the sugar estates, the plantation owners were not supportive of compulsory education, and worried about the possible effects of such a policy on the labour supply. In addition, the cost to the public treasury was likely to be high, and in a time of economic crisis and government cut-backs in spending, there was little chance of its adoption by the legislative assembly. The legislators in the region continually suggested that the colonies were in a state of bankruptcy and were already spending as much money on education as they could afford. In addition, some argued that parents were not very interested in education, as evidenced by their unwillingness to pay school fees.

Commenting on the issue of compulsory education, the *Mitchinson Report* expressed preference for a system of "indirect compulsion," whereby the achievement of a certain level of education was to be made a condition for the employment of any child up to the age of 12. This recommendation was not adopted, however, partly because of the inaccessibility of schools to some children, especially those in the more remote areas.

Nevertheless, while education was not made compulsory in Barbados, the legislature eventually introduced an enabling Act in 1883 which conferred on the board of education the power to enforce compulsory education, if it was found to be necessary. But by then, about 75% of the school-age children were said to be attending school, due to "the anxiety manifested by the public, particularly in the rural districts to participate in the benefit held out to them, by the opening up of elementary schools."[16] This positive attitude to education was said to preclude the necessity of enforcing the compulsory clauses of the Education Act. This was also the stance taken by the Bree Commission of 1894, which reported that parents were generally quite willing to send their children to school when they were able to do so. It therefore refused to recommend the enactment of a compulsory education ordinance, suggesting that it would simply introduce an element of discord between the labouring poor and the ruling authorities.

In Grenada, it was also suggested that any scheme for the education of the working class was unlikely to succeed unless the attendance at school of children between certain specified ages was made compulsory and a special rate levied for the support of the schools. However, while a Compulsory Education Act was passed in 1888, it did not effect any major change, partly because it was not strictly implemented. Thus, in 1891, according to the census report, only about 46.6% of those of school age were enrolled in schools on the island, and moreover, the average attendance was quite low — about 23% of enrollment. In St. Kitts, too, President Alex Moir expressed the view that "if real and widespread advantages are to be obtained in the West Indies," then a system of compulsory education, combined with a bona fide programme of industrial education in schools had to be inaugurated and insisted upon.[17]

With school attendance on the island of Dominica still on average around 40% in 1875, compulsory education was suggested as the only answer to the problem, an issue considered to be of vital importance to the future of the West Indies. In 1887 the inspector of schools re-emphasized the point that, in the absence of compulsory education, a speedy solution to poor attendance could not be expected and in the following year again pointed out that

> without proceeding to the extent of enforcing attendance, possibly a simple measure, similar in its provisions to those clauses of the Imperial Factory Act, placing certain restrictions on the employment of child labour under the age of 10 might be attended by beneficial results in those islands where "grass gangs" flourish; but it would not, to any extent, touch Dominica where the existence of hundreds of children that have never been inside a school testifies to the need for compulsory enforcement of attendance. With whatever financial or other difficulties the question may be fraught, it is one to the necessity of which public opinion is gradually ripening, and sooner or later it must engage the attention of the government. Combined with the present denominational system which possesses, in addition to its economy, valuable qualities of its own, compulsion will multiply the value of existing

schools and raise them to a higher standard of efficiency.[18]

In 1890 a Compulsory Education Act which applied to Antigua, St. Kitts, Dominica, Montserrat, Nevis, and the Virgin Islands was passed by the Leeward Islands Federal Council, with only one dissenting voice. The Act made it possible for these colonies to proclaim certain educational districts as those where school attendance would be compulsory, and to appoint attendance officers to enforce the provision of the Ordinance and impress upon parents and guardians the duty of ensuring that their children regularly received an education.

The Act provided for compulsory attendance to be brought into force gradually, with a period of grace, up to July 1891, during which time no prosecution would be made, but the population would be warned about the consequences of any infringement of the law. When the provisions of the Ordinance were applied, it was noted that the most marked increase in daily attendance was in Montserrat and Dominica. To enforce the Act, the need for the appointment of attendance officers was recognized and for the establishment of government schools in districts where no school yet existed. Efforts to prosecute the parents for the non-attendance of their children at school was often not very successful because many members of the ruling groups, including the lay magistrates, were not fully supportive of the Act.

In St. Lucia, a compulsory education ordinance passed in 1889 imposed on parents and guardians the duty of "causing their children to receive instruction" in the 3Rs. However, as happened in most other colonies, it was not possible to enforce this measure, partly for financial reasons. In St. Vincent, even though it was felt that such a measure might help to overcome the problem of poor attendance, the great opposition which it was expected to meet cast doubts as to whether the ordinance could ever be successfully enforced. In the British Virgin Islands, some schools were situated in quite remote places, and this affected school attendance. Even the inspector of schools often found it dangerous and uncomfortable to travel to some of the schools. Nevertheless, the colony's administrator argued for the rapid extension of education to the whole population on the grounds that

> so long as the knowledge of reading and writing is confined
> to one in a hundred of the population, or thereabouts, the
> result of education is, no doubt, to raise the fortunate
> possessors of such exceptional knowledge to such a pitch of
> self-esteem as to make them averse to the use of the hoe or
> other honest labour, and in this they are often encouraged
> by foolish parents. The general diffusion of education will
> cure this evil.[19]

This view was receiving increasing support from many others in the region.

In British Honduras, only about 36% percent of the 5-15 year olds were registered in schools in 1884. But this low level of enrollment was "to a certain extent, to be accounted for by the peculiar circumstances of the colony, the mixture of races, Hispanics, Indians, Caribs and Negro, the want of internal communication, and other causes."[20] The chief administrator therefore felt that "the time . . . [had] not yet arrived" for the introduction of compulsory education, but pointed out that, should "no improvement take place in the numbers attending school, . . . [he would] have no option in the matter" other than recommending its adoption.[21]

In the Turks and Caicos Islands, it was estimated that as many as 62% of the children between 6-13 years of age were registered in schools by the early 1880s and that their average attendance was about 65% of enrollment. The president of the colony suggested that, in view of these high enrollment and attendance figures, it was not yet necessary to implement the compulsory clauses of the Education Act. He also pointed out that the board of education was "well aware of the poverty of many of the pupils and of the possible hardship that it might mean to some parents, to compel them to send their children to school regularly."[22] However, a circular letter was issued to all schoolmasters, urging them to remind parents that "unless they availed themselves of the advantages now given them of good schools, the law will be made compulsory."[23]

Yet while an increasing number of planters and legislators were slowly accepting the need to provide more government financial support for popular education and the introduction of compulsory education, many continued to remain skeptical about the economic outcomes of such a measure. They felt that for the majority of the black population education often implied immunity from labour and partly for this reason they were opposed to the idea of compulsory school attendance. In some colonies, it was considered desirable that the principle of moral persuasion, rather than legal compulsion, should be used to get parents to send their children to school. For example, Governor Higginson of Antigua saw that the problem of poor attendance could not be solved simply by making education compulsory, but would depend on the success of efforts to inspire the Negroes with a "just appreciation of the benefits of education."[24]

Some missionaries also continued to be against compulsory education, partly because they were opposed to any state intervention in the work of their schools. This lack of missionary support made it difficult for a Compulsory Education Act to be enforced. For example, as previously mentioned, the Baptists in Jamaica were among the principal opponents of compulsory school attendance and helped to defeat the House Tax bill which would have laid the foundation for a compulsory state system of primary education in that colony. On this issue, the Baptists originally took the side of the planters, because they saw in compulsory attendance an attempt by the state to assume greater control of education. However, by 1863, with the tight financial situation that they faced, the increased irregularity of school attendance and the rise in the incidence of juvenile crime, even the Baptists had come to agree that this measure was highly desirable. But despite the growing support for compulsory education it was not seriously considered in most of the West Indian colonies, since the planters who controlled the local legislatures were generally reluctant to provide the necessary funds.

There were also some differing points of view about specific aspects of the measure. For example, there was a lack of agreement as to which age groups were to be subjected to any compulsory education ordinance. In British Guiana, some individuals challenged the proposal that 13 years be the upper age limit to which compulsion might apply. They suggested that if children had not acquired the basic rudiments of education by the age of 10 years, it was a sheer waste of time to keep them in school any longer because they also had to become acquainted with the use of the shovel and hoe and that this should not be postponed to too late an age. Thus, despite the lengthy discussion about the desirability of compulsory education, the measure was never rigidly enforced in those colonies where it was introduced. It was less a case of the unavailability of funds than the different priorities of the West Indian governments, although the costs were sometimes considered to be beyond the financial resources of most colonies. Another consideration was that compulsory education would create a shortage of labour on the plantations.

Other social problems militated against efforts at introducing compulsory education, some of which can be appreciated from the following description of the lives of children among the West Indian labouring classes. While referring to the island of Montserrat, the situation described was quite typical of most of the region at the time:

> Small children may be seen morning and evening steadily and regularly fetching, for family use, water from springs and wells, and tying out, bringing home, or driving to the drinking place the horned stock, ponies, sheep and goats, possessed by nearly every labourer in the island. Children carry from the provision grounds, and take round for sale, the produce —vegetable and fruit — of their parents' land. As the children grow bigger their labour is sought by the planters, for whom they work from 6 a.m. to 5 p.m., earning good wages [which swell the family income] in the grass gang under pretty sharp supervision. Grass and other fodder is brought to the mule and cattle pens by these children, who also drive the mules and donkeys carrying cane to the mill and boxes of manure on to the land. Other useful work, both in and out of crop time, is done by the small gang . . . *they are getting educated in the principal industry of their native land* [emphasis added].[25]

The writer went on to suggest that since "the labour of children" in the colony was "so valuable and useful, attendance at school cannot be expected to increase to a large extent at once," even with compulsory education.

In 1857 the governor of Jamaica, who was quite supportive of the idea of providing more financial assistance for education, suggested that "until far more ample and convenient means of instruction than now exist have been placed within their [the children's] reach I certainly think it would be both unfair and impolitic to make education compulsory."[26] An educational tax was also suggested to help finance this compulsory education effort, since it was felt that such a measure would make parents more appreciative of education. However, this was never implemented by the legislatures.

In 1877 the inspector of schools again expressed the view that the indifference of the parents to education and their desire to have their children employed were the major obstacles to the successful introduction of compulsory education. He also observed that the mountainous terrain and remoteness of certain areas in Jamaica would make compulsion difficult to enforce. He proposed, instead, that the island might forbid the employment of children under a certain age and without a certificate to indicate that they had acquired a certain level of education. This, he felt, could be "productive of much good" since from education there would be "spill over" benefits such as a decrease in the crime rate.

In that year, the governor again noted that the children on the island were kept away from school at certain seasons to help their parents in agricultural pursuits because "these little workers are of great use . . . when the little patch of coffee has to be picked, or the crop of peas to be shelled." Therefore, given the existing economic circumstances and bearing in mind that agriculture would be "the chief occupation of the children themselves," he considered that it might not be "an unalloyed good to insist upon the regular attendance at school of this class of children, thus cutting them off from the labour" which they would eventually have to perform.[27] The 1879 Commission on the Condition of the Juvenile Population possibly took this line of argument into consideration when it recommended the adoption of a "half time system" of schooling, which would have required children to attend school for a certain number of weeks every quarter. This proposal was not likely to receive any objection from the employers.

Education of New Immigrants
Soon after the abolition of slavery there was a substantial influx of new immigrants into some of the West Indian colonies, particularly Trinidad and British Guiana, where they were brought to work as indentured labourers on the sugar plantations. The great majority of them came from Asia, mainly India, and initially, the education of their children was also of little concern to the authorities. The planters regarded them as replacements for the unskilled black labourers who had moved out of the estate labour force and therefore felt that it was unnecessary to educate their children, since it was not likely to improve their competence as plantation workers. Even Anderson, the inspector of schools for Trinidad, suggested in 1860 that, so long as the East Indians "could handle the hoe and the cutlass with dexterity and perseverance," it was of no significance whether they "could read or notate figures."[28]

On the other hand the ward schools in Trinidad were open to East Indian children, but very few, if any, of them, attended the schools. In a few cases, schools were provided for them by the sugar estate authorities, the government, or the denominational bodies. The Lothian estate even sent to India for a Christian Indian teacher who became master of a short-lived infant school in Port-of-Spain. But many East Indian parents were suspicious of the Christian denominational bodies, which were largely interested in converting the children to Christianity and depriving them of their cultural traditions. The East Indians were usually unwilling to give up their own culture and religion to adopt Western ways of living or to become Christians. This was one reason why it was observed that "an Indian will not send his child to a Creole school."

The governor of Trinidad advocated the provision of schools for the children of these new immigrants in order to raise their moral standards. He attributed the crimes committed by the East Indians and Chinese, more than half of which were due to "breaches of labour contract," to the moral weakness of these ethnic groups. "This," he claimed, "is the price which the Colony has to pay for adding a heathen element to its population," and suggested that "the surest prospect of amelioration" of such crimes "lies in the gradual assimilation of this element with the bulk of the people, and its consequent subjection to the influence of a higher and more Christian civilization."[29] Since it was among the young that such efforts were likely to be most effective, he recommended that schools under Christian teachers be opened for their children.

As late as 1893 a Protector of Immigrants for Trinidad, D. W. D. Comins, expressed the view that there was a tendency to carry schooling for East Indians too far, by giving the youngsters a high-class education which was entirely unsuitable to their circumstances. He went on to point out that only a limited number of young East Indians would ever be able to secure such occupations as clerks and catechists and, therefore, for the others, the present education was much too advanced. While accepting the view that elementary schooling on an estate could "expand the intelligence and understanding and inculcate habits of regularity, obedience, and respect for authority" among the pupils, it was suggested that such education should not be continued for a prolonged period, since it would only succeed in making the students

> proud and lazy for manual work . . . and they would walk about with their boots on and do nothing. [Therefore] it is a great curse to a rising generation . . . to have a lot of over-educated and effeminate youngsters. The future of the Colony depends on the development of its agriculture, on which the general revenues might be more usefully employed than in the manufacture of clerks.[30]

It was partly because of the objection by East Indian parents to the proselytization of their children that they often refused to send them to the missionary schools. This was why Keenan urged that to improve the attendance of East Indian children, efforts should simply be made to educate them — not to convert them to Christianity.

There was also an economic reason behind the parents' reluctance to send their children to school. Most of them were intent upon improving their financial situation by increasing their incomes and accumulating as much money as they could, especially during and even after their period of indentureship. This is why they were often willing to work for much lower wages than the Creoles, and why they accepted the indignity of employment as indentured labourers in the first place. Therefore, sending their children to school, rather than having them earning an income by working on the sugar estates or assisting with domestic chores while the parents went out to work, ran counter to their primary objective in coming to the Caribbean.

In addition, with the low status which the society conferred on them, their opportunities for social mobility through education were initially even more limited than for the black population. As a result, they saw that any investment in the education of their children was not likely to yield an adequate economic return. Finally, they thought that "by sending their children to school, they . . . [were] conferring a favour, [on the authorities] and that they ought to receive the same amount of money for attending school as they . . . [could] earn by working on an estate."[31]

Campbell[32] noted that it was therefore doubtful if any East Indian child in Trinidad received formal education between 1845 and 1856. Up to 1869, there were only six East Indian children attending ward schools on the island. However, public attitude to the education of these children gradually changed as it became obvious that they were likely to remain in these colonies, rather than return to India on the termination of their indentureship. In addition, the rise in sugar prices during the second half of the 1850s helped to improve the attitudes of some planters toward the provision of education for East Indians.

In 1856 Frederick Burnely, an absentee proprietor, sent out the Reverend Sorby to act as a catechist to the East Indians on his estate in Trinidad. Sorby later started a home for East Indian children who were orphaned as a result of the cholera epidemic of 1850. This became the Tacarigua Industrial School which East Indian orphans were later compelled to attend.

After the 1850s, the Church of England began to exert some pressure on the government of Trinidad to make provision for the education of its East Indian population. The Bishop of Barbados also urged that schools should be provided for the education of these newer immigrants, if only for a few hours on Saturday mornings and Sundays, and that some funds be voted for the remuneration of those who would take on the extra task and responsibility for helping to teach these children.

Another factor perceived to be important in the education of East Indian children was that their parents were seen as only semi-civilized, speaking a barbarous tongue, and worshipping strange gods. Therefore their children were presumed to be in need of Christian enlightenment and to be introduced to Christian values and the tenets of Christianity. For example, at the Tacarigua Industrial School for East Indian children Christian religious education was compulsory because of its allegedly civilizing influence on the Hindu and Moslem students. It was further suggested that "the separation of even a small number of persons of Indian extraction, at an age when lasting impressions are most easily formed, from the debasing influence of caste and heathenism is in itself a gain."[33] Finally, since East Indians had, so far, held strongly to their cultural beliefs and practices, it was hoped that the school would help not only to Christianize them but also to prepare them as appropriate role models for the younger Indians. On this issue it was indicated that

> it will not appear too much to predict that this asylum may prove to be the cradle. . . of a local Indian population, Indian, that is, in descent and natural characteristics, but English in education and feeling, and having no associations beyond the limits of the Colony.[34]

It was within this context that the Canadian Presbyterian Mission (CPM), through the efforts of the Reverend John Morton, opened its first school in Trinidad in 1868 to provide education for East Indian children.

The governor of the island highlighted the mission's dual aim of evangelization and education among this sector of the population which had so far been neglected by the other Christian denominational bodies. While the CPM's schools were not meant exclusively for East Indian children, the services of a teacher from India were obtained for its school in Port-of-Spain, and a Christian Indian and his wife, also from India, were later employed as teachers at another of its schools. Later the Mission extended its activities to East Indian children in British Guiana.

The increasing recognition, throughout the region, that the education of East Indian children had been neglected led to the view that a special educational provision ought to be made for them. In Trinidad, this resulted in the 1889 Education Act which made it possible for free education to be provided for these children. Two years later, the board of education was given powers to establish schools free of charge, specifically for East Indian children. Initially, these schools received substantial financial assistance from the planters, though later they were partly funded by the government. As a result of these efforts, an increasing number of East Indian children began to attend school.

The CPM later had five schools in which about 250 East Indian children were taught in English and Hindustani. By 1887 there were about 37 schools for East Indian children in Trinidad, and by 1892 the number had reached over 50. Nevertheless, the inspector of schools felt that more should be done for the education of these children, since the East Indians had "rendered such good service to the Colony in developing its material resources." Their education should therefore be seen as a "duty which the government and the employers owe to them."[35] By the late 1880s, those attending schools were said to have been making remarkable progress. Not only were a substantial number able to understand English, but some were members of reading clubs started by the CPM, while others subscribed to overseas newspapers, including the *London Times*. A few were also able to secure employment opportunities outside the sugar plantations.

In British Guiana, a school was established in 1849 for the education of East Indian children "whose ignorance of the [English language] excludes them entirely from the ordinary schools of the colony."[36] This was said to represent, along with another such school, "the first instances in this Colony of such undertakings for benevolent purposes, supported by voluntary contributions from the higher classes."[37] Estate schools for these immigrant children were first established in 1861, and by 1872, in addition to the four estate schools which then existed, there were a number of others which received no government aid, but were financed by some estate proprietors or managers of the plantations.

However, the initial unwillingness of East Indian parents to send their children to school continued and, up to 1895, very few East Indian children were receiving any formal education in the West Indies. The efforts of the Canadian Presbyterian Mission in British Guiana were initially not very successful but became so after the turn of the century. One reason for this was that the education of the East Indians continued to have little support from most of the planters who felt that, once these youngsters had received an education, they would no longer remain as labourers on the sugar estates, but would seek other employment opportunities, eventually reducing the size of the estate labour force. School attendance would also result in the immediate loss of the labour which the children provided for the estates.

Many senior government officials supported the planters in their opposition to the education of East Indian children. For example, Charles Bury, the immigration agent-general for British Guiana who was responsible for the welfare of the East Indian population in that colony, was opposed to the inclusion of East Indians under the local Compulsory Education Ordinance introduced in 1876. He argued that "on most estates the big gangs of little children under [the school-leaving] age are employed in light work such as carrying earth, ashes and manure and this is not only a benefit to their parents but also a source of pleasure to themselves."[38] Another immigration agent-general was even more pointed in his objection to the education of East Indian children, arguing that "when an [East Indian] child was educated he looked down upon his father, got beyond control and after that rarely settled down on the land"[39] — a fact which was likely to have adverse consequences for the supply of cheap labour on the plantations.

In Jamaica, the East Indian population was small and scattered all over the island. This made it difficult for educational facilities to be provided for them as a group, as in Trinidad and British Guiana. So, prior to 1879, as Shepherd[40] noted, the educational needs of their children were ignored by both the colonial government and the larger Jamaican society, including the planters. However, in 1875 the government made provision for the Protector of Immigrants to order, with the consent of the parent, any child of an immigrant to attend the nearest suitable day school. This step had little effect on their attendance, however, because the parents did not want to give up the wages which these children earned by working on the estates.

In Vere, the Reverend C. F. Douet opened a school exclusively for those East Indians who were "free and unindentured." The school offered instruction in English and Hindustani, hoping to overcome the "persistent aversion" which East Indians had developed to sending their children to ordinary schools. While it was proposed that the government should provide special assistance to all those who wanted to establish similar schools, Reverend Douet was strongly urged that the estates employing East Indians "should consider it their duty to help in providing suitable schools for the(ir) children."[41] He even suggested that it would be to the planters' benefit to do so. His idea was to introduce these children to Western cultural traditions and the English language so that they could be more readily integrated into the larger society.

Eventually, a few planters in Jamaica became more supportive of efforts to educate the East Indian children and sometimes made estate buildings available for schools. But, up to about 1891, less than 12% of East Indian children of school age on the island were attending school, as compared with 50% among the remainder of the population. As in other colonies, this was partly attributed to the "not unnatural" objection by the parents to losing their children's services, which were financially valuable to them, especially at certain seasons of the year.

However by the following year another school for East Indian children was opened up in Westmoreland, and during the next few years support was provided by the planters. An estate proprietor made a contribution towards the teacher's salary and the cost of maintaining a school operated by the Presbyterians on Ewing's Caymanas estate in St. Catherine. But by the end of this period under review it was still being observed that East Indians were "only partially, as yet drawn into the education system."

In St. Vincent the first of a new class of schools established exclusively for the education of the children of East Indian immigrants was built by the Argyle estate owners. It was hoped that if the school proved a success, others like it would be opened up in the other colonies of the Leeward and Windward group. In St. Lucia, three schools for East Indian children were established — one in 1886 under an East Indian master and two in 1887 by the Canadian Presbyterian Mission. By 1893, the number of these schools had increased to four. In Grenada, the lieutenant-governor noted that "one of the purposes underlying immigration" was that the immigrants "must be subject to continuous labour" and since they had no time to attend school, "their improvement and education therefore must be acquired by contact and habitude."[42] He admitted that there were benefits which they "ought to receive as members of a civilized and Christian community," but mentioned the possibility of their attending Sunday schools, or receiving noon-hour instruction. Nevertheless, the main idea remained, that East Indian labour should not be lost to the sugar estates by having the children attend school.

Summary and Conclusions

During the period 1846-70, there was as yet no consistent pattern of increases in enrollment and attendance in West Indian elementary schools. Instead, the number of children enrolled in schools tended to fluctuate considerably, with an indication of a slight increase during the first 25 years of the period under review. This can be seen in the graphs in Figure 14 (A-F) which provide an idea of the increases and fluctuations in school enrollment in a number of West Indian colonies up to 1870. School attendance was also quite irregular during this period.

There were many reasons for these fluctuations in enrollment and the decline in average attendance. First, a number of schools were forced to close following the termination of the Negro Education Grant. This occurred at a time when the region was experiencing tremendous economic difficulties and the legislatures were unable and/or unwilling to step in and meet the financial shortfall, even if some of their members were inclined to do so. The schools that remained open were less accessible to many children, which no doubt affected their attendance, especially that of the older children who already had some schooling. Further, after emancipation, a number of families moved away from the sugar estates to live in the more remote areas. This increased the difficulties which children faced in trying to secure access to schools.

In addition, some of the better schools in the region which were operated by the Mico Trust, the largest recipient of funds from the Negro Education Grant, had to be closed. This often meant that their students had to attend other schools which were usually providing an education of a lower quality. The generally poor quality of education offered in West Indian schools and the irrelevance of the programme of instruction to the needs of the students were identified as two of the major factors which contributed to the poor school attendance in the region. To these could be added the high incidence of illness reported in many of these colonies, which experienced frequent outbreaks of epidemics.

The economic crisis which the West Indies was experiencing due to the decline of the sugar industry also affected enrollments and attendance in two ways. First, it meant that the legislatures were less able to provide funds to keep all the existing schools open, much less to establish new ones. Second, the reduced incomes earned by the parents meant that they were often in a difficult financial position to meet the direct and indirect costs of sending their children to school. They were less able to pay the increased school fees, which had become fairly widespread in these colonies, and, at the same time, provide their children with the necessary clothing and other requisites to attend school, especially in view of the rapid increase in the cost of cotton goods. During these financially difficult times, parents were also more in need of their children's labour to help meet the family expenses, either through part-time work on the sugar estates or elsewhere, or by assisting on the family farm. Finally, even though pupils remained away from school for long periods, teachers were reluctant to strike their names off the registers, since their teaching incomes were often linked to school enrollments. This practice was reflected in the poor school attendance rates.

However, during the period from 1871 to 1896, primary school enroll-ment and attendance improved and fluctuations in attendance were somewhat less marked. This can be seen in the graphs in Figure 15 (A-E). The percentage of children who were registered in schools and the regularity of their attendance continued to vary from one colony to another, from one region to another, and from one socio-economic group to another.

Some of this had to do with the availability of schools within easy access of the population. Attendance was usually better in the towns and other areas well supplied with schools than in the more remote, rural areas where school accommodation was either inadequate or not easily accessible to all children. The level of school attendance also depended on the age of the children and the time of the year, so that when students were very young or when there was little work to be done on the farm, attendance was highest.

In this context, and with the enactment of a Compulsory Education Ordinance in Britain in 1870, there was growing local interest in making attendance at school compulsory. However, some legislatures decided that, with the economic difficulties which the population was facing, and the increasingly favourable attitude of many parents to education, it was unwise to make school attendance compulsory. Some of these colonies, such as British Guiana, the Bahamas, and the Leeward Islands, did introduce a Compulsory Education Ordinance, but the Act was never rigidly enforced, largely because of the poor economic conditions of the parents.

The payment of school fees by parents was increasingly insisted on by the authorities in order to help ease the financial burden which the colonies were experiencing in funding education. After the 1870s, however, many legislatures began to relax this requirement, a step which resulted in increased school attendance. Further, although the number of children enrolled in schools was increasing, especially after the 1870s, the percentage who were actually attending school was declining somewhat.

Finally, while the flow of immigrant labourers from Asia increased, the education of their children was generally not encouraged by the authorities on whose sugar estates the immigrants worked. The planters felt that education was likely to encourage the children's mobility outside the sugar estate work force since they were more likely to seek higher status employment in other industries. For economic and cultural reasons, the parents also were not very keen to send their children to the existing denominational schools. Nevertheless, largely through the efforts of the Canadian Presbyterian Mission, increasing numbers of East Indian children gradually received some form of schooling in Trinidad and later in British Guiana.

FIGURE 14 (A)*
Grenada: Enrollment Figures, 1850-70

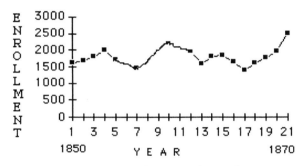

Source: *Annual Reports of Grenada.*

FIGURE 14 (B)
Montserrat: Enrollment Figures, 1846-71

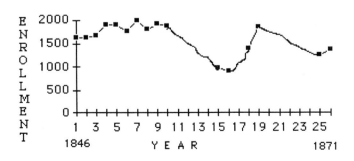

Source: *Annual Reports of Montserrat.*

Note re the graphs in Figures 14 and 15: The data in the annual reports which provided the basis for these graphs were sometimes not comparable over time or were missing. Therefore these graphs were prepared simply to show the trend which was emerging in school enrollment and attendance in some of these colonies. Too much reliance should not be placed on the actual figure for any one year.

FIGURE 14 (C)
St. Vincent: Enrollment Figures, 1848-70

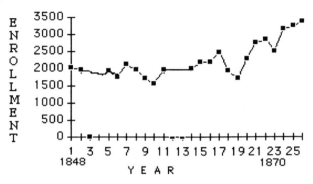

Source: *Annual Reports of St. Vincent.*

FIGURE 14 (D)
Antigua: Enrollment Figures, 1848-68

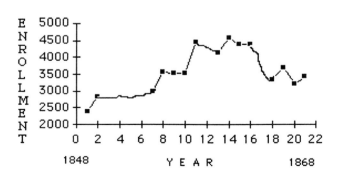

Source: *Annual Reports of Antigua.*

FIGURE 14 (E)
St. Lucia: Enrollment Figures, 1846-71

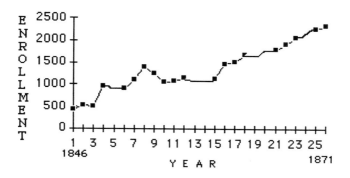

Source: *Annual Reports of St. Lucia.*

Figure 14 (F)
St. Kitts: Fluctuations In Attendance, 1846-70

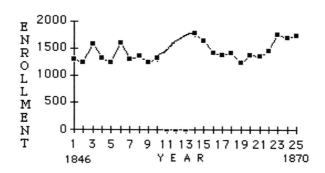

Source: *Annual Reports of St. Kitts.*

FIGURE 15 (A)
Jamaica: Rise in Enrollment, 1868-95

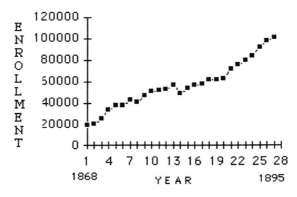

Source: *Annual Reports of Jamaica.*

FIGURE 15 (B)
Grenada: Rise in Enrollment, 1871-96

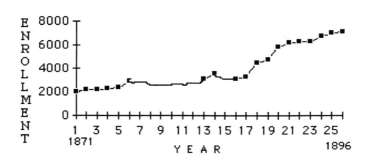

Source: *Annual Reports of Grenada.*

FIGURE 15 (C)
Barbados: Rise in Enrollment, 1870-96

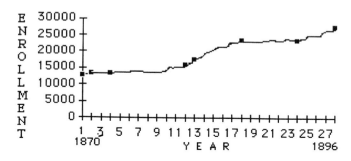

Source: *Annual Reports of Barbados.*

Figure 15 (D)
Bahamas: Rise in Enrollment, 1873-96

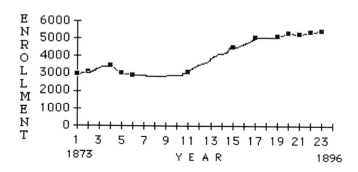

Source: *Annual Reports of the Bahamas.*

FIGURE 15 (E)
British Guiana: Rise in Enrollment, 1870-96

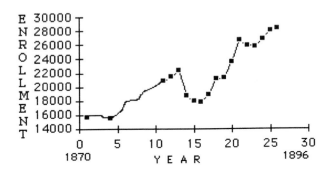

Source: *Annual Reports of British Guiana.*

Notes

1   Carl Campbell, "The Development of Primary Education in Jamaica, 1835-1865" (M.A. thesis, Univ. of London, 1963).
2   Donald Wood, *Trinidad in Transition: The Years After Slavery* (London: Oxford University Press, 1986), 225.
3   Ibid.
4   Government of Antigua, *Historical Notes on Education in Antigua, 1834-1984* (St. Johns, Antigua: Government of Antigua, 1984).
5   Campbell, "Development of Primary Education," 83.
6   Report of the Government of British Guiana, *British Parliamentary Papers*, Vol. 62: *1852-53* (London: Government of Great Britain), 12.
7   Report of the Government of Jamaica, *British Parliamentary Papers*, Vol. 46: *1871* (London: Government of Great Britain).
8   Government of Jamaica, *1883 Report on the Blue Book* (Kingston, Jamaica), 123.
9   B. Brereton, *Race Relations in Colonial Trinidad*, 67.
10   Letter from D. McLean to Edinburgh University's Student Missionary Society, U. P. Miss. R., 1860, 39; also in Ryall, "The Organization of Missionary Societies," 325.
11   CO 31/56, Circular Despatch by Secretary of State to Governor Reid and other West Indian Governors, 29 September 1847.
12   Report of the Inspector of Schools for Antigua for 1875, *British Parliamentary Papers*, Vol. 51: *1876* (London: Government of Great Britain), 87.
13   This was a reference to the indentured immigrants who were arriving in the colony, mainly from India and China.
14   Report of the Government of British Guiana, *British Parliamentary Papers*, Vol. 44: *1882* (London: Government of Great Britain), 135.
15   Government of British Guiana, *Report of the Inspector of Schools for British Guiana, for the Year 1896–97* (Georgetown, 1897), 11.
16   Report of the Government of Barbados, *British Parliamentary Papers*, Vol. 52: *1884-85* (London: Government of Great Britain), 123.
17   Report of the Government of St. Kitts, *British Parliamentary Papers*, Vol. 44: *1874* (London: Government of Great Britain), 89.
18   Report of the Inspector of Schools for Dominica, *British Parliamentary Papers*, Vol. 72: *1888* (London: Government of Great Britain), 35.
19   Report of the Government of the British Virgin Islands, *British Parliamentary Papers*, Vol. 37: *1865* (London: Government of Great Britain), 93.
20   Report of the Government of British Honduras, *British Parliamentary Papers*, Vol. 52: *1884-85* (London: Government of Great Britain), 38.
21   Ibid.

22   Report of the Government of the Turks and Caicos Islands, *British Parliamentary Papers*, Vol. 52: *1884-85* (London: Government of Great Britain), 50.
23   Ibid.
24   CO 31/56, *Papers of Earl Grey Presented to the Legislature*, 25 January 1848.
25   Report of the Government of Montserrat, *British Parliamentary Papers*, Vol. 50: *1878-79* (London: Government of Great Britain), 110.
26   Report of the Government of Jamaica, *British Parliamentary Papers*, Vol. 10: *1857* (London: Government of Great Britain), 54.
27   Ibid., Vol. 44: *1882*, 108.
28   CO 299/10, *Report of the Inspector of Schools for Trinidad, 1860* (Government of Trinidad).
29   Report of the Government of British Guiana, *British Parliamentary Papers*, Vol. 37: *1865* (London: Government of Great Britain), 27.
30   D. W. Comins, *Note on Emigration to Trinidad* (Trinidad: 1893), 35. Cited in Errol A. Furlonge, "The Development of Secondary Education in Trinidad and Tobago" (Ph.D. diss., Univ. of Sheffield, 1968), 200.
31   Government of British Guiana, *Report of the Inspector of Schools for 1893-94* (Georgetown, British Guiana); Gordon, *A Century*, 125.
32   Carl Campbell, "The Development of Education in Trinidad 1834-1870" (Ph.D. diss., Univ. of the West Indies, Mona, Kingston, Jamaica, 1973).
33   CO 295/193, *Keate to Labouchère*, 6 July 1857: 54 (London: PRO).
34   CO 295/208, *Governor to Secretary of State*, 30 March 1860, no. 43 (PRO). Cited in C. Bhagan, "A Critical Study of the Development of Education in Trinidad" (M.A. thesis, Univ. of London, 1964), 207-208.
35   Report of the Government of British Guiana, *British Parliamentary Papers*, Vol. 72: *1888* (London: Government of Great Britain), 12.
36   Report of the Government of Grenada, *British Parliamentary Papers, 1849* (London: Government of Great Britain), 272.
37   Ibid.
38   M. Kazim Bacchus, *Education for Development or Underdevelopment* (Waterloo, ON: Wilfrid Laurier University Press, 1980), 78.
39   Bacchus, *Education for Development*, 78.
40   Verene Shepherd, *The Education of East Indian Children in Jamaica, 1879-1949* (Library of the University of the West Indies: Mona, Jamaica, December 1983).
41   Report of the Government of Jamaica, *British Parliamentary Papers*, Vol. 51: *1875* (London: Government of Great Britain), 27.
42   Report of the Government of Grenada, *British Parliamentary Papers*, Vol. 36: *1850* (London: Government of Great Britain), 22.

CHAPTER 3

FACTORS INFLUENCING SCHOOL ENROLLMENT AND ATTENDANCE

Introduction

As previously indicated, between 1846 and the late 1860s primary school enrollment and average attendance in the British West Indies were not only low, but were characterized by marked fluctuations on a daily, weekly, monthly, seasonal and annual basis. An idea of these monthly and annual fluctuations in average attendance in Jamaican primary schools between 1892 and 1897 can be seen in Figure 16 below.

FIGURE 16
Monthly Variation in Total Average Attendance in the Public Elementary Schools Of Jamaica, 1892-97

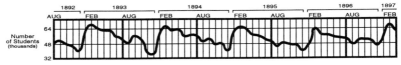

Source: *Annual Reports of Jamaica*.

While attendance improved somewhat after the 1870s, the percentage of those enrolled who were regularly attending school shows a noticeable decline in most of these colonies. A number of factors contributed to this situation, including the economic decline following the removal of the British preferential duty on West Indian sugar. This placed the treasuries of nearly all the West Indian governments in a tight financial squeeze and, consequently, there were heavy cuts and annual fluctuations in government expenditures, including those on education.

Different Levels of Funding for Elementary Education

As pointed out earlier, there were differences in the attitudes of the various West Indian legislatures toward supporting elementary education, as reflected in their varying per capita expenditures on students and the proportion of their national budgets allocated to education. For example, in 1877 Trinidad was spending 42s. 2d on each child in average attendance, while Jamaica and Barbados each spent only 12s., and Antigua, 7s.7d. In British Guiana, the average grant per student examined in government-assisted schools dropped by 47% at current prices, between 1880 and 1894-95, while in Jamaica, the amount provided per student in average attendance more than doubled between 1870 and 1895. Yet by 1896, the per capita grant for students in British Guiana was still about 20% higher than in Jamaica.[1] Further evidence of these differences in the amount of national resources allocated to education can be seen in the following graph, which compares the percentages of government revenues spent on education in the various colonies.

FIGURE 17
Percentage of Government Revenue Spent on Education in Different West Indian Colonies, 1877

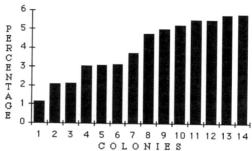

Key: 1. Nevis 2. Jamaica 3. Antigua 4. Honduras 5. St. Vincent
6. St. Lucia 7. St. Kitts 8. Dominica 9. British Guiana
10. Barbados 11. Bahamas 12. Grenada 13. Turks Islands
14. British Virgin Islands
Source: *Annual Reports of the Colonies.*

Per pupil expenditures on education also varied from one district to another within the same colony. For example, in Trinidad, the ratio of expenditures on pupils in the best and worst financed districts was about 6:1. These variations also helped to account for the differences in enrollment and attendance between districts in the same colony — or as in the case of the Bahamas, between various islands in the archipelago.

Factors Contributing to School Enrollment and Attendance
A number of factors contributed to the low enrollment and poor attendance of children in the West Indies, and among these were:

The Poor Quality of Education Provided in Schools
This resulted partly from the employment of poorly qualified and incompetent teachers and the very limited amount of instructional materials available, due to the inadequate funding for education. The irrelevant curriculum of schools which often failed to stimulate the interests of the children added further to this problem and to the desire amongst students to quit school early. In Tobago, it was noted during the early 1860s that "the inferiority and inefficiency of some of the teachers appointed to the rural schools must, in many instances, retard the progress of education, for not only is their training defective, but the effect on the children is adverse, resulting in their withdrawal from the schools altogether."[2]
The general decline in the number of students during the early 1850s was also attributed to the inefficiency of the teachers in these schools. But, to secure the services of a better class of teachers, a higher level of salary would

have been required, and with lack of funds it was impossible for such increased emoluments to be provided.

Campbell also indicated that the falling off of school attendance in Jamaica was due to the type and quality of the education which most pupils were then receiving. Therefore, when the average attendance in these schools increased by nearly 18% between the school years 1886-87 and 1888-89, the inspector of schools attributed it to "the proper appreciation by the parents" of the better quality of instruction that had become available.[3]

Low Rate of Return on Investment in Education
The poor rate of return that most blacks were receiving on their investment in their children's education was another factor contributing to poor attendance and low enrollments. Immediately after emancipation, many parents were anxious to give their children "book knowledge," with the hope that this would provide them with an opportunity for occupational mobility, outside the role of agricultural workers, with the hope of improving their economic position. But by the mid-1840s, they were beginning to realize that this was not an easily attainable goal and, as a result, their enthusiasm for education subsided.

In 1840 the *Blue Book* reported that working class parents in British Guiana had expressed a strong desire to have their children taught to read and write. However, by 1848, the inspector of schools suggested that they had developed a negative attitude to education, due to the inability of their children to find suitable jobs when they left school. This itself was partly due to the poor quality of the education they had received.

The Depressed Economic Condition of the Population
The substantial reduction in workers' wages due to the decline of the economy affected quite considerably the ability of the parents to meet the direct and indirect costs of sending their children to school. Thus, in 1849 the administrator of Montserrat observed that education among the working classes had greatly fallen off due to the limited financial resources of the government and the people. Labourers were "most irregularly and unsatisfactorily paid" and therefore unable to meet the costs of educating their children. In this situation it was simply hoped that "better times" and the "punctual payment" of wages might increase parents' means of "conferring this blessing" of education on their offspring.[4]

In Barbados, the inspector of schools observed that the substantial drop in school attendance in 1864 was due to the straitened circumstances of the classes whose children mainly attended the public schools. In 1866 it was again pointed out that the economic plight which faced the parents on the island had "prejudicially influenced" the number of students in attendance "in a manner not to be mistaken." This was because education was considered to be of lesser importance than "the feeding, clothing and housing" of their families and further, "so great has been the pinch experienced almost throughout the [past] twelve months" that with many, even "the absolute necessaries of life have been, with great difficulty, procured."[5]

In Trinidad also the inspectorate indicated that the main problem in connection with school attendance revolved around the provision of food, clothing and other essential items of support, "to which the lower orders always turn their attention in the first instance, before thinking of education of the mind." It was, therefore, not so much a matter of parents "not appreciating the value of education for their children as one of economic survival or improvement which got the better of their ambition."[6] In 1847 the governor of Antigua observed that the withdrawal of financial support from "home, the absence of assistance from the local government and the more straitened pecuniary means of parents combine to circumscribe the diffusion of useful and suitable instruction."[7]

In British Honduras, labourers' wages fell between one-quarter and one-third during this period and even the "upper classes" were struggling to maintain themselves. In many cases they, too, were "unable to afford to pay for the education of their children."[8] In the British Virgin Islands, the continuing poor economic circumstances also caused school enrollments and attendance to decline steadily. In Bermuda there were a number of parents, both white and coloured, who were in such dire economic circumstances that they were unable to afford the means of education for their children. In the Turks and Caicos Islands, school attendance was also very unsatisfactory, even up to the early 1870s, due to poverty brought about by "the absence of trade" and a "severe drought." Poverty was said to be so universal that parents had to employ their children in collecting shell-fish, herbs or anything with which "to stay the pangs of hunger" since "food for the body" was "of greater importance than food for the mind."[9]

In some colonies there was a tendency among the parents to keep their children at home unless they could dress them smartly and give them shoes and stockings to wear to school. Therefore, the high price of cotton goods also meant that parents could ill-afford to buy the clothes needed for their children to attend school properly clad. As a result, children were sometimes kept away from school "for want of clothes and others have been irregular for want of food supplied in time for their breakfast or their lunch, which the children . . . [were] in the habit of bringing with them to school."[10]

The Levy or Increases in School Fees
With the depletion of the public treasuries which resulted from the economic decline of the region most legislatures in the region expected parents to make a larger contribution to the cost of their children's schooling through the payment of school fees. In Barbados the Mitchinson Commission, after commenting on the high quality of the private fee-paying schools on the island, recommended that the payment of school fees should be enforced in the government-aided schools. The Commission felt that this was likely to induce a better attitude toward elementary education on the part of parents, and the public in general.

In St. Lucia, when the government acquired the Mico schools, it passed an ordinance which required every child to pay school fees in an effort to recover some of the costs of assuming this added financial responsibility. From 1855 school fees were also levied in British Honduras, and with the introduction of the Leeward Islands Education Act in 1875, the payment of fees became compulsory, even in those colonies like Barbuda, where school fees had not previously been charged. Some of the local elites and even a few clergymen also argued that the levying of fees would create a greater appreciation of the value of education.

But the insistence on payment of school fees often resulted in some parents withdrawing their children from school. In 1847 the superintendent of the Moravian Missions in Antigua noted that the imposition of fees caused many parents to withdraw their children from schools while in Grenada, it was later observed that "the rigid exacting of fees" resulted in an increasing "drop-out of the children" from school.[11] A similar outcome was reported in the Bahamas, especially in the Out Islands. In St. John's, Harbour Island, the numbers attending schools declined in 1849 because the payment of school fees was enforced. In Long Cay, Crooked Island, children were also leaving school because of the fees being levied.

In Trinidad, prior to 1875, school enrollment figures were somewhat higher than in some of the smaller West Indian colonies, partly because up to then, school fees were not charged for those attending the government ward schools. However, with the introduction of the 1875 Education Ordinance, it became a condition for schools receiving government grants to raise a certain proportion of their revenues by levying fees. This created hardships among the poorest sections of the society and resulted in a drop in school attendance. For example, in 1885 the head teacher of the Chacon Street School pointed out that "many parents had told him that they kept their children away from school because of the fees."

However, in 1890 an ordinance was introduced which provided for the government to meet the fees of the children of the very poor because of the deterioration in the economic situation which occurred in the late 1880s. This step helped to improve the attendance of children from poor families. The government began to remit fees for the children of indentured Indians, and steps such as these helped to increase school attendance.

In 1862 the lieutenant-governor of Dominica also pointed out that the exaction of school fees was prejudicial to the interests of education on the island, since it contributed to a reduction of enrollments and attendance. In St. Vincent only about one-third of the eligible population was going to school in 1877, partly due to the insistence on the payment of school fees.

Further, when schools had to be closed for a day, especially during a four-day school week which operated in places like Jamaica, parents kept their children away from school for the week so that they would not have to pay a full week's fees for less than a week of instruction. In the minor schools established by the Wesleyans, teachers were even expected to supplement their salaries with the school fees which they collected. They therefore continually exerted pressure on parents to pay their children's fees regularly and promptly. However, this also had adverse effects on school attendance because, with the economic difficulties which many families faced, they found it financially difficult to meet these costs and often withdrew their children from school.

While some parents could ill afford school fees others resented paying them because of the poor quality of the instructional programme offered in schools. It was even noted that there was "a lurking idea" among some parents "that schools, being largely aided by government, the people have a right to share, without cost, in their advantages."[12] A number of parents even registered the names of their children on the books of different schools and sent them to one or another, "as the master may be more or less exacting in the matter of fees."[13] In other cases, such as in the Leeward Islands in 1878, they simply removed their children from school.

To overcome the hurdle presented by higher school fees, the government of the Turks and Caicos Islands decided to abolish them temporarily and even to refund the payments already made by some parents. Yet, even this measure did not bring about any substantial improvement in school attendance in the colony due to low returns which parents saw were accruing from education for their children.

The proportion of school costs made up from fees was never very high, but with the financially straitened circumstances of the parents it became more difficult for school authorities to collect a high percentage of these fees. It was partly because of this that some colonies began a move toward their total abolition in government and even in government-aided schools. As early as 1890, fees were not levied in the 38 Bahamas government schools, while in Jamaica, fees were gradually reduced and finally abolished in 1892. Contrary to expectations, the abolition of fees in Jamaica and other colonies resulted in an immediate and substantial increase in enrollment. As the Jamaican inspector of schools noted in his 1893/94 report, the prediction by some that with the abolition of school fees attendance would drop "has been signally falsified and . . . the reverse has been the result."[14] By the end of the decade fees continued to be eliminated or reduced.

The Indirect Costs of Education

In addition to the direct costs of schooling that parents had to meet such as expenditure on school books, clothes and school fees, the indirect costs were also becoming unbearable for many families. The latter arose mainly from the loss of the benefits which families received from their children's work on the plantations or their assistance with the cultivation of the family farm. Since many parents were struggling for economic survival, they could not easily afford to do without the assistance of their children who had reached productive age.

For example, in Antigua, it was repeatedly noted that considerable irregularity of attendance resulted from the fact that parents often required their children for domestic purposes and at other times to perform paid labour. In St. Vincent also it was noted that although attendance in the free schools had improved by 1851, there was still a drop in enrollment in the regular fee-paying schools. This was largely due to the extended cultivation of arrowroot, which caused some children who were *fitted for this light labour* to be withdrawn from school.

Because of the shortage of labour in the Turks and Caicos Islands, very good incomes were earned by children working in the salt pond, and this made parents even more reluctant to send them to school. As a result, the inspector of schools expressed surprise, not at the fluctuations in attendance, but at the fact that the schools had not been entirely deserted by the children of the labouring classes on these islands. It was this need by parents to have their children contribute to the economic survival of the family that led Anderson, the inspector of schools for Trinidad, to suggest that the "evil" of poor school attendance would only be overcome with a gradual improvement in the economy and an increase in the level of education among the population.

To reduce the opportunity cost of education, some parents sent their offspring to school at an earlier age, so that their formal education would be completed before the children had advanced too far in their economically productive years. Therefore, they did not have to be taken out of the work force for longer than was necessary when they reached the age at which they could be employed. This strategy was based on the assumption that there was a fixed amount of knowledge that students had to acquire before they could be regarded as "learnt done" and that the learning process could take place at any time, regardless of their age.

This was partly why the average age of those attending school declined and, as the Baptists in Jamaica noted, the children were being sent to school quite young with teachers being regarded chiefly as nursemaids. For example, in 1849 the average age of students attending the Methodist schools in Jamaica was nine years and this soon dropped to eight years. In St. Vincent, where attendance in the capital city of Kingstown tended to be of a respectable number, rarely were children 12 -13 years of age to be found in schools, since they were removed as soon as they could be of domestic assistance.

The private secretary to government house in Antigua summarized the situation by noting that the fluctuating and irregular school attendance on the island was likely to persist as long as poverty continued to force parents to seek employment for their children and teachers insisted on the payment of school fees.[15]

The Scattered Distribution of the Population
The geographical distribution of the population also contributed to low enrollment and poor attendance. It was sometimes impossible to find a suitable central location for a school such that all children in an area would have fairly easy access to it, so the more remote areas remained without schools. Therefore in Trinidad, for example, the overwhelming majority of those who received an education lived in towns such as Port-of-Spain and San Fernando, while "intellectually the countryside was arid."[16] Children in the less inhabited districts were said to have been growing up in "ignorance" and "in habits and with ideas" which bordered on "utter barbarism."[17] The few who were persistent in seeking an education sometimes had to walk considerable distances to reach their schools and during the rainy seasons this became very difficult. In Tobago, it was also noted that any attempt to build additional schools to bring all the children within the reach of instruction was likely to pose additional financial problems beyond the resources of the government.

In the Bahamas, because of the sparseness of the population, the cost of administering the schools on some islands had increased to the point where it was necessary for the government to cut back on the extra grant which it had earmarked for new schools This was one of the reasons why, in 1871, the governor of the colony urged the legislature to encourage residents to live within close proximity to one another by amending its land-distribution policies. The provision of education for more clustered groups would make it possible for a larger number of children to receive an education.

Illness Among Children and Poor Climatic Conditions
The high incidence of illness among children in these colonies also contributed to their poor school attendance. For example, in the 1850s there were fatal outbreaks of smallpox, yellow fever, and cholera and these reached epidemic proportions in many islands, especially Jamaica and the Eastern Caribbean. In Barbados also there was a heavy drop off in school attendance in 1894, due to the epidemics of typhoid and dysentery.

In addition, children attended schools less regularly during the heavy rainy season. Hurricanes often wrought destruction on school buildings and made the closure of schools necessary, sometimes for extended periods. In 1880 there was an unprecedented cyclone followed by a prolonged drought in Jamaica, which led not only to diminished enrollments and increased irregularity of attendance but also to a decline in the level of pupils' academic performance. In British Honduras, it was observed that river floods, the want of roads, the scattered distribution of the population, and the difficulty of communication at certain seasons all affected the attendance of children.

Inadequate Numbers of Denominational Schools
Operated by the Roman Catholics
On some islands with a large Catholic population but only a few Catholic schools, the priests were often fearful of the proselytizing possibilities of the education that was being offered in schools operated by other denominational bodies. Therefore, they often advised parents not to send their children to these schools, even though they did not have access to a Roman Catholic school. In some cases, the priests even threatened to refuse the rites of the Church to those who did not follow their advice. It was this practice which led the president of the predominantly Catholic Island of St. Lucia to describe the Catholic priests there as "a secret hostile influence" on improved school attendance.

Racial Prejudice
Most white parents still remained prejudiced against sending their children to schools attended by black pupils and therefore preferred to "forgo the advantages offered by the board of education" to provide their offspring with an education "rather than suffer their children to learn their lessons in the same room with those of the coloured and black population."[18] In the Green Turtle Cay School in the Bahamas, for example, it was noted that "an insurmountable difficulty has been encountered, in associating the white and black children in the school, from a deep felt aversion, manifested by parents of the former."[19] The governor himself admitted that, despite his personal efforts, "the seeds of this unhappy disease [racial prejudice] . . . [were] not yet extirpated from the Bahamian community."[20] This was also marked in the islands like Abaco and Harbour Island. To prevent their children from mixing at school with those who were coloured or black, a number of parents, if they could afford it, sent them to private schools.

In Bermuda white lower class parents often refused to send their children to schools "frequented by the coloured race"[21] despite the fact that they were unable or unwilling to make "any sacrifice, to maintain separate schools."[22] In 1874 the governor expressed regret that time had done little to remove from the white population this "unreasonable and obstructive prejudice" against the black and coloured population, even though many of the latter were "scarcely distinguishable in complexion" from whites, and the children associated very freely with each other in their sports, out of school. A similar situation existed among the poor whites or "redlegs" of Barbados.

Low Level of Financial Support from the State for Education
As previously indicated, West Indian legislators were initially hesitant to provide funds to meet the growing local demand for education, fearing that it would raise the occupational aspirations of the students to unrealistic levels. This in turn would create disappointment and even unrest among those who had received an education and were unable to find higher status jobs. In addition, educated individuals were more likely to move into other jobs, thereby bringing about a further depletion of the estate labour force. This concern was obvious in the views expressed by planters about the education of East Indian children, who they considered to be inevitably destined for the unskilled labour force on the sugar estates.

However, there were some changes in the planters' attitudes to education for the masses from about the late 1860s, and this was reflected in the gradual increase in the educational votes in these colonies. Between 1868-70 and 1880-82, the overall expenditure on education by the Windward Islands group nearly doubled, while the increases for Jamaica during this period were considerably higher. From 1882 to 1896 the total grants to education by all West Indian colonies also rose substantially, and this contributed to an increase in school enrollment and attendance. Nevertheless, the increases in educational expenditures barely kept up with the rise in the overall budgets and in some cases fell behind. This can partly be seen in Figures 18 and 19, which attempt to compare the rate of increase between the overall budgets and the budgets on education for the Leeward and the Windward Islands between 1868 and 1882. In Figure 18 it can be seen that while there were fluctuations in the percentage of the budget allocated to education in these colonies, the overall expenditures in some Leeward Islands were rising somewhat faster than those on education. Among some Windward Island colonies there was a tendency for these increases to take place at about the same rate. Overall, the amounts spent on education were small, a fact recognized by the 1882 Royal Commission on Public Revenues which, while proposing a reduction of 9.2% in the overall budget for the Windward Islands, felt it necessary to recommend a 74.3% increase in its allocation for education.

FIGURE 18
**Comparing Rate of Increase in Total Expenditure and Expenditure on
Education in the Leeward Islands of St. Lucia, St. Vincent,
and Grenada, 1868-82**

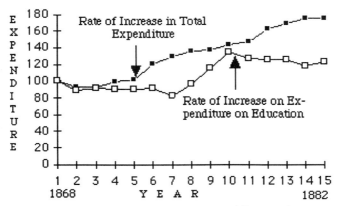

Source: *1882 Royal Commission Report on Public Expenditures.*

FIGURE 19
**Comparing Rate of Increase in Total Expenditure and Expenditure in the
Windward Islands of Antigua, St. Kitts, Nevis, Montserrat,
British Virgin Islands, and Dominica, 1868-82**

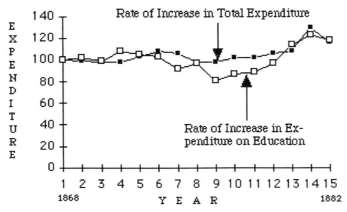

Source: *1882 Royal Commission Report on Public Expenditures.*

Attitude of Blacks to Education
Finally, a major explanation that continued to be advanced for the low school
attendance in the region was the negative attitude to, and the generally
narrow view of, education shared by most black parents. The enthusiasm
which they displayed for education immediately after emancipation had
subsided from about the late 1840s. By 1854, for example, it was observed

that the schools in Trewlawny, Jamaica, were almost deserted, despite the heavy concentration of missionary activities in the parish. In Trinidad, there was said to be no urgent demand for education in the mid-nineteenth century and, as Wood noted, it was rare to find liberated Africans among the pupils in the Ward schools.

The explanation usually put forward was that, since many of these parents had not been formally educated themselves, they had a very limited conception of what constituted a good education. As a result, they often withdrew their children from school as soon as their own narrowly perceived educational goals were met. Children in Trinidad and in other colonies therefore started school at any age and left at the "whims of their parents." A Scottish catechist and teacher observed that, among the adults, a "lamentable ignorance prevails as to what constitutes the necessary amount of education" for a student. "If a child can stammer over a chapter of the New Testament he is what they call 'learnt done' and consequently withdrawn from school."[23] Many parents considered that their children's education was complete after their third year at school, when they could be put out to work.

In Grenada, it was reported in 1852 that there was a great indifference to education among a large portion of the peasantry. These parents considered their children's education was complete after they had spent about two years in school. Following this, they were removed to learn a trade or handicraft or to help in the field. In Trinidad, parents decided to withdraw their older children from school as soon as they could read "in the third book." In British Guiana, when pupils "obtained some smattering of reading and writing," they were taken out of school and bound to a "trade, or for the purpose of having their services at home."[24]

It was even suggested that many parents were not fully appreciative of the value of an education and were therefore quite reluctant to make the necessary sacrifices in order to send their children to school — even if they could afford the costs. In Dominica, it was observed that, in general, there was "an unfavourable disposition on the part of the peasantry" to contribute to "so useful and laudable a measure" as their children's education.[25] Around the same time attention was drawn to the fact that, "all attempts to persuade the peasantry [in Montserrat] . . . to contribute towards the instruction of their children have hitherto failed"[26] on account of the parents' negative attitude to education. In 1854 Davy, too, argued that "the parents, not having received the benefits of education, are not able to impress on the minds of their children a due appreciation of its advantage, nor prepared to make any sacrifice to obtain it." [27]

In 1848 McSwiney, the inspector of schools for British Guiana, advanced the view that even though parents could afford the very moderate cost of educating their children, they were very reluctant to pay for it. Later, he commented on the determined feeling among the black population to avoid such expenditures as school fees, because of their predisposition to amass money, even though this meant sacrificing the education of their children. He also drew attention to the poor attitude toward education of the recent immigrants and suggested that non-attendance of their children at schools

> may be traced to the cupidity of many parents in availing
> themselves of their children's labour or their total and

> lamentable indifference as to whether their children receive any education or none. I did not find at any of the schools which I have visited any Portuguese, Coolie, [East Indian] or African[28] children in attendance, except in two or three instances.[29]

In 1851 the Council of Education in British Guiana also reported that the adult population had become very indifferent toward education, while in St. Vincent the governor noted that

> the reluctance to pay so small a sum [as school fees] arose, certainly not from want of means, nor . . . altogether to total absence of interest in the education of their children. It must be referred I think, *to habit*, and *a want of knowledge of reflection* upon the subject [emphasis added].[30]

In the Bahamas, it was noted that while petitions for the establishment of schools were being received by the government from the residents of the more sparsely populated areas, when the schools were established there was a great disinclination on the part of the parents to supply copy books or any other materials for their children's education.

In 1856 the president of the British Virgin Islands indicated that while school attendance in the colony was "tolerably good," he "should be glad to see the black people show a more earnest desire to avail themselves of the facilities afforded them for educating their children."[31] The poor interest of some parents in their children's education was still seen in 1863, when it was estimated that more than half the children of school age were not in school and were growing up in utter ignorance. In the Turks and Caicos Islands, where attendance had dropped by about 35% between 1868 and 1869, it was noted that

> education in this colony seems hardly to be appreciated as much as might be desired, owing to the fact of parents being able to make the labour of their children remunerative at the age of thirteen, when the boys of the family can then be employed in driving mule carts laden with salt.[32]

Love of money among West Indian blacks was said to be so much greater than their appreciation of education that they were willing to sacrifice their children's education rather than pay their school fees. For example, in Trinidad, comments were made about the greedy disposition of parents of the agricultural class, who sought to make money from their children's labour, rather than having them educated.

In Barbados, Reverend Rawle added that, "next to the apathy of the public, the greatest difficulties with which schools have to contend arise from the untowardness of parents, who . . . [were] not generally aware of the necessity of regularity"[33] in school attendance.

Parental indifference to education, which was considered to have been quite common in the region, was deplored by several leading individuals, both within and outside the West Indies, including Earl Grey and some missionaries. They made every effort, "in sermons, society addresses and private conversation," to persuade parents to appreciate the value of sending their children to school, canvassing them in the various districts and offering free schooling to the children if they could not afford to pay the fees. They even made book prizes available to the children for regular attendance. Lord Elgin of Jamaica also initiated a system of prizes for parents who could show a certificate stating that they had educated large families. Mr. Dyett, in a letter to the president of Nevis, underlined the importance of these incentives in motivating parents to send their children to school regularly. He recommended that, "if possible, it would be desirable to provide rewards or prizes payable in money, to the children for their regular attendance" because "the labourer makes use of his children in the cultivation of his canefield," and "he is not willing, without some inducement, in the shape of a visible return, to part with the labour of his child which brings him immediate return."[34]

But the explanation that parental attitudes toward education were responsible for the low rates of school attendance was inadequate, since it failed to account for the fact that, between 1858 and 1865, there was a substantial improvement in the numbers attending school in many of the islands. Therefore, other reasons for poor school attendance were put forward. For example, in 1884 the governor the Leeward Islands pointed out that

> it is not always selfish anxiety to secure the wages, [which are] earned by the children that causes their parents to keep them from school, but it is often the *necessity* [which] labourers and handicraftsmen, having several children, find themselves under, of adding to their own moderate gains the earnings of the elder children to provide food and clothing for the family.[35]

As a result, parents continued to keep their children, especially the older ones, away from school, since their services were needed to contribute to the family's economic welfare. This resulted, as Inspector Cargill pointed out for Jamaica, in school attendance rates continuing to be low, particularly on Fridays, when children usually spent the day on the family farm helping their parents prepare for the Saturday markets.

Conflicting Views about Parental Interest in Education

Despite the comments of a number of individuals about the poor attitude of the black population toward the education of their children, there were other completely opposite observations on the matter, appearing almost concurrently. While on one hand, there were repeated suggestions that parents needed to develop a more positive attitude to education, on the other, there were some reports which indicated that children were not in school because of the inadequacy of school accommodation. This shortage of school places in many colonies seemed to have resulted from an improvement in the parents' appreciation of the advantages of education, and their growing disposition to provide some schooling for their children. In many rural districts, there was an increasing number of requests for schools to be established because the children were not within easy reach of one.

In Jamaica, the governor pointed out that, as early as 1845, the ex-slaves were very interested in education because they had very high expectations of its outcomes. They prized schooling "as a means of enabling the child of the labourer to emancipate himself from the pursuits in which his parent had been engaged."[36] As he noted,

> During the apprenticeship and immediately after the establishment of freedom, undefined expectations of the advantages which book learning would confer were excited in the breasts of parents and children — it was looked to as a means of obtaining political privileges and advancement in life.[37]

In 1845 also, the working classes in Montserrat were reported to have been "not insensitive" to the benefits of education, and when it could be obtained, readily embraced every opportunity of "gratuitous instruction" for their children. In Nevis, many private schools were springing up in the 1840s, because it was said that there was "no unwillingness [of parents] to obtain instruction for their children."[38]

Despite the impoverished conditions of the people of the British Virgin Islands and the absence of a government grant, education in this colony advanced satisfactorily during the immediate post-emancipation years. For example, in 1845, the labouring population, most of whom were Methodists, "evinced a praiseworthy readiness to aid and assist in the erection of . . . schools."[39] Ten years later, the administration still reported that it was very gratifying to observe that the masses appeared fully appreciative of the advantages of schooling for their children.[40] The parents' desire to give their children an education was also reflected in the number of private schools on the island, and when denominational schools were established, these were also well attended.

The number of schools in Antigua in the late 1840s was increasing, and the regularity of attendance was improving, because of a growing desire on the part of parents to have their children educated. This positive attitude of the population toward education was again commented on in the 1850s, and this was partly reflected in the very numerous private schools in the capital city, which increasingly accepted coloured and black children. Few streets were then without a private school of one kind or another.

In the Bahamas in 1847, parents in some of the Out Islands such as Rock Sound and Eleuthra were so anxious to secure an education for their children that they promised to pay their children's school fees punctually and even volunteered their services "to wattle and plaster" any school building to standards which complied with the by-laws of the board of education. As a result of their efforts schools were erected in Bluff Settlement, Current Settlement, Spanish Wells, and Eight Mile Rock. By 1850, after eight schools were opened in the colony with the assistance of the local population, the board of education received the "grateful acknowledgments" from the inhabitants of these communities "for the advantages which their children . . . [were] permitted to enjoy in the advancement of knowledge."[41] In his response, the governor observed that

> in no part of the world have I ever seen greater proof of anxiety on the part of the parents to have their offspring educated, and when I add that children of tender age are to be seen in almost every island walking four or five miles a day through rocky and rugged paths to and from school, it

would be at once apparent that so laudable a disposition ought to be encouraged by every possible means.[42]

In British Honduras it was suggested in 1856 that while parents still did not fully appreciate the value of education as "a purchasable necessity," nevertheless, their desire to secure schooling for their children was increasing. In 1857 the governor of Jamaica pointed out that the "peasantry" of that island were no more indifferent to the education of their offspring than those in Great Britain.[43]

In Trinidad, it was observed in 1859 that even though the masses were still displaying signs of having been "degraded by slavery," nevertheless, they were increasingly appreciative of the value of education. Evidence of this "laudable" and "growing desire" by the labouring classes for education was seen in the petitions that were "continually being received from the inhabitants of remote districts for the establishment of schools, within reach of their homes."[44] In British Guiana, also, it was noted that "the mass of the people, having just emerged from slavery, evinced an almost insatiable desire to secure for their children the advantage of education."

In 1860 the President of St. Lucia, after noting that he knew of no other country where the poorer classes were expected to bear such a large proportion of the expense of educating their children, expressed satisfaction with their disposition to contribute towards their children's education. In 1865 a great degree of interest in education was also noticed among parents in the Turks and Caicos Islands, while in 1868 "the poorer classes" in Dominica were "beginning to see the advantages of education." Therefore, the administration felt that if more money could "be afforded from the revenue" to establish more schools, there would be "no difficulty in obtaining additional scholars."[45] In 1892 there were, throughout the Leeward Islands Federation, "distinct and encouraging signs that the advantages of education . . . [were] being, more and more, appreciated by all classes."[46]

The Commission which inquired into the conditions of the juvenile population in Jamaica in 1879 also observed that the parents exhibited "a fair inclination to secure education for their children," and that the low attendance observed at the time, due to the temporary disruption of their economic and social conditions, did not affect their basic attitude to schooling. The Jamaican inspector of schools also supported this view, by suggesting that the benefits of elementary education were, as a rule, fully appreciated by the "peasantry of the island."

In 1880 a destructive cyclone struck the island, and because of the low school attendance which followed this event, it was suggested that this indicated a disinclination among the parents to send their children to school which shows up when any pretext arises. Low school attendance continued in 1882 when it was again reported that there were "large numbers of children of the Colony who . . . [were not [yet] taking proper advantage of the means of education."[47] But this retrogression in enrollment was only of a temporary nature and, as the governor insisted, not a reflection of any change in parents' attitude to the education of their children. The correctness of his assessment was seen in the fact that by 1883 there was a "quick recovery [in school enrollment] from the temporary depression [in attendance] of the previous year."[48] By then the administration was noting that "the anxiety manifested by the people, particularly in the rural districts, to participate . . . in the benefit held out to them by the opening of elementary schools is so great as to preclude the necessity of enforcing the Compulsory clause of the Education Act."[49]

In Barbados, the Bree Commission of 1894 reported that parents were generally willing to send their children to school when they were able to do so, and therefore suggested that there was no need for a compulsory education ordinance to be introduced on the island. While the legislature did grant the board of education the power to make education compulsory, the use of this measure was considered unnecessary, partly due to the parents' desire to have their children attend school, "wherever circumstances permitted."

Explaining These Different Perceptions of Attitudes to Education
An interesting question which arises from the above observation is why was there an inconsistency in the assessments about the value which the Negro population placed on the education of their children? Fairly evident is the fact that black parents were quite rational about their decision as to whether or not they should send their children to school and the amount of investment they were prepared to make in their children's education. "Uneducated" as the parents were, they tried to ensure that their investment in schooling would eventually pay off, either in higher incomes or enhanced prestige which their children would receive.

They often had their own views about the type of education which they wanted for their children and when these expectations were not met they did not want to continue sending their children to school. For example, in the British Virgin Islands it was noted in 1881 that parents who were not formally educated could nevertheless discern whether or not their children were benefiting from the education they were receiving, and this affected their willingness to send their children to school.

In making their decision to provide schooling for their children they realized that the better-paying job opportunities that were open in these societies to non-whites and particularly to blacks were quite limited. As a result, many of them initially felt that the returns on an investment in their children's education would not be economically worthwhile. Therefore, when the opportunity arose, they used whatever resources were available to them to acquire wealth rather than invest in their children's education. This explains why they were often reluctant to send their children to school, particularly the older ones for whom the opportunity cost of their education was higher. In other words, whenever economic and educational objectives were in conflict, parents were more interested in pursuing the former.

In British Guiana the outcome of this approach was evident in the fact that up to the mid-1840s, "education . . . [had] not improved amongst the Creoles *in proportion to their independent possession of property.*"[50] Similarly, in 1848 when a school was approved for Duncan's Town, Ragged Island, in the Bahamas, the local population did not want to lose this opportunity for their children's education. They therefore promptly paid their school fees, rented a school house, and subscribed over £16 for the erection of a new building. But in November of that year, they withdrew their children from the school and their subscription to the proposed new school, "assuring the teacher that they acted thus" in order to be able "to secure the repurchase of their shares, at the approaching sale of the salt ponds."[51] As a consequence, the school had to be temporarily closed.

In the early post-emancipation years parents began to find that education was not the instrument of occupational mobility which they had expected, and this accounted for the negative attitude to schooling which developed among them during this period. The inspector of schools for British Guiana, in commenting on this point, drew attention to

> the mortifying disappointment of the extravagant expecta-
> tions . . . indulged in by the people as to the striking effect
> which they believed education would have in promoting the
> future advancement of their children to situations of
> respectability. . . . Now that they have ascertained that the
> mere instruction, so imperfectly imparted by the schools will
> not ensure that complete emancipation from the labours of
> the field and not appreciating any other advantage which
> their children might derive from it, they conceive that they
> consult their own interest, without sacrificing that of their
> children by sending them to work at a very early age.[52]

However, as some more opportunities for upward mobility through education became available to the children of the black population, their parents' attitude to schooling improved.

But this was not the only reason for the apparently conflicting views on the interest which the black population showed in the education of their children. Another was the increasing degree of social differentiation taking place among the non-whites in the West Indies. There were two quite noticeable sub-groups emerging among them. One consisted of the somewhat better-off coloureds and blacks who were experiencing a certain degree of social and economic mobility. The second comprised the mass of the black population who were still estate labourers, or were eking out a marginal existence operating their small farms. The desire to have their children receive a better primary education was most marked among those who belonged to the first sub-group. Davy, writing in 1854, observed that the "skilled Negroes" were generally averse to having their children work on the plantations at an early age since this would interfere with their schooling.[53] On the other hand, the second group tended to display some degree of apathy toward education for their children, as observed by the various individuals mentioned above.

This poorer section of the black population often saw little chances of securing adequate returns on their investment in education and were less inclined to send their children regularly to school. Among them it was said, as in the case of Jamaica, that there was an "insuperable repugnance to contribute the smallest sum for the purpose" of educating their children.[54] In Barbados, too, it was noted that the lukewarmness to education among the non-whites tended to have been confined to the very lowest class, while there was a strong desire to learn among the young coloured people of the island. The avidity which they displayed in their use of the public library was also considered to be some evidence of their growing desire for information and self-education.

Despite the large percentage of manual workers in the West Indian labour force — it was estimated to be around 95% in most of these colonies — only about 50% of the children attending school in Trinidad were from families drawn from this occupational group. The inspector of schools noted in 1851 that a relatively small percentage of the children of the unskilled workers on the sugar estates was at school, and that their attendance was irregular, being particularly low in the planting and harvesting seasons. He therefore concluded that the attitudes which prevailed on the sugar estates — possibly referring to the attitude of both parents and planters — were not propitious to the education of the lower class.

In 1857 he again reported that, on enquiry, he found a low level of school enrollment and attendance among the children of the agricultural labourers. On the other hand, there was a high demand for education among those who made up the higher echelons of the working class, especially those who lived in the towns and in the larger centres of population where "the advantages which accrued to those with an education" were more visible. Two years later, there was still said to have been little or no sympathy for education among the parents of children in the lower socio-economic groups, and that only about one-fifth of them remained at school until they could read, write and spell, in the third and fourth books.

Up to 1862, while the children of the rural labouring classes in Dominica were not attending schools regularly, there was emerging "a class of independent small scale farmers," who were becoming "alive to the benefits of education."[55] In St. Vincent, it was observed that, while amongst the "lowest classes" there was not a great desire to send their children to school, yet "there is a class growing rapidly into existence, which may be called the yeomanry of the country, and composed of the purchasers or lessees of land and the occupiers of villages, who, from their improving intelligence, are becoming more alive to the benefits of education."[56]

The poorest sections of the black population therefore became very disenchanted with the low level of economic and social returns that were accruing from their children's attendance at school. While there were a few white-collar jobs available to non-whites with a limited, primary education, these positions were often filled on the basis of one's skin colour. As a result, the demand for "educated black individuals" was very limited, which made it difficult to convince the poorer black parents of the need to make a greater investment in their children's education, by sending them to school more regularly or for a longer period.

To make it more attractive for the economically disadvantaged sections of the labouring class to send their children to school, it was necessary to reduce the cost of education to them, or otherwise increase the rate of return on their investment, by providing jobs with higher incomes and status for their children who were being educated. The parents themselves attempted to reduce the cost of schooling in a number of ways, including enrolling their children in schools at an earlier age, when the opportunity cost of their education was lower. Other measures included the waiving of school fees, and even providing clothing, books, and prizes for those poor children who were attending school regularly.

But on the other hand the ruling groups were increasingly insistent that parents should contribute more to the cost of their children's education by a compulsory levy of school fees. This obviously had a negative effect on the efforts, especially among the poorer sections of these societies, to give their children an education. In addition, many members of the elite still considered these lower class blacks and, later the East Indians, to have been destined to continue in their traditional role as unskilled plantation labourers. They therefore put a number of obstacles in the path of those who, having received some formal schooling, tried to move into other occupations.

As more opportunities for upward mobility through education became available to blacks, parents' interest in their children's education improved, and this was reflected in the increased attendance in the elementary schools, especially after the 1870s. This was most obvious when the West Indian governments began to provide a limited number of secondary school scholarships for children of the lower classes attending the primary schools. Williams emphasized this point in reference to Barbados, where he noted that increased enrollment in primary schools was

> partly due to the impact of the new "scholarship scheme" for children from the poorest homes, irrespective of colour or class, who had now been given the opportunity to proceed by their own efforts, in small numbers to the "second grade" schools and in even smaller numbers to the "first grade" schools, if they succeeded in rising to the top in various competitive exams conducted for entry to such schools.[57]

This observation could also have applied to other colonies in the region.

The education received by students who were not able to secure white-collar jobs was often considered of little use to them in their everyday lives. The values of the community and those which the teachers attempted to pass on to the children were often in such contrast that schooling sometimes did not do much to improve the quality of life of the school-leavers. This point was emphasized in British Honduras where it was noted that the values, beliefs and morals which the schools attempted to transmit to their pupils were very different from those which they learnt in the community and in their homes. As a result it was said to have been "hardly surprising to find that [their formal] education . . . [had so] little effect" on them.[58] This further reduced the motivation of poor parents to send their children to school.

Another issue of importance was the irrelevance of the knowledge which students often acquired in schools in terms of helping them to cope with the realities that would later face them when they left school. It was therefore reported that after children had been to school for some years, their parents were often sadly disappointed at their achievements because they had learnt little of practical use. Many were unable to read the newspaper, write a short note, or keep simple accounts. As a result, lower class parents in particular concluded that education was of little use to their children and that it would be more profitable to send them to work in the fields, instead of school.[59] In the Bahamas, for example, it was observed that the "apathy" of the parents to education was mainly due to the "merely literary acquirements" of students who had been to school and which were of little use to them in real life. This situation contributed further to the annual variations in primary school attendance and the slow rate at which this situation was improving between the late 1840s and 1870.

To overcome this deficiency in the "usefulness" of the education which the children were receiving, the provision of "some kind of technical instruction that was likely to be of practical benefit to them in their daily pursuits"[60] was often advocated. However, for various reasons, such efforts at making the curriculum more relevant to the needs of the population through the introduction of industrial training in schools were not very successful. Many planters still did not want the aspiration levels of the workers to rise unduly because they were afraid that those who were being educated would no longer be available to work on the plantations. These factors together contributed to the "growing disinclination of parents to send their children to school."[61]

Nevertheless, an increasing number of parents realized that education was the main and sometimes the only means by which their children could achieve some degree of occupational and social mobility. This was why, despite the odds, they persisted in their efforts to send them to schools in increasing numbers, especially after the 1870s. These increases in enrollment continued even though, as indicated above, the basic education which the students received was virtually irrelevant in terms of providing them with the skills that were likely to be directly useful to them later in life. Their parents were still hoping that, despite the lack of practical use to which this education could be put, it would nevertheless help them to move up the occupational and social hierarchy.

Summary and Conclusions
While school enrollment and attendance gradually improved over the entire half-century covered by this study, attendance continued to fluctuate considerably, and the overall enrollment in most colonies still did not normally exceed 50% of the population of school age. Further, while elementary school enrollments increased quite substantially after the 1870s, the percentage of average attendance tended to decline in many of these colonies. There were a number of reasons for this. First, a number of schools were forced to close following the termination of the Negro Education Grant. This occurred at a time when the region was experiencing tremendous economic difficulties, and the local legislatures were unable or unwilling to step in to meet the full impact of the financial shortfall. The closure of schools meant that fewer children had ready access to education.

Further, after emancipation, a number of families moved away from the sugar estates and began living in the less accessible areas. This increased the difficulties which their children faced in getting an education, especially since parents were often less willing to send them to schools located some distance from their homes. The closure of some of the smaller schools, the absence of roads, the heavy rainfall, the frequency of river floods, and the high incidence of childhood diseases all contributed to reducing school attendance .

In addition, some of the better schools in the region which were operated by the Mico Trust were also closed. The Trust was the largest single agency providing educational services to the region, and the closure of its schools often meant that students had to attend other schools of a lower quality — a factor that also had a negative effect on their attendance. In fact, the generally poor quality of the education and the irrelevance of the programme of instruction to the needs of students were identified as two other factors contributing to some parents' lack of enthusiasm for educating their children.

The economic crisis which the West Indies was experiencing due to the continuing decline in the sugar industry also affected enrollments and attendance in two ways. First, it meant that the legislatures were unable or unwilling to provide additional funds to keep all the existing schools open, much less to establish new ones. Second, as the incomes earned by the parents were reduced, they were often in a difficult financial position to meet the direct and indirect costs of their children's education. This meant that they were less able to pay the increased school fees which had virtually become compulsory in most of these colonies.

Finally, even though pupils remained away from school for a long time, teachers were reluctant to drop their names from the attendance registers because grants were often related to the level of school enrollment. Teachers hoped that by keeping the names of long-term absentees "on the books" these pupils might be encouraged to return to school. An outcome of this practice was that the records showed very low attendance rates.

The following reasons which Wood advanced for poor school attendance in Trinidad were also applicable to the other colonies in the region. He noted that

> fevers and other illnesses, the conflicting demands of the land and the schoolroom, the scattered distribution of the population, overgrown and neglected roads, impassable tracks for children on the heavy clays in wet season as well as parental indifference and the sheer delights of truancy all contributed to the dispiriting state of affairs for teachers who could never plan a regular course of instruction.[62]

One of the most significant points to be made is that there seemed to have been emerging two groups of working-class parents with somewhat different attitudes to their children's education. First, there were the economically better-off blacks and coloureds who were keen to ensure that their children received a good education. One could describe these as forming part of an emerging middle class who were fairly ambitious for their children and were in a somewhat better economic position to help meet the cost of their education.

On the other hand, there was a group which comprised the mass of the black population, who were still estate labourers or were eking out a marginal existence from farming. It was among this second group that low enrollments and irregular attendance were most marked. In other words, the black population as a whole did not become less interested in the education of their children. However, with low wages and the rising cost of education, some parents were less able than others to raise the funds necessary to send their children to school on a regular basis. It was largely for this group that compulsory education was seen to be necessary.

An important factor which helped to develop a more positive attitude toward education on the part of the population and increased the regularity of attendance by pupils was the limited, though increasing, opportunity for upward mobility which education was beginning to provide. This was further stimulated by the few scholarships which became available in most of these colonies to students from the primary schools to enter a local secondary grammar school and eventually through this route eventually enter a tertiary-level educational institution in the metropole.

Notes

1 These figures were obtained from the *Annual Reports* from these colonies.
2 Report of the Government of Tobago, *British Parliamentary Papers*, Vol. 44: *1860* (London: Government of Great Britain), 61.
3 Report of the Government of Jamaica, *British Parliamentary Papers*, Vol. 54: *1889* (London: Government of Great Britain), 20.
4 Report of the Government of Montserrat, *British Parliamentary Papers*, Vol. 46: *1847-48* (London: Government of Great Britain), 119.
5 Report of the Government of Barbados, *British Parliamentary Papers*, Vol. 49: *1866* (London: Government of Great Britain), 85.
6 CO 299/11, Government of Trinidad, *Report of the Inspector of Schools for the Year 1860*, 1 March 1861 (Trinidad: the Royal Gazette).
7 Report of the Government of Antigua, *British Parliamentary Papers*, Vol. 34: *1849* (London: Government of Great Britain), 217.
8 Report of the Government of British Honduras, *British Parliamentary Papers*, Vol. 34: *1849* (London: Government of Great Britain), 286.
9 Report of the Government of the Turks and Caicos Islands in *British Parliamentary Papers*, Vol. 42: *1872* (London: Government of Great Britain), 49.
10 Letter by J. Cox, Private Secretary to Government House. *British Parliamentary Papers*, Vol. 46: *1847-48* (London: Government of Great Britain), 113.
11 Report of the Government of Grenada, *British Parliamentary Papers*, Vol. 10: *1857* (London: Government of Great Britain), 113.
12 Report of the Government of Jamaica, *British Parliamentary Papers*, Vol. 54: *1889* (London: Government of Great Britain), 20.
13 Report of the Government of St. Vincent, *British Parliamentary Papers*, Vol. 48: *1873* (London: Government of Great Britain), 131–32.
14 Report of the Government of Jamaica for 1893–94, *British Parliamentary Papers*, Vol. 69: *1895* (London: Government of Great Britain), 19.
15 Letter by J. Cox, Private Secretary to Government House. *British Parliamentary Papers*, Vol. 46: *1847-48* (London: Government of Great Britain), 113.
16 Wood, *Trinidad in Transition* 226.
17 CO 295/232, Government of Trinidad, *Report of the Inspector of Schools for Trinidad, 1864* (Port-of-Spain, Trinidad: PRO).
18 Report of the Government of Bahamas, *British, Parliamentary Papers*, Vol. 36: *1850*, 163.
19 Ibid.
20 Ibid.
21 Report of the Government of Bermuda, *British Parliamentary Papers*, Vol. 44: *1874* (London: Government of Great Britain), 37
22 Ibid.
23 Robert Gregory, *Report of the Scottish Missionary Society, 1846*, 25.
24 Report of the Government of British Guiana, *British Parliamentary Papers*, Vol. 46: *1847-48* (London: Government of Great Britain), 144.
25 Report of the Government of Dominica, *British Parliamentary Papers*, Vol. 37: *1847* (London: Government of Great Britain), 53.
26 Report of the Government of Montserrat, *British Parliamentary Papers*, Vol. 46: *1847-48* (London: Government of Great Britain), 119.
27 Davy, *The West Indies Before and Since Slave Emancipation* (London: W. & F. G. Cash, 1854), 231.
28 This refers to recent immigrants from Africa, not West Indians of African descent.
29 CO 111/259 (McSwiney), 55.
30 Report of the Government of St. Vincent, *British Parliamentary Papers*, Vol. 46: *1847-48* (London: Government of Great Britain), 91.
31 Report of the Government of British Virgin Islands, *British Parliamentary Papers*, Vol. 42: *1856* (London: Government of Great Britain), 171.
32 Report of the Government of the Turks and Caicos Islands, *British Parliamentary Papers*, Vol. 47: *1871* (London: Government of Great Britain), 38.

33 Report of the Government of Barbados, *British Parliamentary Papers*, Vol. 34: *1849* (London: Government of Great Britain), 169.

34 Isidore L. Dyett to the President of Nevis, 14 May 1857.

35 Report of the Government of Antigua, *British Parliamentary Papers*, Vol. 44: *1884* (London: Government of Great Britain), 201.

36 Lord Elgin, Despatch with the Blue Book, 7 May 1845; Gordon, 59.

37 Governor Lord Elgin, *Confidential Despatch to the Secretary of State, 5 August 1845*; Gordon, 59.

38 Report of the Government of Nevis, *British Parliamentary Papers*, Vol. 37: *1847* (London: Government of Great Britain), 56.

39 Report of the Government of the Turks and Caicos Islands, *British Parliamentary Papers*, Vol. 29: *1846* (London: Government of Great Britain), 109.

40 Ibid. *British Parliamentary Papers*, Vol. 40: *1857-58* (London: Government of Great Britain), 131.

41 Report of the Government of Bahamas, *British Parliamentary Papers*, Vol. 36: *1850* (London: Government of Great Britain), 162.

42 Ibid.

43 Report of the Government of Jamaica, *British Parliamentary Papers*, Vol. 10: *1857* (London: Government of Great Britain), 54.

44 Report of the Government of Trinidad, *British Parliamentary Papers*, Vol. 51: *1875* (London: Government of Great Britain), 41.

45 Report of the Government of Dominica, *British Parliamentary Papers*, Vol. 49: *1870* (London: Government of Great Britain), 100.

46 Report of the Government of Leeward Islands, *British Parliamentary Papers*, Vol. 55: *1892* (London: Government of Great Britain), 16.

47 Report of the Government of Jamaica, *British Parliamentary Papers*, Vol. 45: *1883* (London: Government of Great Britain), 21

48 *British Parliamentary Papers*, Vol. 46: *1871* (London: Government of Great Britain), 18.

49 Government of Jamaica, *1883 Report on the Blue Book* (Kingston, Jamaica), 123.

50 Report of the Government of British Guiana, *British Parliamentary Papers*, Vol. 48: *1847-48* (London: Government of Great Britain), 143.

51 Report of the Government of the Bahamas, *British Parliamentary Papers*, Vol. 46: *1847-48* (London: Government of Great Britain), 57.

52 CO 111/259 (McSwiney), 30-38.

53 Davy, *The West Indies* 231.

54 Report of the Government of Jamaica, *British Parliamentary Papers*, Vol. 10: *1857* (London: Government of Great Britain), 54.

55 Report of the Government of Dominica, *British Parliamentary Papers*, Vol. 36: *1862* (London: Government of Great Britain), 104.

56 Report of the Government of St. Vincent, *British Parliamentary Papers*, Vol. 34: *1851* (London: Government of Great Britain), 84.

57 A. G. Williams, "The Development of Education in Barbados With Special Reference to the Social and Economic Conditions, 1834-1958" (M. A. thesis, Univ. of London, 1964), 211-12.

58 Report of the Government of British Honduras, *British Parliamentary Papers*, Vol. 54: *1884* (London: Government of Great Britain), 135.

59 Government of Jamaica, *Report of the Inspector of Schools*, 14 December 1863.

60 Report of the Government of the Bahamas, *British Parliamentary Papers*, Vol. 54: *1884* (London: Government of Great Britain), 171.

61 Report of the Government of Jamaica, *British Parliamentary Papers*, Vol. 44: *1882* (London: Government of Great Britain), 36.

62 Wood, *Trinidad in Transition*, 228-29.

CHAPTER 4

THE DOMINANCE OF RELIGIOUS EDUCATION IN THE CURRICULUM OF THE PRIMARY SCHOOLS

Introduction

In the immediate post-emancipation years, there continued to be much discussion about the most appropriate education for the children of the ex-slaves. The legislators and planters expected that, like their parents, these children would eventually "become estate labourers"[1] and therefore suggested that their education should specifically prepare them for this role. Others had a broader view of the role of education in the West Indies after emancipation, as can be seen in the request made by E. Burke to the government of British Honduras for a school in the northern district of that colony.

In his request[2] Burke pointed out that the numbers who could read and write in the area for which he was requesting a school were very small. In addition, several individuals who had appeared as witnesses in court cases were found ignorant of the nature of the oath, the existence of the Divine Being, and of a "future state of reward and punishment." Added to this was the "desecration of the Sabbath" by many members of the local community, their total "disregard for the marriage vows," and their constant "gambling and intemperance." In general, the masses were living under "depraved moral and social conditions."

The children were therefore in need of a school which would help to bring them "under the influence of secular teaching and sound religious training." Through the instruction which they were to receive, "good principles would be fixed and good habits formed — habits of industry, sobriety, and economy which would produce a revolution in the moral, social and physical conditions of these classes."[3] In other words, education would prevent them from emulating the "vicious courses" and practices of their parents. Those engaged in providing an elementary education for the black population wanted (1) to develop in them the idea that hard work was a social and moral obligation on their part; (2) to inculcate in them the belief that the existing order of society was fixed by "divine precept" and for "wise purposes"; and (3) to teach them to accept as "given" their own place within the social and occupational hierarchy.

For these concerns, an elementary curriculum focussing on religious and moral education on one hand and industrial training on the other was thought to be crucial. This was partly why the imperial government earlier insisted that any educational programme which was to be financed from its Negro Education Grant was to consist of a combination of religious and practical instruction. According to the secretary of state for the colonies, education for the masses was to produce individuals who would become "animated by a . . . spirit of patient industry," which he felt should always accompany good instruction.[4]

In a communication to the West Indian governors in 1846, the secretary of state suggested that there ought to be two dominant motives — a higher and a lower one — influencing all educational programmes for the "Negro race." The first of these was to contribute to their "moral and spiritual enlightenment." If emancipation was to result, "not merely in exemption from physical suffering and brutalizing oppression," but in "a moral and spiritual freedom," the first element of education had to be based "on a stronger foundation than that of human laws." This would necessitate an "advancement in Christian virtues and happiness" that could only be secured "through the channel of education and [particularly] religious instruction."[5] This inculcation of Christian religious values was also considered to be the best way of impressing on the masses the importance of being "diligent, faithful, patient and useful workers," while developing in them a "humble and subordinate carriage."

The second and lower motive stemmed from the recognition that the continued economic prosperity of the West Indies depended on providing the young with the appropriate attitudes, knowledge, and skills for their future role as agricultural labourers. This educational focus obviously had direct economic implications which were appreciated by the planters. An active programme of industrial training was considered necessary to achieve these goals, since it was likely to make labour "more intelligent and orderly." Commenting on this point, the *Royal Gazette* of Jamaica suggested that, since indolence was "the besetting sin" of most workers on the island, the ex-slaves had to realize the importance of industry and hard work in order to make "sensible" use of their freedom. This was particularly important for the new generation of blacks who, unlike their parents, would not have been brought up under the discipline of compulsory labour.

In stressing the need for such practical education Earl Grey drew attention to the economic circumstances of the region by suggesting that it was probably impossible to find another colony in which the agricultural and commercial prospects were so absolutely dependent on the achievement of some level of education by the lower orders, as the West Indies. He therefore proposed that both these motives — the higher and the lower — should underlie any elementary school curriculum in the region. The educational programmes of local schools needed to place a strong emphasis on practical or industrial education, which should have as its base the teaching of sound Christian principles. These were to stress the duty of individuals to work diligently, fulfilling the wishes of their employers and all those whom "God" had placed in a position of authority over them. This educational focus was similar to that for the labouring classes in the metropole and was to be directed, not at producing ladies and gentlemen but "honest, industrious, self-respectful, and God-fearing gardeners, servants, cooks, or housekeepers."[6]

While doubts were occasionally expressed about the intellectual capacity of the Negro population, by the 1850s, the view was gradually shared that they were capable of levels of learning comparable to any other group. For example, in commenting on the situation in Montserrat, the president indicated that the educational progress among the children was extremely satisfactory and that there was no natural inferiority of intellect on the part of the African in comparison with other races of mankind. What was occasionally being challenged was their *capacity for moral development*. But even here, there was a growing acceptance of the view that the ex-slaves were capable of acquiring "powers of mind and a course of good behaviour," which was in "no way inferior to the children of European descent."[7] With a proper education "these dispositions and habits [acquired during slavery could be] altered for the better and the African [could] stand forth as a being equally capable of mental culture as other human beings, both intellectual and religious, [with] equal powers of observation, reflection and aspirations after the good."[8]

Elementary education therefore needed to focus on the development of both the affective domain — through moral and spiritual training — and of the cognitive domain — through basic instruction in the 3Rs along with a programme of industrial education. These were said to have been the goals of all the better schools in the region and while they could not be achieved by schools alone, especially considering the environment from which most students came, nevertheless, it was strongly believed that through proper education a moral, social, and economic transformation of the young black population could be achieved.

Support for Religious Education

Religious and moral education, as McBean Hartley pointed out, involved instruction in the doctrines of the Christian religion, along with the basic skills in reading which would provide the "keys to the Scriptures and the history and ethics of the Christian religion."[9] This type of education was considered by the upper class in these societies to be important for the children of the labouring classes and hence it came to be the central focus of the curriculum of West Indian schools. As late as 1880 the governor of St. Lucia was still raising the question that, if the benefits of education, of which religious instruction was an important element, "are felt to be absolutely necessary in all free and civilized communities how much more requisite are they in a colony like this, that has lately emerged from the darkness of slavery into the full light of freedom?"[10]

In 1846 the governor of Tobago argued that "the soundness of the fruit to be gathered from the tree of freedom mainly depends on the Christian moral instruction of the Negro population."[11] Prescod, a coloured Barbadian legislator, who was very interested to see "our people well educated," argued in 1846 that

> no scheme of education for them or for any human being can be complete, or at all deserving of the name of education, unless broadly based on moral and religious principles. [Therefore the children should not only be taught] the knowledge of their duties as accountable human beings . . . but they should also be carefully instructed and trained into the habits of performance, intellect, and feelings. The[ir] passions as well as the[ir] reason should be carefully cultivated and trained in the habits of virtue and an education such as this we should rejoice to see our people receiving. It would be a noble act worthy of the Christian community, in the proper sense of Christianity.[12]

The president of Montserrat, too, suggested that, whatever might be the future occupations of the children of the ex-slaves, they still needed a heavy concentration of Christian religious education to ensure a proper moral upbringing. In Antigua, it was observed that the teaching of religious education in the schools was very important because "the force of religious principles on the . . . community has prevented much moral evil and inspired contentment and patience."[13]

Governor Barkly of British Guiana commented on the social benefits that were to accrue from a sound religious education by noting that without such an education, "it will be in vain to look for a race of *steady* and *industrious* labourers and still more in vain to expect *skill* and *intelligence* in the application of labour which is almost as important as *steady industry* to West Indian agriculture in the present time [emphasis added]."[14]

In addition, he observed that it would be impossible to answer for the peace and safety of the society without the religious education of the younger generation.

In Barbados, the introduction of the 1851 Education Act, which was to provide a somewhat broader education for the masses, prompted members of the legislature to express the hope that the increased attention to a more general education "will not in any way impair, but improve the religious instruction given, and help to fit the rising generation, both in mind and character, for the satisfactory and cheerful performance of their unavoidable duties," as estate labourers.[15]

In 1856 the president of the Agricultural Society of that island, the Honourable E.G. Thomas, in discussing the importance of religious education, pointed out that "we see the Negro demoralized and crippled in mind by the injury which slavery has inflicted on his mental conditions, but what we see is not his natural character." He also noted that the children's intellectual and moral development was negatively affected by their morally and educationally debilitating home environment, characterized by the "ignorance, idleness and prejudices," of their "semi-barbarous and uneducated parents." As a result, he felt that they were likely to "indulge in all kinds of vicious propensities, unless there can be some countervailing principles, some controlling discipline to restrain them."[16] Hence, he emphasized the importance of Christian religious teachings to enable the young to rise above the confines and restrictions imposed by their environment.

The 1857 report of a local legislative committee also reiterated that if education was to produce the kind of individuals needed by the society, it should combine intellectual and religious training. It also recommended that the "teaching of the Holy Scriptures in the Authorized Version" should be one of the conditions which must be fulfilled for any school to be given a public grant. In fact, in most colonies government financial assistance to the local denominational schools was usually made on condition that religious instruction, founded on the Holy Scriptures, would be formally provided for the pupils.

The government of St. Kitts stressed this dual function of education in its 1855 Education Act, which noted that "intellectual culture" was "not the only or even the chief requisite in public instruction." Rather, its focus should be "the cultivation of moral faculties." Therefore, the legislature made it quite clear that its grants to schools were to "ensure this moral development" of the pupils and it instructed its board of education to see that "the education imparted in each school shall be religious, plain and useful." It was also "to prohibit, under a forfeiture of the State allowance any [other] practice or course of studies which experience has proved to be . . . unsuited to the children of the industrial classes."[17]

Even though governors McLeod and Harris were responsible for the introduction of a secular system of education in Trinidad they both recognized the importance of religious education in the upbringing of children. For example, Lord Harris himself had pointed out that he acknowledged "to the fullest, the immense importance" of religious education, because without religion "no society of men can flourish." It was needed to "purify, arouse and almost create motives," "direct the will," "affect the moral sentiments," and modify the "impulses and habits" of the black population. In fact, he saw that "the energies," "the conduct," and the "welfare" of whole communities could be affected by religion.[18]

But it was for social and political reasons that these two governors decided that religious education should not be offered as part of the regular instructional programme of schools. With such diversity in the island's population, they believed that an important function of education was to contribute to socio-cultural integration among these various groups. Religious instruction in the schools was likely to inhibit this process by exacerbating the divisiveness among the various religious and ethnic groups in the colony.

In 1859 the inspector of schools for the island drew attention to the many examples of "ancient degraded character" which were engendered by slavery and which he felt always accompanied the absence of religious education. In 1875 the *Mitchinson Report* also referred to the need for inculcating

> the habit of obedience, order, punctuality, honesty etc. which a child ought instinctively to acquire in his progress, be it ever so slow, through a well-disciplined school. [These] are likely to stick all through his life and make him a better labourer than he would have been without that training. [19]

As a result, an amendment in the Education Act was introduced during the following year, requiring that all students be examined in religious education.

In 1880 the governor of the Bahamas saw that schools should assist not only with the task of inculcating habits of "neatness, cleanliness and order," but also contribute to the peace and stability of family life. For this they needed to offer a sound programme of religious education. As the governor noted, "I am certain that much of the unhappiness and sorrow which sometimes exists in families is from the rebellious nature of children and I am also sure that nothing is so likely to prevent this as the good [religious] education and corrective discipline which are to be found in schools."[20]

He therefore urged parents to avail themselves of the advantages of schooling for their children since it would increase their happiness and the success of their families and would contribute towards building a society on the "sure foundation" of an intelligent and Christian people.

In Jamaica, all schools were required to offer religious education which involved teaching the facts set out in the Old and the New Testament. As late as 1892, the government was said to have still been "anxious to encourage every educational effort, either by societies or individuals . . . to impart sound practical instruction, and a good moral training to the children of the working classes."[21] Such education was to be distinguished by its thoroughness and in it "a prominent place" was to be given "to the chief or necessary subjects," [22] including religious education.

Reasons for the Dominant Role of Religious Instruction in Schools

In review, one sees that religious education was considered important because it was expected to contribute to the moral welfare of the *individual* by laying a sound Christian foundation among the upcoming generation. The missionaries who were mainly responsible for providing education in the region stressed the contribution which religious education could make in helping the masses *overcome some of the[ir] more "sinful" practices.* Writing in 1854, Davy also argued that "a general system of education, accompanied with *moral and religious training* must form the basis of any future improvement" of the 'Negro' population [emphasis added].[23] Religious education was also intended to foster the overall development of the *society* through inculcating in the young those attitudes that were likely to help them acquire the appropriate social behaviours and favourable attitudes to work.

Commenting on this expected outcome of education in Jamaica, Campbell noted,

> The planter classes hoped that *moral and religious education* would help to teach the newly emancipated Negroes their divinely ordained place as agricultural labourers and the wisdom and blessing of peacefully and orderly executing the duties of the labouring class [emphasis added]. [24]

Since most black parents had themselves never been to school nor had received any formal education in the principles of Christianity they were considered incapable of providing their children with the requisite moral instruction needed for their proper upbringing. Therefore the school and the church were seen as the institutions which had to fill this need.

It was also noted that West Indian children were being influenced by the many examples of immoral behaviour which were daily confronting them on the plantations and in the villages. The result of their growing up in such undesirable social and moral environments was often their discreditable regression toward the uncivilized behaviours of the older generation. This, it was argued, would continue unless they were provided with an effective programme of religious education. The 1851 *Report of the Joint Committee on Education in Barbados* argued that religious and moral training was even more important at the infant rather than at the primary school stage, because it enabled the teachers to work on the children before their bad or immoral habits were developed. This point of view was shared by many missionaries who often suggested that an early intervention should be made in the education of the young through the establishment of nursery and boarding schools providing a vibrant programme of religious training .

To keep the children away from the morally corrupting environments of their homes, the establishment of model boarding schools was also proposed. Here, black children were to come under the more prolonged and supposedly superior religious influence of Europeans who would very likely have been in charge of such institutions. However, for financial reasons, such schools did not materialize, and the responsibility of providing formal religious instruction to elevate the moral standards of the upcoming generation continued to rest with the regular day and Sunday schools.

Another consideration for stressing the importance of religious education was that the post-emancipation generation in the West Indies was said to be growing up in the most "unbounded freedom" and "independence" and, as a result, their behaviours left much to be desired. While during the earlier years, the region was said to have had "an exceedingly well-behaved and orderly people," as evidenced by the "peculiarly rare instances of crime, beyond that of petty thefts, occurring amongst them," allegations began to be made that this situation was changing, especially among the young.[25] For example, in Barbados, it was reported in 1848 that problems associated with the lack of discipline were more apparent among the rising generation than the adult population, "who have been schooled into obedience, industry and regularity of habits by a discipline which is now happily at an end," i.e., slavery.

Among the young, this upbringing was "not yet effectively replaced by influences more consistent with nature and the gospel."[26] Therefore, in 1857 the Association for the Improvement of the Religious and Social Condition of the Labouring Poor on the island petitioned the legislature to suggest that there had been a retrogression in the moral and social conditions of the labouring population on the island, one of the alarming consequences of which was an increase in juvenile delinquency. This was further compounded by the difficulty youths had in finding work, especially those who migrated to the urban areas. For example, it was estimated that in the 1870s nearly 40% of children between 4-15 years of age in this colony were not in school and were out of work. In addition, a large number of children in the region were illegitimate, receiving no support or care from or by their fathers. They had therefore become "a sore burden" on their mothers and were often left destitute of all moral training and other "wholesome influences."

The governor of British Guiana noted that there was a "marked change in the respectful demeanour of the population during the early days after emancipation, particularly in the younger of the Creole race." As a result, he found it necessary to keep a mounted police patrol in areas of Georgetown where "respectable" citizens went "for rides and drives," in order "to check the jeering and impertinent remarks of the loungers in the neighbourhood of the town."[27] In commenting further on this problem, he observed that "our Asylums and our poor lists are crowded with men and women who, having been neglected in their own childhood [and] through[out] their maturity [have] been utterly idle and dissolute, living upon society and producing their own kind."[28]

The dominant view, as reflected the 1857 *Report of a Barbadian Legislative Committee* was that intellectual secular education alone was highly inadequate to lay a sound moral foundation in the pupils. This, it was suggested, would only change "the character of a crime" but not "the heart of the criminal." Hence, "to educate the head and sharpen the faculties, without at the same time educating the heart, would be to inflict a curse upon rather than to benefit the people."[29] The young needed to be taught "the common duties of humanity" in time, so that their liberty might become a blessing rather than a curse to themselves and to the colony. Without such an education it was said that they would grow up to become "mere African savages." This *Report* therefore recommended that primary education with a strong religious foundation should be the key factor in helping to curb the "rebellious nature" of the youths in the region by giving them a solid moral foundation in Christianity. This was likely to produce an overall social stability in these societies and add to the economic and social "success of the children" and the "happiness" of their parents.[30]

Governor Hincks of Barbados saw that the provision of religious education was particularly important for the destitute children and had urged the legislature that, in extending the blessings of education more generously among the population, special provision should also be made for their religious and moral training since it was from among them that young criminals were most readily recruited. The need for moral upliftment of the female population was also obvious because the number of illegitimate children in the society exceeded those then being born in wedlock. These young females therefore needed to acquire a higher moral tone through a sound programme of religious instruction which would provide an important restraining influence on their sexual desires and teach them to reject the sexual advances of adult males.[31]

A higher level of Christian morality was also seen as particularly important among the middle-class blacks, especially those who were being put in positions of responsibility and trust. For example, male teachers, who were among the more educated of the black population, were often accused of immorality with the older female students, with consequent evil effects on all the children at school. This pointed to the need for higher moral standards which would teach these individuals to abstain from such immoral activities.

One of the planters' hopes was that religious education would produce a superior class of worker who would become a role model for the remainder of the black population. They therefore saw that "to train up" the young children "in habits of industry, to teach them *the truths of religion*, and . . . *to implant in their minds the fear of God* cannot but be a work productive of good" [emphasis added].[32] This was especially important since it was also likely to imbue them with the attitudes and values that could prepare them psychologically to follow the occupation of their parents, as workers on the sugar estates.

Christian religious education was also expected to instill in the young something of a "European character and *energy*," so that by the time they reached adulthood they would be prepared to act like leaven upon the mass of society, and thereby raise the moral tone of the whole community. It was also seen as a necessary ingredient in maximizing the outcomes of the industrial education programmes that were being introduced in West Indian schools. As previously suggested, religious education was to teach individuals those values that would provide a moral underpinning for the skills, behaviours, and attitudes considered necessary for the economic growth of these societies. This was why Kay Shuttleworth placed the subject at the centre of his educational programme for *Day Schools of Industry for the Coloured Races of the British Colonies.*

An example of the type of responsible attitudes toward work which religious education was to help inculcate among the young was said to have been reflected in the restraint which the older population had shown during the period of declining wages. In Antigua, it was noted that in 1848 the force of religious principle on the community had not only prevented much moral evil but also inspired contentment and patience. In Barbados, it was suggested that

> the labouring classes deserve commendation for the very proper spirit in which they have yielded to the altered circumstances of their employers; they seem quite sensible of the inability of the planters to continue the former rate of wages and work cheerfully at a reduction of more than one half. [This was the result of] the force of religious principles on the . . . community [which] has prevented much moral evil and inspired contentment and patience.[33]

It was often emphasized that education of the masses was not intended to "raise them above their station and business in life . . . but to . . . fit them for that business." Within this context, religious instruction was deemed "a noble device for uplifting the human spirit, controlling passion and *preserving the prevailing social order."* [emphasis added].[34] As Earl Grey suggested, the major means by which emancipation might be made to result in true spiritual freedom for the Negroes was in their religious education, which would lay a solid foundation for human laws. Because of this perceived importance, it was recommended to the government of Barbados that it should develop an adult education programme, based on religious and moral teachings, to be offered in the homes of the labourers.

Another reason for religion maintaining its dominant place in the curriculum stemmed from the fact that initially the missionaries played a crucial role in the establishment of the schools in the region. This resulted in the development of a denominational system of education throughout the region — with the exception of the ward schools in Trinidad between 1851 and 1870. Given the crucial role which they occupied in the management of education, the missionaries exerted a considerable influence on the curriculum content offered in the schools under their jurisdiction, and to them, religion was the most important subject to be taught to the younger generation.

For example, the 1851 Commission on Education in British Guiana had recommended that, in view of the great religious diversity of its population, a secular system of education should be introduced in the colony. The Church of England, with its powerful influence, immediately petitioned against the move, on the grounds that

> to present to the Children of the Peasantry, as a substitute for Scriptural Education, a system of instruction from which would be excluded the very highest wisdom, that which the word of God contains, would be to offer to them a very imperfect or doubtful good, and they have no confidence it would even accomplish what its advocates anticipate from it, the training of a Moral and Industrious people.[35]

As a result the Anglican authorities argued that funds should not be given for the establishment of schools in which the "revealed will of God does not form a component and essential part"[36] of the education of the children. To them it was necessary to make "the rising generation acquainted with those truths which should be their guide through life and their comfort in death."[37] On account of this active opposition to a secular system of education, the commissioners were asked to draft a new bill that would ensure that religious instruction founded on the precepts of the Holy Scriptures would be offered in all schools receiving public support.

Because of their control of the elementary school system in the region, the religious bodies were also responsible for the selection and appointment of teachers, who were recruited largely on the basis of their religious background. Therefore, most teachers in the region were generally considered to have the necessary competence to provide catechistical and other religious training for their pupils and, with the exception of the teachers in the ward schools in Trinidad, had an obligation to do so, as part of the terms of their appointment. Teachers were also expected to be regularly present at church and to encourage their pupils to attend church services and Sunday School. These extracurricular activities further indicate the crucial importance which the missionary bodies who controlled the schools attached to the religious education of the young. Attention was also drawn to the 77th Canon of the Duty of Schoolmasters, which was adopted in practice by teachers in the West Indies, and which stated that "they shall train them [their pupils] with such sentences of Holy Scripture as shall be most expedient to induce them to all godliness."[38]

The strong influence which the churches exerted in education can also be seen in the fact that in Barbados, when the legislature created the position of inspector of schools, it was specified that any appointee must receive the assent of the Anglican bishop. Furthermore, the inspector was not to interfere with the management of the schools or the content of the education provided but was simply to tender his advice to the appropriate legislative authorities.

There were certain other social and political benefits which it was believed would accrue from an education strongly focussed on the teaching of religion. Many legislators continued to consider a basic knowledge of Christianity as one of the best means of preparing the West Indian masses for the new political society in which they were supposed to become full members. As indicated earlier, Earl Grey had suggested that religious instruction provided the only solid foundation for human laws while the *Barbadian* newspaper argued that

> civilization without mental and moral culture only makes men [*sic*] discontented with the institutions of their country, restless, vain, and ambitious, whereas religious educa-
> tion . . . brings men up in the fear of God, teaches them that
> *obedience to the law* of the land and *the government of the*
> *country* is due, not as a matter of compulsion, but as *a*
> *principle of conscience.* [Therefore] no education is of value
> which is not based on religion [emphasis added].[39]

Governor Barclay thought that evidence of the positive impact which religion might have on the development of West Indian societies was already obvious in Jamaica. After making a tour of some settlements, he observed that "the mountain villages have a decided air of progressive civilization and comfort about them." This he attributed to the teachings of the missionaries, which he said had, "on the whole, been productive of great good." Barclay went on to add that his observation "is now, I think all but universally admitted and I am bound to state that I have found their congregations well dressed and orderly and with every appearance of being — as I believe they are — the most civilized portions of the emancipated population."[40]

Another reason advanced for the continued emphasis on religious education related to the moral drain that was said to be occurring in these colonies with the steady emigration of their white population. It was suggested that such migration meant that "a generation is growing up, uninfluenced by the daily spectacle of any higher civilization than their own" and unless the effects of such a development were countered by religious education then, by the time the current generation reached adulthood, their behaviour was likely "to degenerate into a state of barbarism . . . worse than any that obtained in the days of slavery."[41]

In 1867 the lieutenant-governor of Dominica suggested that there was a great need for religious education because of the absence of upper-class individuals who could exert some positive moral influence on the masses on the island. The decline in numbers of the white population also meant that many of the civic duties which they had performed, including their role in the legislature, would eventually fall to the more progressive elements among the non-whites. If these people were to govern wisely, they needed an education rooted in religion and morality.

The number of immigrants, especially those from the East such as the Chinese and East Indians, who were arriving in the region was also said to be creating some serious moral problems for the authorities. Many Christians, including governor Lord Harris of Trinidad, doubted the "moral and mental" capabilities of these newly arrived indentured workers and their ability to act "upon the same motives . . . as labourers . . . in more civilized countries." Their needs were said to be limited. "Luxuries, they do not generally know of or require" and hence their motivation to work was considered to be not very great. While the European labourer was said to regard industriousness as a "duty and a virtue," such motives "are unknown to the[se] fatalist worshippers of Mahomet and Brahma and to the savages who go by the name of liberated Africans."[42] They therefore had to acquire Christian values if they were going to make a more positive contribution to the overall development of these societies.

Further, they had little fear of the law and, as evidence of this, it was pointed out that the Indian and Chinese immigrants frequently breached their indentureship contract. The conclusion was that they were incapable of fully understanding the moral obligations of a contractual agreement. In such a situation the surest prospect of ameliorating this problem was the gradual assimilation of these non-Christian elements within the dominant culture of these societies and subjecting them to the influence of the higher Christian civilization. This was also to help overcome the threat to the moral fabric of these societies which Dennis, the inspector of schools in British Guiana, felt was posed by large additions of the semi-barbarian element to the population that the country was receiving from the East.

It was also hoped that some of the East Indian children who were being educated at the Industrial Training School at Tacarigua in Trinidad, where they were required to convert to Christianity, would eventually become teachers among their "heathen countrymen." The governor of Grenada, too, expressed fears about the moral standards of the immigrants coming to that island and urged that they should be instructed in the duties and obligations of a Christian community.

For these various reasons mentioned above, it was almost universally acknowledged throughout the British Caribbean colonies that religious instruction was the most effective instrument for laying the foundation in the population of good principles and good habits, such as industry, sobriety, and economy, which would produce a revolution in the moral, social, and physical condition of the lower classes. The importance of religious and moral values was to be fully impressed upon the minds of all pupils, in order to develop in them sound morals, orderly conduct, and punctuality. As Peter Fraser noted, this knowledge of moral and religious truth which religious education would provide was expected to inculcate in the masses a respect for the laws of the land, their responsibilities as citizens, and the need to be industrious.

In summary, religious education was to have an important elevating effect on the character and behaviour of the rising generation and was to teach them that to be industrious is a duty and a virtue. This would eventually bring about a higher and kindlier tone to the life of the community in its moral and social relations, diminish crime, and produce a race of industrious, God-fearing colonists.

While teachers in the ward schools in Trinidad were forbidden to provide instruction in religion, the subject still formed a crucial part of the curriculum of their schools, including, as shall be seen later, the schools of Trinidad.

Implementation of the Programme of Religious Education

As part of a programme of religious instruction, the morning sessions in most primary schools in the British West Indies normally started with the Lord's Prayer and the afternoon sessions closed in a similar manner. In addition, it was quite usual for a substantial portion of the morning's activities to be devoted to formal religious instruction. For example, in the Bahamas, on account of "the paramount importance" which the board of education attached to "inculcating a thorough knowledge of the Holy Scriptures, a chapter of the Bible is read daily by every class sufficiently far advanced in the power of reading, and the children are examined upon it immediately afterwards, so as to ensure their understanding of what they have just been reading."[43]

Barbados provided a not untypical example of the time and effort devoted to religious instruction in the primary schools. Rawle had suggested that it was not too much to allocate the first hour of the morning to religion, during which time a portion of the Holy Scriptures was read, and verses of a selected psalm or a hymn were recited or sung. For him, it was also important that a Scripture lesson should be impressed daily on the minds of the children — "one truth set in a fitting frame of natural imagery and practical illustrations . . . to be fixed like a picture in the memory." In various ways, elementary schools tended to follow the essence of this recommendation.[44] The Ten Commandments and the Decalogue were usually taught as part of the children's reading lessons, which, in any case, continued to be directed towards giving them the skills that they would eventually need to read the Holy Scriptures.

From the results of the 1864 examinations conducted on Barbadian primary schools, one gets a further idea of the dominant place of religion in the instructional programme of these schools. The following were the results for that year:

1. Reading: Children able to read the New Testament with some degree of fluency: 2,336 out of 4,697: 49.7%.
2. Dictation: Children able to write a dictation from the Psalms: 8.7%.
3. Catechistical Religious Instruction: Children able to say the texts of the Ten Commandments well: 13.9%.

The results for the infant schools were as follows:

1. Reading: Children able to read a verse from the New Testament: 502 out of 2,423: 20.7%.
2. Dictation: Children able to write at dictation the 8th Commandment: (One mis-spelling granted): 7.3%.
3. Catechistical Religious Knowledge: Children able to repeat intelligibly the Lord's Prayer: 12.3%.
4. Singing: Children able to start and sing alone intelligently a verse of some hymn or school song: 5.9%.

Incidentally, the instructional programme adopted in Barbados was similar to that followed in most of the other British colonies in the region.

The content of the examination demonstrated that religion continued to permeate nearly all other subjects on the curriculum, in addition to occupying its own dominant position in the timetable. However, in the higher grades of the primary school there was beginning to be an observable differentiation between the curriculum content of the religious education programme and that of other subjects.

During the school year 1847-48, it was noted that in nearly all schools in the Bahamas, the Holy Scriptures or selections from them formed the basis of the reading lessons. Later, the governor of the island, having replaced members of the various religious orders on the board of education with lay individuals, wanted to assure the missionary societies that religious education would not, as a result, be de-emphasized. To this end, he encouraged the clergy to visit the schools in order to see for themselves that the subject still formed "the very basis of all our system of tuition."[45] The board of education continued to recognize the "paramount importance" of providing children with a thorough knowledge of the Holy Scriptures. Each school day opened up with the Lord's Prayer and closed with pupils repeating three or more verses of a hymn or psalm. The Ten Commandments and the Decalogue were also to be taught to all children as part of their reading lesson — at least during one day of each week.

The 1852 Bahamas Education Act clearly indicated that the Holy Bible and other religious and secular works which the education board specified would be the *only* books or lessons permitted to be read in any of the public schools. In addition, all ordained ministers of religion in that colony were *ipso facto* declared visitors of all government-aided schools, and no book which they protested against was allowed to be used in schools. The government even proposed that one day per week should be set aside exclusively for religious instruction. In British Honduras it was still being reported, as late as 1853, that reading in schools was largely confined to the Bible.

Other colonies faced with a tight financial situation examined the proposal that schools be allowed to teach only religious subjects, without charge, in the mornings, while during the afternoons the teachers would offer secular subjects for which they would charge full tuition fees. The Bahamas Education Act of 1864 specified that the following subjects of instruction should be offered in schools — the 3Rs, Outlines of History, Scripture and Practical Work (Needlework and Industrial Arts). Elements of religious instruction would have formed the core of most of these subjects, as was noted in the 1864 examination results for Barbados.

In Antigua and other colonies, it was one of the stated responsibilities of the board of education to ensure that the teaching of religion occupied a dominant position in the curriculum of all schools which received government financial support. As a result, the 1866 report for that island noted that religious instruction continued to be given considerable attention and that the students in the higher classes of several schools had even acquired "a very fair knowledge" of Scripture History. At the close of the year, "38.6% of those pupils on the books were able to read the Scriptures" and "in no other subject . . . do our students improve so rapidly"[46] no doubt because of the amount of time devoted to it.

In 1879, when the Mico Trustees gave up their schools in St. Lucia to the government, the main condition was "that the Bible must be read in the schools daily and Religious Instruction given [though] in an unsectarian manner."[47] In St. Vincent in the late 1840s, most schools offered only the 3Rs plus Religious Instruction. This, it was suggested, was the type of education "that can be expected, or perhaps, even desired, for the great mass of the population."[48] In Dominica, the 1863 School Act required that all schools be opened and closed with the Apostle's Creed, the Lord's Prayer, and the Doxology. A similar requirement existed among the schools in most of these colonies.

In British Guiana, the inspector of schools reported in 1848 that religious instruction offered from the Holy Scriptures, catechisms, and other religious books composed the principal feature of the education offered in the schools. Two years later, the examination conducted on the rural Wesleyan schools revealed that, of the 686 students enrolled, all were taking "Scriptural Catechism," while 274 (about 40%) were engaged in reading the Scriptures. Admittedly, this focus on religious education was largely due to the efforts of the Reverend Dennis, the first inspector of schools for the colony, who, like many others, believed that religious instruction was crucial in helping to overcome the "gross ignorance" and "moral obliquity" of the labouring classes. In the Turks and Caicos Islands, religion also remained a key subject in the primary schools. During his examination of the scholars at the East Harbour school, the president of the colony considered it important enough to suggest in his report of 1864 that the schoolmaster should exercise the pupils more thoroughly in "sacred" history.

The secular education provided by schools in Trinidad was sharply criticized by the various denominational bodies for being godless and creedless. But despite the clear provisions of the Education Act that no religious instruction be given in schools, it was difficult for teachers, especially with the kind of education and training which they had received, to ignore the subject entirely. Some of these teachers were even paid catechists even though this was contrary to the Education Ordinance. In addition, as Campbell noted, the schools most often used the Irish National Readers, which, though allegedly neutral between the various Christian denominations in their content, were, however, crammed full of moralizing and religiosity.

The ordinary reading material used in schools combined Bible History, Old Testament stories, and New Testament meanings of sin, repentance, and salvation. The use of these books indicated that religious instruction most decidedly crept into the curriculum. As the inspector noted, the schools were expected to bring "moral enlightenment" to the black population by exposing them to "civilized culture" and behaviour. Religious education was also expected to teach children to "work hard, respect their social betters and to be contented with their lot in life."[49] The subject was often seen by teachers as the basis of all education, and this was why the rule against its inclusion in the curriculum was often informally ignored.

Reports indicated that religious instruction in government schools was being offered in combination with certain secular subjects. For example, in 1852 Trinidad's inspector of schools noted that religion was still being taught in many schools and in one of them he found that the head class read and spelt the words in the various chapters in the New Testament very well. He pointed out that by their very knowledge of the subject the students proved that great pains had been taken to teach them "Scripture history." In one girls' school, he also observed that, in the first class (grade) some children fluently read a chapter from the Epistle to the Corinthians, while in the second class, during a Scripture history lesson, they read a chapter from the Epistle of St. James.

The practice of teaching religion in the primary schools of Trinidad was so marked that the governor's secretary felt it necessary to remind the wardens of the provisions of the Education Act, pointing out that the aim of the ward schools was "to inculcate . . . the habits of cleanliness, neatness and decency and of mutual courtesy and forbearance and the full obedience to the law and the dignity of industry and independence," rather than giving them any direct religious instruction.[50] As late as 1870, Keenan was still observing that "the principle of no religious instruction in the ward schools" was being violated by the Protestants. Pupils in some ward schools even used the New Testament to learn to read and spell.

Wednesdays and a half-day on Saturdays were, in addition, set aside in the ward schools for religious education, with the only stipulation being that such classes should not be conducted on school holidays, or by the regular school teachers, but by individuals provided through the various missionary groups.

The private, non-aided, denominational system which consisted of about 35 schools (13 Roman Catholic and 22 Protestant) obviously also offered to their pupils religious instruction with a denominational bias. For example, in all the Roman Catholic schools, the denominational version of the Scriptures was read, and paraphrases in French of the catechism of the Church of Rome were also being taught.

Despite the fact that some religious instruction was illegally offered in the ward schools of Trinidad, Governor Gordon regarded its lack of formal recognition as a "serious evil." He therefore attempted to overcome this problem by insisting that every clergyman in receipt of a stipend should be required to conduct regular classes in religion at the ward schools on the days officially assigned for the teaching of the subject, risking forfeiture of part of their salaries if they failed to do so. He also appointed two commissioners to review the situation, and they observed that the children's level of religious knowledge was quite unsatisfactory. Gordon therefore asked the Colonial Office to send an impartial educational expert to review the education provided on the island. The outcome was the appointment of Keenan, whose report led in 1870 to government grants being made to denominational primary schools. In these schools religious education was undoubtedly a key subject in their curriculum.

From the evidence presented above, it can be seen that religion occupied a crucial place in the instructional programme of West Indian primary schools — even in Trinidad, where it was legally forbidden during regular school hours. But although a considerable amount of time was devoted to the teaching of the subject the instructional strategies used often came in for severe criticism. For example, in Nevis, it was noted that religious instruction consisted of the repetition of verbal answers to questions, rather than "in the cultivation of moral qualities or the real enlightenment of the mind to the duties and responsibilities of life."[51] This rote system of learning in religious education was characteristic of the method of instruction used throughout the region in all other subjects taught in schools.

Summary and Conclusions

Two major concerns dominated the curriculum of the primary schools in the West Indies during the latter half of the nineteenth century. One focussed on the moral and religious development of the children of the ex-slaves, while the other was concerned with their preparation to continue working, like their parents, as agricultural labourers on the sugar estates. This chapter examined mainly the first of these concerns.

Substantial support for the teaching of religion came from many individuals and groups in these societies, including the local governors, the missionary societies, the legislators, and other members of the local elite. There were a number of reasons for granting religious education such a prominent place in the curriculum of schools. Chief among these was that it was considered necessary for promoting the "much needed" moral development among those who were recently emancipated from slavery. Moreover, religious education was expected to lay a foundation for social stability by teaching the upcoming generation that the rigid hierarchical structure of these societies was divinely ordained, as was their place within it. Therefore, the subject was considered to be so important that, during the period under review, it continued to dominate the curriculum of the primary schools, and while it was often taught separately, it was also integrated with virtually every other subject offered in schools. However, an assessment of the instructional strategies used indicated that attention tended to focus more on children committing to memory certain portions of the Scriptures, and their ability to repeat them or give verbal answers to specific questions culled from the scriptural lessons. Less emphasis seemed to have been placed on the inculcation of moral qualities among the children.

Notes
1 Gordon, *A Century* ,44.
2 Report of the Government of British Honduras, *British Parliamentary Papers*, Vol. 36: *1862* (London: Government of Great Britain), 16.
3 Ibid.
4 Colonial Office, Government of Great Britain, Circular Despatch to West Indian Governors, October 1838 (London).
5 Letter by Earl Stanley, 26 January 1847, Collection of the Colonial Department 1841-47, Vol. 3.
6 *Port of Spain Gazette*, 5 December 1885.
7 Report of the Government of Trinidad, *British Parliamentary Papers*, Vol. 40: *1861* (London: Government of Great Britain), 38.
8 Ibid.
9 Dorothy McBean-Hartley, "The Jamaican Educational System and the Maintenance of Existing Class Boundaries" (Ph.D. diss., State Univ. of New York at Buffalo, 1964; 1977).
10 Report of the Government of St. Lucia, *British Parliamentary Papers*, Vol. 48: *1880* (London: Government of Great Britain), 84.
11 Report of the Government of Tobago, *British Parliamentary Papers*, Vol. 39: *1846* (London: Government of Great Britain), 53.
12 CO 33/81, *The Liberal* 1846-47, Editorial, 18 April 1846; also in Goodridge, "The Development of Education in Barbados, 1818-1866" (M. Ed. thesis, Univ. of Leeds, 1966), 141.
13 Letter by James Cox, 1 June 1848, *British Parliamentary Papers*, Vol. 46: *1847-48*(London: Government of Great Britain), 113.
14 CO 111/259 (McSwiney), 30-38.
15 Government of Barbados, Response of Legislature to Opening Address of the Governor on the 1851 Education Act, 27 May 1851; Gordon, *A Century*, 57.
16 Hon. G. E. Thomas, President of the Agricultural Society of Barbados, "Address", *British Parliamentary Papers*, Vol. 42: *1856* (London: Government of Great Britain), 61.
17 Report of the Government of St. Kitts, *British Parliamentary Papers*, Vol. 10: *1857* (London: Government of Great Britain), 196.
18 *Port-of-Spain Gazette* [Trinidad], 2 February 1847.
19 *Report of the Commission on Education in Barbados (The Mitchinson Report)* , 6.
20 Report of the Government of Bahamas, *British Parliamentary Papers*, Vol. 48: *1880* (London: Government of Great Britain), 179.
21 Government of Jamaica, *Government Regulations With Regard to Grants in Aid of Elementary Schools* (Spanish Town, Jamaica: Government Printer, 1867), 9.
22 Ibid.
23 Davy, *The West Indies* 231.
24 Campbell, "The Development of Primary Education in Jamaica", 93.
25 See, for example, the Report of the Government of the Leeward Islands, *British Parliamentary Papers*, Vol. 37: *1847* (London: Government of Great Britain), 41.
26 Report of the Government of Barbados, *British Parliamentary Papers*, Vol. 62: *1852-53* (London: Government of Great Britain), 170.
27 Report of the Government of British Guiana, *British Parliamentary Papers*, Vol. 46: *1847-48* (London: Government of Great Britain), 144.
28 CO 111/410, *Longden to Secretary of State for the Colonies* (PRO:1874).
29 Report, Barbadian Legislative Committee, 1857; R. V. Goodridge, "The Development of Education in Barbados, 1818-1860" (M.Ed. thesis, Univ. of Leeds), 198.
30 Goodridge, "The Development of Education," 198.
31 CO 111/406, *Governor Longden to the Secretary of State* (PRO: 27 November 1875).
32 CO 111/410, *Longden to Secretary of State for the Colonies* (PRO: 1874).
33 Report of the British Virgin Islands to Governor Higginson, *British Parliamentary Papers*, Vol. 46: *1847-48* (London: Government of Great Britain).
34 Green, *British Slave Emancipation*.
35 *Memorial of the Clergy and Laity of the Church of England*, 1851; Gordon, *A Century*, 51.
36 Ibid.

37   *Memorial of the Presbytery of Demerara and Essequibo*, 1851; Gordon, *A Century*, 51.
38   77th Canon of the Duty of Schoolmasters," *British Parliamentary Papers*, Vol. 34: *1849* (London: Government of Great Britain), 170.
39   *The Barbadian*, 6 May 1856.
40   CO 137/323, *Barclay to Newcastle*, 26 May 1854, no. 75 (London: PRO).
41   Report of the Government of the British Virgin Islands, *British Parliamentary Papers*, Vol. 40: *1864* (London: Government of Great Britain), 88.
42   Report of the Government of Trinidad, *British Parliamentary Papers*, Vol. 46: *1847-48* (London: Government of Great Britain), 174.
43   Report of the Government of the Bahamas, *British Parliamentary Papers*, Vol. 36: *1850* (London: Government of Great Britain), 162.
44   Report of the Government of Barbados, *British Parliamentary Papers*, Vol. 36: *1849* (London: Government of Great Britain), 170.
45   Report of the Government of the Bahamas, *British Parliamentary Papers*, Vol. 36: *1850*, (London: Government of Great Britain), 163.
46   Report of the Government of Antigua, *British Parliamentary Papers*, Vol. 48: *1867-68* (London: Government of Great Britain), 93.
47   Report of the Government of St. Lucia, *British Parliamentary Papers*, Vol. 48: *1880* (London: Government of Great Britain), 209-10.
48   Report of the Government of St. Vincent, *British Parliamentary Papers*, Vol. 46: *1847-48* (London: Government of Great Britain), 92.
49   CO 299/12, *Report of the Inspector of Schools for Trinidad for the Year 1861*, 1 March 1862 (Port-of Spain, Trinidad).
50   Government of Trinidad, Report of the Board of Education (Port-of-Spain, Trinidad), 18; Bhagan, "A Critical Study," 144.
51   Report of the Government of Nevis, *British Parliamentary Papers*, Vol. 40: *1857-58* (London: Government of Great Britain), 124.

CHAPTER 5

THE ROLE OF INDUSTRIAL EDUCATION IN THE CURRICULUM OF THE PRIMARY SCHOOLS

Support of the Elites for Industrial Education

The second most important factor which influenced the content of the elementary school curriculum was the expectation that the students, after leaving school, would follow their parents' footsteps as agricultural workers on the sugar estates or as small-scale peasant farmers. Therefore, it was considered necessary to develop in them a willingness to accept the inevitability of their future role as manual workers by providing them with an effective programme of practical, industrial, agricultural, or manual training. Such a course of instruction was expected to develop the attitudes, skills, and knowledge necessary to increase the students' efficiency in their destined role by inculcating in them the idea that it was their social and moral obligation to work hard.

Most members of the West Indian elite would no doubt have subscribed to the views of C. J. Latrobe, who was sent by the British government to undertake a comprehensive inspection of West Indian schools between 1837-38. In his report Latrobe expressed doubt about the "wisdom" or "kindness" in providing an education for the black masses which would lead them to "reason falsely" about its value, by failing to impress upon them "the necessity of submitting to labour." The British government therefore suggested that West Indian education should be geared towards helping the masses become "animated" with the spirit of "patient industry," since this would ensure that, for the ex-slaves, "the boon of freedom will not have been bestowed on them in vain."[1]

Lord Elgin also urged the introduction of a course of instruction which would provide a link between the "academic" subjects and the "vocation of the husbandman," because this would render the labour of the West Indian worker valuable to himself and to his employer.

Earl Grey was convinced that the right type of education "not only makes labour intelligent and orderly, but creates new wants and desires, new activities, a love of employment, and an increased alacrity, both of the body and the mind." Consequently, he was of the view that "there is probably no example of a well-instructed population which is not also active and eager for work" and saw education as "the most certain of all methods for equalizing the supply of labour with the demand."[2] He regarded the agricultural and commercial prosperity of the West Indies as being dependent on the nature, purpose, and outcomes of the education provided for the masses and believed that workers with some industrial training would contribute more to the economic development of these colonies. Grey therefore felt that a more industrially educated labour force would make it easier for the planters to promote scientific and mechanical improvements in agriculture. For him, a science-based industrial education would also bring about a cultivated and intelligent race of proprietors, who would further help to produce civil order and the "advancement of all Classes."

Towards the Development of a Programme of Industrial Education

But despite the views of the ruling groups and the support provided by some missionary societies, efforts at giving industrial or practical education a prominent position in the curriculum of the primary schools were not very successful.

The Reverend J. Sterling had very early realized that the inclusion of practical subjects in the curriculum, especially agriculture, would discourage the ex-slaves from sending their children to school and therefore urged that too heavy an emphasis should not be placed on the teaching of the subject in the immediate post-emancipation years.

The British colonial authorities, too, encouraged the inclusion of practical education in West Indian schools, even though they were not prepared to provide financial support for it. For example, the secretary of state for the colonies offered to make the educational experiences obtained in Britain, in the field of industrial education, available to the West Indies. He also tried to inspire the "Influential Classes" to recognize the importance of such education for the spiritual and economic well-being of the labouring population, and for the continued prosperity of the planters themselves.

In the effort to foster the development of an industrial education programme the Colonial Office requested the Committee on Education of the Privy Council to prepare a memorandum "disseminating in the West Indies such knowledge of industrial systems as the experience of this country could afford, in so far as it might appear to be applicable to the state of society in the colonies."[3] The task fell on James Kay Shuttleworth, the well-known English educator, who presented in 1847 his *Brief Practical Suggestions on the Mode of Organizing Day-Schools of Industry, Model Farm Schools, and Normal Schools as Part of a System of Education for the Coloured Races of the British Colonies*. This was the first comprehensive proposal on the subject to be put forward for the region or for any other British colony.

The Kay Shuttleworth Report

In carrying out its assignment, Kay Shuttleworth recognized that, with the withdrawal of the British government support for "Negro Education," the problem of financing any new educational project would be of major concern to the local legislatures. He therefore tried to develop a financially self-supporting industrial education programme — one which aimed to "combine intellectual and industrial education" in such a way as "to render the labour of the children available towards meeting some part of the expense of their education."[4]

In order to achieve this goal it was necessary for all areas of instruction to be "interwoven with labour . . . so as to render the connection as intimate as possible." He felt that the more effectively this was done, the greater the likelihood that the programme could become self-supporting. Further, he wanted to ensure that the practical training which the students received would prepare them to become more efficient in the "cultivation of the soil," after they left school. This attempt to link practical experience with relevant classroom instruction, so as to make the industrial education programme largely self-supporting was considered a particularly attractive feature of the proposal. But while Kay Shuttleworth was primarily concerned with industrial education, his proposed scheme was quite comprehensive. This can be seen in the broad range of educational objectives which it addressed and which included the following:

The Moral Development of the Black Population

Kay Shuttleworth wanted "to inculcate the principles and promote the influence of Christianity" among West Indian school children through their "instruction in the Holy Scripture and training in the duties of a religious life." The aim was to have the pupils develop strong moral discipline as a basis for acquiring habits of self-control. In fact, religious education was to provide the moral underpinning for his proposed industrial education programme.

The Improvement of the General Standard of Living among the Black Population

To Kay Shuttleworth another important objective of education was to help improve "the condition of the peasant," by providing those in school with "practical training in household economy, in the cultivation of a cottage garden, as well as in the production of common handicrafts," in an effort to improve their domestic comfort. For example, students were to be taught the elements of scientific agriculture which would help them replace some of the poor farming practices of their parents that were resulting in the "exhaustion of the virgin soils" of these colonies. They were also to be instructed on "how health may be preserved by proper diet, cleanliness, ventilation and clothing and by the structure of their dwellings."

Even such subjects as writing and arithmetic were to be taught in a manner which would ensure direct application to "the pupils' wants and duties," eventually enabling them to economize and live within their means.[5] The instruction was also to provide the students with the skills required "to enter into calculations and agreements," a particularly important need for those who would eventually become estate labourers. In other words, it was to be education for sustainable development.

The Development of Social Skills and Political Awareness

Another objective of the Kay Shuttleworth proposal was "to diffuse grammatical knowledge of the English language, as the most important agent of civilization for the coloured population of the colonies." In addition, the report recommended that efforts be made to inculcate acceptance by the pupils of the existing social arrangements and the belief that these should be maintained and strengthened. The books produced for use in the schools should therefore "teach the mutual interests of the Mother-Country and her dependencies" and give the pupils a better grasp of "the rational basis" of this connection. They were also to explain "the domestic and social duties of the coloured races" so that the black students would get a better understanding of their expected role in the society. The importance of government for the "personal security" and "independence" of the individual, and for the preservation of "order" in the society as a whole, was to be stressed. Finally, topics dealing with the relationship between "wages, capital, and labour" were to be introduced to help further the understanding of "the domestic and social duties of the coloured races" within the existing social and economic structure of these societies.

To achieve these objectives, Kay Shuttleworth proposed a system of Day-Schools of Industry, Model Farm Schools, and Normal Schools of Industry. The Day-Schools of Industry were to combine academic and practical training, in order to prepare the students "for the duties of their station in life." Each school was to have a large garden plot that was to be divided into two sections. The school plot would be communally cultivated to provide vegetables for daily school dinners, of which all students would partake. The communal cultivation was to demonstrate to students that their cooperative efforts could benefit from "order, method, harmony, and subordination." The second plot was to be the scholars' plot, where students would work on their individual sections. This was expected to develop in them a "sense of personal interest and responsibility."

In the Model Farm Schools, the instruction was to be more advanced. The students were to be taught the elements of scientific agriculture as well as basic construction skills that would enable them to build a simple cottage, along with "rude but substantial furniture and the most healthy bedding, together with the outbuildings required for domestic animals and the family." Since academic and practical skills had to be interwoven, the students were to be instructed in keeping accounts and preparing for their garden operations an annual balance sheet showing details of their expenditures and overall profits. A knowledge of weights and measures was also to be acquired from the day-to-day operations of cultivating the garden. The girls were to be taught to carry out efficiently "the duties of a skillful housewife" in a "cottage [type] economy." These skills, meant to complement those acquired by the boys, consisted of laundering, mending, and ironing clothes, taking care of cooking, nutrition, domestic and personal cleanliness, and the management of infants.

The other subjects were to be integrated into industrial training. For example, reading skills were to be taught, not from the Holy Bible, but rather from "class books appropriate to an industrial school." Arithmetic and language skills were to be more functional and related to the practical activities since, according to Kay Shuttleworth, "nothing is learned so soon, or retained so surely, as knowledge, the practical relation of which is perceived." In consonance with this principle, students were to learn how to "compose simple letters on the business of the school, the garden or kitchen." In addition, if time permitted, they were to be given an "acquaintance . . . with the art of drawing plans, and those of land surveying and leveling," skills which they might need later for constructing their own homes. Some instruction was also to be provided in geography, to enable the students "to better understand the Scriptures," as well as the connection between the colony and the mother country.

According to Kay Shuttleworth, this educational program could not "fail to raise the population to a condition of improved comfort," since it would provide them with "such habits of steady industry" that were likely to produce "a settled and thriving peasantry." In time, this would lead to the development of "a native middle class" which was considered important for the long-term stability of these societies.

The Model Farm Schools were to be established specifically to aid the development of a strong, independent peasantry whose members would eventually form the "middle class," and who would occupy a position between the black estate labourers and the white population. These schools therefore were intended for "the class of labourers who have accumulated sufficient money to become small farmers." Since the students were to be between 14-15, and 18-19 years of age, those admitted would be among the select few — either those whose parents had enough resources to help establish them as independent farmers or those who had such a degree of motivation that they could eventually achieve that status by their own efforts. The Model Farm Schools would be conducted along the same lines as the Day-Schools of Industry, especially in terms of the content of the education which they were to offer. Their overall objective was to provide small farmers with the knowledge and skills which would better equip them to make sensible allocative decisions in farming and thereby enable them "to employ their capital to greater advantage."

Courses in scientific agriculture started in the Day-Schools of Industry were to be continued at a more advanced level in the Model Farm Schools, with students being taught to carry out such additional tasks as testing the quality of soils, and being given "some acquaintance with veterinary science," which would better equip them to care of their livestock. They were also to acquire the basic skills of wheelwrights and blacksmiths, in order to be able to "mend the carts, wagons, farm machines and implements, to repair the farming premises and to shoe the horse."

The Normal Schools of Industry were to prepare industrial education teachers for these proposed new schools. Only the best and most advanced students were to be selected for this training, and the subjects offered were to be a continuation of those covered at the Day-Industrial and the Model Farm Schools. In addition, other subjects directed at the general education of the teacher were to be included, with some attention paid to methods of teaching and classroom organization. The curriculum of these Normal Schools of Industry was to include the following subject areas:

1. Religious Education: Biblical Instruction and the Evidence of Christianity.
2. Agricultural or Industrial Education: Chemistry and its Application to Agriculture, Theory of Natural Phenomena in Relation to Agriculture, Theory and Practice of Agriculture and Gardening, Management of Farming Stock including the Treatment of their Diseases.
3. Other "Practical" Subjects: Rudiments of Mechanics, Art of Land Surveying and Leveling and Practical Mensuration, Drawing from Models and Plan Drawing.
4. Language Arts: English Grammar and Composition.
5. Arithmetic and Book-Keeping:
6. Social Studies: English History, Geography.
7. Aesthetic Subjects: Vocal Music.
8. Professional Subjects: The Art of Organizing and Conducting an Elementary School.

Despite this long list of practical and academic subjects, the principal objective of the proposed industrial teacher education programme was "the formation of character" and the development of the students' intellect.

According to the report the aim was "to train the student in simplicity, humility and truth and at the same time to strengthen his mental powers, to inform his intelligence, to elevate his principles and to invigorate his intellect, are the objects of his education."[6]

Thus, in the professional training of these teachers, great emphasis was to be placed on measures aimed at preventing them from becoming psychologically or culturally alienated from their own social group. Such alienation, it was felt, would adversely affect their performance as "teacher[s] of the children of the poor." Steps therefore had to be taken to ensure that, in both the selection and training of a teacher, "instead of [his] being repelled by their [i.e., the labouring population's] coarseness and poverty, and thus unfitted for daily conduct with them, he would have a sympathy with their condition."

This, to Kay Shuttleworth, was very important, because few things would be more injurious to the professional development of the intending teacher "than to do anything that might tend to sever such sympathies, or take . . . an educated peasant out of his sphere of life." Therefore, the student's entry into the Normal School was not to be accompanied by any change in lifestyle likely to separate him from "his own class in society." The teacher trainees had to be taught to be humble and not to perceive themselves as superior to the parents of the children whom they would be teaching. One of the ways suggested for them to achieve this humility was to insist that they "should continue, during three hours daily, to partake the rudest toils of the field and garden."

Such practical work would also help to broaden the knowledge that students would acquire from their academic studies, i.e., it would "build all . . . [their] intellectual acquirements on the experiences of the life of those [who are] supported by manual industry." The meals provided for the students at the Normal School were not to be above that which they would eventually be able to purchase for themselves on the salary of a teacher. Similarly, their accommodation and their dress were to be simple, and "any pretension beyond the ordinary peasant's dress . . . should be discouraged and . . . [they] should strive to teach by [their] example how that common dress could be worn with frugality and neatness." Finally, the atmosphere that existed in the Normal Schools was to be similar to that of a good Christian family, and the relationship between the principal and the students was to be one of "filial piety."

The *Kay Shuttleworth Report* was meant to be a blueprint for a comprehensive system of industrial education, albeit on predominantly agricultural lines. The Day-Schools, which were to be open to all, were to provide an integrated practical, intellectual, and religious education. This combination was considered central to the work of the primary schools in the West Indies, since "Christian civilization comprehends the complex development of all the faculties." Therefore, the school for the ex-slaves, whom Kay Shuttleworth described as "a semi-barbarous class" which "readily abandons itself to excitement . . . should be established on the conviction that these several forms of training and instruction mutually assist each other."

The secretary of state strongly supported Kay Shuttleworth's proposals, particularly the suggestion that, apart from the small salary of the school master, the proposed educational institutions would eventually become self-supporting. The emphasis on linking practical, academic, and religious studies also appealed to him. In his covering letter to the various West Indian governments which enclosed copies of the report, he pointed out that this feature should make the proposal particularly attractive to some local groups which would be quick to discern the value of the link between education and industry. Finally, he felt that, with the implementation of the programme, even the parents would have less motivation to withdraw their children from school prematurely "to cultivate provision grounds or otherwise earn a living," since "the principal part of the children's food [would] be provided at School from the produce of their own labour."

But despite its comprehensiveness the Kay Shuttleworth proposal had many weaknesses, and its effect on educational practice in these colonies was not very great. It ran into objections from a number of influential groups, including even the planters, who saw it as far too sophisticated and too expensive a scheme, geared more toward producing independent small farmers than agricultural labourers who would be willing to remain on the estates as unskilled workers earning a "reasonable" remuneration. The optimistic vision which characterized the report essentially ignored the economic and political realities of these West Indian colonies. It implied that the planters would favour the development of a black middle class of independent peasants. Instead, as indicated above, they wanted the "Negro population" to be available mainly to work on the plantations and did everything possible to frustrate the early emergence of an independent peasantry.[7]

Some of the religious groups with an entrenched interest in the education of the black masses were also not very supportive of Kay Shuttleworth's proposals because they felt that, if implemented, these would likely threaten their own activities and dominance in education. The Baptists raised direct objections to the plan because they perceived it as an attempt to keep the black population perpetually in agriculture. In addition, the proposal was almost monolithic in its focus on agriculture, virtually ignoring other areas of industrial training.

Some individuals who remained skeptical about the intellectual capacity of the Negro population to undertake further studies were willing to accept the proposals put forward by Kay Shuttleworth. But, as F. A. J. Johnston[8] observed, if the Kay Shuttleworth plan were implemented it would not have resulted in the creation of "new social relationships" between blacks and whites, but would have represented a holdover from slave society, helping to solidify the linkage between class and colour. In other words the occupational future of the blacks was to be inevitably confined to the role of agricultural labourers and small-scale farmers and they were to be relegated forever to the lowest rung of colonial society.

Finally, the proposals came at an economically inauspicious time — just after the Imperial Grant for Negro Education had been terminated and preferential treatment for West Indian sugar was coming to an end. To implement Kay Shuttleworth's recommendations would have required a substantial capital expenditure, even if, as he suggested, the recurrent costs would have been low. The planters were therefore not in a mood to consider any plan involving additional expenditure of funds, especially since the

British government, which supported the proposals, did not offer any financial incentive to the local legislatures to help with its implementation. The overall result was that none of these colonies ever attempted to implement the report as it was presented.

Efforts at Introducing Modified Industrial Education Programmes
Because of parental objection to industrial education for their children and the unwillingness or the inability of the local legislatures to provide funds for a comprehensive industrial education programme along the lines proposed by Kay Shuttleworth, more limited efforts were made in many colonies to introduce a number of "practical" subjects in their primary school curriculum. The secretary of state for the colonies recognized that the apparent magnitude of Kay Shuttleworth's plan seemed to deter West Indian governments from taking action on it and he therefore tried to assure the colonies that Her Majesty's government would "most gladly" promote the adoption of any more "simple and less complete" line of industrial education which "could at once be set on foot, leaving the improvement and completion of it to be the work of time and experience."[9]

Jamaica
In Jamaica, the evident design of the legislature since the 1840s was to encourage the establishment of schools that combined moral and religious instruction with agricultural pursuits. The board of education was expected to stress the expediency of uniting lessons of active industry with other branches of instruction, and schools were to inculcate, by precept and habit, the necessity of honest labour among all those who were under tuition. Therefore, a number of efforts were made to encourage the development of less ambitious industrial training programmes in Jamaica, and special grants were available to schools in which industrial education formed an important part of the curriculum.

The first provision for this purpose was made in 1845 by the board of education. A series of 18-24 lectures in agriculture was delivered at the Mico College, and schools were encouraged to allow their best students to attend these lectures. But in 1847 Cargill, the inspector of schools, reported that little progress had yet been made with industrial training in Jamaica, partly due to the insufficient supply of qualified industrial education teachers.

By 1849 the board of education began to examine the possibilities of providing a suitable industrial education programme on a self-financing basis. A plan was put forward for the organization of centrally located schools for the children who were between 4-7 years of age, and for those between 7-14 years, education was to be combined with labour, with the older pupils performing from 1-6 hours of service in agriculture or in some other useful trade every week. According to this plan, children would acquire the "habits and ordinary skills" of the labourer and would be provided with all the necessary instruction to help them adapt to this course of life by the age of 14.

A Normal School of Industry was also established, and Cargill sought add-itional funding from the board of eduaction in 1848 to increase its enrollment from 11 to 20 teacher trainees. Special grants were provided for schools implementing an industrial education programme, and the board also recommended that schools change their hours of instruction to give pupils time to acquire practical experience by working on the sugar estates, if they wanted to do so. This resulted from the pressures by the planters, who wanted the children on the plantations to be available to work, especially during the busy seasons. But little progress was made with these proposals, and only a few schools applied for the industrial education grants.

Nevertheless, as far as girls were concerned, efforts continued to be made to teach them needlework when a suitably competent teacher could be found. Some of the more enterprising teachers even attempted to arrange for the articles produced in the sewing classes to be sold to the public. However, needlework was not often regarded as a subject in the industrial education curriculum, but was considered a part of the general education for girls.

In 1857 the Jamaican legislature introduced another bill to aid the establishment of Industrial Schools that were to be Reformatories for delinquent children and those "in need of care and protection." As a result of this measure, a Reformatory School for girls was established in St. Andrews with a strong industrial education programme. One gets an idea of the purpose of the school from the third annual report of the Reformatory and Industrial Association for Girls in 1857, which indicated that the institution was

> to train them [the girls] to habits of continuous industry . . . to accustom them to order, obedience, courtesy, modesty and civility . . . to discountenance . . . all disobedience, falsehood, deceit, dishonesty and idleness . . . give them the opportunity of learning, how a life of honest industry drives away poverty [and] makes time pass pleasantly, and usefully, and when combined with the Divine blessing, and united with a good moral and religious education, lays the foundation of character, leads to respectability and paves the way to a useful, happy and virtuous life. [10]

In 1869 several other attempts were made to introduce manual work in the elementary schools, and the grants-in-aid system was again directed at giving all possible encouragement to these efforts. Yet, while the outcomes were "not entirely discouraging," they were not very successful. By 1871, attempts were again being made to include manual labour or practical instruction into the curriculum of the government-aided elementary schools. But these efforts were also unsuccessful. Therefore, a more comprehensive bill for the establishment of industrial schools for primary school children was considered but dropped for financial reasons.

Nevertheless, the curriculum of the better primary schools came to include a combination of such subjects as reading, writing, catechism and religious knowledge, geography, arithmetic, needlework, and straw-plaiting. This suggests that the amount of practical work done in these schools was very limited. In 1872 industrial education programmes were still almost non-existent in most schools, although the inspector noted that every effort was being made to induce managers to introduce this focus into their school curriculum and to show to parents the usefulness of this type of education. However, even the teachers lacked competence in these areas and, as a result of the failure of most of these efforts, the industrial grants provided by the board of eduaction were reduced to only £30 by 1877.

There were still two government Model Industrial Schools in Jamaica, one located in Port Antonio and the other in Montego Bay. The former, which was reported to have been doing well, was considered by the authorities as the most hopeful of all government schools, largely because it had two skilled workmen whose services proved to be very valuable in directing the practical labours of the pupils. A third industrial school was operated by the Reverend E. Bassett Key, in St Elizabeth. The students here were also taught useful practical skills and had a few acres of land to cultivate. After a time parents' opposition to the work of the institution declined, probably because, in addition to agriculture, the school offered instruction by trained artisans in such fields as carpentering, coopering, and bricklaying. However, it was generally agreed that the progress of the institution was largely due to the "indefatigable perseverance" of the founder.[11]

Between 1871 and 1874 the grants for industrial education paid by the Jamaican government rose by six and a half times — i.e., from £90 to £586. This largely resulted from the extension of the system of "payment by results" introduced in 1867 to include agriculture after which schools made every effort to improve their work in this area. In some schools girls were taught sewing and plain needlework, with the hope that they might become reasonably competent seamstresses. As instruction in sewing improved, so did the grants for the teaching of the subject. However, this occupational field was becoming overcrowded and some schools were encouraged instead to offer their female students such subjects as cooking, washing, and other work "suited to their sex." In these occupations, there were said to be relatively few trained and efficient individuals and, therefore, those who took these courses were likely to improve their prospects of securing employment.

Since there were no suitable textbooks available in Tropical Agriculture, the governor of Jamaica and the Royal Agricultural Society offered a premium for the best practical but scientifically based elementary textbook on the subject for use in schools and possibly even in the teachers' colleges. A number of entries were presented for the competition, including one by Dr. H. A. A. Nicholl, entitled *An Elementary Textbook of Tropical Agriculture* which was later published as a school text by the Jamaican government printers. Teachers-in-training at the Government Teachers' College at Stony Hill, established in 1870, were also encouraged to take up industrial pursuits as part of their studies in order to teach in this field.

Even though new regulations for industrial education were again introduced, these remained a "dead letter," and much of the effort made to combine manual work with academic instruction in Jamaica was regarded as a failure. Therefore by 1877 there was a considerable reduction in the industrial grants provided by the board of education. In 1880 the inspector of schools, while reviewing the progress that had so far been made, noted

> no satisfactory results from attempts made by several school managers to combine so-called industrial with school labour. . . . The experience of several years of observation and experiment has, at length, clearly shown that we have very little hope with regard to the successful adoption of agricultural pursuits in connection with our ordinary day

schools. The failure of these schools has, in great measure resulted from objection on the part of parents to their children's time being employed, even in ever so slight a way in manual labour instead of in book learning, and in many cases the nature of the industry was not calculated to overcome the objection. . . . The people naturally feel unwilling to pay for the pretence of instruction, which in most cases they could better impart themselves.[12]

To mark Queen Victoria's Jubilee in Jamaica in 1887, it was proposed that a Model Farm be established to serve the dual purpose of promoting industry and "civilizing" the majority of the population. The *Colonial Standard* [13] suggested that from such a farm, "people would learn to regard labour as a thing no longer to be ashamed of." In addition, the experience would lead them to develop "new wants and to feel the restless stir of new ambitions" which were considered necessary for the development of the country. This did not come to fruition, however, and the inspector of schools concluded that "the experience of several years of observation and experiment has at length clearly shown that we have very little to hope for with regard to the successful adoption of agricultural pursuits in connection with our ordinary day schools."[14]

In 1890 it was again reported that there was still "an almost total want" of industrial schools on the island. In response, another industrial school for girls, developed in connection with the Shortwood College, was opened in 1892. There were also three such schools run by the government and one operated by the Roman Catholics. Despite the earlier unsuccessful experiences with these institutions, hopes were still high that they would make an important contribution to the development of the island. Jamaica even appointed an inspector of schools, specially for Industrial Education, and in 1893 it was still optimistically being noted that "the work of the industrial school promises to become an important factor in the training of the juvenile population of the Island."[15] But this training was now focussed on those "in need of care and protection" and was outside the mainstream of primary education.

Barbados

The governor of Barbados noted in 1848 that the elementary education being provided on the island was not at all suited to the wants of a community which had just emerged from slavery and was "ill calculated to render workmen more intelligent."[16] He suggested that agriculture and sugar manufacture should be approached as scientific pursuits and that "the rudiments of those sciences required for it, should be taught in schools." He also noted that practical geometry, suitable for mechanics, was already being introduced in some schools and rudimentary chemistry in one of them — a development of which he obviously approved.[17]

Further, when a legislative committee recommended that the government provide some additional financial assistance for education, it proposed that regular instruction should be restricted to three hours daily, since this would give the children a chance to obtain practical experience by actually working on the sugar estates for the remainder of the day. This arrangement would ensure that learning to read could in fact be combined with learning to work. It was even argued that those of the labouring classes who wanted a different type of education, which might lead their children away from manual work on the sugar estates, should pay for such education themselves. However, despite the many efforts that were made to render their education more useful through the introduction of practical training in schools, these attempts, too, were largely unsuccessful.

The governor issued a reminder in 1857 that the state should take care not to educate a man beyond his station in life, since this would only increase his dissatisfaction with his "natural position." He therefore suggested that primary education should always be directed toward the training of the peasantry to work hard and steadily and to carry out their domestic tasks and social duties. A more academic focus was likely to result in the masses attempting to imitate the higher class in society, thus raising their levels of aspiration and creating artificial wants, which would eventually produce dissatisfaction with their present situation. In that year also, in a letter to the governor, the Bishop of Barbados welcomed the idea of adapting education in the colony to the "real wants" of the island's agricultural population. He proposed the establishment of schools of a humbler and less ambitious character, which would emphasize the importance of practical or industrial training, and be of particular benefit for girls.[18]

In 1876 it was still being argued that if there was an error in the programme of education for the lower classes, it was in the omission of industrial instruction and training. Therefore, the *Mitchinson Report* recommended that more than one industrial school be established near the capital city, where children who were leading an idle and vagrant life might acquire the rudiments of learning, morality, religion, and a regular trade. In addition, it suggested that attendance at such a school should be made compulsory. The *Report* also put forward a proposal for a new and possibly more scientific approach to technical, including agricultural, training and, while recognizing that this could not have been immediately achieved because of cost, the members noted that it was worthy of future consideration.

The Bree Commission, which was appointed in the late 1880s to suggest ways of restricting expenditure on elementary education proposed that the school curriculum should be limited to the 4Rs — intelligent reading, fair writing, elementary arithmetic, and a thorough grounding in religious knowledge. Industrial education was not included in its recommendations, partly because of the costs involved. By 1892 most Barbadian schools still did not offer practical subjects, an omission which continued to be condemned, because this unfitted young people for life and work in their local communities. This point was made very clearly in the following excerpt from an article in the *Agricultural Reporter* in January 1892:

> In our elementary schools we are teaching Geography and Grammar and History and Singing and so forth. . . . We are neglecting studies which would teach the rising generation, not only about the dignity of manual labour but how to labour freely to get their living in that sphere of life into which it had pleased God to call them. . . . The sons and daughters of the labouring classes had become impregnated with the idea that the education which was imparted to

them makes them better than their fathers and they have
begun to look with disdain upon mere manual labour. Field
labour in particular they regard as an abomination. Rather
than work in the fields they prefer to gravitate to towns and
be recruited in the army of loafers to be seen about
Bridgetown. . . . We are far from saying that the people
should not be educated. But what we do advocate and insist
upon is that the present system of education should be
remodelled and be remodelled in such a way as will put an
end to the teaching of mere words. . . . Let us teach our
children something about things. . . . In short let us educate
their hands as well as their heads.[19]

The rise in the incidence of juvenile delinquency also prompted the
suggestion in the 1890s that a Reformatory offering industrial education
needed to be established on the island. It was hoped that such a school, if
well conducted, could become self-supporting and so make the cost of crime
prevention cheaper than the cost of punishment. In 1892, the Executive
Council also established a Committee on Technical Education to consider the
"necessity" and "feasibility" of providing technical education in schools in
Barbados. With the exception of needlework and sewing, which had almost
become a compulsory subject for girls in the aided elementary schools, the
Committee noted that no attempt was being made to teach a trade or manual
skills. Therefore, it recommended the establishment of a central school at
which boys would be kept under apprenticeship. However, with the further
deterioration of the Barbadian economy, the proposal was not pursued, and
schools restricted their practical activities to the teaching of handicrafts.

Trinidad
In Trinidad, there was even less success with the introduction of industrial
education programmes in the primary schools. As C. Bhagan pointed out,
there were two points of view about practical or agricultural education in the
colony. One was expressed as follows in a letter to the *Trinidad Spectator* in
1845:

Men should not be trained for any particular calling mainly,
and left barricaded by ignorance of all else that might be
known to their advantage . . . to educate them for a
particular sphere as though they were never designed by the
Almighty to travel out of that state. . . . But [education
should] impart power and vigour to the minds of the poor
whereby they might emerge from their degradation and
misery if opportunity is offered.[20]

The other point of view which was shared by most planters was stated in
an editorial in the *Port of Spain Gazette* in 1850. While it advocated the
inculcation of "sound notions of religion," it also asserted that "the
dissemination of knowledge among the poorer classes . . . beyond a certain
point might engender ideas which, in after life, [i.e., after school] may be the
ruin of those who are to earn their bread by the sweat of their brows."[21]
Stating that "the common man has no right to look to government to
raise himself to a more elevated sphere of life," the editorial suggested that
all that the students needed was an education which provided basic literacy

and numeracy, along with some practical skills, because "beyond the primary degree of instruction, the institution of schools will ultimately encourage in the lower orders an aversion and contempt for the labour of agriculture."[22] This was clearly considered undesirable.

In 1846 C.F. Stollemeyer suggested that the government sponsor an agricultural scheme to encourage and train the labouring class to become small-scale farmers. Gladstone, who was in general agreement with the proposal, urged that "whatever plan may be approved of, as far as the intellect is concerned . . . it should be joined to a system of industrial occupation and teaching."[23] However, nothing came of this proposal. In 1846, Model Farms were proposed by Governor Harris as part of a general scheme of education for Trinidad and in 1850 A. A. De Verteuill, in his *Suggestions for Organizing a Central Agricultural Committee and Establishing Model Farms in the Island of Trinidad*, proposed an industrial education plan similar to that recommended by Kay Shuttleworth.

In 1851 Lord Harris suggested that primary education in Trinidad should be of "a rudimentary nature," consisting of subjects which were generally important to "all men" such as reading, writing, spelling, arithmetic, and grammar, although this could be supplemented by geography and history for the more advanced students. He also recommended the "establishment of industrial schools" to teach subjects "which [were] generally useful to the labouring classes," and without which they would be "deprived of taking advantage of circumstances" which could improve "their conditions of life."[24] These subjects included chemistry, botany, geology, and practical mechanics. Harris wanted to put industrial training on a more scientific basis, and his proposals in this field were generally more advanced than those shared by most planters. But with the economic conditions which the island was facing at the time, little action was taken on this proposal.

In 1862 Anderson, the inspector of schools, tried to include agricultural science in the curriculum of the model schools and made a strong plea for some form of higher technical training in agriculture for boys at the Woodbrook model school. His argument was that

> the days are gone when the management of a sugar estate can be considered a mere matter of routine requiring little or no exercise of reflective powers. The sugars of this colony . . . are subjected to extensive and powerful competition and . . . the race in the end will be won by skill and science. . . . It would be a matter of importance to the colony if lads could be procured from Woodbrook, who besides being able to read, spell, write and cypher correctly, could measure a cane piece and calculate the number of tasks in it of so many rods each; who could temper cane juice and take off a strike; who would understand the general outlines of agricultural chemistry and particularly the vegetable economy of the sugar-cane and the general principles connected with the manufacture of sugar.[25]

The school inspector further suggested that the island's educational policies should be directed toward ensuring that the masses receive an education in the basic elements which would not elevate their ideas above their station of life "in which they are "bound to labour" for their support and improvement." Such a focus should render them "industrious, contented and happy" in the tasks which they would inevitably undertake.[26] This point of view was reiterated the following year when it was stated that

> every system of popular education should be based on the principle of fitting a man to perform his daily task of labour, whether of mind or body *in the sphere of life where Providence has placed him* and at the same time of exercising and improving those higher faculties and aspirations with which he is endowed [emphasis added].[27]

But the scientific basis of agriculture which Anderson suggested for the model school was to prepare future managers and overseers of sugar estates. As such it was not really meant for children of the masses but for those of the primary and secondary whites, because there was then little opportunity for non-whites to be employed in managerial or supervisory positions.

The Trinidad government also became increasingly concerned about the rise of crime among the young and believed that industrial training would make an important contribution toward helping to curb the problem of juvenile delinquency. Further, in the industrial schools, which were residential institutions, parental opposition did not have to be taken into account. However, the association of industrial education with the education of delinquents and orphans which occurred in the region helped to lower, even further, its status in the eyes of the public.

In 1856-57, an Industrial Training school with 64 East Indian orphans and young vagrants as students was established at Tacarigua, through the efforts of a private individual, William Burnley. One year later, the government passed an ordinance to make the attendance of East Indian orphans at this school obligatory. It placed the institution under government control and supervision and later permitted the admission, not only of abandoned children, but also those whose parents allowed them to attend. In 1860, a general ordinance for craft apprentices was enacted which gave permission for these children to be legally bonded for training for up to seven years. The major aim of the school was to provide children with the necessary skills to remain part of the local labour force of manual workers. The subjects taught included general agriculture and the cultivation of a garden, carpentry, shoemaking, and masonry, while girls were instructed in cookery, needlework, and laundering. Christian religious education was also provided, and the admission of children to the school was conditional upon their being brought up in Christianity.

Despite all the efforts or exhortations to have industrial training included in the curriculum, the inspector of schools noted in 1861 that "nothing useful, in an industrial way was taught in the primary schools."[28] This point was again made in 1869 by Keenan, who observed that in the ward schools there was still a complete absence of industrial instruction. In addition, he suggested that laziness and a negative attitude to work were chronic among the lower classes on the island. To overcome this problem he recommended that industrial education be introduced in schools. For this, "schoolmistresses should be appointed who are competent to teach needlework and other industrial pursuits," while attached to every boys' school, "there should be a little workshop and a garden where the boys could learn to cultivate vegetables." But, "above all, they should be taught from their earliest days to take kindly to labour, to persevere in it and be proud of it. Once and for all it must be laid down that education in its thoroughly practical sense is to take the place of mere book instruction."[29] In 1892 a local Committee on Agricultural Education called for the training of primary school teachers in agriculture, but their recommendations were ignored.

Other West Indian Colonies

In Tobago, the Moravians tried to introduce a much more modified industrial education programme. Their schools had started to inculcate in the very young a system of work habits "suited to their tender age" by involving them in practical work, while the older age groups were required to

> sweep the school rooms, trim the walks and ornament the grounds within the confines of the mission establishment, plant and weed Guinea grass, raise Indian corn, bananas and other fruits and vegetables. To the elder pupils are assigned small plots of land, for their own exclusive benefit. . . . In many cases the boys are not infrequently at work in their gardens, early [in the mornings] and late [in the afternoons]. By such means as these, industrial habits are implanted, and obedience and regularity inculcated imperceptibly on the minds of the rising generation—elements of instruction [which are] almost as necessary to the future comfort and happiness of the labouring classes as the intellectual acquirements as reading and writing.[30]

The efforts of the Moravians, described as a modest imitation of the Kay Shuttleworth scheme, were founded on the principles of the industrial schools at Hofyl in Switzerland. This system had the advantage of extreme simplicity and cheapness and could, it was felt, be easily implemented in rural schools. Commending these efforts to the West Indian governments, the secretary of state noted that, while the programme in Tobago was not as perfect as the scheme proposed by Kay Shuttleworth, the approach to the subject was an excellent one in itself and well worthy of general imitation by other colonies in the region. However, he still urged that, in their efforts to introduce modified industrial education programmes, the better system should not be entirely forgotten.

The Governor of Antigua reported in 1850 that he seized every opportunity

> to press upon the consideration of the Legislature, the paramount obligation of fostering and disseminating a sound . . . industrial system of instruction amongst the working class, and the valuable benefits, both moral and material, that must inevitably flow from it.[31]

His efforts were not very successful however, largely due to lack of funds rather than any attempt by the legislature to under-rate the importance of the issue. Seven years later, the governor was still hoping to get financial support for a sound religious and industrial education from a legislature that so far had not made any financial provision for such education. But little success was achieved with the proposed curriculum change, and in 1866 the Commissioners of Education again drew attention to the need for schools to provide children with a firmly practical education.

In 1883 the question of industrial or technical education once more engaged the attention of the legislators in the Leeward Islands, and funds were voted for it in Montserrat and Antigua. Judging from the report of a clergyman who had worked in the West Indies and later retired to Britain, it seemed that Antigua had experienced some success with its agricultural education program. The clergyman observed that he had "seen a great many schools lately of various kinds, [in Britain] but I have not often met with agricultural schools which, on the whole were better . . . than the dozen schools I could name in Antigua."[32] In Montserrat, in the early 1870s, the Sturge family established a school in Olveston that had the reputation of providing a good pratical education. It was hoped that, in course of time, it would provide a model education for the labouring classes.

As late as 1864 no industrial education programme was being offered in any of the 32 aided schools in St. Kitts and, a few years later, it was reported that the education offered was still best suited to the requirements of an agricultural population. In 1874 the island's chief administrator repeated his conviction that, "if real and widespread advantages are to be obtained in the West Indies, a compulsory [scheme] combined with a *bona fide* programme of industrial education must be inaugurated and insisted upon."[33] Yet, despite this official support, little success was achieved in this area during the years which followed.

In 1864 the administrator of Dominica indicated that, in most cases, the attempts to make education more useful had not been particularly successful. He therefore argued for a change in the primary school curriculum in the colony, claiming that

> it is of little service to the agricultural labourer to cram his head with high mathematics, or with any science whatever which he cannot apply to his future daily pursuit. His ordinary converse is of as humble a character as his occupation, and while opportunity may be afforded by some other means to [those with] really promising capacities and elegant tastes to distinguish themselves in the world of letters and science, it appears to me to savour of cruelty to make the field labourer waste the best years of his life at a village school . . . [acquiring] knowledge which he can scarcely ever hope to put to practicable account.[34]

Industrial training in Dominica, therefore, came to focus on teaching agriculture to boys and sewing to girls. In the orphanage attached to the Roseau Convent, which had a girls' industrial school established by the Roman Catholics, the 3Rs were taught along with sewing and embroidery. Instruction in embroidery, in particular, was said to be very good. The suggestion was made, however, that other subjects might be offered which could be of greater practical advantage, and in 1890 it was proposed that special grants should be made available to help schools willing to offer an industrial education programme.

In Nevis, President Seymour noted in 1856 that the education offered in the primary schools was impractical, quite unrelated to the life experiences and the future occupational roles of the students. But efforts to introduce a more relevant industrial education in this colony also failed. While the Catholic schools offered their girls instruction in sewing and other plain needlework, the market for seamstresses, as in Jamaica, was already saturated. The suggestion was therefore made that schools should teach their students other practical tasks such as cookery and laundering which were considered suited to their sex.

In St Lucia, official pressure for the introduction of industrial education increased after a number of those who had attended schools tried to secure non-existent white-collar jobs. The more literary curriculum was often blamed for the unrealistic aspirations of these youths, and the introduction of an industrial element in their education was seen as the best way to overcome this problem.

In St. Vincent, the establishment of industrial schools that would eventually become self-supporting was recommended in 1847-48, because of the effect they were expected to have both on the cognitive and the attitudinal development of the young. As the governor suggested, "In addition to the useful and practical knowledge to be gained [from such schools] a highly beneficial effect may be expected to follow their operation, upon the character of the people, by inducing habits of regularity and steady industry."[35]

However, despite this emphasis on industrial education, additional funds were not provided to offer the relevant subjects. Therefore, only the 3Rs, along with religious instruction, were taught in most primary schools. In explanation, it was observed that "in the existing state of the community this . . . is all that can be expected, or perhaps even desired, for the great mass of the population."[36] But the governor continued to emphasize the importance of offering practical or industrial education at the primary level.

In the British Virgin Islands, an industrial school established on Anegada around 1846-47 was reported to have been quite successful. The practical activities in which the students were engaged included walling in and cultivating a garden, making fishing nets, and plaiting straw for hats. However, much of this was made possible only because the teachers were actually engaged in these occupations and gave of their leisure time to assist with the projects.

In British Guiana, an early attempt was made by a Presbyterian minister in New Amsterdam to unite work and study as part of an industrial education programme, in a school that would also properly cultivate the students' minds by training them to be humble, obedient, and useful. This school was originally hailed as a model institution, having been developed along the lines of the industrial schools in Switzerland and England. But the experiment was not successful. In the late 1840s, the inspector of schools reported that there was no other school in the country in which industrial training for boys was being provided and very few in which such instruction was provided for girls.

McSwiney, the inspector of schools, reported that the general feeling among all those with whom he had conversed was that any plan for establishing and conducting schools of industry would be impractical as long as the children resided with and were under the jurisdiction of their parents. He therefore recommended the establishment of an industrial training school for the older pupils which he considered was likely to face less opposition from parents. Nevertheless, in 1885 A. A. Thornereported that some "successful attempts were made at industrial education on a small scale in some primary schools."[37] Later, it was still being suggested that special industrial schools, including an agricultural school, should be established in the colony and that any child for whom the government was paying fees should be made to attend one of them. As a result, an industrial school was opened in 1892 which offered instruction in carpentry and agriculture, but it closed after only two terms partly because the parents still objected to agriculture being a school subject.

In 1847 the government of British Honduras had hoped to establish a self-financing industrial school like the one operated by the Moravians in Tobago. However, there seemed to have been little success with the project, and in 1887 the assistant inspector of schools noted that sewing was not even taught to all girls, though every effort was made to offer plain needlework as a means of "domesticating and civilizing" them.

The importance of industrial training was also recognized in the Bahamas, and persons competent to teach "navigation, tailoring, and shoemaking" were employed at the Boys' Central school in Nassau, where students were trained to become teachers. The 1845-46 Education Act had indicated that it was the intention of the government that the children in the 20 schools which were to be established receive instruction in the "mechanical arts" or agriculture. Therefore, at a school in the eastern district of New Providence, a piece of land was acquired for agricultural purposes, a teacher of agriculture employed and an agricultural class was formed.[38] But almost as soon as these provisions were made, the programme began to run into financial difficulties because of the expenses involved in providing the instructional facilities for these practical subjects. Further, the schools were not able to make their activities self-supporting because the articles produced in the tailoring and shoemaking classes did not find a ready market. By 1847-48, one of the schools had to dispense with the services of one teacher and it was noted that the whole programme might be abandoned unless the legislature provided additional funds.

Although it was difficult to secure more money for education in view of the financial state of the islands, a modicum of activities in this area was continued in some schools. The Boys' Central school carried on its industrial classes in shoemaking and tailoring, while the Girls' Model school offered needlework. However, by 1852 the section of the board's by-laws on agricultural and horticultural education had to be discontinued because it was expensive and "difficult of execution."[39] The situation deteriorated to such an extent that, by 1857-58, the governor felt it necessary to comment that the instructional program of the schools was defective because it did not "strongly inculcate in the minds of the pupils the duty of industry or at any rate [did] not adapt them to its habitual exercise . . . which could mould their habits to a life of steady labour." He therefore went on to urge the clergy and teachers to "recognize the expediency of blending that imperfect book learning . . . with special branches of skilled or unskilled labour," because of the need to induce the population to "devote their energies to the continuous and systematic prosecution of agricultural, horticultural and pastoral industry."[40]

Later, in 1876, the governor again criticized the instructional programme offered in the local schools. He noted that "sufficient provision is not made for that kind of instruction which would mould the habits of the . . . pupils to a life of steady labour, such as falls to the lot of a similar class in other countries."[41] He commented on the marked inefficiency of domestic servants and the "paucity of skilled labour" in the colony and expressed his desire to see industrial schools established in which the students could be "trained to be more useful members of society than under the present" system. His overriding conviction was that there was "no surer way of raising the people in the social scale and of diminishing crime than by extending the benefits of education [especially industrial education] to them." He also drew attention to the need for practical or industrial training for girls.[42]

In 1883 the governor once more expressed the hope that the board of eduaction would ensure that students received "some kind of technical instruction that may be of practical benefit to them in their daily pursuits."[43] As a result of these repeated suggestions, regulations were introduced in 1884 to encourage, where practicable, classes for teaching agriculture, needlework, plaiting, netting, or any other industrial subjects "which the Board might direct." In an effort to strengthen its industrial education programme, the board of education hired an Italian cameo cutter for two years to teach his art to about eight or nine boys. The experiment was not very successful, since only four candidates presented themselves for training. However, it was still hoped that the cutting of conch shells into ornaments would turn out to be a "useful and remunerative" industry.

In Bermuda, pupils were still being taught the usual elementary subjects, though needlework was offered to girls. But apart from this subject, it was noted that, even after the mid-1870s, technical instruction was still deficient, parti-cularly because of the absence of navigation. However, a "superior" school in connection with the Mechanics Institute was opened in the capital city, Hamilton, to train those who had already completed their primary schooling for various trades.

Reasons for the Continued Insistence on Industrial Education by the Elites

There were a number of reasons for the continued insistence by the West Indian elites that industrial or practical education should be given a prominent place in the curriculum of the elementary schools. One of these was to overcome what some planters and others regarded as a tendency towards idleness and indiscipline by the Negroes. For example, in 1847 the governor of St. Lucia pointed out that the problem with labour on that island was characterised by instability and inconsistency. In Trinidad, it was suggested that the population needed to obtain "some notion of the value of time and money," if they were going to be induced to work, and "some faint ideas of comfort and decency, *some glimmering perception that work is not dishonourable* and that truth and morality are not badges of degradation" [emphasis added].[44]

In British Guiana, also, it was suggested that there existed among the rising generation a "vast amount of idleness . . . [and] a lamentable disinclination [among the youths] to do anything for themselves."[45] In the Bahamas, the governor referred to the "wayward habits" of the younger generation, "their antipathy to the habitual exercise of work" as hired labourers, and the "extortionate price" which they charged for the "occasional labour" that they performed. In the British Virgin Islands, it was suggested that, because only a minority of children were attending school, this boosted the self-esteem of those who received an education "to such a pitch . . . as to make them averse to the use of the hoe or other honest labour, and in this they are often encouraged by foolish parents."[46] Similar attitudes to work were said to have existed throughout the West Indies and were most apparent among the youths.

The type of "literary" education provided in the elementary schools was supposed to be largely responsible for this "idleness, indifference and extortion" which was being "imputed to our labouring classes." Such education was alleged to have inspired the children of the masses with ideas "above their station in life" and omitted to impress upon them "with sufficient earnestness the duties of their condition, *the dignity of honest labour* and the compatibility of civil freedom with the recognized gradations and orders of civil society."[47] The result, as one report argued, was that "the emancipated Negro had been so flattered, and his vanity so excited that he scarcely yet understands his position in society." In the efforts made to "verify his emancipation, humility has been forgotten."[48] Practical training was therefore seen as a means of overcoming these poor attitudes to work.

The editor of *The Colonist* expressed the view that industrial education would motivate the students to work and respect authority and would teach them that idleness was a crime against a "higher law," as well as an "infraction of the social duty." Through it, students would also learn that the commandment which urged them to keep the seventh day holy was equally explicit in requiring them to labour during the remaining six. The *Kingston Chronicle* of Jamaica had earlier suggested that students should begin their education by being introduced, not only to the 3Rs and religion, but also to the mechanical arts, which involved the use of the plough and harrow, the plane, and the adze, the awl or needle.[49]

In addition, there were problems with the way the West Indian youths were conducting themselves in society. For example, the governor of British Guiana suggested that a very noticeable deterioration had occurred in the demeanour of the young Creoles. In Dominica, similar observations were made by members of the dominant group, one of whom remarked that

> under the present [literary] system of education the scholars do not improve in habits, manners or conduct, whilst the want of respect for any superior, and the evident absence of discrimination between the honest assertion of liberty and the overbearing swagger of licence, is painfully observable amongst the younger portion of the population; and ministers of religion state that the difficulties in controlling them from a moral point of view are daily increasing.[50]

To counteract this problem, it was proposed that the educational programme for West Indian youths should consist of both moral and practical training in addition to reading, writing and arithmetic. Such an education would socialize the upcoming generation to accept their role in the occupational and social order by developing among them the understanding that everyone is sent here to carry out their duties in a certain sphere of life.

Nevertheless, even though the programme of instruction in some primary schools in the British Caribbean gradually came to include aspects of practical or industrial training, greater emphasis continued to be placed on

academic or literary subjects which, it was said, contributed to a dislike for
"honest industry." It also led to the development of "false and extravagant
ideas of their position and claims, and an absence of right feeling of relative
station and subordinacy which they imagine inconsistent with self-respect
and independence."[51] The failure of the literary subjects to implant the right
values and dispositions among the children of the masses, which industrial
education was to foster, was one reason why many planters were not
supportive of education of the black population.

Another point advanced by employers in support of practical education
in the schools was the growing shortage of skilled artisans and good
domestic servants. During the days of slavery, there were institutionalized
systems for training such workers. Selected young slaves were apprenticed
to older trained craftsmen, and after some years of supervised training, the
young slave would become a skilled artisan. Domestic servants were also
able to acquire their expertise by learning on the job, within the household of
their master. But with emancipation, these opportunities no longer existed,
and the school began to be looked upon as the only available institution
which could offer this training.

For these various reasons the planters continued to insist that West
Indian elementary schools should attempt to provide a sound industrial or
practical education, which would not only elevate the pupil's moral and
physical condition, but would also help to produce a more "intelligent,
trustworthy and industrious" labourer, thereby augmenting the value of his
services. It was even suggested that the importance of industrial education to
the rising generation could not be over-estimated, either in terms of the kind
of individuals it was likely to produce or the influence that they were likely
to have on the long-term prosperity of the region. It was therefore pointed
out that, unless there was a change in the prejudices and dispositions of the
mass of the people, particularly in their negative attitude to work and to the
practical education of their children, European capital and enterprise would
be frightened away from this part of the world forever and bring about its
economic ruin.

The authorities continued to recognize the need to solve this problem
and, as indicated above, made many efforts in this direction. Some planters
and legislators continued to stress the value of industrial education, even
though they were unable and/or unwilling to provide adequate funding to
implement such programmes. However, the governor of the Bahamas raised
the question for those who seemed to have been losing faith in all education
that if the youngsters who had the benefit of some education had grown up
"in many cases indolent, indifferent to the interests of their employers, and
rude, if not subordinate in their demeanor, what were they likely to become
when deprived of all mental and moral cultivation?" He even went on to
argue that

> to expect that, untaught and untrained, they would
> voluntarily resort to the submissive deportment of slaves,
> and exhibit the mild docility of newly captured Africans,
> [which was what was desired by some planters] is absurd.
> They are free men and they know it. The question therefore
> is "Should we have free barbarians [which was what the

Governor felt they would become without education] or civilized free men living and multiplying among us?"[52]

He did not hesitate to give his own answer to this question, suggesting that while the negative attitudes of the Negro population to work was an ongoing and thorny problem, it could largely be mitigated by the appropriate education, i. e., one which stressed "practical" subjects.

Problems Affecting the Implementation of Industrial Education

Many problems adversely affected the introduction of an industrial education programme in schools, including the inadequate financial provision made for the effective introduction of the subject in the primary schools. The cost of such education was a major consideration in the efforts to introduce self-financing industrial education programmes. For the parents, who were generally reluctant to pay school fees, it was adding insult to injury if their children were engaged in industrial activities as part of their education.

Secondly, there was strong popular objection to such education. The inspector of schools for Jamaica observed that parents were opposed to their children's time being employed, even slightly, in manual labour instead of studying. This was particularly so since industrial education was often synonymous with agricultural training, which the parents viewed as an attempt to persuade their children to follow in their occupation as estate labourers. To these parents, a good education should have nothing to do with agricultural work. Because of its association with slavery, it was a field of employment from which they most wanted their children to escape. Even though the pupils who joined the industrial education classes had their fees remitted, their enrollments continued to decline.

The inspector of schools for British Guiana noted that the lack of success in the introduction of an industrial education programme was not entirely the fault of the educational authorities, but was partly due to the repugnance of parents to the involvement of their children in practical pursuits at school where they were not even being paid for their labour. Their point of view was that "their children were sent to school to read their book and not to work for the schoolmaster and that if they were required to work at school they might as well be kept at home to work for their parents."[53] Similar sentiments were expressed in other West Indian colonies.

The parents' objection to such education had to be taken seriously, because education was not compulsory, and parents had to pay school fees for their children. They were therefore in a position to register their support for, or their objection to, the content of the curriculum by sending or refusing to send their children to school. Further, the survival of schools and the level of teachers' incomes depended very much on the number of children in attendance, and this put parents in a position to influence the programme of instruction which teachers offered. As one observer noted,

> The teaching is by no means what one would wish it to be, for the schoolmasters are obliged, under a voluntary system, to conform more than is desirable to the wishes of the parents in order to prevent the withdrawal of their children [from school. Because of this situation] the fathers and

mothers born in slavery are [now] the principal directors of public education [in these colonies]. [54]

Another factor which adversely affected the successful introduction of industrial education was the lack of qualified teachers in this subject area. It was only in Jamaica that an attempt was made to establish a Normal School of Industry. But the number of teachers which it trained annually was inadequate to meet the needs of the schools on the island, Further, after about four years this Normal School was eventually closed.

In an effort to help meet the costs incurred by teaching practical subjects, schools attempted to produce articles in the industrial education classes that could then be sold to the public. But in most colonies great difficulties were experienced in finding remunerative outlets for the sale of these articles, making it difficult for the schools to recover even the cost of the materials used.

Some educators disagreed with the view that the type of education being offered was having a negative effect on the public disposition towards work. The inspector of schools for Trinidad, for example, argued that there was not "the remotest prospect of knowledge acquired at school" having the effect of "puffing [up]" the pupils "in their own conceit or withdrawing them from working for wages." [55] He later reiterated the point that "teaching a boy to read and spell and write and cypher, and know something of the world in which he lives, can never incapacitate him from applying his physical powers, whether to till the soil, or to engage in any other agricultural or mechanical operation." [56]

The inspector of schools for Grenada probably made the most insightful observation on this issue when in 1857 he noted that

> an opinion is prevalent among certain parties that schooling renders the labourer unfit for tilling the soil, [but] this does not seem to be borne out by the facts, for it appears that the great majority do resort to agricultural pursuits after leaving school. True, they do not readily flock to the sugar estates to work, because from a laudable ambition, they prefer to rent patches of land and to cultivate the minor products on their own account, with a view of eventually procuring their own independent homestead; but this is not to be attributed to the influence of the schools solely; it is the natural aspiration after progress and advancement implanted by the Almighty Creator in the breast of every member of the human race, and it will manifest itself, and must ultimately prevail, in spite of every obstacle to prevent it. [57]

The suggestion was even made that, rather than offering a literary education to all students, as was then being done in most schools, it would be better to differentiate the educational programmes according to the aptitude and abilities of the children. So that,

> instead of labouring to drive on, in an even line, the idle and the industrious, the boy of ready aptitudes and him whose dull brain becomes fancied and confused in an effort to master the simplest problem, we propose to assume a different position; and by holding inducements which only the more intellectual would appreciate, draw forward the

lad who may live by the labour of his brain, or the special skills of his hands, from him who should, for his own benefit . . . be taught that he has only his muscles and good temper to depend on.[58]

But despite this lack of popular support for industrial education, the local planters were in a strong position to influence its inclusion in the curriculum of the elementary schools. The local legislatures were increasingly asked to provide funds for elementary education, and their members saw this as a useful lever to influence the content of the education offered in the primary schools. The great majority of planters continued to believe that the advantages to be derived from the introduction of an industrial education programme were likely to be great and of tremendous value to the economic development and social stability of these societies.

However, this field of study was still in its infancy in most colonies up until the early 1890s, even though school managers were encouraged to introduce a modified version of the programme recommended by Kay Shuttleworth. The purpose was to demonstrate its usefulness, despite the parents' abhorrence for manual labour. Teachers were therefore encouraged to look at the popular objection to industrial education as an obstacle that was surmountable and were urged to persist in their efforts to include the subject in the instructional programmes of the children of the black population. The Colonial Office continued to give support to the introduction of industrial education in schools, and this became quite obvious in the funding it provided for the teaching of agricultural education after 1895.

Summary and Conclusions

The second major concern which dominated the curriculum of the primary schools in the West Indies was how to prepare students with the appropriate skills, values, and predispositions to ensure that they would accept with equanimity and possibly even with contentment their "inevitable" role as agricultural workers on the sugar estates. As a result, many members of the dominant groups strongly supported practical or industrial training as an important part of the education for the children of the masses. James Kay Shuttleworth, an eminent English educator, was therefore appointed to prepare a programme of industrial education for the schools in the British West Indies.

In his recommendations, Kay Shuttleworth proposed the establishment of Day-Schools of Industry, Model Farm Schools, and Normal Schools of Industry as part of a comprehensive system of industrial education for the "Coloured Races of the British Colonies." Although the report focussed on agricultural education, it was otherwise quite wide ranging in its coverage. However, it did not find much support from among the planters, nor even among the general population of the region. The parents were opposed in principle to any type of agricultural training for their children which they saw as a strategy for keeping them as labourers on the plantations.

On the other hand, the planters considered Kay Shuttleworth's proposal as a programme for training small-scale independent farmers, rather than for preparing students to become labourers for the sugar estates. In addition, the initial cost of implementing the programme was likely to be quite high. When the proposal was received, the British West Indies was undergoing a period of economic decline, and since the imperial authorities offered no financial aid to help with the introduction of the programme, there was no serious attempt by any one of these colonies to implement these recommendations.

Nevertheless, the British government and most West Indian governors urged the local legislatures to support the introduction of an industrial education programme, and on account of its perceived importance, efforts were continuously made by various boards of education to have practical subjects included in the curriculum of the primary schools in the region. The Moravians even developed a modified industrial education programme in Tobago which the secretary of state commended to all the West Indian governments. But the various attempts at this major curriculum change were not very successful. One of the major reasons for this was the continuing strong parental opposition to their children's involvement in any form of agricultural education. Nevertheless, the ruling groups insisted on the importance of the subject, and over the next half-century (1896-1945), renewed attempts were to be made and funds provided by the imperial government to introduce agriculture in the instructional programmes at all levels of the educational system of the British West Indies.

Notes

1   Circular Letter from the Colonial Secretary to West Indian Governors, 10 October 1845 (London: PRO).
2   Letter by Earl Grey, 26 January 1847, collection of the Colonial Department 1841-47, Vol. 3.
3   CO 318/138, *The Kay Shuttleworth Report* (1948).
4   Ibid.
5   Ibid.
6   Ibid.
7   George L., "Persistent Poverty". London: Oxford University Press, 1972
8   Johnston, "Education in Trinidad and Jamaica."
9   Report of the Government of Tobago, The Secretary of State's Circular Despatch, 25 January, 1847, *British Parliamentary Papers*, Vol. 37: *1847* (London: Government of Great Britain), 28.
10   CO 137/353, The Third Annual Report of the K & A's Reformatory and Industrial Association for Girls, 19 October 1857 (London).
11   Ibid.
12   Report of the Government of Jamaica, *British Parliamentary Papers*, Vol. 48: *1880* (London: Government of Great Britain), 65.
13   *The Colonial Standard*, 9 June 1887.
14   Ibid.
15   Report of the Government of Jamaica, *British Parliamentary Papers*, Vol. 59: *1893-94* (London: Government of Great Britain), 123.
16   Report of the Government of Barbados, *British Parliamentary Papers*, Vol. 46: *1847-48* (London: Government of Great Britain), 65.
17   Ibid.
18   CO 295/197, Letter by the Bishop of Barbados to *Parliamentary Papers* Governor Keate, 8 September 1857 (London: PRO).
19   Gordon, *A Century of West Indian Education*, 125.
20   *Trinidad Spectator*, 10 December 1895 (PRO).
21   *Port-of-Spain Gazette* [Trinidad], 1850.
22   Ibid.
23   CO 295/151, C. F. Stollemeyer in Enclosure from Harris to Secretary of State, 31 July 1846, no. 35; Bhagan, "A Critical Study," 49.
24   A. A. De Verteuill, *Trinidad, Its Geography, Natural Resources, Administration, Present Conditions and Prospects* (London: Ward and Lock, 1850); Cited in ibid.
25   CO 300/72.
26   Ibid.

27   Government of Trinidad, *Report of the Inspector of Schools, 1862* (Port-of-Spain, Trinidad).

28   *San Fernando Gazette*, 14 March 1868. Letter from Robert Guppy. Cited in Brereton, *Race Relations*, 78.

29   Patrick Joseph Keenan, "Report Upon the State of Education in the Island of Trinidad"(the *Keenan Report*, 1869) *British Parliamentary Papers*, Vol. 50: *1870* (London :Government of Great Britain]), 21.

30   Report of the Government of Tobago, *British Parliamentary Papers*, Vol. 37: *1847* (London: Government of Great Britain), 28.

31   Report of the Government of Nevis, *British Parliamentary Papers*, Vol. 36: *1850* (London: Government of Great Britain), 43.

32   Report of the Government of Antigua, British *Parliamentary Papers*, Vol. 55: *1878* (London: Government of Great Britain), 79.

33   Report of the Government of St. Kitts, *British Parliamentary Papers*, Vol. 44: *1874* (London: Government of Great Britain), 89.

34   Report of the Government of Dominica, *British Parliamentary Papers*, Vol. 40: *1864* (London: Government of Great Britain), 100.

35   Report of the Government of St. Vincent, *British Parliamentary Papers*, Vol. 46: *1847-48* (London: Government of Great Britain), 93.

36   Inid., 92

37   A. A. Thorne, "Education in British Guiana", *Timehri* 1, 18 (1923): 113-19.

38   Report of the Government of Bahamas, *British Parliamentary Papers*, Vol. 46: *1847-48* (London: Government of Great Britain), 52.

39   Ibid.,Vol. 31: *1852* , 54.

40   Ibid.,Vol. 40: *1857-58* , 25.

41   Ibid.,Vol. 51: *1876* , 80.

42
43   Ibid.,Vol. 51: *1876* , 80.
      Ibid., Vol. 54: *1884* , 171.

44   *Keenan Report*, 21.

45   Report of the Government of British Guiana, *British Parliamentary Papers*, Vol. 47: *1871* (London: Government of Great Britain), 46.

46   Report of the Government of the British Virgin Islands, *British Parliamentary Papers*, Vol. 37: *1865* (London: Government of Great Britain), 93.

47   Report of the Government of British Guiana, *British Parliamentary Papers*, Vol. 46: *1847-48* (London: Government of Great Britain), 144.

48   Ibid., Vol. 46: *1847-48* , 144.

49   *Kingston Chronicle and City Advertizer* [Jamaica], 3 November 1835.

50   Lieutenant Governor Blackwell to Governor in Chief, Leeward Islands, despatch, 12 April 1856, *British Parliamentary Paper*, Vol. 10: *1857* (London: Government of Great Britain), 213.

51   Report of the Government of St. Kitts, *British Parliamentary Papers*, Vol. 10: *1857* (London: Government of Great Britain), 196.

52   Address by Governor to the Legislature, *British Parliamentary Papers*, Vol. 44: *1860* (London: Government of Great Britain), 14.

53   Ibid.

54   Ibid.

55   Ibid., 43.

56   Government of Trinidad, *Report of the Inspector of Schools for Trinidad, 1874* (Port-of-Spain, Trinidad).

57   Report of the Inspector of Schools for Grenada, 22 April 1856, *British Parliamentary Papers*, Vol. 10: *1857* (London: Government of Great Britain), 115.

58   Report of the Government of British Honduras, *British Parliamentary Papers*, Vol. 44: *1860* (London: Government of Great Britain), 6.

CHAPTER 6

OTHER DEVELOPMENTS IN PRIMARY EDUCATION

Other Educational Concerns at the Primary Level

As indicated in the previous chapters, the groups involved in providing and/or financing education in the British Caribbean colonies initially attached the greatest importance to the religious and industrial education of the masses. But by the 1890s, other subjects were assuming a more prominent position in the curriculum of schools, particularly the 3Rs. The instructional programme of schools in Antigua was typical of those in the other colonies.

There, the infant and dame schools offered mainly reading, spelling, writing on slates, and learning hymns. In the juvenile schools, the main subjects were arithmetic and writing on paper, though the elements of grammar, geography, and religious instruction were also offered in some schools. "Particular stress" was placed on the 3Rs, since failure in any two of these subjects was regarded as a failure in the entire annual examination, "however excellently the remainder of the work had been done."[1]

It was reported in 1868 that in almost all schools the older children were able to read "readily and correctly" and their progress in writing was satisfactory. The results of the written examinations showed acceptable performance in spelling, while in arithmetic "great intelligence and considerable proficiency [were] frequently met with."[2] The children's knowledge of scriptural history was also considered to be good. But such levels of academic achievement were not typical of all schools in the region. In addition to providing basic literacy and numeracy skills, and a knowledge of the fundamental tenets of Christianity, efforts were made for primary schools to contribute to such areas as the following.

The Development of a Sense of Loyalty to the New Colonizers through Education in English

The ruling groups felt that there was a great need to develop and/or strengthen a sense of loyalty to the imperial power among the masses, especially in those colonies which had been more recently taken over from other European colonizers. Efforts were therefore made, through the choice of subjects offered, the language of instruction used, and the sources of the instructional materials, to help the young switch their political loyalties from their previous colonizers to their new ones.

In such colonies very few individuals spoke English, the language of the new governing elite. In St. Lucia, for example this was only about 4% of the population. Therefore, all instruction in schools was compulsorily conducted in the new imperial language. In fact, education generally became an integral part of the process of Anglicization. West Indian governments stressed the need for the young to learn the language in which their laws were written and through which the entire business of the state was conducted. A rivalry also developed between the traditional local elite and the new ruling class for cultural hegemony in these colonies. For example, despite the strong French heritage in Trinidad, a law was introduced in 1833 which required local legal practitioners to be graduates of a British law school — a requirement which did not exist in the traditionally English-speaking colonies of the West Indies.

Some members of the French Creole population in the Eastern Caribbean were still sending their sons to Martinique or Paris for their education, partly because of their lack of facility in English. But the British authorities regarded this as poor preparation for those who were later likely to occupy important positions in an English colony. This was another reason why the colonial authorities were keen to see that more active efforts were made to spread a knowledge of the English language among the population. In 1846, the governor of St. Lucia commented on the great contribution which schools were making to the society by giving the population an acquaintance with the English language and in the same year, the secretary of state, Earl Grey, indicated that he was very satisfied with the success of the island's infant schools in diffusing a knowledge of English. For him, few things were "more essential than this, to the progress and good government of the colony."[3]

In addition to the political considerations, the acquisition of a knowledge of English was seen to have been of great economic importance, in part because it was the means of communication among most employers. Even to those who traditionally spoke French in colonies such as St. Lucia, it was becoming obvious that "without a knowledge of the English language and a notion of English laws, commerce and literature," there was little chance of securing better paid employment, in either the public or the private sector.[4] In 1863 the governor of Trinidad indicated that the Roman Catholic schools were not adequately preparing their pupils for future employment because they were "not being sufficiently English." However, he expressed the hope that "this very radical *defect* will be remedied before long,"[5] because many parents were beginning to demand an English education for their children.

The French *patois* spoken in the Eastern Caribbean proved to be a major obstacle to the children's education, which was conducted only in English. In 1852, Trinidad's inspector of schools reported that the standard of the school work was particularly poor in those areas where children were unacquainted with English before entering school and had to be "laboriously carried," step by step, in the "simplest rudiments" of their education.[6] In 1859 and again in 1860, the school inspector repeated his earlier comments about the learning difficulties which these children faced and drew attention to a school at Erin which had recently opened with 29 pupils, not one of whom understood a word of English. Their home language was Spanish and occasionally French and to communicate with them, the schoolmaster had to learn the locally spoken language.

In St. Lucia, where the language at home was *patois*, a French-based Creole, most children only heard English while at school. In church they heard only French since their priests were mainly from France.[7] Teachers discouraged the use of the local language, both in and out of school, and made every effort to eradicate its use, not only from the school room but also from the playground.

In British Honduras, where the children were largely of Spanish or Mayan descent, and spoke only the local language or Spanish, their schooling, too, was conducted entirely in English. This contributed to their slow academic progress, since for many of them reading in English was a difficult task. The pupils had such great difficulties completing their lessons that it was sometimes said that their minds were not capable of learning. Their teachers also needed to persevere patiently to teach the children systematic habits.

Despite these problems, nearly all West Indian governments continued to insist that English should be the sole medium of instruction in schools. In 1867 the government of St. Lucia introduced a regulation which stated that no grant would be made to any school in which the English language was not effectively taught and that all classroom instruction *must* be given in English. In British Honduras, also, the education authorities mandated, in the late 1860s, that English should be the language of instruction in the aided elementary schools of that colony. In 1876 the authorities in Dominica, too, stressed that teaching should be conducted in English *only*. It was considered "desirable to have a definite and recognized language spoken in the Colony," and it was believed that only through the constant use of this language could there be any expectation of "eliminating, within a moderate number of years, the patois now currently used by the population."[8]

In Trinidad, Patrick Keenan observed that while he shared the desire of the colonists to see that all the inhabitants spoke English, yet the methods of instruction used in the teaching of the subject were extremely poor and not very helpful to children who were trying to learn the language. He noted that teachers who had minimal knowledge of French or Spanish were often placed in charge of schools where the children only spoke one of these two languages. They were therefore unable to communicate with the children.

Further, among those teachers who did speak French it was nevertheless considered inappropriate to translate unfamiliar English words or phrases for the children. Efforts to diffuse the English language therefore resulted in

> French and Spanish speaking children having been set to learn English alphabets, English spelling and English reading, without the slightest reference whatever, in the explanation of a word or the translation of a phrase, to the only language which they could speak or understand.[9]

In view of the difficulties which these students faced, Joseph P. Keenan recommended that reading be taught first in the local language and English acquired afterward. Other individuals had also expressed support for this recommendation. In 1874, the island's inspector of schools suggested that a schoolmaster ought first to teach the children to understand and speak the English language before attempting to provide instruction in any other subject. However, this approach was never accepted as part of the official policy of the board of education.

In an effort to improve the students' knowledge of English, the teaching of grammar was often made compulsory. This occurred in the schools in the Leeward Islands during the early 1870s, even though the inspector questioned the advisability of introducing such a measure. In 1877, it was noted that the Mico schools were sticking to the traditional practice of teaching in English only, and nearly two decades later the issue was still being discussed as to whether the teaching of English grammar might not be discontinued, "with advantage."

All teachers also had to demonstrate competence in English, and a satisfactory level of performance in this language was required from students seeking to enter the Normal Schools. For example, in 1849 all applicants for entry into the Teachers' College near Spanish Town in Jamaica were able to express themselves "in a correct manner on any plain subject and some also had a fair knowledge of English Grammar."[10]

In an attempt to overcome the difficulties posed by the children's lack of English, some teachers devoted much time to the teaching of the subject, recognizing that without facility in the language, the pupils would not benefit from any of the other instruction provided. In addition, teachers occasionally spoke the local language in school so that the children could understand what was being taught. Even the inspector of schools found it necessary to advise teachers to make some use of the local language in instructing the children to ensure better academic progress. However, while these students displayed "as much advancement as could be reasonably expected," they were, because of their language difficulties, said to be "far inferior" in their achievement to the children "in English schools of a corresponding character."[11]

Improving the Relevance of the Primary School Curriculum
Pupils often experienced difficulties with the content of the readers used in West Indian schools since these were usually written for pupils in England, or in the case of the Irish Readers, for those in Ireland. The objects and events which they described were peculiar to the European environment and were entirely unfamiliar to the students in the West Indies. These books of interest to European children therefore had no appeal to children in a tropical country, who could not fully grasp the allusions made to unfamiliar seasons, places, birds, animals, and scenes. The poor academic performance of West Indian students was sometimes attributed to their lack of acquaintance with the materials referred to in their books.

The irrelevance of the curriculum content was also commented on by Rawle, who suggested that, to overcome the problem, special efforts had to be made to familiarize West Indian pupils with the objects and the issues dealt with in the English schools. What Rawle seemed to have ignored was the fact that the educational interests of West Indian students would have been better served by the production and use of teaching materials and books which drew upon their own experiences, interests, and the objects with which they were familiar, rather than by trying to develop in them a second-hand acquaintance with the materials referred to in the books from the United Kingdom or Eire.

This need for developing local West Indian reading materials was gradually recognized by individuals like Lord Harris, and later by Keenan, who, for example, while noting the excellence of the publications of the Irish National Board, observed that these books were not suitable for children of the region. Instead, he suggested that what Trinidad needed were materials that were "descriptive of its history, of its resources, of its trade, of the natural life of its trees, plants, flowers, fruits, birds, fishes."[12] In 1872 it was noted in St. Lucia that,

> the reading books in use are . . . unsuited to the country. Many of their illustrations and allusions refer to objects, with which [the students']. . . familiarity is taken for granted, but which neither pupils or teachers have ever seen, and most of them are never likely to see; while, on the other hand, no instruction is conveyed nor interest excited with reference to the phenomena around them.[13]

But very little effort was made over the years to overcome this deficiency and in 1884 there was still in Jamaica, a dearth of books suitable to children of that island.

Preparing a Few Individuals for Higher Education

Another concern of the local elites stemmed from the realization that, while education was to be an important instrument in socializing working-class children to accept their lowly position in an extremely unequal social order, this alone was not likely to achieve the objective of pacifying the masses. In addition, there was the need for a reward system which appeared to compensate those who accepted the beliefs and adopted the behaviours which the dominant group expected of them. There were a number of steps taken to achieve this goal. One of these was the provision of a broader curriculum in some elementary schools which gave students the type of education that enabled them to move into some lower-level white-collar jobs.

Governor Harris had proposed that a variety of new subjects, including science, be offered at the primary level. While his recommendations were not fully accepted, they did influence the development of the curriculum of some primary schools on the island. By 1852, the colony had instituted an entrance examination for its normal schools, and potential teacher trainees were expected to have covered a range of subjects, including the following:

1. Reading: To read with correctness, ease, fluency and intelligence any passage from an English author.
2. Writing: To write a bold free hand, and to exhibit a knowledge of the principles of penmanship and of the rules for teaching writing.
3. Spelling: To write from dictation with correct spelling, any passage read slowly from any English work.
4. Arithmetic: To be familiar with the principles of the elementary rules, and with proportion, and to be able to work sums in these rules.
5. Grammar: To parse any short easy sentence in prose, and to exhibit an acquaintance with the elements of Grammar.
6. Geography: To be acquainted with the general outline of the great divisions of the Globe.
7. Scriptural History: To be conversant with Scriptural History generally, and more particularly that of the New Testament.

It was even expected that some of the students — probably those of a lighter complexion — from the better elementary schools would eventually fill some supervisory positions on the estates and other comparable jobs previously held by whites. For these jobs, also, a broader education was considered necessary because the management of a sugar estate was increasingly regarded as requiring some technical or scientific knowledge and good judgement

A broadening of the school curriculum at the primary level was particularly obvious in the model and the borough schools in Port of Spain and San Fernando. In these schools it was noted that the students

> can work sums in the four rules, simple and compound; some of the sums in proportion, practice and reduction. Their knowledge of the geography of the four quarters of the globe is extensive. They can write fairly and generally correctly, passages by dictation; while in some schools there are pupils who can parse sentences very creditably.[14]

Students at the Woodbrook School also had to achieve a satisfactory level in written English. In general, the model schools were intended for those hoping to become teachers, although they also provided an education for other children so as to fit them to fill any position in life, except those requiring classical attainments.

While the system of classifying schools in Jamaica was largely based on students' performance in the 3Rs, the range of subjects offered in some schools was nonetheless quite broad. For example, in the Fairfield Moravian School, it was noted that children were doing grammar, geography, universal and ecclesiastical history, geometry, arithmetic, zoology, natural philosophy, and Bible knowledge, both historical and doctrinal. Those who had the opportunity of continuing their basic education usually studied additional subjects to a level which was to be considered creditable to anyone wanting to be a primary school teacher. These subjects included writing from dictation, cyphering in the simple and compound rules and at times doing proportion and practice, geography of Europe and the world, and grammar.

At the schools on the Codrington Estate in Barbados, Rawle taught his monitors a range of subjects, including grammar from *Wilson's Elements of English Grammar*, geography, and singing. In Antigua, the better primary schools offered instruction in the 3Rs, scripture, history, geography, grammar, natural history, and singing, while girls also took sewing.

In Montserrat, however, the children were instructed mainly in reading, though in 1855 there were five schools which offered writing and arithmetic also. The ordinary primary schools in St. Kitts failed to provide a more useful education because the teachers as a body did not possess the proper qualifications for the task. However, with their limited knowledge and a great deal of vanity, they succeeded in impressing their pupils with the superiority of their rather limited learning. They considered themselves competent to instruct, but did so very poorly.

This tendency toward increasing the range of subjects was observed throughout the West Indies but, as in Montserrat, the outcome was often a poor quality of instruction, consisting of useless studies. In St. Lucia, for example, it was observed that

> too much is attempted by teachers. . . . Were the instruction imparted limited to the rudimentary and elementary branches of education, more real practical benefits would be

> derived, than by inculcating lessons in astronomy and . . .
> Scriptural Geography. Reading, Writing, and the first
> rules of Arithmetic, with some slight knowledge of
> geography are all that is required. To attempt to give more
> is not only fruitless in its results, but is . . . manifestly
> injurious, and calculated to unfit the pupils for that station
> in life which they are destined to fill.[15]

However, many parents preferred this broader education for their children since it was believed to lead to an improvement in their occupational prospects. Therefore, in 1846, when the bishop of Barbados decided to limit the instructional programme traditionally offered at St. Mary's, the school's management committee, which consisted mainly of non-whites, refused to accept the bishop's aid on these terms. By 1857, the demand for a broader range of primary school subjects had increased to such a point that the Barbados Joint Committee on Education eventually recommended the establishment of middle schools with better qualified teachers, similar to those in the central schools. These were to provide a higher level of instruction for some of the intellectually more promising students. Partly as a result of this recommendation, a few private middle schools were established in 1858, with some of them even receiving government loans. In addition, a new Act was passed in that year which expanded the curriculum to include not only the 3Rs and Scripture but also the elements of grammar, geography, history, and music.

Problems in Providing a Broader-based Curriculum

Despite the strong desire among parents to give their children a broader-based curriculum, there were a number of problems which often made the achievement of this goal difficult. First, suitably qualified teachers for these additional subjects were usually unavailable. In 1845, there were still a few European teachers in the region who were products of some of the newly established teachers' training colleges in Britain, but their numbers had declined after the termination of the Negro Education Grant, increasing the shortage of suitably qualified instructors for these subjects.

Even when teachers were available their teaching strategies left much to be desired. Some of them tried to demonstrate the breadth of their own learning by using language which was often unintelligible to the students. They also attempted to deal with topics about which they themselves probably knew very little and which were usually meaningless to the pupils. For example, Anderson, the inspector of schools for Trinidad, reported that one of the teachers attempted to explain the meaning of the concepts "latitude" and "longitude" by identifying the Latin origins of the words — "a mode of illustration" considered to be "faulty" not only because it went beyond the children's level of comprehension but also because it took the teacher outside the limits of his own knowledge. This was not an unusual practice by teachers who often took "occasional flights to the magnitude and distance of the sun and moon" while others tried to explain the revolutions of the earth — topics which the children found difficult to comprehend.

Governor Keate of Grenada also commented on the unsuitability of the teaching methods used in schools on that island, noting that teachers tried to put "into children's mouths long, obsolete words and expressions rarely used in daily life."[16] This, along with other factors, contributed to the low standards of achievement which Noble, the island's first inspector of schools, reported in 1858. He noted that even the more advanced pupils were ignorant of the common arithmetic tables, while in many schools the pupils were unable to count up to 20 or name the days of the week or months of the year. Their performance in reading was also highly unsatisfactory. Further, all the students, regardless of their age or attainment, were provided with the same instruction — a factor which he attributed to the poor quality of the teaching force.

Another factor which sometimes impeded the efforts at developing a broader curriculum for West Indian schools was said to be the pupils' own background, which was usually seen as a limitation rather than a challenge for the teacher. The students found it difficult to understand the materials in their books, which often presented concepts and images that were totally foreign to them. Rawle, in commenting on how the limited experiential background of the pupils presented a problem for teachers, suggested that with

> the absence of manufactories, the want of variety in the employment of the people, the sameness of tropical seasons and scenery and the dearth of intelligent conversation, the children can get no idea to attach to terms which, in the Bible and most other books, are familiarly used, on the presumption that these things referred to are of common notoriety [i.e., are commonly known].[17]

He considered that the West Indian world was too small and too much of a "limited colour" to supply children with a "sufficient stock of fundamental ideas to fully understand the language in the books" which they used. He therefore argued that unless

> education enlarges the horizon and endows the mind's eye with telescopic power to see the things and customs and the social state of the country from which books come, not only will most little story books, meant particularly for children's edification, appear full of enigmas, but the Bible, the Liturgy and Sermons will in great part remain in language not understood by the people.[18]

Another difficulty experienced in efforts to broaden the curriculum was the parents' limited view of education. Even though their role in curriculum development was small, they had acquired their own ideas about what should constitute a good education. For example, as previously noted, the parents were opposed to having their children engaged in practical training as part of their educational programme, largely because of its association with slavery. As one Scottish catechist noted, there were some parents who sent their children to school with utmost regularity and who would not willingly permit them to do any kind of job, either for themselves or others, because they considered it demeaning for them to work.

Bewley, the superintendent of the Methodist mission in Jamaica, had earlier criticized the parents' narrow conception of education. He noted that any teacher who agreed with their views of education was "lauded and extolled," while any other who, instead of yielding to the "ignorant self-delusion" of the parents, "truly strives" to provide an instructional programme that would be of direct benefit to their children, was held in great contempt. Parents, therefore, increasingly exerted pressures on teachers to offer the type of education which they considered important for their children. Their views usually had to be taken into consideration, since they were required to make a larger contribution to the cost of operating the schools through regular and punctual payment of higher school fees.

Further, education was not compulsory, and many pupils were withdrawn from school after attending for about two to three years. Moreover, those who operated schools expected children to acquire certain behaviours, attitudes, and values which they considered more important than any form of academic knowledge. This made it very difficult for schools to aim at any set levels of academic achievement among all children and constrained them in the range of subjects they could offer. For example, in Trinidad only about one-fifth of those who started school remained until they could read, write and spell "well into the third and/or fourth [reading] books." During this time, a few of them might have acquired some elementary knowledge of geography and scriptural history, but on the whole the level of their education was quite limited.

Some of the more ambitious parents wanted a broader education for their children, and this was often provided, despite the irrelevance of many of the subjects taught to the lives, experiences, and the future occupational needs of the majority of the labouring population. For example, the children in Nevis, who were "born without a prospect of inheriting property of any kind," were being taught to "draw up imaginary bills of exchange." This demonstrated that they were getting an education which began "at the wrong end."[19] However, as teachers' incomes depended largely on the pupil's attendance and the willingness of the parents to pay school fees, it was in the teachers' economic interest to be responsive to parental demands.

There were also differences between the missionaries and the parents about the nature of the education which they thought to be important. The parents were not as concerned as were the missionaries with religious education as a means of raising the moral standards of the students. Rather, the parents wanted to see their children acquire reading and writing skills and have "enough appearance of learning" to raise themselves above the level of manual workers.

Most missionaries, on the other hand, did not share the same hopes as the parents for the occupational mobility of the children. They continued to see their role as mainly to help improve the moral standards of the young black West Indians who would later work as agricultural labourers on the sugar estates. This was reflected in the limited range of subjects which were offered in most schools. For example, in Trinidad, the children in the Roman Catholic schools were usually taught only reading, spelling, arithmetic (as far as division), and sewing, but not geography or grammar.

Another factor which affected the range of subjects offered in the primary schools was the poor economies of the colonies. To cope with this new economic reality, many primary schools, particularly those located in the more remote areas, could only offer a narrow curriculum. This was seen in the dame or infant schools in Trinidad which, because they provided instruction in so few subjects, were cheaper to operate than the ward schools. In Jamaica, Burke noted that one outcome of the reduction of expenditure on education was that curriculum offerings were sometimes restricted to the basics. References to the need for such subjects as grammar, geography, and history were fewer during these financially difficult years, and rudimentary instruction became more general.

When the bishop of Barbados decided in 1846 to limit the programme traditionally offered at St. Mary's School, he proposed that the free instruction offered in the morning sessions should be confined to teaching students to read the Scriptures and learn the catechism. After midday these children were expected to go out and learn some trade or work on the estates. Those parents who desired secular instruction in writing, arithmetic, grammar, and other academic subjects for their children were to pay for it out of their private means.

In the 1850s and up to 1860, the ward schools in Trinidad offered mainly the 3Rs, although some of them taught geography and sewing, and in some cases, English grammar. Up to 1857, the Port of Spain Borough Council School for boys taught nothing but reading, writing, arithmetic, and some English grammar, in accordance with strict orders from the council.

In British Guiana, the instruction in the primary school in 1848 was usually confined to reading, spelling, and catechistical exercises, to which were added the "rudiments of writing" for some children, and reading of the Scriptures for others. In a few cases, instruction was also given in such other branches of knowledge as grammar, geography, and arithmetic up to the advanced rules, with religious instruction as "the principal feature" of primary education.

In Grenada, in 1855 the education offered was still of a very elementary nature, often not beyond the 4Rs. Subjects such as grammar, geography, and history were reported to have been unknown in most primary schools. Towards the end of the nineteenth century, the Bree Commission in Barbados, in pursuit of its cost-cutting mandate, criticized the trend for schools to offer higher subjects, since it saw this as not only adding to the cost of education but also as detrimental to pupils' achievement in the basic primary school subjects.

The geographical location of schools also influenced the range of the subjects offered. In the towns and other fairly well-populated districts, more parents wanted their children to receive a broader education. Hence, the curriculum of the urban schools was not as restricted as those in the rural areas. A limited curriculum was also more likely to be offered in the smaller islands, especially those in which government aid for education was not yet forthcoming.

Individuals with interests in the sugar industry, such as Mr. Sproston in British Guiana, continued to criticize the efforts by schools to offer a broader curriculum. They argued that if the children of the labouring classes knew how to read and write, it would be enough. Such views acted as another restraining force on efforts to introduce a range of subjects in the curriculum.

Effect of Inspection on the Work of Schools

Another development in education during this period was the increasing use and growing popularity of the annual examinations conducted by the inspector of schools. These were introduced to monitor the work of the pupils and to determine whether the government funds allocated to education were being well spent. The examinations were regarded with interest by the students, parents or guardians, teachers, school managers, and even by the denominational bodies, which were usually keen to have their schools presented to the government inspector "in the best possible manner."

Assessing the quality of education provided in schools through the results of formally conducted examinations became institutionalized in the West Indies from about the late 1860s when the system of "payment by results" was introduced in most of these colonies. While this represented a change in the way in which the work of schools was assessed, the objective was virtually the same as before, i.e., to link students' performance more directly to the amount of the grants their schools received.

This method of evaluating the efficiency of schools had an impact on their instructional programme and resulted in a gradual movement away from the almost complete dominance of religion in the curriculum. Those aspects of religious instruction that could be assessed by formal examination remained an important part of the work of most schools, but teachers placed increasing emphasis on the subjects for which the remuneration for passes tended to be higher.

In many primary schools in Jamaica, the subjects were classified into two groups for evaluating and rewarding the work of teachers — a practice which was followed in many primary schools in the region. First, there were the basic subjects such as reading, writing from dictation and arithmetic, which were considered most important at the primary level. Each of these carried a maximum of 12 marks, and the final performance by any school was assessed mainly according to the students' achievement in these three subjects. Second were the subjects of somewhat lesser importance for examination purposes, which included Scripture, general knowledge, grammar, and geography. These carried only half the number of marks each — six as opposed to 12 for the basic subjects. The overall academic performance of students had to reach a certain level before their school could become eligible to receive grants.

Teachers tended to place much of their instructional effort on the subjects in the first group which were likely to help their schools secure the highest assessment score. Reading, writing, and arithmetic were usually assigned a much higher proportion of the marks that schools could earn at their annual inspections — sometimes up to 2.5 times more — than "Scripture, including the Teaching of Morals." The payment for passes in any one of the subjects of the 3Rs was $1; for two subjects, $4; and for all three subjects, $7 as compared with only $1 for passes in each of the other subjects approved by the board of education. This made it financially worthwhile for teachers to devote more attention to the teaching of reading, writing, and arithmetic.

The relatively higher fees levied by private schools for instruction in the 3Rs also illustrates the value attached to these subjects by the public. In some schools, the following fees were charged: (1) 25¢ per month for teaching of the alphabet and spelling—which were considered pre-requisites to the development of reading skills; (2) 50¢ per month for the teaching of reading; and (3) $1.00 per month for the teaching of writing.

One of the effects of the annual examination on the work of the school was that the instruction provided was "too much narrowed by the teachers, to the mere object of obtaining passes in the minimum [number] of subjects."[20] Since the content of the subjects offered was also prescribed by the examination this, too, contributed to the narrowing of instructional programmes. In addition, the teaching strategies used to bring students' level of performance up to that required by the examination tended to be mechanical and lacking any challenge or intellectual stimulation.

The system of payment by results also caused teachers to direct more of their instructional efforts to the brighter pupils to the detriment of those whose academic performance was generally poorer. This was because it was financially more rewarding for them to pay greater attention to the "high flyers" and to discourage the weaker ones from attending school on the day of the inspection. Through this means they hoped to raise the average scores obtained by children taking the examination in the various grades, thereby achieving a higher position for their schools on the order of merit list and increasing the amount of government grant which they received.

Another factor which made teachers more willing to concentrate their efforts on the brighter students was the development of secondary education in the region and the award of a limited number of scholarships for primary school students to attend secondary schools. These awards were granted earlier in Barbados and Trinidad but in Jamaica they only became available in 1892. One outcome of this was that the teacher's prestige in the local community and the reputation of his school were usually enhanced if one of the students won a scholarship to a secondary school. Therefore, in their efforts to secure one of these awards teachers often devoted much of their time and attention to the more advanced children, often to the detriment of those in the lower grades. The practice was condemned by the inspector of schools of Antigua who, in 1876, suggested that

> what the Government has to aim at securing, is that for *all* children not materially below the average capacity, there should be established in *all* elementary schools a course of training calculated to bring them to a standard of useful practical efficiency, so far at least as regards reading, writing and arithmetic.[21]

In 1888 it was reported that some teachers in Trinidad were still directing more of their energies toward, and taking pains with, the brighter children or those in whom they were specially interested.[22] The report on this issue in the Turks and Caicos Islands reflected the situation in other colonies where the primary school student had a chance of securing a scholarship to attend a secondary school. In the primary schools of that colony it was noted that

the masters are inclined to take pains with the brighter
children or those in whom they are especially interested
and to give up much time to teaching them a smattering of
higher, and to them useless subjects, at the expense of the
more elementary training. The general efficiency of the
school suffers from this and the children thus taught, think
themselves, as a rule, above manual labour, while they are
really almost ludicrously ignorant.[23]

Other Effects of School Evaluation Based on the Annual Examination
The attempt to assess schools simply by focussing on the students'
performance at the annual examination conducted by the inspector also
resulted in little tangible effort being made to improve the academic and
professional competence of the teacher. This was probably due to the
difficulty of assessing the work of teachers, except through their students'
results. The authorities tended to see students' examination performance as
the best measure of teacher competence. As a result, they became less
concerned with the qualifications or training of the teachers and the
instructional strategies which they used.

One consequence was that the teaching continued to be quite
mechanical, with rote learning remaining the most popular instructional
strategy. This method was originally used in the teaching of the
catechisms and hymns and came to be practised in the teaching of nearly
all subjects in the curriculum. For example, in his 1846 *Report*, Inspector
Savage of Jamaica noted that the children's memories were still being
stored with "scraps of unrelated knowledge" and that there was nothing in
the methods used by the "ill-qualified teachers" which induced "real
thought, observation or reflection." Later, another of the island's inspector
of schools, Capper, also reported in 1877 that "the quick and showy pupil,
with glib answers learnt by rote is too often the product of a school" under
ill-qualified teachers. This often resulted in the "neglect of a solid
foundation of useful learning."[24]

The prevalence of this method of instruction by repetition was also
alluded to by the inspector of schools for Trinidad in 1852, where "modern"
teaching methods were said to have been adopted. In fact, this modern
approach was quite similar to rote learning, since it consisted simply of a
"system of simultaneous answering, of elliptical questioning and teaching,"
which was done by impressing on the minds of the young the importance of
"a knowledge of facts, of singing, and of arresting and controlling the
attention and attitudes [of the children] on the word of command."[25] In
1869, Keenan too commented on the fact that teaching in the colony was not
only conducted on "a haphazard principle" but was purely mechanical—as
it was in most primary schools in the region at the time. As he noted, "with
the words of their prayers and catechisms the pupils' heads are
abundantly crammed, but of the meaning of those words very few have the
slightest comprehension."[26]

The inspector of schools in Barbados observed in 1863 that the practice
of learning by rote was still the most common means of instruction and that
the habit of committing bits of information to memory, by repeating words
whether or not they were understood, continued. Reverend Moxly also
criticized the work of the elementary schools on the island, noting that

"the children learn very little and what they learn, they learn by rote as moderately intelligent parrots."[27]

In Nevis, too, it was noted in 1856 that the teaching of religious education still consisted of "repetition of verbal answers to questions," rather than in the cultivation of moral qualities or the real enlightenment of the mind to the "duties and responsibilities of life."[28]

Reading was also taught through rote learning — with children learning "sound without sense." As a result, the inspector of schools for Antigua reported in 1876 that "it has occurred in the course of this year's examination [1876] that a child was able to go on with its so called *reading* just as fluently after the book had been closed." He further noted that this was not "a rare occurrence."[29]

There were often criticisms made of this method of teaching, but these had little impact on changing the situation. The inspector of schools for Trinidad, in commenting on the instructional strategies used by teachers, observed out that they were only concerned with the cognitive and not with the affective development of the children. On this point, he argued that it was not sufficient that a child's mind be supplied with information, but that he should also be taught to "behave himself," "acquire an active desire to do what is right and avoid what is wrong" and that his education should also fit him "to perform his duties . . . in whatever position he might be placed."[30]

In Grenada, the knowledge which the scholars often acquired was said to be very "limited and superficial." Many of them, having learnt by rote, were in "entire ignorance" of the meaning of the words they so glibly read and repeated. The Moravians, with their emphasis on industrial education, made a somewhat similar point, suggesting that teachers needed to be imaginative, and not cram their pupils "with endless strings of facts, assuming them to be so many passive creatures to be filled by so much unsavoury meat. Our children have minds, and these must be actively engaged." Teachers, they pointed out, are "educators of the mind not donors of it."[31]

Nevertheless, despite these criticisms, the practice of rote learning continued, and nearly a decade and a half later, H. Marshall found it necessary to pose this challenge to teachers in St. Kitts: "Let it be borne in mind by all teachers, that development of intelligence is of much greater importance than storing a memory with crude facts, which generally turn out [to be] of no valuable application."[32]

Other Outcomes of the Examination System

The rigid examination system also encouraged an authoritarian discipline in schools and suppressed any incipient signs of initiative and self-reliance among the children — features which were just beginning to be considered desirable outcomes of education. The payment by results system also helped to strengthen the barriers between teachers and inspectors by placing the teachers' financial future, including their chances for promotion, almost entirely in the hands of the school inspector. This autocratic relationship continued to pervade the atmosphere of the primary schools in the Caribbean throughout the entire period under review.

The inspector of schools for Trinidad observed in his 1859 *Report* that, as a result of the system of evaluation, the "better tendencies and dispositions of self-reliance" among young children were often "cowed and kept down" by the harsh treatment and repeated flogging administered by the teachers. While the annual examination system obviously was not the root of all these deficiencies, it nevertheless contributed to them.

Because of the negative outcomes of the system of evaluating the work of schools there were increasing pressures for a modification of the practice of basing school grants entirely on the average performance of the students at the annual examinations. The suggestion was to substitute it with a more comprehensive method of assessment.

As a result, there was a gradual broadening of the basis on which school inspection and evaluation came to be carried out. School grants were to depend, not only on the annual examination results of the students, but also upon the amount and the nature of the entire work of the teacher, including the organization of the school and the discipline and academic performance of the students.

In Antigua, for example, while primary schools were under regular inspection by the 1870s, only a portion of their aid was contingent on their examination results. In Barbados, school grants were eventually based on both the pupils' average attendance and their attainment at the annual examinations, and in 1877 provision was also made for surprise visits to schools by the inspector. In 1875 the Bahamian board of education adopted the "standards of attainment" approach, introduced in Britain in 1863, which was a modification of the system of payment by results. This was said to have resulted in an improvement in the achievement of pupils and was very popular with conscientious teachers. The outcry against the system of payment by results in Barbados also led the Bree Commission of 1894 to recommend a change in favour of fixed salaries for teachers.

In 1878 the government of Montserrat established an order of merit list for its inspected schools, based on the overall performance of the students at the annual examination. This list was published in the *Royal Gazette*, in the hope that it would create a feeling of rivalry among teachers which would be good for the school system.

In Bermuda, all schools were technically regarded as private institutions to which the government granted subsidies towards the salaries of the teachers. It was therefore the duty of the inspector to visit each school frequently rather than annually and to ascertain, once in each quarter, the progress made by the scholars in the various subjects. Since this was the only basis on which these subsidies were granted to schools, the assessments which were based on these quarterly examinations were taken seriously.

These modifications in the system of payment by results had some positive outcomes. They were reported to have facilitated the development of a certain amount of discipline among teachers, encouraged them to devote more time and energy to their work and pay more attention to the education of all children in the class, however backward or dull they might be. This represented a shift in the approach to teaching from the earlier days when, in an effort to obtain greater financial support for the work of a particular school, a few bright students were paraded at the annual examinations before some of the more distinguished members of the public to exhibit their knowledge.

The new method of assessment used in schools therefore provided an impetus for teachers to help all students improve their academic performance, especially since their salaries still heavily depended on the outcomes of the annual inspections. Around 1875 the inspector of schools for Jamaica, while noting that the insufficient pay received by most teachers had been a matter of complaint, argued that "the remedy, in most cases, lies in the hands of the teachers themselves, for, as they, by earnestness and close application to their work bring up their schools to a higher standard, so will their earnings from Government and from parents . . . increase." However, he admitted that the "lack of professional ability in many of the teachers was a discouraging defect in the schools, not alone among the untrained, but also among the trained teachers."[33]

The inspector of schools for Barbados also agreed that the modifications to the payment by results approach gave new vigour to teachers and resulted in a marked improvement in school attendance, in greater regularity in the hours of work, and in a "nearer approach to faithfulness" in teaching. The new system was considered so successful that it was extended even to the infant schools, and in 1868-69, it was reported that there was an improvement in the performance of the pupils at this level also. The better examination performance of students was seen as visible evidence that value was being received for public expenditure on education, and this helped to strengthen the case of those who were advocating that more funds be allocated to the primary schools. In an effort to improve the educational standards of the government-aided primary schools in Barbados, Governor Reid suggested that they be regularly inspected and that funding be made conditional upon schools achieving and maintaining good standards, somewhat more broadly defined. He therefore sought to encourage teachers to improve their level of performance by trying to emulate the work of the better schools and teachers on the island.

Despite these efforts at changing the methods by which school grants were allocated, they still tended to depend heavily on the individual subject passes of the pupils rather than on the general merits of the "whole bulk of teachers." In making this observation, the inspector of schools for Barbados quoted from Inspector Savage's report on the situation in Jamaica, where the practice was said to have had

> the inevitable effect of narrowing down the examinations [conducted by the school inspector] to the mere mechanical results by which passes are secured, and thus no time is left for testing intellectual development. . . . Besides this narrowing effect on the general teaching and intelligence of the children and the want of wholesome stimulus to the teachers to do more than cultivate a bare uniform level of mediocrity, this microscopic, not to say tedious process of individual examination consumes so much of the Inspector's time that it prevents the possibility of that frequent and regular testing of the work of all the schools which is so necessary to secure continuous effort on the teacher's part and sustain efficiency in the schools.[34]

The Low Level of Professional Competence among Teachers

Another factor which adversely affected the quality of education offered by the primary schools was the limited professional training of teachers. This was affirmed by various authorities throughout the region. For example, in 1847 the governor of the Windward Islands suggested that the low level of achievement among the pupils in those islands was due to poorly qualified and inadequately equipped teachers. Therefore, many students left school with only some knowledge of reading and of the Scriptures, a poor grasp of the "rudiments of writing and arithmetic" and just a "smattering" of grammar, geography, and history. The governor went on to add that for this situation to be corrected there was need for additional funds to pay teachers the level of stipend for their services which would ensure the supply to the profession of an "efficient" and "well qualified class of men."

Despite their poor academic and professional preparation, the absence of suitable teaching materials in the schools and the dilapidated buildings in which they worked, teachers were expected to carry out their teaching tasks with efficiency and effectiveness. A number of them performed their duties with dedication and commitment and, as a result, brought about some improvement in the practice of education though others showed "little sympathy" for the "advancement of knowledge among the lower classes."

School Buildings and Instructional Supplies

The poor physical condition under which the teaching took place also had a negative effect on education. In general, school houses were in "a discreditable state" and, with a few exceptions, the amenities received little attention. The rented buildings often used to house schools were usually dilapidated, and the equipment was "limited and inferior" in quality. Sanitary facilities were also absent.

In describing the condition of school buildings and school supplies in Barbados, Rawle noted that in many cases a school consisted essentially of "four walls and a man inside." Some of them had two benches, a book and a half, and perchance half a slate. In describing the school accommodation provided by the school on the Codrington Estates, which was probably better than most other elementary schools on the island, he noted that 60 pupils occupied a room measuring 13 feet by 12 feet, while another 120 were located in a room measuring 16 feet by 35 feet. In addition, the school was renovating an old kitchen, measuring 5 feet by 8 feet, to accommodate 20 infants.

In 1849, in the Moravian School at Bethabara, in Jamaica, the actual school equipment consisted of the following:

> Two boards fastened against the wall, planed, with a ledge to serve as writing desks; six battered leaden inkstands; one dozen Bibles and one dozen Testaments . . . eight Fenning's and Dillworth's Spelling books . . . three dozen slates, framed and unframed; one ink-bottle; one small bell; one dozen spelling-lessons [including "A B C" sheets] pasted on boards; eight or ten copybooks, belonging to the children, which they received as rewards in

January; one hymn book, borrowed from the communion table.[35]

In 1852 the inspector of schools for Trinidad was still commenting that several schoolhouses on that island were in a wretched condition, a situation that continued on for years. In 1861 the premises rented for schoolhouses were still of "a rude description" — usually cheaply and poorly constructed, sometimes with mud floors covered with palm leaves. In 1868, the reports continued to note that very few schools, if any, were "in good order." In some cases, the buildings were in such need of repair that "during a shower it was hard to find dry places in the school room."[36] In other instances, schoolhouses were dirty, the floors full of holes, the wall decayed, and the furniture deficient, imperfect, or broken. Quite often, it was noted that schools had been operating "in a make shift manner" from year to year, without any effort being made at improving their physical condition.

In the following year Keenan observed that nearly half of the ward schools were unsuitable and in bad repair, while four years later, "one of the greatest hindrances to the advancement of education . . . [was still] the unsuitable character of many of the ward school-houses and their deficiency in many of the most essential requirements of furniture and even in the most necessary convenience" such as toilet facilities.[37]

In Rock Sound, Bahamas, a school was established in a hut which measured 18 feet by 21 feet and into which were crammed 85 children. In addition, the roof leaked and there were no school supplies.[38] Davy reported that schools in Grenada, too, were of a "miserable description." In Tobago, considerable damage was done to schools by a hurricane in 1847 which further reduced the conditions of the school buildings.

Not infrequently, schools in the urban and other centres of high population concentration were too small to accept all the pupils who sought admission. In addition, there was some living space attached to the school in which the teacher was accommodated rent-free. Internal connection between the school-room and the teacher's residence was, as Huitt[39] noted, not uncommon, and members of the teacher's family ran in and out of the school, thereby interrupting its work. The teacher himself was often distracted from his school duties to look after his domestic affairs and sometimes even gave in to the "seductive temptations of the hammock" which often formed part of his home furniture.

Supplies and Equipment

In addition, there was a tremendous shortage, sometimes almost a complete absence, of instructional materials and supplies. In some schools not even a slate or a copybook could be found. In the model schools, also, the instructional materials were either unsuitable or inadequate, and the supply of books was, in most cases, deficient.

In British Guiana, the Bible and *Fennings Spelling Book* were the only two books regularly used in the schools during the early 1850s. Rawle observed that in the schools in Barbados, the facilities were very poor and that books and desks were in short supply. It was pointed out that "the want of class-books, apparatus and fittings" was "felt by all the masters as a serious obstacle to the improvement of their schools."[40]

The inspector of schools for Trinidad noted that in 1852 the schools throughout the island were generally very poorly supplied with books, maps, and materials, a state of affairs then quite common in most of the West Indies. About a decade later, in 1861, he again commented on the lack of books and other instructional materials available in the ward schools which the government was responsible for financing.

In 1855 when a teacher from Tarpum Bay in Eleuthera, Bahamas, asked the board of education for funds to purchase a school bell to summon the children to school, he was not provided with the money but was told to blow a conch shell instead.

In Grenada, it was reported in 1855 that, "very little appears to have been spent for books, maps and other school furniture" over the years.[41] Over three decades later it was still being noted that the assisted schools on the island were "very indifferently supplied with books and other school requisites" and not one school manager was reported to have sent in an order for school materials during the year.[42]

When the Commissioners of Education reported on the state of education in Antigua in 1858, they observed that the only reading book in common use was still the Bible. In the Turks and Caicos Islands, three or more pupils were reading out of one book and a row of children were writing in copy books with only one pen between them, which they used in turn.

In Bermuda, where government expenditure per head of population was substantially higher than in most other colonies in the region (with the exception of Trinidad), it was still reported in 1874 that most of the schools were very poorly provided with maps, wall pictures, and other school apparatus and that there was not one school which was fully equipped with desks. Similar observations were again made in 1875, when it was noted that the small private schools, including those for the poorer sections of the white population, were conducted under the "most dreary" and "discouraging" conditions and were almost "destitute of every appliance."[43]

Under these conditions, it was said to have been a surprise that teachers did not abandon in despair the struggle to provide instruction for their pupils. The most outstanding need was for suitable reading materials, and as a result, the Bible, which was often supplied free of cost, still continued to be the principal book for teaching reading and spelling, in addition to being a major source book of information and guidance for the pupils.

Towards Some Signs of Improvement

Modest improvements in the quality of teachers and their working conditions did take place in many colonies, and these were reflected in the overall educational standards achieved by some of the primary school students. This partly resulted from the efforts of a few young individuals who had the proper and "correctly laid elementary foundation" to be teachers. Their improved academic background was the result of the quality of education offered in some of the better elementary schools. Particular emphasis was placed in these schools on the education of those who were likely to become pupil teachers or monitors. For example, in Barbados, the standard of the work carried on in the central schools was higher than in most other primary schools on the island, and the additional legislative grants which they received for their role in the preparation of potential teachers helped to improve further the quality of the instruction offered.

Rawle, in reporting on the educational activities at the Codrington Estates schools, noted that they were getting "a good deal of work" done, despite "the undisciplined state of the monitors." He went on to observe that the first classes of boys and girls in Barbados were of the same standing as those at school in Cheadle, Surrey, England and were reading as well. While the situation he was describing was not altogether typical of elementary schools in the West Indies, the inspector of schools for Trinidad reported in 1867 that the many teachers on the island were doing good work, and that this bore testimony to the "zeal, perseverance and success" with which they were carrying out their "useful labours." In the Turks and Caicos Islands also, some teachers were said to be still "diligent and painstaking," despite the fact that they were so poorly paid, even in comparison with those who worked in the salt mines.

Somewhat similar developments occurred in other colonies in the region. For example, after the governor of the Bahamas had visited a number of schools in the colony he mentioned that he found the children to be

> evincing an amount of intellectual acquirement generally, and of Religious Knowledge in particular which will do credit to any of the National schools in England. . . . The general intelligence of the Negro children and the quickness with which they answered the numerous questions of myself and others upon a variety of subjects, struck me very forcibly throughout my inspection of the schools.[44]

The inspector of schools in Trinidad was also quite convinced about the rising standards of primary education on that island, as can be seen in his 1864 report. As he put it,

> My belief is that the great majority of the Ward schools may be favourably compared with the primary schools of any country, notwithstanding the great drawback the masters have to contend against, in children coming to school not understanding a word of English.[45]

In Jamaica the somewhat higher academic standards of those who applied to enter the Normal School of Industry in Spanish Town in 1849 was said to have been an indication that some improvement had taken place in the primary education offered in the colony. Among these who applied for admission as teacher trainees it was reported that

> in every case [the students had] a fair knowledge of the various branches of learning, which comprise reading, writing and arithmetic and most had some idea of English Grammar, at least, so much as to express themselves in a correct manner on any plain subject. They are deficient in geography, in English Composition, in geometry, and the more advanced rules of Arithmetic . . . [but] on the whole

> their acquirements were such as to warrant the
> anticipation that with one or two years' training, all
> would be fully qualified to undertake the duties of school
> masters. [46]

This represented an improvement on the past when most normal schools had to provide sub-junior classes for those students who did not have a satisfactory basic foundation before being admitted for training as teachers. For entry into most normal schools, candidates were expected to read with "correctness and fluency" any passage in English, to write a "bold free hand," to exhibit a knowledge of the "rules of penmanship," to write "from dictation," to be familiar with the elementary rules of arithmetic and to be acquainted with the divisions of the globe. Primary school students intending to become pupil teachers were, in particular, expected to have already acquired these competencies. This brought about an improvement in the academic standards of the government-aided schools and was said to have provided a stimulus for the private schools to raise the quality of their own work in order to compete for students with the national system. Incidentally, it should be noted that the improvements in primary education which were reported took place in a limited number of schools only.

The Education of Girls

The provision of education for girls during a decade or more after 1850 followed the pattern established in the previous period, though with some gradual changes. The primary whites who were in a position to afford it still sent their daughters to school in the metropole, often at an earlier age than their sons, possibly to remove them from the corrupting influence of plantation life. They also attended finishing schools where they were able to acquire the social graces considered important and appropriate for their station in life. In addition to reading and writing these girls were taught embroidery, how to play the piano and the harpsichord and even horseback riding. Geography and history were sometimes included in their programme of studies. A few coloured girls whose parents were well off were also provided with this type of education.

But the great majority of coloured and black girls who received an education attended local primary schools where their percentage was somewhat lower than for boys. This difference seemed to have widened in the 1850s, partly due to the colonies' poor economics. However, the difference gradually narrowed by the end of the period covered by this study. For example, in 1833 girls made up 45.7% of school enrollment in Barbados. But by 1850 this figure had fallen to 41%. By 1860 the percentage of girls in all schools on the island increased to 48.9% and by 1891 the figure had reached 49.6%. This was somewhat similar to the situation in some other West Indian colonies.

One reason for the early low enrollment among girls as compared to boys was that many parents anticipated a higher rate of return of the education of boys than girls. Another factor was the limited number of girls' schools in most of these colonies. Many parents preferred separate schools for their daughters, especially as they became older, since they were afraid that male teachers in mixed schools would sexually "interfere" with their daughters. Over the period under review the number of girls' schools increased in some colonies, and this helps to explain the rise in the enrollment of girls. In 1858 Barbados had 6 girls' schools but by 1889 this figure had increased to 30.

While the education provided for middle-class girls was to make them good mothers and good wives, the education of non-white girls, particularly those from the working class, was to prepare them for such lower-status jobs as domestics in the household of more well-to-do families, seamstresses, and sometimes even hucksters and shopkeepers. Because of the likely occupational destination of most of these girls it was felt to be a waste of time for them to study the more academic subjects such as geography when what they really needed was domestic subjects such as cooking, needlework and sewing and housework.

As late as 1875 the Mitchinson Commission of Barbados was still observing a concern among those providing education on the island about whether girls had the same capabilities as boys and if so whether they should receive the same type of education. After noting that there was no adequate facility for the education of middle- and upper-class girls on the island, the Commission recommended the establishment of such a school. It was to be under the charge of a female English principal with governors who had received their education "in one of the excellent Girls Colleges now at work in England."[47] Further, the subjects on the curriculum were to be divinity, English language, composition and literature, history, geography, arithmetic, one branch of science, class singing (with music, drawing and singing as extras). The classical subjects which enjoyed such high academic prestige at the time were not to be offered in this premier girls' school. However, the later 1895 Educational Commission recommended the provision of a scholarship for girls which was tenable at an institution of higher education abroad and as a result suggested that Latin, which was then necessary for entry into a British university was an indispensable subject in the education of girls.

In the ordinary primary school girls studied some academic subjects, but great emphasis was placed on the acquisition of practical skills. Therefore when industrial or practical education was offered girls were expected to do handicrafts such as basket weaving, fibre work, and twine work. In schools which offered agriculture girls were often engaged in the lighter duties: weeding, harvesting of crops and tending flower borders.

Summary

While efforts continued to be made to ensure that religious and industrial education occupied the most prominent position in the curriculum of the elementary schools, the teaching of the 3Rs was increasingly emphasized throughout the region. These subjects had a key place in the instructional programme of schools, in part because grants made to schools on the basis of students' passes in these subjects were higher than for other subjects.

Additional curriculum goals were also emphasized, including the development of a greater sense of loyalty to the new colonial power, especially in those colonies which were only recently acquired by Britain. In addition, the teaching of English was a key concern among those who only spoke French or Spanish. For this reason, English was made the sole language of instruction in schools throughout the region. This posed many problems both for the teachers and the pupils, especially those who came to school not knowing a word of English. Another challenge facing teachers and pupils was the irrelevance to West Indian children of the curriculum, as it had been developed for schools in Europe. Teachers, however, added to these difficulties by attempting to teach a range of subjects beyond the 3Rs in areas in which they often did not have the necessary competence.

Evaluation of schools for the purpose of determining their grants increasingly relied on students' academic performance at the annual examination conducted by the inspectors of schools. This focus on examination results had a number of adverse effects on the instructional programme of schools and the teaching strategies used. Nevertheless, the introduction of the system of payment by results was said to have increased the teachers' opportunities to raise their incomes by their own efforts.

This shift also led to less attention being paid to the formal professional preparation of teachers, a fact which negatively affected improving the instructional strategies used in schools. Teachers continued to rely on rote learning as the main means of instruction and often focussed most of their attention on the education of the brighter children in their classes.

Finally, school buildings throughout the region were often in a dilapidated condition, while instructional materials were non-existent or very limited and inappropriate. Such poor physical conditions under which teachers had to work added to the problems which they faced in trying to improve the effectiveness of their teaching. However, despite these difficulties there were some indications that teachers paid more attention than previously to the quality of their students' work. Judging from the reports available, and based on the method of evaluation used at the time, there seemed to have been a modest improvement in the level of education among those attending some schools and in the teaching methods used. However, a realistic overall assessment of the quality of education which most primary school students received during this period would have to conclude that, while the educational standards of a few, such as those preparing to become teachers or to take the scholarship examinations for entry into a secondary school, might have been higher than in previous years, this was not necessarily so for the great majority of pupils.

Notes

1   Report of the Government of Antigua, *British Parliamentary Papers*, Vol. 49: *1866* (London: Government of Great Britain), 116.
2   Ibid., Vol. 48: *1867-68* ,93.
3   *Despatch from Earl Grey to Governor Reid*, 27 August 1847.
4   Report of the Government of St. Lucia, *British Parliamentary Papers*, Vol. 29: *1846* (London: Government of Great Britain), 86.
5   Report of the Government of Trinidad, *British Parliamentary Papers*, Vol. 37: *1865* (London: Government of Great Britain), 27.
6   Government of Trinidad, *Report of the Inspector of Schools for Trinidad for the Year 1852* (Port-of-Spain, Trinidad).
7   Report of the Government of St. Lucia for 1891, *British Parliamentary Papers*, Vol. 60: *1893-94* (London: Government of Great Britain), 15.
8   Report of the Government of Dominica, *British Parliamentary Papers*, Vol. 51: *1876* (London: Government of Great Britain), 103.
9   *Report of the Inspector of Schools for Trinidad for the Year 1852* (Port-of-Spain, Trinidad).

10 Report of the Government of Jamaica, *British Parliamentary Papers*, Vol. 34: *1849* (London: Government of Great Britain), 110.

11 Report of the Government of British Honduras, *British Parliamentary Papers*, Vol. 42: *1856* (London: Government of Great Britain), 35.

12 *Keenan Report*, 114.

13 Report of the Government of St. Lucia, *British Parliamentary Papers*, Vol. 42: *1872* (London: Government of Great Britain), 123.

14 Report of the Government of Trinidad, *British Parliamentary Papers*, Vol. 40: *1861* (London: Government of Great Britain), 37.

15 Despatch from Governor Hincks to Rt. Hon. H. Labouchere, 22 May 1856.

16 Brizan, *Grenada*, 154-55.

17 R. Rawle, *Printed Papers* (n.p., n.d.), 172.

18 Ibid.

19 Report of the Government of Nevis, *British Parliamentary Papers*, Vol. 42: *1856* (London: Government of Great Britain), 171.

20 Report of the Government of Barbados, *British Parliamentary Papers*, Vol. 59: *1877* (London: Government of Great Britain), 60.

21 *Report of the Inspector of Schools of Antigua for 1875, British Parliamentary Papers*, Vol. 51: *1875* (London: Government of Great Britain), 102.

22 Report of the Government of the Turks and Caicos Islands, *British Parliamentary Papers*, Vol.72: *1888* (London: Government of Great Britain), 35.

23 Ibid.

24 Report of the Government of Jamaica, *British Parliamentary Papers*, Vol. 59: *1877* (London: Government of Great Britain), 19.

25 CO 259/181, Enclosure in *Papers and Reports on Secular Education*, 1853.

26 *Keenan Report*, 13.

27 Rev. J. H. Sutton Moxly, *An Account of a West Indian Sanatorium and a Guide to Barbados* (London: Sampson Low, Marston, Searle and Rivington, 1886), 175.

28 Report of the Government of Nevis, *British Parliamentary Papers*, Vol. 40: *1857-58* (London: Government of Great Britain), 124.

29 *Report of the Inspector of Schools of Antigua for 1875*, 101.

30 Report of the Government of Trinidad, *British Parliamentary Papers*, Vol. 40: *1861* (London: Government of Great Britain), 41.

31 Report of the Government of Tobago, *British Parliamentary Papers*, Vol. 40: *1861* (London: Government of Great Britain), 43.

32 Report of the Government of St. Kitts, *British Parliamentary Papers*, Vol. 51: *1875* (London: Government of Great Britain), 77.

33 Report of the Government of Jamaica, *British Parliamentary Papers*, Vol. 59: *1877* (London: Government of Great Britain), 19.

34 Report of the Government of Trinidad, *British Parliamentary Papers*, Vol. 59: *1877* (London: Government of Great Britain), 60-61.

35 Ryall, "The Organization of Missionary Societies," 342.

36 CO 299/19, Government of Trinidad, *Report of the Inspector of Schools for Trinidad for the Year 1868*, Vol. 37: 16 (Port-of-Spain, Trinidad, 2 February 1869; London: PRO).

37 Report of the Government of Trinidad for 1871, *British Parliamentary Papers*, Vol. 48: *1873* (London: Government of Great Britain), 94.

38 M. Craton, *A History of the Bahamas* (London: Collins, 1968), 211.

39 Homer Carroll Huitt, "The British West Indies in Eclipse 1838-1902" (Ph.D. diss., Univ. of Missouri, 1937).

40 Report of the Government of Barbados, *British Parliamentary Papers*, Vol. 34: *1849* (London: Government of Great Britain), 167.

41 Government of Grenada, *Report of the Inspector of Schools for 1855* (St. George's, Grenada, 22 April 1856).

42 Report of the Government of Grenada, *British Parliamentary Papers*, Vol. 57: *1887* (London: Government of Great Britain), 9.

43 Report of the Government of Bermuda, *British Parliamentary Papers*, Vol. 51: *1875* (London: Government of Great Britain), 7.

44 Report of the Government of the Bahamas, *British Parliamentary Papers*, Vol. 36: *1850* (London: Government of Great Britain), 143.

45 Government of Trinidad, *Report of the Inspector of Schools for Trinidad, 1864* (Port-of-Spain, Trinidad).

46   Report of the Government of Jamaica, *British Parliamentary Papers*, Vol. 34: *1849* (London: Government of Great Britain), 110.
47   *Mitchinson Report*, 25.

CHAPTER 7

TEACHERS: THEIR SUPPLY
AND STATUS

Introduction
The low level of education and professional training of teachers also affected the quality of primary education offered in the schools of the British Caribbean colonies. To cope with the substantial increase in primary school enrollment which occurred throughout the region at the end of the apprenticeship period, a large number of local individuals were recruited as teachers. They received little or no training, and the opportunities to improve their skills diminished considerably after the termination of the Negro Education Grant, which led to the closure by the Mico Trust of all its teacher-training institutions, with the exception of those in Jamaica and Antigua.

Despite this deficiency in teachers' educational and professional background, most colonial legislatures did not provide support for the establishment of new normal schools to assist with the training of teachers. Therefore, the teachers' opportunities to improve their competence were very limited and, in addition, their salaries were entirely inadequate to attract better educated individuals to the profession. Further, the general conditions under which teaching was carried out were unsuitable, with limited and often irrelevant instructional materials. Together, these factors would have presented an extreme challenge even to well-educated and trained teachers, but for the poorly qualified West Indian teachers, this was almost a recipe for failure in the use of effective instructional strategies.

The Supply of Qualified Teachers
Jamaica
In Jamaica, as in some other West Indian colonies, teachers were initially recruited from Britain immediately after the post-emancipation period. However, after this, as Campbell[1] noted, there were some efforts by the government of Jamaica to provide training opportunities for local teachers in the post-1838 period, but these were inadequate to meet the educational needs of the island. While Jamaica benefited from the early establishment of a Mico normal school, the number of teachers produced by this institution was very limited. In addition, some of the trainees were from the other West Indian colonies to which they returned after the completion of their training. Between 1836 and 1858 only about 278 teachers were trained at the Mico institution — an average of about 13 per year. In 1870 this normal school had 30 trainees in a two-year programme, allowing for a maximum output of only 15 teachers per annum.

However, these efforts were supplemented, in a limited way, by the teacher-training initiatives of some missionary bodies, such as the Moravians and the Baptists. But in 1868, Jamaica still had only 90 students in training at its five elementary teacher-training institutions. Further, not all these trainees were being prepared for teaching. Colleges like Calabar trained both ministers of religion and teachers, and since the church had more prestige than the school, some of the better teachers eventually became preachers.

The denominational schools wanted teachers of their own religious persuasion, with the result that the training provided by their colleges was so "denominationalised" that their teachers were not particularly welcome to teach in other denominational schools. There were also a number of Model Schools which helped to prepare some better educated primary school students to become monitors and pupil-teachers.

The board of education recognized that if its proposed industrial training programme was to be successful, specially trained teachers were needed for the various practical subjects. Consequently, in 1847 it agreed to establish a Normal School of Industry near Stony Hill. This institution was to produce teachers of a quality at least comparable to those teaching the literary subjects. To increase the prestige of its teachers the board wanted the Normal School of Industry to attract trainees who possessed *"remarkable talents or fitness* for the exercise of *intellectual rather than corporeal energies"* [emphasis added].[2] But there is evidence that the programme of studies which it provided was as classical as that of other normal colleges.

Shortly after this normal school opened, the inspector of schools recommended and the board approved an increase in the number of its trainees. In 1848 efforts were also made to get the Mico Normal School to convert to a Normal School of Industry. But the Mico trustees, who were still opposed to the introduction of agricultural education in the primary schools, objected to the change. However, after August 1849, the Normal School of Industry was temporarily closed due to lack of funds. It was reopened briefly in 1850 but, with the government's retrenchment policy, the institution finally ceased its operations in 1852, after about five years of "shaky existence."

Suggestions were also made for well-regulated infant schools that were to be placed under the care of "pious, properly educated female teachers." The need for trained teachers for these schools led to the proposal for the establishment of a normal school for female teachers. The Moravians, however, who established a seminary to train such teachers at Bethabara in 1861, were the only group which immediately responded to this proposal. A proposal for the establishment of four model schools, in place of the "inefficient vestry schools" which was made in 1866, was repeated in 1869. These were to be staffed with "good and efficient masters" from England who were to play a role in the training of teachers.

The difficulty of securing competent teachers often prevented a number of schools from being ready for inspection, and this proved an "obstacle" to the efforts to provide education as widely as possible on the island. Therefore, to help meet the "rapidly increasing demand" for elementary school teachers, the board of education established the Stony Hill Teachers' Training College in 1870. In addition, an increase in the number of teachers in training at the Mico Normal School in Kingston was proposed.

Despite such efforts, it was again observed in 1880 that the "want of skilled teachers" in sufficient numbers had been retarding the progress of education in the colony, and this concern was expressed repeatedly in the inspector's annual reports. A training college for female teachers was also considered a pressing need, and in 1885 the Shortwood Teachers' College for girls was established to fill this gap. At this time, it was the only one of Jamaica's six training colleges exclusively supported by the government. In 1885 a commission recommended that more grants be made available for teachers' colleges with the view of doubling the number of students under training, "as soon as possible." Therefore, even though the male Teachers' College at Spanish Town was closed in December 1890, by the turn of the century, the number of teacher trainees in Jamaica had risen to 191, from 75 in 1885.

In 1892, the board of education again drew attention to the "great want" of properly trained female teachers and noted that qualified male teachers, too, were "not in sufficient supply." Therefore, in an attempt to improve the educational standards of the new recruits to teaching, the board ruled that no new person could be registered as a teacher without having passed the teachers' examination, and unregistered persons were to be only temporarily employed.

Another Approach to Improving Teacher Quality

A number of years elapsed following the closure of the Normal School of Industry in 1852 without the government taking any new initiative in the field of teacher education. Thus, many who held teaching positions were really quite "useless" and "incapable" of performing their jobs competently. The board of education therefore decided to "rectify this defect" by introducing a measure to encourage practising teachers to improve their education through their own efforts. The main element in the plan was indicated in the Competitive Examinations Bill of 1861, which provided for the institution of Teachers' Certificate Examinations and the establishment of a Board of Public Examiners. The board was responsible for conducting these examinations, which were aimed at encouraging teachers to improve their professional skills largely by self-study and with little cost to the government. The Bill also stipulated that, after three years, no school would receive aid unless its teachers held certificates, in compliance with the new regulation. This was the first attempt by the government to establish a minimum level of education for teachers.

Additional motivation was provided for practising teachers to improve the level of their qualification by the offer of higher incomes for those who were successful at these examinations. Therefore, the amount of the school grant became partly dependent on the level of certification which teachers obtained. This measure aimed at making the profession more attractive to better educated personnel and won some official support because it was considered likely to ease the pressure on the government to establish more normal schools.

The efforts to establish certain minimum levels of education for teachers through a common examination system met with poor overall response. Teachers did not usually study on their own for these examinations. For example, even as late as 1882, the inspector of schools was still commenting on the fact that teachers in Jamaica did not spend any time reading. He pointed out that "a book is rarely read and a stray newspaper comprises almost their sole literature . . . [even though] with the price of printed material so cheap today the excuse of prohibitive cost no longer exists."[3]

Teachers, however, criticized the examination on the ground that its standards were too high and the curriculum most inappropriate. They saw, for example, that of the 11 teachers who sat for the examination in the first year, several were reported to have exhibited "great ignorance," especially in Scripture and arithmetic. Only four teachers were successful — two in the second class and two in the third class. The missionaries also did not particularly welcome government involvement with their teachers as they saw happening through the examination system, since they regarded it as an official attempt to encroach upon what they regarded as their special area of jurisdiction. They also thought that the emphasis on formal qualifications as a factor in determining teachers' income levels would result in a decline in the importance of school inspections which might lead to a reduction in the quality of instruction offered in schools.

Further, the denominational bodies did not accept the view that a high academic attainment was necessary for success as a teacher. They preferred to emphasize the religious and moral calibre of the individuals seeking teaching positions — factors which could not be assessed by formal examinations. As Savage noted, the church leaders shared the view that "moderate literary attainments" plus "good teaching power" were preferable to "brilliant scholastic attainments," especially since the teachers were expected to teach only the "simple rudiments." This point was also made in Grenada, where it was suggested that "to simply give catechistical instruction, and teach spelling, reading, writing, and the first principles of arithmetic does not require any great scholarship."[4] In Trinidad, Anderson, the inspector of schools, also noted that steadiness and perseverance were more valued in a teacher than academic qualification.

Finally, some of the planters were unhappy about the use of formal examination results as a means of rewarding teachers, on the grounds that the country could ill afford additional public expenditure on education. They realized that the linking of school grants to teachers' success at these examinations was likely to result in increases in the financial subvention to education over which they might have no control. Therefore, by 1869 school grants were still largely dependent on the number of pupils in attendance and their performance at the annual examination conducted by the inspector of schools.

Barbados

The number of teachers being trained in Jamaica may have been inadequate to meet the colony's educational needs, but the situation was worse in most other British West Indian colonies, with the possible exception of Antigua. Barbados did not have its own normal school, despite the efforts of many well-known individuals to persuade the legislature to establish such an institution. When Rawle, the principal of Codrington College, arrived on the island in the 1840s, he found that, with the exception of St. Paul's, the education provided by nearly all the elementary schools was quite unsatisfactory. He determined that the children were failing in their academic work because their teachers were untrained, and for this reason, he became heavily involved in helping to improve teachers' academic and professional competence, through in-service training. He emphasized the point that knowledge and good habits alone were not sufficient criteria for assessing whether an individual would be successful as a teacher. For him the craft of teaching had to be acquired as part of a course of instruction which provided "practice under guidance" by competent instructors. He therefore suggested that, until there was a normal training school in Barbados to supply "rightly instructed and disciplined teachers," no sound basis could be laid for an efficient system of education for the island.

The teaching force in Barbados also depended for its recruits largely on the graduates of its better primary schools who, initially, took up positions as monitors and pupil-teachers. Providing professional training for these individuals, up to the level where they could become reasonably competent as teachers was still a major problem. However, Rawle recruited a trained master from England who was attached to the central school and helped with the education of these potential teachers. Further, he persuaded the director of the two central schools to convert their schools into model primary schools for the systematic training of pupil-teachers. He was also able to convince the authorities to open these central schools to pupils of all complexion, so that non-white pupil-teachers could also benefit from the education and training which they offered. The legislature also substantially increased the grants to the central schools to help them undertake these additional responsibilities. By 1852 it was reported that "with staff from England" they were already producing "good fruit." In 1864, it was again pointed out that the Boys' Central School was being "efficiently conducted" as a "training school for teachers."

Rawle also started in-service training courses for practising teachers. Provision was made for instruction in grammar, parts of speech, etymology, growth of language, geography, history and chronology. They also had "debates" on Old Testament history, and school management. Rawle further helped to establish an Association of Anglican Schoolmasters which allowed one denominational group of teachers to meet and discuss professional matters. He even suggested the institution of annual examinations at which schoolmasters might voluntarily compete for prizes, offered as a stimulus towards their self-improvement. The idea was accepted, but by 1865 all headmasters were required to take what became the Teachers' Certificate Examinations. The aim was to assess and reward teachers for their level of academic and professional competence.

The Barbados Association of Schoolmasters was so appreciative of Rawle's efforts at in-service teacher-training that, in 1847, it proposed the establishment of a teachers' library, a collection of "school apparatus" for use by its members, and the holding of quarterly meetings to listen to lectures and/or to have discussions on educational subjects. But despite Rawle's earlier efforts to improve teacher education, progress in this field continued to be very slow. As a result, criticisms were continually made about the quality of the teaching staff in the primary schools. While the importance of training monitors was stressed, the establishment of a normal school receded further from the horizon.

In 1850 Bishop Parry indicated to the governor that the lack of competence among the teachers was an evil with which the colony had contended for the past 25 years. He attributed this situation to the overall neglect of popular education by the government, and the resulting scarcity of educated and trained persons to conduct schools. Governor Hincks urged the Barbadian legislature to pay attention to the educational achievements and remuneration of teachers so that the profession could be made attractive to more "respectable" groups in the society and in 1857 reiterated the view that the first step in building a proper system of education was the provision of competent teachers. To this end, he urged the establishment of an efficient training school.

The Joint Legislative Committee on Education also stressed the need for more and better teacher-training facilities and recommended the introduction of the pupil-teacher system, which was seen as a means of obtaining an adequate supply of teachers at a "reasonable price." Therefore, the 1858 Education Act which followed made provision for students who were at least 14 years of age to be apprenticed as pupil-teachers. The adoption of this system imposed a duty on the Education Committee to provide in-service courses for these young teachers during the school vacation. The "sad inefficiency" of schoolmasters in general came in for criticism again in 1860, and the hope was expressed that, through the training of pupil-teachers, the situation would eventually be corrected. The decision to focus on the recruitment and in-service training of pupil-teachers indicated that in the selection of a system of teacher-training in Barbados, as in other West Indian colonies, the question of cost took precedence over the issue of quality.

Local teachers were constantly encouraged to improve their qualification and incomes by preparing for and being successful at the Teachers' Certificate Examinations which were introduced in Barbados and other West Indian colonies. Those who were able to improve their level of certification became entitled to a yearly premium in addition to their regular incomes. About two years after the introduction of these examinations, Elliot, the inspector of schools, commented on the great satisfaction and eagerness with which "uncertificated" teachers sought to qualify themselves for certification and increased pay.

But with Rawle's departure from the island, problems began to arise with his plan to have the central schools recognized as the centre for the training of local teachers. The master of the Boys' School observed that of the 30 boarders to pass through the institution during his time only one had become a teacher. This was probably because the occupation of a clerk was often much more lucrative than that of a schoolmaster. It was therefore argued that the central schools could not, by themselves, provide the motivation for their pupils to take up teaching as a career and that the training of teachers should no longer be regarded as their main aim, as Rawle had envisaged. The headmistress of the Girls' Central School also felt that the plan for training infant teachers at her school was a waste of time, both for the school and its pupils. Therefore, by 1876, the scheme to provide teacher-training to students at the central schools was officially described as a failure.

Later, the government threw open its annual vacation courses to all who wanted to attend them in an attempt to help teachers prepare for the Certificate Examinations. But the impetus which Rawle gave to the in-service training scheme subsided and the need for a separate teacher-training institution became even more marked. However, despite the many pressures that continued to be exerted on the government, it did not provide the necessary funds to establish a normal school. In 1876 the Mitchinson Commission observed that teachers in Barbados "labour under the disadvantage of deficient training." Therefore, around 1880, a training institution for schoolmasters was finally opened at Mission House, which was part of Codrington College. But in 1886, the Reverend Moxly was still noting that primary school teachers on the island were "in many cases [still] woefully ignorant and even if they knew anything they have no power or skill in imparting information." He therefore went on to suggest that until "well-taught and well-trained teachers can be obtained," the money which was being spent on primary education in the colony was "in great measure wasted."[5]

Trinidad

In Trinidad, too, the teachers were poorly qualified, both academically and professionally. A Mico normal school was in operation on the island for about nine years and produced only about 20 teachers before it was closed in 1845. By 1847, the government began to express interest in re-establishing its own teacher-training institution. But little more was done at the time to ensure the development and implementation of a plan for a normal school. The colony was thus left without any formal teacher-training facility until 1852.

Because only a few educational facilities were initially provided for the black population, the early demand for teachers was limited, and the island did not experience much difficulty in recruiting staff for its schools. A number of teachers were brought from Europe and they, along with the missionaries and some local personnel, were enough to staff the schools. However, by 1848, the governor commented on the poor moral and intellectual qualifications of many of the local teachers. To improve the quality of elementary education he suggested the recruitment from Sierra Leone of young Africans who were educated by the missionaries for the express purpose of becoming schoolmasters. But this proposal was abandoned because of the costs involved.

In his 1851 report, Governor Harris noted that he could not give a "very satisfactory account" of the general progress of education because of the "scarcity of efficient teachers" which he saw as the "principal impediment" to the improvement of education on the island. He therefore proposed the establishment of a teachers' college to serve as the central teacher-training institution with model schools ancillary to it. These model schools were to provide the ideal conditions for the trainees to do their teaching practice. But this proposal was never fully implemented, although in 1852 the governor hired someone to take charge of the Normal

School for Boys in Port of Spain and to establish a model school on the nearby estate of Woodbrook.

While about 40 pupils initially applied for entry to this training institution, many did not meet the entry requirements, largely because of their generally low levels of academic achievement. The teacher-training institution was poorly equipped, lacking sufficient books and other equipment and a library. Further, there was no specified length of training which the trainees had to undergo, nor any examination they had to pass before they were regarded as qualified teachers. Finally, relatively little attention was paid by the institution to help teachers improve their teaching techniques.

The first batch of graduates was produced in 1853. However, after the superintendent, Roger Dixon, died it was said that the standard of the work of the institution deteriorated even further and in 1879 Keenan even recommended its closure after commenting on its poor standards.

As in the other West Indian colonies, the model schools of Trinidad were eventually used not only for teaching practice but also to meet the need for some secondary education among the trainees — a factor which often detracted from their value as teacher-training institutions. However, the borough council schools, which were attracting students of higher levels of ability, were important sources of teacher trainees for the primary schools. In 1856, a Girls' Model School was also established, with a teacher from England brought to serve as its first principal. This school was intended to help meet the need for good female teachers, but its output was very limited.

In an effort to attract more teacher trainees, their allowances were doubled in 1857, and a limited number of places were even made available in the normal schools for students who were not receiving training subsidies. The increase in the training allowances was an important step for the profession, since it made the intellectual ability of applicants a more important criterion for selection as teacher trainees than their sponsorship by a religious organization.

In 1860 the governor again drew attention to the need for a proper normal school, in addition to the two existing model schools, and once more argued that it was impossible to maintain an efficient system of education without the establishment of a well-organized and effective training institution for school masters. In the following year, the inspector of schools continued to report that the general calibre of teachers left much to be desired and in 1868 he attributed the weaknesses of the ward school system to the deficiencies of the teachers, who tended to be "short of knowledge, industry, and even cleanliness of habits."

At any one time only a relatively small number of individuals received training as teachers, since those who were trained tended to be employed only at the government schools and there were usually more trained teachers for these schools than there were positions available for them. By the late 1860s, Trinidad's two model schools were also reported to have been doing a "creditable job" in helping to prepare primary school teachers.

By 1869, the monitorial system, which had fallen into disuse, was revived and, despite the fact that some trained teachers were not employed, the brighter students from the primary schools were still attracted to the teaching profession as monitors and later as pupil-teachers. The importance of these monitors was stressed because of the help they provided with the management of large classes and because they represented a potential source of raising a "properly trained corps" of teachers. Incidentally, in compensation for their services, these unpaid monitors normally received extra instruction and became eligible for promotion to paid studentship in the normal school.

In his report on education in Trinidad in 1870, Keenan drew attention to the fact that the salaries of teachers were still inadequate for the profession to attract "really superior men and women" who wanted to make teaching their life's career. Therefore, individuals continued to be admitted into teaching with levels of achievement lower than that required to enter the normal school. In addition, they were still not recruited from the classes which, it was said, "should have furnished them." Keenan suggested that every effort should be made to attract "a better class" of individuals to the profession. He also felt that, although the teachers laboured under the disadvantage of the deficient training, some of them turned out to be quite "good and efficient" practitioners. Since they would have come through the pupil-teacher system this was an implied positive assessment of the system.

Nonetheless, this method of preparing teachers had severe limitations. At most it was able to impart only "a bare modicum of knowledge" to those in training and got them accustomed to "teaching by practice." It was also criticized because it was pointed out that

> there can never be any study of education as a theory; no attempt at an analytical study of man's moral and intellectual nature, with a view of bringing this knowledge to bear on the formation of children's characters — above all no subjecting of the would-be teacher to those refining and moulding influences which can alone be got by instruction and contact with superior minds.[6]

Keenan recommended that model schools should cease operations because individuals were entering teaching with "qualifications of the humblest character," and the programme did not provide them with the adequate training to become competent teachers. One major deficiency was that "pedagogy was practically ignored" in their training. In its place, Keenan suggested the re-introduction of the monitorial system because he felt that the effects of "bad schoolmanship" in Trinidad was aggravated by the absence of monitors who could help teachers with their large classes. Further, he felt that the monitors would be more highly motivated to become teachers since they were not likely to be "driven to teaching by laziness, by disappointment or by their failure in other callings,"[7] as was the case with others who had been directly recruited into teaching. In 1876 the pupil-teacher system was adopted in the colony, and the number of pupil-teachers rose so rapidly that by the 1890s they made up about half of the teaching force.

In the 1870s Governor Gordon introduced the Teachers' Certificate Examination which all teachers in Trinidad had to pass in order to obtain their certification. Teachers without such certificates, which had to be secured within a four-year period, could not be placed in charge of a school. Yet, despite these efforts, it was still being noted in the 1890s that the status and qualification of teachers needed to be raised before there could be any "general improvement" in education. Therefore, another ordinance was passed that year, providing for the employment of certificated teachers only. Those who were already teaching were allowed five years to obtain their certificates.

The ordinance also permitted denominational bodies to offer their own teacher-training programmes and, as a result, the Canadian Presbyterian Mission established the Naparima Teachers' College in 1894. The aim of this institution was to further the Mission's efforts at training East Indian teachers which commenced with the offer of in-service training courses in the 1870s. The Roman Catholics also set up two residential teacher-training schools — one for males and the other for females. However, despite all of these efforts, the number of individuals undergoing teacher training in any one year remained insufficient to meet the colony's need for qualified teachers.

Other West Indian Colonies
In Antigua there were about 25 teacher trainees at the local Mico normal school, but some of them were from other parts of the Eastern Caribbean. In 1847 another training school was established, in addition to the two operated by the Moravians — one for males and the other for females. The need for qualified female teachers resulted in an agreement between the government and the Moravians whereby, in return for a government grant, their college accepted female teachers for training, irrespective of their denominational affiliation.

Although the Boys' School at Cedar Hall (which had about 25 students in attendance) was not a Normal School of Industry, it tried to prepare students to become industrial education teachers by combining their classroom studies with manual work. A training school for girls was originally opened in 1840 by Bishop Westerby of the Moravian Mission and was moved to Spring Gardens in 1854. In 1855 a teachers' college was also established, and the importance of this institution increased after the closure of the Mico teachers' college towards the end of the century. Antigua, therefore, eventually had more teacher-training facilities than most other colonies in the British Caribbean, with the possible exception of Jamaica. But the total output from these various institutions also did not meet the island's overall need for trained teachers.

In 1859 the governor, while recognizing the need for improved systems of teaching and for the training of teachers and monitors, observed that the lack of funds made it impossible to tackle this problem effectively. Therefore, all that could be done at the time was for the government to encourage the self-education of teachers by distributing books and pamphlets which provided them with some information on "the conduct of their labours." Nevertheless, the governor realized that the issue was not simply one of finding funds for teacher training, but was linked to the problem which was then common throughout the region, viz, the profession was still attracting mainly "an inferior class of teachers" since the salaries that were offered were "not so large as to induce many of superior ability to apply for the office."[8]

In 1862, due to the shortage of qualified teachers, most of the instruction in the schools was carried out by monitors whose parents sometimes unwillingly permitted them to be used in this largely unpaid role. But the Educational Commission of 1866 regarded their assistance as being of little or no value because the service was irregular and therefore could not be entirely depended on. Hence, it was suggested that unless more effective help was obtained, in the form of qualified teachers, the standard of work in the schools was likely to remain low. The inability of the colony to afford trained teachers, however, continued to be a problem.

Two approaches to help improve the supply of better qualified teachers for the profession were recommended by the 1866 Education Commission. The first was to follow the development already initiated in some of the other colonies, i.e., to institute an external Teachers' Certificate Examination. The aim was to help teachers widen their knowledge base and improve their professional competence, both in teaching and classroom management, through their own efforts. With the introduction of these examinations, it was decided that schools under the charge of uncertificated teachers would eventually not be granted any government aid. Commenting on this approach, the Commission argued that

> believing that the first essential of a good school to be a well-qualified teacher, we have, with a view of encouraging the more competent [teachers] and stimulating the rest, held a public examination of teachers in charge of schools, in those subjects which enter into the course of instruction in a good elementary school. [Particular stress was laid upon the] Holy Scripture, Reading, Spelling, Writing and Arithmetic. [The other subjects included were] English Grammar, the Elements of Geography, the Outlines of English History, Vocal Music, the Elements of Physical Science, and the Principles of Teaching. Each successful candidate was entitled to receive a gratuity, with the amount depending on the level of certificate which he or she was able to achieve. [And] small as these amounts are, it has been . . . a great source of pleasure to be able to make even so slight an addition to the narrow incomes of deserving teachers.[9]

The Commissioners of Education also passed rules in 1867 that prevented the appointment of individuals as teachers unless they obtained a professional certificate of competency. School managers, therefore, tried to hire only certificated teachers. But the lack of a sufficient supply of such individuals remained a major obstacle and therefore, when the Mico Charity intimated its intention in 1880 to close its Teachers' College, which had been almost the sole source of trained teachers for the island's schools for about 40 years, the government stepped in to prevent this catastrophe by voting funds to assist the institution.

The second approach was to introduce the pupil-teacher system as soon as funds were available. This became a reality a few years later, as the demand for "more thoroughly competent men" as schoolmasters continued.

The objective was to give some assistance to teachers in the larger schools and prepare a "better class" of individuals for teaching.

In St. Lucia, the educational authorities also regularly complained of the difficulty of obtaining good schoolmasters, because of the lack of adequate facilities for their training. In 1853 it was pointed out that the standard of education on that island was not as high as it should have been, due to the continued lack of qualified masters. Therefore, in 1857 a normal school was established for the purpose of educating "a sufficient number" of teachers to meet the needs of the local schools. However, for many reasons, including costs, the institution was closed two years later. From then on, there was no other teacher-training institution on the island, and schools were forced to depend on the Mico normal school in Antigua for their supply of trained teachers.

In Dominica, qualified teachers were also in short supply, and to ensure that a satisfactory standard of work in schools was maintained, the 1857 School Act was passed making compulsory the examination of all denominational schools receiving aid. Grants to these schools were to be continued only if the teachers were found to be competent. But this measure did not help to solve the problem of the inadequate supply of qualified teachers. Therefore, in 1864 it was again reported that the schoolmasters and mistresses in most parts of the island were not "competent to lead the rural youth of Dominica beyond reading, writing . . . and the first rules of Arithmetic."[10] In 1876 it was once more noted that education was at its lowest ebb in the colony, due mainly to the poor quality of the teaching staff that was available. The untrained teachers were reported to have induced apathy among teachers, children, and parents alike. As an example of the poor quality of preparation which teachers received, the 1882 Royal Commission on Expenditures in these colonies drew attention to the case of a much respected schoolmistress on the island who was referred to as Mother Young. Whenever her students had difficulties with a "rare word or difficult passage," which probably she herself did not comprehend, her "curt solution" was to suggest to the reader "Jump 'im, my child jump 'im."[11]

In Grenada, also, where no "sound system" of teacher-training existed, the want of properly trained teachers was considered a major factor contributing to the inefficiency of the schools. In 1857 the school inspector attempted to lay the blame for the overall situation squarely on the shoulders of the legislators and other influential groups in the community, due to their negative attitude toward the education of the black masses.

Lieutenant-governor Keate agreed that the root of the problem was in the poor quality of teachers available on the island and recommended the establishment of a secular central teachers' training school which was to be open to persons of all denominations. While clergy and ministers would be allowed to provide religious instruction for the trainees, this was not to be a part of the school's regular instructional programme.

By 1857, an Education Act was introduced which provided for the establishment of a normal school, although its principal was required to hold concurrently two other positions — principal of the grammar school and the inspector of schools. The school, which opened in 1858 with 12 pupil-teachers in training, was financed by the board of education, although the trainees were required to pay the cost of their education when they started to work. Each parish priest was allowed to select one person from his young teacher-volunteers for training at the normal school. On the completion of their course, these individuals would return to serve in schools in the parishes from which they were selected, if vacancies existed. However, this institution did not survive very long.

Again in 1882, because of the continued shortage of qualified teachers in the colony, an Act was introduced that permitted individuals to teach, on probation, in primary schools receiving government aid. These individuals were required to pass, within a given time, the examination for certification conducted by the board of education, failing which, their services were to be terminated. This caused the dismissal of several individuals who were teaching before the new Act was introduced, because they failed to obtain the necessary certification. Despite these measures aimed at improving the quality of teachers, success was limited.

In St. Vincent, while the need for facilities to improve "the systems of teaching and training" was recognized, the major problem here was also the lack of finance to provide the required facilities. It was accepted that the salaries, in most cases, were not attractive enough to keep trained teachers in the profession and would have to be improved, if the qualified individuals were not to be lost to other occupations or to the other colonies. In this situation, the board of education resorted to distributing books and pamphlets on the subject of teaching in the hope that teachers would study them during their spare time and improve their instructional strategies by their own efforts.

In 1864 an Act was passed which set out the standards of attainment that schools were required to reach before government grants would be given. A board of education was established with a salaried inspector of schools to supervise and conduct the examinations by which teachers' levels of remuneration were to be determined. In other words, the focus on improving teacher competence shifted, as it had in other West Indian colonies, from the professional training of teachers, to the assessment of students' performance at the annual examinations conducted by the school inspector.

In St. Kitts, where up to the late 1870s grants to school did not yet depend on examination results, the poor quality of the teaching staff was also a regular subject of comment. Further, even though some teachers were not considered efficient enough to be placed in charge of schools, a number of them were nevertheless appointed to such positions, due to a shortage of qualified staff. This happened even in cases where the schools had a daily attendance of between 50 and 100 pupils. However, by 1876, amendments to the Education Act were passed requiring that provision be made for the training and examination of practising teachers. But no new facilities for teacher training materialized from this measure.

In 1851 it was observed in Tobago, also, that while there was an adequate supply of schools, the quality of education in schools was poor because the teachers were "comparatively uninstructed." This problem of finding proper persons to serve as schoolmasters was also continually mentioned over the years. Here, too, the want of means to pay for a better quality of teachers was at the root of the problem. The outcome was that primary education continued to be far from satisfactory. For example, some of the teachers were so poorly educated that they could not speak even moderately good English and were commonly making such grammatically incorrect statements as "Where did Moses born?" or "I did came yesterday."

To overcome this problem, it was suggested that the Anglicans, who were the main missionary group involved in providing education on the island, adopt a policy of training teachers locally, as the Moravians had done in Antigua. However, in view of the economic conditions, the authorities were not very optimistic about this possibility and indicated that there was little reason to expect any considerable improvement in the supply of better qualified teachers for the primary schools. But an attempt was made, through the system of payment by results, to improve teachers' incomes with the hope that this would help to overcome the problem of teacher shortage. However, this resulted in a de-emphasis on the professional preparation of teachers, since the assessment of the work of the school depended on the examination results of the students and much less on the teaching strategies used.

Even this system of payment by results, as the inspector of schools noted, was likely to pose some financial problems. He realized that with additional efforts on the part of the teachers and the increased numbers of pupils who attended school, the amount voted annually for education was likely to be exceeded when the system of payment by results was introduced. The over-expenditure of the education vote would eventually necessitate a reduction in the premiums paid to teachers which would have a negative motivating effect on their efforts to improve their own levels of education. The unpredictability of costs which accompanied the system of payment by results was also mentioned by the governor, who noted that "year by year, according to the efforts of the teachers and the increase in the schools the amount voted has been exceeded by the premiums, necessitating reductions to bring it within the grant."[12] This measure, which was aimed at motivating teachers to work harder, also had to be cut back because of lack of funds.

In British Guiana, efforts were made to provide a formal teacher-training facility but these also did not have any long-term success. In 1847-48 a minister of the London Missionary Society established a normal school in New Amsterdam without the aid of the government. However, this institution did not last very long. Bishop's College, originally established as a theological seminary, became a local centre for the training of pupil-teachers when the system was introduced in 1852, after the closure of the local Mico normal school. This institution made its greatest contribution as a normal school between 1877 and 1882 but after several years it was closed for financial reasons. For the remainder of the century, there were many half-hearted attempts to re-establish a teacher-training institution, but again none of these were successful. The result was a steady decline in the actual numbers and percentages of teachers with some form of professional training.

In this colony, too, suitably educated individuals were not attracted to the teaching profession because of low salaries. Nevertheless, by the 1850s, the Combined Court modestly boosted its education budget in order to provide a financial incentive for teachers to acquire higher qualifications. In 1852, they were placed on fixed salaries, according to the class of certificate which they held. In addition to the extra emoluments which certificated teachers received, their incomes were supplemented by the school fees that were paid under the existing Education Ordinance. It was expected that these measures would attract and/or retain superior quality individuals to the profession. But since the facilities to help them prepare for the local teachers' certificate examinations were not readily available, few benefited from this provision, and the measure was not as effective as had been hoped.

In order to raise the quality of the work offered by the teachers at its central schools, the government of British Honduras passed an Act in 1855 that required head teachers of these schools to be certificated from one of the institutions in the United Kingdom. However, this requirement was dropped in 1863 because of the difficulties and costs involved. By 1868, the government had abolished its central schools and introduced a new system of funding whereby the only aid to education was to be an allowance for each pupil in attendance. This sum was to be paid to all teachers who had been certified as competent to teach by the board of education.

The government of the Bahamas also regularly acknowledged the need for a teacher-training institution. A commission had earlier recommended the establishment of a normal school in Nassau, and in 1847-48, the legislature made liberal provision for such an institution by remodelling the central schools to convert them into a permanent and efficient teacher-training institution. In effect, two normal schools were created — one for boys and the other for girls. A master was appointed from "that excellent seminary," the Normal Institution in Glasgow, to undertake the duties of principal. To support the activities of this school, the board of education resolved not to engage anyone as a teacher unless the person had successfully attended a normal school. Five pupil-teachers were sent there for training and on completion of their course they were put in sole charge of schools.

Due to the low salaries paid to teachers here also, the profession was not very attractive to potential recruits. However, the quality of the work at the central school began to show a marked improvement and, as early as 1849, the attainment of the boys in the 3Rs and geography was said to bear comparison with that of boys in similar schools in Europe. Around 1849, the system of paid monitors and paid pupil-teachers was introduced in the colony as an attempt to attract a better quality of candidate into teaching. This proved fairly successful, and the project was said to have been highly stimulating to the efforts of the scholars.

The establishment of a regular normal training school was reconsidered by a legislative committee in 1856, although without any positive results. In 1864 the inspector of schools again emphasized the importance of teacher-training if there were to be well-organized and efficient schools. He further pointed out that, up to then, the colony had only one teacher who had received a systematic course of training as a pupil-teacher in the Central School. In 1870 the need for "a good general training school" for teachers was again mentioned, since this was seen as the "greatest defect" of the colony's educational system.

Yet the establishment of such an institution once more failed to materialize. Instead, monitors selected from the most suitable pupils over 11 years of age continued to do much of the teaching in schools. In return for their help they were provided with special instruction by their teachers out of school hours and eventually became pupil-teachers themselves. However, the supply of such apprentices to teaching was inadequate.

The board of education had also resolved that it would not engage any unqualified teacher and preferred those who had attended a normal school. But the implementation of this measure over a short period of time had an immediate negative effect on the local educational situation. It resulted in the dismissal of a substantial number of unqualified teachers whom the board was unable to replace immediately. As a result, a number of publicly supported schools had to be closed.

The board, recognizing that the low salaries of teachers were still largely responsible for the poor quality of the candidates attracted to the profession, informed the government that there was a great need to improve teachers' emoluments if the colony was to secure a "better and more efficient class" of teachers. The government's response was not very positive. However, an in-service teacher-training programme was tried out in 1866 and, as in some other colonies, teachers were encouraged to improve themselves by their own efforts. To this end, the inspector of schools gave each teacher in the government and government-aided schools three books on school management — *Dunn's Principles of Teaching, Girls' School Management*, and *Handbook to Model Schools*. Such attempts to improve teaching were not very productive, however, and up to the late 1860s, the school inspector still reported that, while there were "some zealous and sufficiently competent teachers . . . in general their qualifications . . . [were] but meagre. Few, if any . . . [were] acquainted with the recent improvements in the methods of instruction and management." The result was that "the amount of education in its true sense, and of instruction in its more limited sense, acquired in these schools . . . [fell] short of the intention and liberal provisions of the Legislature."[13]

However, it was hoped that this problem would be solved, since several young men were being trained as teachers and were expected to replace the incompetent ones when their training was completed. But in 1882, teacher-training was suspended and in 1884 it continued to be observed that, in several of the schools in the Out Islands, the teachers were "incapable of the task" of teaching, either due to their inadequate education or their lack of those qualities essential to being a good teacher. In 1892 a Normal Training Institute for Teachers was therefore opened, under the direction of one G. H. Smith, who was sent out to the colony by the British and Foreign Schools Society. However, this institution was closed after operating for only two years.

In Bermuda, also, the financial assistance provided for schools was insufficient to attract good teachers, and a shortage of qualified staff existed in most schools throughout the colony; this was most pronounced in girls' and infant schools. As a result, the idea of training local teachers in model schools was suggested, but with a private system of education, this was difficult to translate into practice. For this reason no normal school was established in this colony.

Elements of Teacher Preparation

Three of the most important aspects in the professional life of teachers were their religious and moral background, their general level of education, and the training they received. Of these, greatest emphasis was placed on the first area; the second was given less attention, while the third was often neglected. In Jamaica, candidates for admission to the Government Teachers' Training College at Stony Hill were expected to be well acquainted with the fundamental doctrines of Christianity. In addition, their "love of the work, regular habits, gentleness and religious consistency" were "more important than attainment and experience" in their selection for teaching positions. In other words, "moral qualities" were "to rank above mental" ones for those wanting to enter the teaching profession.[14]

The education levels of teacher trainees had improved over the years, judging from those who applied for entry into the Stony Plain Normal School. However, their overall academic standards were still quite low. This resulted in a continuing gap between the trainees' level of education after leaving the primary schools and that which was required to start the regular training programme at a normal school. In addition, it was pointed out that teachers, due to their limited training, lacked the tact and talent to impart what they knew.

The following were the expected levels of educational attainment at the various Teachers' Certificate Examinations:

1. The Third Class teacher would know how to read, write, and spell. In addition, he[15] would have enough knowledge of grammar to identify the parts of speech in a simple sentence. In arithmetic the teacher would be capable of working sums — both simple and complex — in the four rules.

2. The Second Class teacher would, in addition, be able to parse a simple sentence and work sums based on reduction, proportion, and practice. He would have a slight knowledge of history and geography, and know the weights and measures tables.

3. The First Class teacher, who was usually the product of a teacher-training institution, would have mastered all that was expected of a Second Class teacher and, in addition, would be capable of doing mental arithmetic, have a knowledge of "roots, prefixes and affixes" in English composition, and be able to produce and reproduce a short essay. Male teachers at this level were also expected to have some knowledge of book-keeping and geometry, while female teachers were to have some competence in Needlework. Credit was also given to those teachers who could teach singing from musical notes.[16]

In the teachers' training programmes in Jamaica the curriculum offered was even more ambitious. As previously pointed out,[17] in addition to moral science and a thorough preparation in Bible studies, the Mico normal school offered such subjects as "Sacred and Universal History, Geography, the Elements of Astronomy, Entomology, the Elements of Science as Applied to the Common Purposes of Life, Grammar, Composition, Mental Calculation and the higher branches of Arithmetic." The principal was even instructing his teacher trainees in the rudiments of Latin and Greek "in order to more successfully communicate to [them] the elements of an English education. This object is pursued whether the young men are able or incapable of speaking or writing their Mother tongue with propriety."[18]

Status of Teachers in the West Indies

Prior to 1845 the status of primary school teachers in the British Caribbean continued to remain very depressed, for the same reasons noted above. These included their low rates of pay, their inadequate academic and professional training, and the low status of most of their part-time colleagues, who were mainly manual workers.[19] Their poor social standing, to which the Reverend Josiah Cork of the Church Missionary Society referred in 1845, did not change very much during the second half of the nineteenth century. Cork[20] compared the status of teachers with that of other occupational groups and observed that, while a number of these groups, including the clergy, the customs, police and immigrations officers, and even the gaol-keepers had "a suitable provision and an honourable rank in society," the same could not be said of the public school teacher. He noted further that the government had neglected teachers and that the public showed little respect for the profession. Under these conditions, he suggested, no one would become a teacher if he/she could avoid it.[21]

In Grenada, it was pointed out that the status of teachers had not improved over the years, despite the increased demand for their services. As a result, primary schools continued to draw their teaching staff from the lower socio-economic groups and "the profession of pedagogy . . . [was] not infrequently adopted as a last resort when everything else had failed."[22]

In Trinidad, also, temporary masters came from among those individuals who were shoemakers, house-servants, and others who had difficulties in finding jobs elsewhere. Governor Harris and others recognized that the low status and poor pay of the teaching profession made it difficult to secure recruits from members of the "higher echelons" of society. Even the coloureds who had some level of education and wanted to become teachers tended to establish private schools where they enjoyed more prestige than in the state-aided schools.

The governor therefore felt it necessary to look to the clergy and to individuals from the lower class who possessed a "sense of mission" as potential recruits to teaching. In 1852, the inspector of schools noted that of those teachers who still remained in temporary charge of schools,

> two had abandoned the trade of shoemakers and turned
> schoolmasters, another had been elevated from the
> position of a house-servant to that of a teacher of youths,
> and some of the others had evidently adopted their
> present calling in consequence of other avenues of
> livelihood having been closed to them.[23]

In British Honduras, many individuals with enough education to become teachers preferred to work in a store, behind a desk or in a bank, rather than take on the "monotonous lonely and somewhat mechanical position" of a "town or village schoolmaster."

One inspector of schools reported that he had found a man teaching who had previously been a cart driver and "whose capabilities consisted of his wearing glasses, looking wise, being of a very plausible address, able to scratch his name and repeat — we cannot say read — the Lord's Prayer and most of the ordinary portions of the Church of England service."[24] Reference was also made to someone who was taken directly from the field and put in charge of a large country school but had subsequently returned to his hoe and was seen in the market "with provisions on his head." Another was dismissed for immorality, became a boatswain in a jail, but later resumed the office of a teacher, in charge of the very school from which he had been discharged. The writer further commented that such an individual, would, without doubt, disgrace the "school master's desk."

Teachers' Remuneration

The salaries of teachers had not markedly improved over the years, although a number of them were able to secure relatively high incomes, especially following the introduction of the system of payment by results. In some cases their salaries were as low as £10 per annum while others earned as much as £60 p.a., plus school fees which they were allowed to collect. The average annual income of schoolmasters as compared with other occupations in Jamaica in 1847 is indicated in table 1.

TABLE 1
Average Annual Incomes of Various Occupations in Jamaica, 1847

Merchants	£700
Planting Attorneys	£600
Professional People (Doctors, Lawyers), Bankers, Public Servants	£500
Ministers of Religion	£400
Surveyors & Tavern Keepers	£300
Architects	£200
Master Tradesmen	£150
Clerks	£120
Schoolmasters & Miners	£ 70
Journeymen	£ 50

Source: Douglas Hall, *Free Jamaica* (Yale University Press, 1959).

In 1884 teachers' incomes in Jamaica were still about the same as those of messengers or porters in the public service. However, the revised Education Codes of 1893 and 1895 tried to ensure that a teacher would earn enough to maintain himself respectably, despite the size of the school. As a result, the salaries earned by those in charge of the smallest schools were increased by between 50 and 100%. Some teachers earned substantially more with the introduction of payment by results[25] in 1866, and this often led to marked differences in incomes even among teachers in the same district. Because of this, the inspector of schools refused to believe that small salaries were the chief reason for the profession attracting an inferior class of individuals. He suggested that those with a sound educational background and a willingness to work hard could earn quite substantial incomes as teachers. In 1881 he even pointed out that, "the master of one of our average first class schools earns a much higher income here than a teacher of equal knowledge and capacity would do in Germany and England."[26] In Germany, the better teachers were said to be paid the equivalent of £45 p.a., while in Jamaica, where the living costs were much lower, they could receive up to £60 p.a. for working four days per week.[27]

Teachers' incomes were also differentiated on the basis of colour, sex, and marital status, with whites often being paid between 50 and 100% more than non-whites and married couples receiving higher salaries than single individuals. In Bermuda, for example, in 1875 the lowest paid teachers, who were mainly blacks, received one-tenth the amount paid to teachers at the highest end of the salary scale, who were usually whites. In British Guiana, a first-class female teacher received an income about one-third lower than that of her male counterpart. Such pay differentials were found in most of these colonies.

There were also cases in which teachers did not even receive a basic salary, but had to depend for their livelihood on the school fees they collected, plus part of the government grant that was given to the school. These low rates of pay also made it necessary for schools to continue employing, on a part-time basis, individuals who were often paid at even lower rates than the regular staff. This obviously had an influence on the quality and the social status of those who could be secured to teach part-time. Since they could not afford to maintain the more respectable appearance which was usually expected of the regular teacher, it was felt that their employment helped to depress the already low status of the profession.

Criticisms of the employment of these part-time teachers at low salaries were not uncommon. In a correspondence in the *Morning Journal* in Jamaica in December 1864, a writer accused those who were responsible for hiring such individuals of being, "highly culpable in sustaining a spurious system of education." He went on to claim that it was

> a positive injury to the cause of education . . . to have men as day-school teachers who are only fit for the field, carpenter's shop and cobblers' bench. By such a farcical patronage, qualified schoolmasters cannot succeed because the salaries with which pseudo teachers are satisfied, are spurned by those who respect their abilities as teachers of the young.[28]

The consequence of employing these "cheap, bargain-priced" schoolmasters, these "ignorant pretenders" to office, was that the job of the teacher was almost always despised. Many individuals relinquished their teaching positions for other employment because the salaries which were acceptable to these "schoolboy" teachers — being mere "monkey allowance" were insults to the more qualified individuals, Therefore, it was suggested that the sooner schools were freed from the "£8-£40 men," the better it would be for the teaching profession, parents, and students.

In view of their low salaries, it was little wonder that there was no strong sense of professional commitment by many teachers to their jobs. As

Governor Harris noted, it was "utterly futile to expect effective teaching from such materials" and he pointed out that, "the consequence has been that the drudgery of daily school teaching has been gone through, for the mere purpose of receiving the monthly allowance of government, without any active interest being manifested by the teacher for the progress of the children."[29]

In some cases, they even sought other employment opportunities to supplement their meagre incomes, such as becoming the district registrar of births and deaths. In the Bahamas, the involvement of teachers in outside commercial activities was obvious from the fact that the board of education found it necessary to rule in 1854 that no teacher in its employment was permitted to keep a retail store.

In 1875 the inspector of schools for Trinidad, recognizing that teachers' incomes on that island were often inadequate to meet all their living costs, suggested that there were additional opportunities open to industrious teachers to earn extra incomes during their leisure time, especially since they worked less than half the days of the year. They were even permitted to purchase books from local agents and sell them for 10% above their purchase price, keeping the profit for themselves.

In some colonies, other attempts were made to ease the financial burden faced by schoolmasters, especially those in the rural areas. Accommodation was sometimes provided for them rent free, they were allowed keep part of the school fees which they collected, and were permitted to accept private tuition fees from those who wanted extra lessons.

In 1849 the *Barbadian* newspaper[30] questioned whether the island could continue to obtain an adequate supply of competent teachers, if their current low rates of pay continued. By the mid-1860s, it was observed that teachers' incomes were further reduced due to declining economic circumstances of the region. As parents were experiencing difficulties in paying school fees, a substantial drop occurred in school enrollments, resulting in even further reductions in the grants to schools and, consequently, in the income levels of teachers. In 1875 the *Mitchinson Report*, after stating that the salary of a teacher in Barbados was "not sufficient to attract really superior men and women to make education their profession," also noted that a

> considerable number of pupil-teachers . . . diverge as soon as
> possible into other walks of life and become clerks in stores
> etc., not finding Education as a Profession sufficiently
> remunerative to attract them to it, in preference to other
> openings in life. . . . [Therefore] until education is elevated
> to an honourable and fairly lucrative profession, it is idle
> to expect those who have brains and energy to devote
> themselves to it [on a continuing basis].[31]

In 1848 the inspector of schools for British Guiana reported that the salaries of teachers were so low that they provided "insufficient encouragement" for persons of "any moderate attainments or practical ability to devote themselves to the arduous but respectable office of teachers of youths in this colony."[32] Referring to "the miserable pittance" which they received, he noted that this often fell far short of the sum that could be earned with little effort by the "common field labourer" or "ordinary mechanic."

The government also admitted that the funds allocated to education were insufficient to pay good teachers. Teaching, then, was the last resort of an individual who had failed in other attempts at earning his bread. In 1853 the school inspector again commented on the poor quality of teachers resulting from the grievous deficiency in the level of their academic and professional attainments which, in turn, were due basically to the low salaries which they were paid.

However, the situation improved after the 1850s when teachers were placed on fixed salaries that were supplemented by the allowances earned through the system of payment by results and by school fees collected in accordance with the existing ordinance. But, despite these developments, teaching at the elementary level remained one of the most poorly paid white-collar occupations in the colony — a fact which thereby continued to depress the status of the profession.

In 1874 Governor Longden appointed an Education Commission under the Chief Justice, Sir W. Snagg, to report on the educational situation in the colony. One of the factors to which the Commission attributed the low standards of the primary schools was the inefficiency of the school teachers. Because of the low salaries offered, the profession was failing to attract suitably educated individuals, and the Commission therefore recommended not only that teacher-training facilities be provided but also that teachers' salaries be improved in order to make the job more attractive to "a better class" of individuals, both socially and educationally.

In Tobago, in 1850, the small education grant had to be distributed among the different denominational bodies, so that teachers were paid even less than labourers who were engaged in "digging cane holes." Up to 1857, their situation had hardly improved, and the total emoluments of schoolmasters, including their pay from the government grant, the fees they collected from the children, and the stipend they received from the missionary society operating the school, remained on par with sugar plantation labourers. Incidentally, up to 1880, teachers in Tobago were still being paid quarterly, and the inspector urged the government to pay them monthly, since such a long time span between payments was a source of additional hardships for them.

In St. Vincent, a teacher's pay was not even equal to that of "an ordinary tradesman." Their low salaries were partly due to a proliferation of schools in some areas, which resulted from the persistent desire of the denominational bodies to establish their own institutions, even in communities where public schools already existed. The government would have preferred to have one good school in an area, offering a "respectable" salary to the schoolmaster and the pupil-teachers rather than a number of small schools in which the staff received meagre incomes. Therefore, a scheme for building Central Schools was eventually proposed, the aim of which was to reduce the number of smaller schools and teachers in each district and increase the emoluments of those who remained employed. But with the denominational control of schools, this change was difficult to implement.

The governor of the Leeward Islands, in commenting on the poor salaries of teachers in that colony, pointed out that there was need for additional funds to pay them the level of stipend that would ensure the supply to the profession of an "efficient" and "well qualified" class of men. Archbishop Jermyn also reported, around the mid-1850s, that "the class of persons employed as teachers, both male and female was "anything but satisfactory" due to the fact that "the salaries paid . . . [were] so small . . . and the payment even of these, . . . [was] so precarious and irregular that persons of intelligence, and sufficiently educated for the purpose, . . . [could] hardly be found to undertake the office."[33]

In 1890 attention was again drawn to the fact that "nothing has more retarded the progress of education in the [Leeward Island] colony than the want of skilled teachers in sufficient numbers,"[34] due largely to their low incomes. As a result, the Federal Council took steps to improve the situation, by introducing an Education Act which gave the Governor-in-Council the power to pass rules and regulations to adjust the salaries of teachers according to their assessed level of competence, as judged by their performance at the Teachers' Examinations. The Council used its authority to attract better qualified teachers by considerably augmenting their incomes through providing additional grants for those with certificates.

In St. Kitts, where, in the years immediately after 1849, there was no government grant to education, it was even more difficult to recruit suitable individuals as teachers because of the limited salaries which the missionary societies could afford. When the government suspended its contribution to schools because of lack of funds, teachers were the first to suffer. Their stipends were reduced further, despite the fact that their incomes were "already sufficiently scanty."

In Grenada, when the legislature failed to provide money for education, many teachers had to continue their jobs without the part of their incomes that usually came from government grants. In the Turks and Caicos Islands, teachers' incomes were also very low, especially in comparison with workers in the salt mines. This made it especially difficult for schools in this colony to secure the services of suitably educated individuals to become teachers. Up to the 1880s, salaries in the British Virgin Islands were so depressed that many teachers either left the colony for other islands, or took up other, more remunerative, but less respectable employment, usually as labourers. Some of the best teachers were therefore lost to the profession, and as a result, low morale prevailed among those who remained.

Due to the "insufficiency of funds" to pay them reasonable salaries, the government of British Honduras was unable to find properly qualified teachers to implement its planned changes to improve the colony's educational system. To raise the quality of its teaching staff, an Act was passed in 1855 which initially required a headmaster or mistress of its central schools to be a certificated teacher from one of the institutions in the United Kingdom. By 1868, the government introduced a new system of funding whereby grants to schools were to be paid only to teachers who had been certified as competent to teach by the board of education. But this new policy had the adverse effect on the income levels of uncertificated teachers who had to be employed because better qualified ones were unavailable. The alternative was to close the schools, and this often happened in the rural areas, thereby defeating the efforts to extend primary educational facilities throughout the colony.

In 1884 the council of education again tried to attract a better type of individual into teaching by increasing the allowances paid to those in the rural areas. But in 1892 there was a keen competition for the services of the few available teachers. The introduction of the system of annual examinations in 1894 was partly aimed at giving teachers the opportunity to improve their income levels by their own efforts.

In 1847 the governor of the Bahamas drew attention to the low salaries paid to teachers in that colony and the effects of this on recruitment to the profession. He therefore argued for an improvement in their emoluments in order to secure a "better and more efficient class" of teacher. Yet, almost two decades later, the newly appointed inspector of schools found that, due to the low status and pay, the profession still attracted a number of undesirable characters, among whom he found "considerable drunkenness and immorality." In 1871 he again noted that "good men can obtain higher wages as clerks or mechanics, than that paid to teachers. One accepts the office of schoolmaster because he can do nothing else."[35]

Other Effects of Low Level of Teachers' Salaries

With such low salaries paid to teachers the profession often had to accept as recruits individuals of questionable "moral quality." In 1845 the Anglican missionary J. Clark pointed out that the office of schoolmaster was not an honourable one, with the result that, "men of honour and integrity, intellectual power and moral worth" are not attracted to it. [36] This fact made it necessary for the governments of the Leeward Islands to state openly that they would deny the annual grant to a school if the teacher was known to be leading "an immoral and disreputable" life.

Many teachers throughout the region were falsifying their pupils' attendance registers in order to increase their emoluments — an act which was considered to be a reflection of their poor moral character. In Grenada, for example, the inspector of schools observed that there was "gross falsification" of attendance returns by teachers. The number of pupils recorded as present in school was always much lower on the days when the inspector visited the schools. While teachers tried to give some explanation for the "exceptionally low numbers" in school on these days, it was often regarded as a reflection of their dishonest practice in reporting higher attendance during the other days of the school year.

But the system of awarding grants to schools, as the inspector of schools noted, was itself "a thoroughly unsound one," "perfectly rotten to the core" and provided much temptation for teachers to falsify their attendance figures. For example, if attendance at a school fell below a certain minimum, the teacher received no payments at all, while payments went up, sometimes substantially, after that minimum number was reached. Those teachers who were honest, therefore, sometimes worked without salaries for one or perhaps two months in succession, or for a pittance, hardly enough to "keep them and their families on bread." On the other hand, those who were unscrupulous could and did make "fair salaries" by falsifying their records. While these assertions by the inspector were "strong" and "harsh," they were, as he pointed out, "not in the least exaggerated."

The difficulty of attracting suitable teaching recruits meant that even when teachers lost their jobs with one denominational body, they often found employment with another. This was quite common in most West Indian colonies and led the inspector of schools for Antigua to call for some general agreement among ministers of all denominations not to re-employ those who had been dismissed for immorality or other serious cause.

Another development was the increasing feminization of the teaching profession. Women were increasingly recruited as teachers partly because they were less costly than their male counterparts and partly to avoid any acts of immorality between male teachers and older female students. As a result, female enrollment in the training colleges in Jamaica, for example, rose from 11.2% in 1870 to 46.7% in 1894.

The low salaries also contributed to the fact that the profession often recruited individuals who had no real interest in teaching and who were poorly motivated. The inspector of schools in Trinidad often drew attention to teachers' disinclination to perform their work properly, while Keenan pointed out that, since their homes were invariably attached to the schoolhouses, their domestic duties and comforts frequently took precedence over their school work. They "indolently passed away the hours in their hammocks between the quarterly visits of the Inspector of Schools."[37]

A comment about the teachers in Grenada in 1857 suggested that some of them did make an effort to do well at their jobs, given the circumstances under which they worked. But most of the others lacked "that love of the work for its own sake which would animate them with a missionary spirit, and a deeper interest in the success of their labours."[38] Obviously, many people, including the missionaries, had high expectations of teachers. Strong religious commitment was also considered necessary, to give them the stamina to continue the task of teaching "in spite of a low salary."

Many local teachers also had the opportunity to serve as catechists and lay preachers, and the additional stipend for this extra responsibility made the job more financially attractive. The Anglicans even recruited their teachers for the joint roles of schoolmaster and catechist. For this reason, did not like to employ teachers from other religious faiths to serve in their schools. These opportunities to earn extra income made teaching somewhat more attractive, even to individuals of a "higher class" who saw it as a stepping stone to the ministry.

In fact, the inspector of schools advanced the view, in his 1861 report, that teaching in Trinidad need not be a "dead-end" job, since a number of the more successful teachers had experienced no difficulty in moving to other positions. Elaborating on this point, he noted that the lot of the local schoolmaster was not intended to be fixed "unalterably" to the "destiny of a school." Instead, he suggested, teachers might reasonably aspire to other jobs in the public service and promised that the government would be inclined to consider favourably their prior experience as teachers when making appointments.

The inspector's point was proven when, as of 1867, entrance to jobs in the public sector in Trinidad were made available through open competitive examinations which teachers also could take. Probably the most outstanding of the black teachers who were able to move out of the profession and into the civil service via this system was J. J. Thomas, who became the most senior black civil servant of the time. He was the son of, probably, an ex-slave and received his education in an ordinary primary school. Later he was trained as a teacher but continued to improve his education by his own efforts. Thomas won first place at one of the Civil Service Competitive Entry examinations, eventually becoming secretary to the board of education. Although he was even regarded as a prospective successor to the inspector of schools, Anderson, Thomas was not promoted to this position because of his colour. As the author of *Creole Grammar* and *Froudacity* , he was, however, regarded as a scholar, a "man of letters."[39]

But the exodus of the more successful individuals from teaching had adverse effects on the profession. Those who left teaching probably possessed the kind of leadership qualities that would have made a difference to the professionalization of elementary school teaching in the Caribbean. Since some of them became catechists or priests and in these roles were often appointed school managers or were otherwise still involved in the work of the elementary schools, it was not the case that their services were completely lost to the field of education. But they were no longer in a position to revitalize the profession from within its ranks, which was most needed.

Despite the various prejudices they experienced, primary school teachers in the Caribbean tended to enjoy a fair degree of respect from parents and other local community members, largely because many of them made an important contribution to the educational, social, political, and religious life of their communities. For example, in 1853 the governor of the Bahamas, drawing from his experience with the local teachers, went so far as to suggest that the colony could set an example of what could be done, through "the agency of the public schoolmaster, in elevating the intellectual and moral condition of the Negro."[40]

In addition, the fact that teaching was a white-collar job gave it considerable prestige in the eyes of the black manual workers in the region. Therefore, even with the extremely low levels of remuneration which many part-time teachers received, individuals continued to seek teaching jobs to supplement their incomes and possibly even enhance their status in society. Many black parents were also keen to see their children become full-time teachers because it was one of the few respectable occupations to which blacks could aspire.

Finally, there was some indication that teachers were beginning to develop a degree of professional pride in their work and were intent on taking measures to improve their prestige and status in society. They began to establish teachers' associations aimed at helping to improve the quality of their professional practice. In 1852 the British Guiana Teachers' Association was formed with the objective of working closely with parents for the improvement of their children's education. In 1882 the teachers in Jamaica also established professional associations throughout the island to promote "the interests of teachers to advance their profession, to increase the efficiency of their work, and generally to further the cause of elementary education in Jamaica."[41] The major organizer of the association identified its two major activities as "the dissemination among its members of educational books and periodicals and the holding of educational meetings."[42] Teachers in other West Indian colonies were soon to follow in the same direction.

Summary and Conclusions

The lack of professional training among teachers in the West Indies proved to be an important factor impeding the quality of education offered in the schools. The closure of all but two of the Mico normal schools in 1845 was a further drawback to efforts at improving the educational levels among teachers in the region. Various attempts were made to influence the local legislatures to provide funds for the establishment of more normal schools, but these were generally not very successful.

The other strategy to improve the quality of teachers in the region was to recruit those students who had a good primary school background to become monitors and subsequently pupil-teachers. This was possible because a few better primary schools had developed in these colonies, especially the model schools, which became increasingly important sources for the supply of monitors, pupil-teachers, untrained teachers, and teacher trainees. The pupil-teacher system, which eventually superseded the monitorial system, was also introduced during this period. The system was very popular and, in view of the lack or shortage of alternative teacher-training facilities, became the most important means by which teachers received some "practical" training in these colonies. This lasted the next three-quarters of a century.

Another step taken to improve teachers' educational standards was the introduction of Teachers' Certificate Examinations. Teachers were expected to study on their own for these examinations, although, in some cases, attempts were made by the local boards of education to provide in-service courses covering certain academic subjects, methods of class teaching, and school management. These courses were aimed at helping teachers improve both their knowledge of the subjects they taught and the quality of their teaching.

Based on the results of these examinations, teachers were awarded certificates of the first, second, third, or fourth class and, as an incentive, those who were successful were usually rewarded with higher incomes. In addition, school fees were often shared with the teachers so that, in Jamaica, it was estimated that a first class teacher with a school of 60 pupils could earn £77. 10s. p.a. A second or a third class teacher, in a school of the same size and with students who performed just as well, could earn between £50 and £60 p.a., and a fourth class teacher under the same conditions could earn £37. 10s p.a. Therefore, while grants to schools were paid on the basis of overall attendance and pupils' academic performance, the class of certificates obtained by teachers was increasingly taken into account in deciding their level of remuneration. This new reward system became quite popular among some conscientious, hard-working individuals.

Generally, the schools in the British Caribbean were, therefore, staffed by young, untrained, but slightly better educated ex-students from the primary schools who were expected to improve their standards either by self-study and/or "apprenticeship" through the pupil-teacher system. But despite this change, the most important factor which made it difficult to attract better educated recruits to teaching still remained the low incomes of teachers. This in turn affected the status of the profession and the socio-economic levels from which its members were drawn. Teaching tended to recruit individuals from the lowest socio-economic levels of the society and a few others from a higher status level who saw it as a useful means of upward social mobility, since it could enable them to become priests.

Some of the elites tried to underplay the gravity of the situation brought about by the low levels of remuneration offered to teachers by attempting to focus attention on the educational improvements that teachers had made possible over the years. For example, the governor of Grenada, in discussing the teaching situation on that island in the mid-1850s, suggested that "as a class the teachers are sufficiently qualified for the work at present before them. Many, having had the experience of several years, [of teaching] are fully competent to instruct" the children under their charge. But having made this point, he immediately admitted that

> if the labouring classes are to progress in life, and the standard of education is to be raised, and a more extended system of instruction adopted, as sooner or later must be the case, then a higher class of teachers will certainly be necessary. At present the existing staff is sufficient, only in so far as it prepares the way for a better one in the next generation. To simply give catechistical instruction, and teach spelling, reading and writing and the first principles of arithmetic does not require any great scholarship. It is the tact and talent to impart what little he knows that is the great desideratum in a teacher; and when we consider that several of them are élèves of these very establishments, and that the profession of pedagogy is not infrequently adopted as a last resort when everything else has failed, the surprise is not that we number so few of the literati in the corps [of teachers], but that so many are at all able to teach.[43]

While the quality of the instruction provided in some primary schools, especially the model schools, had improved somewhat, the standards in the other primary schools remained deplorably low. One of the reasons for this was the generally poor condition under which teachers laboured. In his 1857 report on education in Grenada, the inspector of schools attempted to give a composite picture of the problems which teachers faced and which affected the performance and the attendance of the students at school. The situation it described was not unlike that in the other West Indian colonies, and these conditions changed only very slowly over the next few decades. The report noted that

> condemned by the drudgery of a most laborious employment, with a mere pittance of a salary, with no cheering prospect of rising in his profession or bettering his

condition, and with hardly the countenance or sympathy of the public, the teacher is doomed to waste his energies frequently on a barren field, unaided, unnoticed and unknown. Is it any wonder then, that men of talent and education are unwilling to labour in the cause, and that [among] those who do many, after years of ineffectual struggles in an enervating climate, failing in their efforts to reduce into a beauteous shape or form, the rude intractable material they have to work upon, sink into apathy and indifference, and abandon at last their unprofitable labour in sheer disgust and utter disappointment.[44]

Nevertheless, by the mid-1880s, a certificated teacher was reported to have been in charge of every or nearly every school in some of these colonies, even on a small island like Grenada. This was regarded as an important indication of the progress that had been made in education. By then a new system of evaluating teachers' performance was in place which included a payment by results component. This brought about a substantial increase in the income levels of some teachers. But while these increases were enjoyed by relatively few teachers, by the late 1880s it was generally agreed, as the inspector of schools for Grenada observed, that there was "no master now who does not considerably better his position under the recent change in the manner of giving State aid" to education.[45] In other words, the conditions under which teachers laboured were slowly improving, and this was reflected in the higher academic performance of a small percentage of the students attending primary schools in the region.

Notes

1   Campbell, "The Development of Primary Education."
2   Report of the Government of Jamaica, *British Parliamentary Papers*, Vol. 34: *1849* (London: Government of Great Britain), 98.
3   Ibid., Vol. 44: *1882* (London: Government of Great Britain), 108.
4   Report of the Government of Grenada, *British Parliamentary Papers*, Vol. 10: *1857* (London: Government of Great Britain), 112.
5   Moxly, *An Account*, 175-76.
6   *Keenan Report*, 4.
7   Ibid., 28.
8   Report of the Government of Antigua, *British Parliamentary Papers*, Vol. 44: *1860* (London: Government of Great Britain), 79.
9   Report of the Commission on Education, Antigua, ag. C. Davis, Chairman, *British Parliamentary Papers*, Vol. 49: *1866* (London: Government of Great Britain), 116.
10   Report of the Government of Dominica, *British Parliamentary Papers*, Vol. 40: *1864* (London: Government of Great Britain), 100.
11   Report of the Royal Commission appointed December 1882, *Memo from J. Fadelle, Provost Marshall, Dominica*, 10 April 1883 (London).
12   Report of the Government of Tobago, *British Parliamentary Papers*, Vol. 44: *1882* (London: Government of Great Britain), 56.
13   Report of the Government of the Bahamas, *British Parliamentary Papers*, Vol. 49: *1866* (London: Government of Great Britain), 28.
14   Report of the Government of Barbados, *British Parliamentary Papers*, Vol. 34: *1849* (London: Government of Great Britain), 169-70.
15   Since teachers were mainly males, the masculine pronoun was often used in referring to teachers in general.
16   N. E. Cameron, *The Evolution of the Negro* (Georgetown, British Guiana: Argosy, 1934), 71.
17   Bacchus , *The Utilization* , 321.
18   Ibid.
19   Ibid., 305-310.

20 Josiah Cork, *Six Essays on the Best Mode of Establishing and Conducting Industrial Schools* (London: 1845), 209; Campbell, "The Development of Primary Education," 273-74.

21 Cork, *Six Essays,* 209; Campbell "The Development of Primary Education," 273-74.

22 Report of the Inspector of Schools for Grenada for 1855, 22 April 1856, *British Parliamentary Papers,* Vol. 10: *1857* (London: Government of Great Britain), 112.

23 CO 295/181, *Harris to Secretary of State,* 20 June 1853, 76.

24 Cyril Hamshere, *The British in the Caribbean* (London: Weidenfeld and Nicholson, 1972), 155.

25 Government of Barbados, *Blue Book for 1865* (Bridgetown, Barbados), 46.

26 Government of Jamaica, *Report of the Inspector of Schools for 1881* (Kingston, Jamaica, 1882).

27 Ibid.

28 *Morning Journal,* 13 December 1864; Campbell "The Development of Primary Education," 271.

29 CO 295/181.

30 *Barbadian,* 21 July 1849.

31 *Mitchinson Report,* 4-5.

32 Report of the Government of British Guiana, *British Parliamentary Papers,* Vol. 46: *1847-48* (London: Government of Great Britain), 143.

33 Report of the Government of St. Kitts, *British Parliamentary Papers,* Vol. 42: *1856* (London: Government of Great Britain), 138.

34 Report of the Government of the Leeward Islands, *British Parliamentary Papers,* Vol. 52: *1892* (London: Government of Great Britain), 15.

35 Government of the Bahamas, *Report of the Inspector of Schools for the Bahamas* (Nassau, Bahamas, 1871).

36 Cork, *Six Essays* 209; Campbell "The Development of Primary Education," 273-74.

37 *Keenan Report,* 9.

38 Government of Grenada, *Report of the Inspector of Schools for 1855* (Grenada, 22 April 1856).

39 See Campbell, *The Young Colonials.*

40 Report of the Government of the Bahamas, *British Parliamentary Papers,* Vol. 62: *1852-53* (London: Government of Great Britain), 46.

41 Report of the Government of Jamaica, *British Parliamentary Papers,* Vol. 45: *1883* (London: Government of Great Britain), 21.

42 Ibid.

43 Government of Grenada, *Report of the Inspector of Schools for 1855.*

44 Ibid.

45 Report of the Government of Grenada, *British Parliamentary Papers,* Vol. 52: *1884-85* (London: Government of Great Britain), 134.

CHAPTER 8

PRIMARY EDUCATION, 1846-95:
SUMMARY AND CONCLUSIONS

Review and Assessment

The period from 1846 to 1895 started inauspiciously with the termination of the imperial Negro Education Grant. As a result, the financing of elementary education was increasingly thrown onto the shoulders of the local legislatures, missionary societies, and parents. But even though the British government was no longer willing to contribute to the cost of educating the children of the ex-slaves, it continued to provide moral support for the idea that primary education should be extended as widely as possible among the masses. These colonies were even encouraged to consider the introduction of compulsory education.

During the first part of this period, the extension of educational facilities proceeded very slowly. For example, in Trinidad, between the 1850s and the 1870s, Campbell observed that the school system was virtually in "a stage of stagnation." A number of factors contributed to the slow pace at which education developed, especially prior to the 1870s, as well as to the low level of performance by the pupils. These included (1) the poor academic and professional training of the teachers, which was partly due to their low salaries. Despite their limited education, some teachers even attempted to offer instruction on topics about which they knew little or nothing; (2) the pupils' irregular attendance; (3) the attitude of the parents, who allegedly did not "evince a sufficient appreciation of the blessings of education";[1] (4) the unfamiliarity of students with English, the only language of instruction used in schools; (5) the irrelevance of the reading materials used in schools and the pupils' lack of acquaintance or experience with the objects referred to in these materials; (6) the shortage or almost complete absence of other instructional materials and teaching aids in schools; and (7) the poor physical conditions under which teachers worked, including the dilapidated nature of most of the school buildings and the "lack of sympathy" and support from the public for their work.

The following assessment made by the governor of Antigua in the 1850s applied equally to the educational situation in the other British Caribbean colonies. After noting that school attendance was beginning to rise again, the governor went on to express his doubts about the quality of the work in most schools, indicating that he was

> not aware that any substantial or permanent improvement
> [in the quality of education] has taken place: [and] so long as
> the funds disposable are inadequate to procure the services
> of properly qualified teachers, the efficiency and usefulness
> of the schools must be seriously diminished.[2]

The poor quality of the teaching and the teachers' low level of education meant that the efforts which they sometimes made to broaden the educational background of the pupils were not very successful. Therefore, the subjects offered in most schools were

> in practice confined to the three R's, Reading, Writing and Arithmetic, taught with varying degrees of efficiency, but mostly with a poor degree of success since it did not create a literate population in the West Indies. Where additions were made to the curriculum, such as in Geography, History and Religious Knowledge, they were in fact selections of information to be learnt by heart and repeated verbatim.[3]

Some Positive Outcomes of Primary Education

Three approaches were used to assess the outcomes of primary education during this period. One dealt with the number of students who had acquired some acquaintance with the "elements of learning"; the second was concerned with the quality of instruction that was offered in schools; the third was the impact which the schools were having on the life of the local communities. The available evidence indicates that, despite the many difficulties and drawbacks faced in providing education, a "fair" degree of progress had been achieved in the region in all three areas.

Quantitative Increases in Education

While primary school enrollments and average attendance fluctuated considerably, especially before the 1870s, the number of children attending school rose steadily. However, the rate of increase in average attendance did not always keep pace with increases in enrollments and, therefore, the percentage of those attending school regularly declined slightly as the enrollments increased. Evidence of this "decided improvement" in school enrollments can be seen in almost every island of the British West Indies. For example, in 1861 in Jamaica, about 8% of the island's total population was attending school. By 1891 this had increased to 15.6%. During these three decades, the percentage of those over five years of age who could read and write rose from 31.3% to 52.5%,[4] and the numbers in schools more than doubled between 1871 and 1891, rising from 40,610 to 99,760 — an increase of about 146%.

In 1879 the inspector of schools, in commenting on the "steady progress" that was being made in education, noted that school enrollments had increased by over 160% between 1868 and 1878, even though total average attendance had only risen by about 143%. Further, by the mid-1880s children had, on the average, about three years of elementary schooling, as compared with two years during the earlier years. If those who, for one reason or another, were not even enrolled in schools were deducted from these figures, it would have been seen that the average length of schooling for those who received an education had risen considerably. Moreover, average attendance was rising, especially after the late 1860s, and by 1892 it had reached about 66.4%. While this figure was about 11% lower than England and Wales at the time, it was substantially higher than in the past years. In response to the growing desire of some parents to see their children receive more education, the official age limit for children to remain in school was raised to 16 years in 1894, even though these older children were not recognized by the government for funding purposes.

In 1867 it was reported that the educational facilities in Barbados were becoming so widespread that schools were within easy distance from all, while in Trinidad, too, it was observed that there was some improvement in the amount of education that was being provided at the elementary level. For example, enrollments in the ward schools rose by 11% (or 1.1% per annum) from 1858 to 1867, while average attendance figures increased somewhat more slowly — at an average of 0.22% per annum. In addition, about three-quarters of the children who attended school stayed on to proceed beyond "the second book." Comparable levels of educational expansion were also seen in British Guiana. In 1851 only 10% of the inhabitants of that country were able to read and write. This figure rose to 14% in 1871 and then to 27.8% by 1891. While the numbers of literate and numerate individuals only increased by 4% from 1851 to 1871, they nearly doubled between 1871 and 1891. According to the figures supplied in a government report, school enrollments rose by about 146%[5] during these four decades. In British Honduras, about 70% and 90% increases were recorded in the total average enrollment and average attendance, respectively, between 1871 and 1891.

In 1882 Grenada was said to have succeeded "in placing within reach of the bulk of the people that sound primary teaching and training which is essential from childhood upwards to fit them to participate in the many advantages and employment in a civilized community."[6] By 1889 both enrollment and attendance had improved quite substantially. At that time, a spate of school-building activities was undertaken. Two new schools were constructed, 15 were rebuilt by the government and eight others were repaired or enlarged through a government grant. In order to facilitate the development of education in the "Out Islands," the government of the Bahamas established a grants-in-aid programme in 1883 which provided public funds to establish schools on these islands. This change from previous practice, when the population was expected to build their own schools, resulted in a great boost in enrollments. By 1899 J. W. Root acknowledged that, "excellent educational facilities existed in the West Indies." This, he claimed, was "beyond dispute. There are good schools and colleges [secondary schools] with efficient masters, substantial endowments [these were mainly in Jamaica and to some extent in Barbados also] and a number of scholarships, some of them to English Universities."[7]

This fairly steady increase in school enrollments which began to occur just before the 1870s resulted from a number of factors, including the availability of more school places, an improvement in the quality of education offered in some elementary schools in the region, the introduction of a competitive examination to select more educated individuals for teaching posts, and the scholarships that were made available for primary school students to attend one of the local grammar schools. In 1890, a regulation was passed in Antigua and in other colonies to restrict the employment of children under nine years of age. It also imposed on parents the duty of ensuring that their children receive a sound education. The legislature empowered the governor to erect and maintain proper and sufficient schoolhouses so that no child could be denied an education because of lack of facilities. Overall, this Act, too, resulted in a "dramatic increase in enrollment and average attendance."[8]

However, despite these developments, the number of children benefiting from schooling was limited and usually did not exceed 50% of the 5-12 age group, though the figure was lower in many colonies. If one added those who did not receive any formal instruction during slavery to those who were unable or unwilling to attend school after emancipation, it was evident that the educational challenge that still faced the West Indian colonies was tremendous. Commenting on this point, Ryall noted that

> thousands of children were introduced to popular branches of education. . . . But the *slow pace of progress* and also *the limited number of individuals* who could claim *to be real beneficiaries* were indications of the size of the task of educating a population which had a tremendous backlog of ignorance and illiteracy [emphasis added].[9]

The educational challenge which these colonies faced led fairly early to discussions about the desirability of introducing compulsory education. Little effective action was taken on this issue, though, because the costs were prohibitive. However, some West Indian governments, as indicated above in the case of Antigua, began to enact legislation which prepared the ground for the introduction of compulsory schooling.

It was not so much that money was unavailable to provide compulsory education as it was a question of priorities. For example, expenditure on the repressive state apparatus (RSA), such as the police and the prisons, was considered a more reliable way of controlling the population than was education. Thus, expenditure on the RSA continued to remain many times higher than that on schools, even though the gap between the two areas of spending slowly decreased.

The actual percentage of the school-age population attending school varied quite considerably between colonies and economic groups. Attendance also fluctuated with the season and even with the days of the week, being lowest on Fridays and Mondays. In colonies like Jamaica, schools were usually not in operation on Fridays and in a year there were only about 100 school days in many of these colonies. This figure, while lower than those for the northern states of the USA, was higher than those for some of the southern states. In general, up to the end of the nineteenth century, a great deal still needed to be done to improve the availability of elementary education in the West Indies. In addition there were setbacks due to the poor state of the economy, ill-health among children, the climate, etc. For example, the efficiency of schools in Jamaica was said to have suffered for at least six years after the Jamaican hurricane in 1880. But, as was suggested above, "real progress" had been made not only in the larger colonies like Jamaica, Barbados, Trinidad, and British Guiana, but also in most of the smaller ones.

Qualitative Improvements in Education
Although the availability of educational facilities throughout the region was increasing, the reports of the inspectors of schools were sometimes highly critical of the quality of the instruction offered in schools. Yet the available evidence indicated that some improvement took place in this area also. Around the late 1860s, Savage, the inspector of schools for Jamaica, noted that many students left the primary school with some knowledge of reading

and the Scriptures, a limited grasp of the rudiments of writing and arithmetic, and with a smattering of grammar, geography, and history.

In addition, of the 286 schools that were inspected in 1870, 96 met the required standard for a government grant. But over the next few years, the percentage of these schools increased substantially, as did the number of first and second class schools. Despite his earlier criticism of their work, in 1871 Savage observed that the schools had shown an encouraging improvement in their results. Six years later, after noting that grants to schools now depended "upon the amount and character of the entire work of the teacher," he suggested that "the great increase in grants-in-aid year by year . . . attest[ed to] the progressive improvement in the character of the instruction imparted in the schools."[10] In the early 1870s the inspector of schools noted that,

> It is gratifying now to find that . . . notwithstanding some opposition at first, and a good many difficulties that had to be encountered, we are able to report as a very marked and decided advance, both in the number and conditions of the schools. Generally, the system is working smoothly and giving general satisfaction to all the true friends of education.[11]

In 1882 the governor also noted that while "there is a very great deal yet to be done to improve the elementary schools of the Colony," especially when such factors as the number of "incompetent teachers" employed were taken into consideration, nevertheless, it was evident that "real progress" had already been made. He went on to suggest that "any passer-by today, contrasting his experiences with those of twenty years ago, cannot fail to admit that education of the people has greatly improved."[12]

In 1884 Capper, the school inspector, observed that, considering that freedom had come less than 50 years before, the efforts of the government and of the religious societies in providing a fairly good education in the region had resulted "in great advantage" to the people, and had been highly appreciated. In the following year, Plummer, the assistant inspector of schools for Jamaica, also noted that

> there is an erroneous opinion that no substantial progress in the education of the masses has been made. My opportunity of comparing the present with the past enables me to say most emphatically that a very marked and gratifying progress has been made.[13]

As further evidence of this improvement in the quality of education offered in schools, one sees that in 1887 the number of first class schools had risen by about 30% over the previous years. The inspector of schools suggested that this was not due to any relaxation of standards, but mainly to the annual increase in the number of trained teachers entering the profession. The substantial rise in enrollments which occurred in 1888 was ascribed to the proper appreciation by the parents of the better teaching power that was becoming available in the schools.

In Trinidad, there were indications that improvement in the quality of elementary education had taken place over the years. For example, in 1854, the inspector of schools, in commenting on the educational standards achieved by pupils, noted that in the schools the prominent *points of proficiency are so few* and the symptoms of *mediocrity and ignorance so general* among the pupils, that a detailed statement of their individual acquirements must necessarily be limited. . . . The children meet together irregularly; they are in general badly provided with books, in some cases not at all and *the little acquaintance they show with even the elements of learning,* demonstrate but plainly that their attendance at school has been little better than a matter of form [emphasis added].[14]

Most students were leaving school with only a smattering of knowledge of the subjects taught and without a strong hold on literacy.

However, about seven years later, it was observed that the educational situation had slowly improved and the report on education for the year mentioned that "in the great majority of . . . [elementary] schools the more advanced pupils can read and spell readily and correctly" and "they can work sums in the four rules." In addition, they had some knowledge of the geography of the "four quarters of the globe" and could "write fairly and generally correctly, passages by dictation; while in some schools there . . . [were] pupils who . . . [could] parse sentences very creditably."[15]

Despite this improvement, the inspector of schools still suggested that, judging from the pupils' knowledge of these "elements of learning," their attendance at school had in some cases been little more than a mere formality. However, he did admit that this did not apply in general. Keenan, too, noted that, although the system revealed many weaknesses, if it had not been for the schools, the children in many parts of the colony would have been growing up without any education at all.

But there was a degree of exaggeration in some of the observations about the amount of improvement which had occurred in the educational standards of the primary schools. This can be seen when one considers Keenan's criticisms of the pupils' academic performance in 1869, at which time he observed that education was generally characterized by "bad schoolmanship."

The more glowing references to improvements in pupils' standards of education mentioned by the inspector of schools in the quotation cited above most likely referred to the academic work being done by the more advanced pupils — i.e., those who had stayed in school for longer than the average period of time in the hope of becoming teachers or securing other white-collar jobs. His observations would not have applied to the majority of the elementary school population, who left school after barely acquiring some of the basic literacy and numeracy skills. The real educational condition of the population probably fell somewhere in between the descriptive accounts presented by Keenan and the inspector of schools.

In 1847 Rawle described the educational system in Barbados as "deplorable" and a "wretched failure," with much of the money spent on it as "wasted." But by the late 1860s it was observed that this island had made "considerable progress" in education, not only in terms of the numbers who were attending school, but also in the "passes" the students obtained at the annual inspection. In 1862, the inspector of schools, Elliott, indicated that he was satisfied that the system of education was progressing at a pace equal to that attained in the Mother Country. In addition, the children were being taught by fairly efficient teachers, in decent buildings suitably furnished and quite well supplied with school materials. These developments indicated that there was a greater level of proficiency achieved by the pupils, especially in the higher subjects that were offered in some schools. This was said to have been due to the increased faithfulness in the teaching being carried out and as a result of the efforts made to raise the quality of the teaching staff.

In Dominica, the percentage of schools that failed to achieve the standards set by the government inspector dropped from 81% in 1875 to 30% in 1881. By 1882, the inspector-general of schools for the Leeward Islands commented on the "steady progress" that had been made in the field of elementary education.[16] In Antigua, the school inspector noted in 1876 that, despite all the problems faced by education on the island, "the real wonder . . . [was] that so much should nevertheless have been achieved up to the present time towards the general spread of that elementary knowledge which should be looked upon as one of the birthrights of civilization."[17] A few years later, in the early 1880s, Admiral Sir A. Cooper Key examined two schools on the island and in his report indicated that in comparison with many other schools they were few in the West Indies and North America to equal and none to surpass these two schools in Antigua. In 1877, the island's inspector of schools drew attention to a letter he had received from a beneficed clergyman in England who had worked in Antigua. In the letter the clergyman stated, "I have seen a great many schools lately of various kinds, but I have not often met with agricultural schools which, on the whole were better . . . than a dozen schools I could name in Antigua."[18]

In St. Kitts, it was noted that, by the 1860s, the teachers employed in the elementary schools were superior to those of previous years and that this was reflected in the quality of the education offered in the schools. In St. Vincent, it was reported that by 1883 a general improvement had taken place in the colony's educational system and that a number of inefficient teachers had been weeded out. By that time the schools in the British Virgin Islands which had increased in numbers were also better organized, schoolmasters were provided where necessary, and periodical examinations had been instituted. One of the results of this was that school enrollments, average attendance, and the quality of the work done by the students were reported to have increased quite substantially.

Some Alternative Views about the Qualitative Outcomes of Primary Schooling

However, while there were signs of improvement in West Indian education, the standards achieved were not always considered satisfactory. Improvements were very slow, due partly to a number of external factors. For example, the inspector of schools for Grenada observed that in 1856, although the children in the primary schools were exhibiting "a creditable amount of proficiency" in various subject areas, there was as yet, "abundant room for improvement." He noted that

> most of them read fluently, but do not spell well. Some write pretty correctly from dictation, and in cyphering they understand the rules they have passed. Their copybooks and cyphering books are clean and neatly kept. . . . They all excel in writing. . . . Many show an aptitude for learning but the

short time they are permitted to stay at school, [usually two years] and the irregularity of their attendance prevent them from acquiring the full benefits which the institution is capable of affording.[19]

In Tobago, when R. G. Rice took over as superintendent of the Scarborough Boys' School in 1856, he observed that "on entering the discharge of my duties here I found the boys to evince not only little knowledge of the common branches of an elementary education but also total ignorance of anything like scholastic discipline."[20] In 1884, in British Honduras it was pointed out that with each succeeding generation a slight improvement in the educational levels could be seen. However, it was suggested that when one looked back at the efforts that had been made since 1816, when the first free school was established, and compared this with "the result at the present day," it was obvious that it required "much courage to continue labours having so unproductive results."[21]

Many planters and other members of the elite group also remained critical of the outcomes of education in the region, including its assumed irrelevance to the lives of potential estate labourers. In most of these colonies it was constantly reported that the kind of instructional programme offered by the elementary schools was irrelevant to the needs of the vast majority of working-class students who were likely to return to earn their living from the soil or enter into some skilled or semi-skilled occupation. The president of St. Kitts, in commenting on this point, noted in 1857 that education was still unsuited for those who were destined to be engaged in "agricultural production." Later, he continued to observe that the schools offered their pupils "a useless course of studies when viewed in connection with [the needs of] a labouring population."[22] Similar criticisms were made in many other Caribbean territories. It was often pointed out that some teachers, instead of imparting such useful knowledge as the 3Rs, introduced abstruse subjects into the classroom, and neglected to emphasize the type of instruction that was "most necessary" for the future lives of the students.

In 1857, in a communication with the governor-in-chief of the Leeward Island colony, Blackwell, lieutenant-governor of Dominica, also claimed that, despite the liberal grants made by the legislature, progress in education was unsatisfactory, largely because the curriculum was irrelevant to the needs of the population. He went on to note that, "we have begun in too high a key. The subjects chosen are of too scientific a character, even for a labouring population much more advanced in civilization than ours." What the "rising generation" needed was "a little reading, writing and arithmetic — with strict attention to discipline and developing habits of industry." With the current programme of instruction offered in schools, such discipline and industry were underemphasized and, as a result, "the difficulties in *controlling them* [the youths] . . . [were] daily increasing."[23]

In 1860 Price, the new lieutenant-governor of Dominica, commented on the same issue and suggested that the attempts to make "education subservient to usefulness in after life has not been crowned with success." He went on to point out that "it is cruel to give children knowledge . . . which they cannot put to practical use."[24] Three years later, he again expressed the view that the education provided was not very useful to the students when they left school. He argued that it was of little value to the future agricultural labourers to fill their heads with subjects such as "high mathematics" or even science which they could not later use to earn a living. Price therefore proposed that the primary school curriculum should focus more on subjects which could fall under the description of industrial education.

In Nevis, education was considered "hardly common" and not "practical enough." President Seymour noted that it was "somewhat startling to hear [in West Indian classrooms] the hardest words of the Linnaean Vocabulary — names belonging to the natural history, not of these islands, but of Australia and Siberia — coming from the lips which have nothing to tell you of the commonest methods by which mechanics . . . earn their bread."[25] In the 1880s, also, the inspector of schools reported that he even came across a teacher who was instructing his class in the "theory of Tides," when a knowledge of the 3Rs was all that was necessary. Further, the education being offered was said to have an undesirable impact on the students because it raised their occupational aspirations to an unrealistic level, thereby unfitting them to later engage in agricultural labour.

According to the chief administrator of St. Kitts, this education merely gave students an inflated impression of themselves, making them less willing to accept their subordinate position in the occupational and social structure. In 1860 the administrator noted that some teachers, "instead of imparting that knowledge which is alone necessary to a labouring population such as the 3Rs," attempted to teach their students other subjects, and thereby neglected the type of "instruction which . . . [was] most necessary" for their future livelihood. They offered "a useless course of studies when viewed in connection with [the needs of] a labouring population." Therefore, much of the skills acquired at the elementary level were of little use to them in real life. Such education not only "did little to fit its recipients for the[ir] most ordinary duties" it also provided limited opportunities for the occupational and social mobility which many of these parents "had anticipated and hoped for" as an outcome of their children's schooling. They therefore began to react with "an utter indifference" to education. In fact, "education, or what was called such, having failed to show them [the parents and the pupils] how to cultivate the soil better, to make more money, to *improve their circumstances*, or to *advance themselves in life*, was considered a failure."[26]

In 1877, in St. Lucia, it was observed that although many pupils left school with only a smattering of the 3Rs, they felt that their education should place them substantially above the level of their "illiterate [fellow] countrymen." They despised the manual work in which they were engaged and only wanted occupations of a higher status, even though they were not qualified for these positions.

In 1856, the newly appointed inspector of schools for the Bahamas observed that despite the "sagacious liberality" of the government, the outcomes of schooling were not "proportionate to the liberality." He drew particular attention to the defect that was said to have arisen because schools either did not introduce their students to, or did not sufficiently emphasize, industrial or practical education, which "could mould their habits to a life of steady labour."[27] In addition, he opined that the clergy and teachers should induce the population to devote their energies to agriculture if these islands were to progress.

While the governor was not prepared to accept the extreme view of the negative impact of education on the work attitudes and moral behaviour of the students, he indicated that he thought that the local schools might have erred by not impressing on the students "the dignity of honest labour" and the idea that freedom was not incompatible with the existing gradations of the social order. The major exception, as far as the irrelevance of the curriculum was concerned, was the basic literacy and numeracy that pupils were able to acquire. However, many left schools with very elementary skills in these areas, and soon lost them through lack of use.

However, while the elites saw the lack of a practical course of instruction in schools as evidence of their failure, most parents continued to consider education in terms of the mobility opportunities it provided for their children. But they too saw the schools as failing, since the education which their children were receiving did not open doors to white-collar jobs nor was it particularly useful for their lives after leaving school.

The Impact of Primary Education on Community Life

Schools were generally considered to have a positive influence on the quality of life in their communities. For example, in Trinidad, it was pointed out that popular education helped to improve the overall society by giving "a higher and kindlier tone to the life of the community in all its moral and social relations."[28] In 1868, Guppy, the inspector of schools, observed that "the influence of the education obtained at the government schools" was "not confined to those who have immediately received it, but that the tone of whole districts has been raised by the increased intelligence and the higher views thereby diffused."[29] It was noted that there was a marked difference in the demeanour and mode of life exhibited by inhabitants in districts where there were schools, as compared to those where there were no schools. In the latter the inhabitants were described as "rude and barbarous," while in the former they were comparatively "well behaved and orderly," and possessed of a greater desire to "conform to the manners" and avail themselves of the "convenience of civilized life."[30] The presence of a school in an area also contributed to the spread of the English language, especially in the more remote districts where the language was previously unknown. In 1869 even Keenan suggested that the spread of education throughout the island had produced an "increased intelligence" and a "higher view" of life among the population.

Similar observations were made about the positive influence of schooling on local communities in many of the other colonies. In Jamaica, for example, the inspector of schools suggested the favourable impact of the elementary schools on the self-reliance of the negro population, by pointing out that

> in my tour of the West [of the Island] I visited two schools which have been established by the people themselves without any assistance whatever from any societies or the Government. They had organized their own school committees, laid down rules for themselves, and agreed to pay certain rates to secure this important object. They had, moreover, so far as their scanty means would allow, built tolerably fair school-houses . . . and had furnished their children with fair supply of books and other appliances.[31]

He also remarked upon the growing interest of members of the community in education, noting that

> the amount of annual grants earned by schools and paid by the Government is more than three times as much as in the first year [of the new system of grants, i.e., 1868]. A real interest is awakened among the people of all classes on the subject of education. Trade is evidently beginning to feel an upward tendency, owing to the increased intelligence of the people; and such a start has been given to the enlightening and elevating influences of education, as to afford the cheering prospect of Jamaica becoming in time, a highly civilized and prosperous country. [32]

In St. Kitts, it was suggested in 1863 that, partly as a result of schooling, the "labouring population" was "steadily improving in morals and intelligence." Further, notwithstanding the very severe privations to which they were subjected by the recent droughts, they conducted themselves on the whole, in the "most peaceful and orderly manner."[33] In the Bahamas, the governor reported that he had reason to believe that "teachers are exerting a salutary effect, not only on the children but also on the community."[34]

There was also some evidence to indicate that primary education helped to raise the educational and occupational aspirations of those members of the local communities who had been to school. This was seen by the demand in some colonies for continuing education, which led some governments to establish such institutions as public libraries. These helped to improve or maintain the levels of literacy in the local communities.

Following the provision of a library for teacher trainees, the government of the Bahamas established a public library with 1,860 volumes, along with a reading room and a museum. The library was to include books suitable for the "labouring classes," and readers were to have access to it by paying a "low level" of subscription. In the attempt to develop a more comprehensive programme of popular education, school libraries were also started in 1850, and it was hoped that a further extension of such "useful auxiliaries" would continue. In response to public demand, the government of St. Vincent also encouraged the establishment of a public library and proposed to set up a literary and scientific institute.

In the 1850s a small public library was established in Barbados that contained 700 "well-selected" books. This venture had much public support and received a "meagre" assistance from the legislature. In Grenada, the public library in St. George's had an "excellent collection" of about 5,630 books, which were very much used, and a small library was established in Grenville, the second town on the island. A public library also existed in St. Lucia, though it was reported that only a small minority on the island were members and made use of this facility. This was probably due to the low percentage of the population who were literate in English. Around 1872 the government of Antigua took over a library that had been originally established by a private association.

In 1871 the booksellers in Kingston, Jamaica, reported that sales of school requisites had been much greater than at any previous period in the history of the island, another indication that the educational standards of the population were continuing to improve. The 1882 Royal Commission on the financial situation of the West Indian colonies advocated the opening of reading rooms in rural areas, similar to those in the towns and which secured their supplies of books through their affiliation with the Institute of Jamaica. In 1883 it was noted that very "encouraging success" had followed the establishment of adult and juvenile reading clubs on the island, and it was felt that these would continue to have a generally beneficial effect on the society as a whole. In 1884 the inspector of schools again observed that attendance at these adult and juvenile reading clubs was encouraging and suggested that they were even likely to have a marked influence on the work of the schools. In addition, he commented on the effect they were likely to have on the children who had left school in giving them the incentive that was previously lacking to keep up their "acquirements in reading," and to extend their general knowledge.[35]

The annual report on Jamaica for that year also drew attention to the recent establishment of more book clubs on the island — probably a consequence of increased literacy. It continued to be mentioned that this should further help in "counteracting the tendency" for those who leave the elementary schools to lose their reading skills. With the cheap prices of books that were made available in some of the islands through "American Reprints of English works," the problem of securing funds to purchase books was not as formidable as it was in the past.

However, literature suited to the "capacities and tastes of the humbler classes" was not usually available and was "a bar to the spread of general useful information" on matters and things "outside their little world." The reports on British Honduras in 1883 indicated that there was serious loss of reading and writing skills when students left school after having received a few years of education. This was happening throughout the West Indies, where "the majority of children, having no occasion to make use of the knowledge they had acquired," in school, "soon forget all they have learnt, and the instances are many where scholars who have passed the second and third standards within a few years afterwards, prefer making a cross to signing their names."[36] The establishment of libraries was to help grapple with this problem.

The impact of education was also seen in the increased number of locally published newspapers appearing in the various colonies, and it was hoped that these publications would further stimulate the reading habits of the population. For example, around 1885 three newspapers were started in the Bahamas and although they were mainly concerned with pointing out the grievances of the coloured population, their appearance on the market indicated that there was a certain section of the population able and willing to read them. In the other colonies there were also newspapers which were produced mainly by the middle-class non-white population.

Finally, education was seen to have contributed to the development and strengthening of the sense of loyalty to the British Crown, both among the emerging middle class and the masses, and schools made an important contribution in this area. This was accomplished through the formal curriculum, including the textbooks that were being used, and the informal curriculum, as manifested in such activities as the celebration of the Queen's Birthday or Empire Day. In addition, loyalty to the Crown and to the metropole was inculcated as part of the moral training students received.

Even in Trinidad, it was noted in 1847 that, although the "ties of blood" might not connect the population of that island with that in Great Britain, there was "a general feeling of satisfaction at being under her protection, of confidence in her power and loyalty to her Government."[37] In Jamaica, it was observed that at the Jubilee celebrations for Queen Victoria, the population displayed its loyalty to the monarchy by a massive number of individuals coming down to Kingston to join in the celebrations.[38] It was suggested that the Queen had come to represent a unifying force, not only among the peoples of Jamaica but also among those in the various British Caribbean colonies, despite divisions based on colour, class, culture, and religion. However, it is difficult to say how much of this was the outcome of formal schooling. This loyalty to Queen Victoria could partly have been attributed to the fact that she ascended the throne one year before emancipation and had therefore become a symbol of freedom from slavery and oppression.[39]

While there had been definite progress in the provision of elementary education in most West Indian colonies over the years, the effect of schooling on the community was not always as great as was hoped. For example, it was pointed out that the limited success education had achieved in a colony like British Honduras was mainly due to "the sense of order and morality which a pupil feels in school is so different to what he experiences out of it." It was therefore "hardly surprising to find that education . . . [had] little effect"[40] in that society, where the value systems which the schools tried to pass on differed markedly from those of the community. This was also the situation, to a greater or lesser degree, in most of the other British Caribbean colonies.

In addition, up to the mid-1860s in Trinidad and other colonies, it was said that education had so far "done little to build up a society" in "true, sound and lasting principles." It simply helped to reinforce and increase the social differentiation which existed between different groups in these societies. For example, it was noted that

> a small elite were receiving an efficient training to enter the professions; some near the bottom [of the social hierarchy] were struggling to read and write, [though] a few of them [were] able to rise in the world. But between these two extremes there was no contact, nor were there educational provisions . . . for those in between the rich and the labouring poor. The children of coloured clerks and shopkeepers and others . . . who were expected to form a middle class as time went on were neglected.[41]

This was particularly true up to the 1870s.

Finally, much of the educational progress of this period was largely due to the hard work and dedication of its supporters and providers, under some of the most difficult circumstances. This involved much courage and dedication, particularly because the results were sometimes quite "unproductive," or at least far from satisfactory. Hence, while some improvement in primary education had occurred over the period, it was often a very slow, and sometimes difficult, process.

Notes

1   Report of the Government of British Honduras, *British Parliamentary Papers*, Vol. 34: *1849* (London: Government of Great Britain), 272.
2   Report of the Government of Antigua, *British Parliamentary Papers*, Vol. 36: *1850* (London: Government of Great Britain), 42.
3   Gordon, *A Century* 44.
4   *Quarterly Publications of the American Statistical Association*, Vol. 4: New Series 30, January 1895 (Boston: American Statistical Association, 1895).
5   Board of Education, *Special Reports on Education Subjects*, Vol. 4: col./416 (London: HMSO, 1901).
6   Report of the Government of Grenada, *British Parliamentary Papers*, Vol. 44: *1882* (London: Government of Great Britain), 126.
7   Root, *The British West Indies and the Sugar Industries*, 39.
8   Government of Antigua, *Historical Notes on Education in Antigua, 1834-1984*.
9   Ryall, "The Organization of Missionary Societies," 286.
10   Report of the Government of Jamaica, *British Parliamentary Papers*, Vol. 59: *1877* (London: Government of Great Britain), 18.
11   Ibid., Vol. 44: *1874* , 50.
12   Ibid., Vol. 55: *1882* , 38.
13   Ibid., Vol. 52: *1884-85* , 17.
14   CO 295/181, *Report of the Inspector of Schools for Trinidad 1854* (PRO); Furlonge, "The Development of Secondary Education in Trinidad and Tobago," 49.
15   *Report of the Inspector of Schools for Trinidad for 1861, British Parliamentary Papers*, Vol. 40: *1861* (London: The Government of Great Britain), 37.
16   Report of the Government of Dominica, *British Parliamentary Papers*, Vol. 44: *1882* (London: Government of Great Britain), 126.
17   Report of the Government of Antigua, *British Parliamentary Papers*, Vol. 51: *1876* (London: Government of Great Britain), 100.
18   Ibid., Vol. 55: *1878*, 79.
19   Government of Grenada, *Report of the Inspector of Schools for 1855*.
20   Letter from R. G. Rice to the Colonial Secretary, 16 July 1855; *British Parliamentary Papers*, Vol. 42: *1856* (London: Government of Great Britain), 83.
21   Report of the Government of British Honduras, *British Parliamentary Papers*, Vol. 54: *1884* (London: Government of Great Britain), 135.
22   Report of the Government of St. Kitts, *British Parliamentary Papers*, Vol. 44: *1860* (London: Government of Great Britain), 90-91.
23   Despatch from Lieutenant Governor to Governor in Chief, Leeward Island Colony, 12 April 1856, *British Parliamentary Papers*, Vol. 10: *1857* (London: Government of Great Britain), 196.
24   Report of the Government of Dominica, *British Parliamentary Papers*, Vol. 40: *1864* (London: Government of Great Britain), 100.
25   Report of the Government of Nevis, *British Parliamentary Papers*, Vol. 42: *1856* (London: Government of Great Britain), 171.
26   Board of Education, *Special Report on Education Subjects*.
27   *Report of the Inspector of Schools for the Bahamas, 1856, British Parliamentary Papers*, Vol. 40: *1857-58* (London: Government of Great Britain), 3.
28   Report of the Government of Trinidad, *British Parliamentary Papers*, Vol. 37: *1865* (London: Government of Great Britain), 27.
29   CO 299/19.
30   Carl Campbell "The Development of Education in Trinidad," 438.
31   Report of the Government of Jamaica, *British Parliamentary Papers*, Vol. 44: *1874* (London: Government of Great Britain), 50.
32   Ibid., 50.
33   Report of the Government of St. Kitts, *British Parliamentary Papers*, Vol. 37: *1865* (London: Government of Great Britain), 91.
34   Report of the Government of the Bahamas, *British Parliamentary Papers*, Vol. 49: *1866* (London: Government of Great Britain), 33.
35   Report of the Government of Jamaica, *British Parliamentary Papers*, Vol. 54: *1884* (London: Government of Great Britain), 119.
36   Report of the Government of British Honduras, *British Parliamentary Papers* Vol. 54: *1884* (London: Government of Great Britain), 135.
37   Report of the Government of Trinidad, *British Parliamentary Papers*, Vol. 37: *1847* (London: Government of Great Britain), 120.

38   Kathleen Monteith "The Victoria Jubilee Celebrations of 1887 in Jamaica," *Jamaica Journal 20*: 4 (Kingston: Institute of Jamaica, Nov. 1987- Jan. 1988).

39   Philip D. Curtin, *Two Jamaicas: The Role of Ideas in a Tropical Colony, 1830-1865* (New York: Atheneum, 1975), 125.

40   Report of the Government of British Honduras, *British Parliamentary Papers,* Vol. 54: *1884* (London: The Government of Great Britain), 135.

41   Brereton, *Race Relations,* 235.

CHAPTER 9

SECONDARY AND POST-SECONDARY
EDUCATION, 1845-95

Secondary Education prior to 1845

The British West Indies, in contrast to the North American colonies, initially experienced much difficulty over the establishment of secondary and post-secondary educational institutions, despite the many individuals who generously provided legacies specifically for this purpose. One reason was that the early settlers never considered the West Indies their home and were not interested in developing local public institutions to offer education beyond the basic primary level.

Nevertheless, opportunities for private instruction up to the secondary level were generally available to all those who could afford it.[1] The demand for such education usually arose from among the primary whites who planned eventually to send their children back to Britain, and in some cases to France or to the USA, for further academic and professional training. Most of them sought secondary education for their children in the prestigious British public schools, as a means of helping their offspring achieve higher status within the metropolitan society.

Such schooling brought West Indian students into closer contact with children of the middle and upper classes in Britain which was to prepare them to become members of the elite groups in that society. Their parents also valued this education because it was likely to enhance their own prestige to have educated their children at British public schools .

But there was another consideration. Because of the existing system of primogeniture, only the eldest son of a sugar planter was normally eligible to inherit his father's estate. Therefore, to ensure the younger sons' future they were often given the type of education and training which would earn them a respectable social position — similar to that which their families enjoyed in the West Indies. For this purpose, one of the learned professions such as medicine, law, or the Church was usually considered appropriate, and a secondary grammar school education was normally a prerequisite for such training. Therefore, secondary and more advanced education for the primary whites was a means of status confirmation and also an investment. It served as the equivalent of an insurance policy for the younger sons of the planters because it provided them with qualifications by which they could later earn a "respectable living, if the need arose."

The secondary whites did not initially consider education beyond the elementary level as necessary for the occupational mobility of their children, since this was virtually assured by their skin colour. Further, they filled positions in the West Indies left open by primary whites returning to Britain, often regardless of the level of their education. This was partly why the early efforts to establish private secondary schools in the region for the children of the secondary whites were not very successful and resulted in the under-utilization of many endowments that had been provided for their education, especially in Jamaica.

Through the generosity of their wealthy white fathers, a few coloured children were sometimes able to secure an education at the secondary and even at the tertiary level. However, their upward social mobility usually only occurred in their own socially segmented sector of these societies. They were unable to secure entry into "first" society. For example, in 1861 Sewell noted that "no person with . . . the slightest taint of African blood . . . [was] admitted to white society," and therefore, a white father's status was not enjoyed by his coloured children.[2] Samuel Prescod, a well-educated liberal journalist and a young leader of the free coloured community in Barbados, was ejected from the House of Assembly for merely observing its proceedings. In general, individuals of colour, with "all the advantages that a most liberal education . . . [could] bestow" on them, were excluded from white society, long after emancipation had become a legal reality.[3]

Two Types of Post-basic Education

Two different types or levels of post-basic education, each meant for different strata of the population, were provided in the West Indies after slavery was abolished.

1. The "advanced" primary education was offered in the model, intermediate, or central schools. After emancipation, a growing demand for individuals to fill certain white-collar jobs such as teaching, along with the poor quality of the education offered in the ordinary primary schools, increased the pressure for the establishment of model schools which were initially attended by the children of the secondary whites and later by the upwardly mobile coloureds and blacks. They therefore became a major instrument by which non-whites were able to move into a few lower level white-collar jobs. However, as King[4] noted, the model schools in Jamaica, with one exception, were not as successful in offering advanced programmes as those in some other West Indian colonies.

2. The secondary grammar school education prepared children for a more elevated social standing in society, for admission into institutions of higher education, or for local higher level white-collar jobs. Parents from the upper and more established middle-class groups saw such an education as increasingly valuable for their children's future, especially since it was a prerequisite for entry into tertiary level educational institutions overseas. The growing demand for this more advanced education resulted in the eighteenth-century endowments for secondary schools being better utilized.

Factors Influencing the Provision of Secondary Education after Abolition

While earlier attempts had been made to establish secondary schools in the West Indies, only after the abolition of slavery and the spread of elementary education did a keener interest in advanced primary and secondary education become fairly widespread.

Initially, West Indian legislators objected to providing government funds to support secondary education, because it was felt that the section of the population whose children were likely to benefit from it should be able to meet its cost without having to rely on government assistance. They argued that the public funds available for schooling in the region should only be used to provide elementary education for the masses.

This point of view was shared by many individuals in the Colonial Office, including Henry Taylor. The secretary of state for the colonies also expressed the view that the state should not support schools designed for the wealthy and that if any aid was to be given to them, it should be confined to the "narrowest limits" possible. In 1860 the governor of Grenada also criticized the decision of the local legislature to provide financial aid to a local grammar school by pointing out that

> it appears to be the idea here that . . . a Grammar School for the education of the middle class is of paramount importance, and should be supported by the Colony from funds which would be more legitimately employed in educating the children of the working class. Although I do not deny the utility of a Grammar School I do not admit the principle that it should be a charge to the public, especially when a large portion of the very small grant usually made for educational purposes is absorbed in the head and assistant masters' salaries, to the prejudice of the parochial schools.[5]

An unstated objective of this reluctance to provide government aid for secondary education was to discourage any rise in the educational and occupational aspirations of the lower classes. The planters believed that secondary education was likely to affect their supply of agricultural labourers for the sugar estates. The Royal Commission of 1897 noted that the advanced educational programme provided by these colonies had greatly crippled the labour supply and deprived agriculture of the services of the "younger portion of the labouring class."

But some legislators and an increasing number of middle-class educators and missionaries gradually took a different stand. They advanced the following reasons for West Indian governments to help provide secondary education:

1. It was inequitable to provide only for the education of the masses and not for the children of the middle classes in their educational efforts. It was suggested that with the declining prosperity of the sugar industry, many middle-class parents were unable to meet the full cost of secondary education for their children and hence they, too, were in need of help. In 1867 the inspector of schools for Barbados, in advocating the need for a further expansion of secondary educational facilities on the island, suggested that

> while the legislature is assisting on an average six or seven schools for the poor in each parish at the rate of £20 or £30 a year each . . . it would appear to be no more than just that one school in each [parish] should be aided to at least that amount, in which a superior Education for the children of such of the Middle classes as are unable to board them from home, should be provided.[6]

In the following year the governor of the island continued with his argument that

the condition at which this colony has now arrived . . .
suggests, or even demands that some considerable effort
should be made for the better instruction of the classes
socially above those who have hitherto monopolized the
pecuniary aid of the legislature [for elementary
education].[7]

Similarly, in Jamaica, the Secondary Schools Commission suggested that it would be unjust for any system to provide a free education for the children of the masses at the cost of the general body of taxpayers, if it did not also provide equivalent or proportionate financial aid for the children attending the middle and higher class schools. In the late 1880s it was pointed out that, "it appears to the Commission that the time has arrived when it should clearly state its conviction that the middle class of the island has a strong claim on the government for attention to its educational needs."[8]

This was becoming a politically important issue due to the slowly expanding size of the middle class and was a point of view shared by others, such as Bishop Enos Nuttall of Jamaica, later chairman of the Secondary Schools Commission. He proposed that financial assistance should also be made available by the government to secondary schools on an equitable basis without destroying their private or religious links.

2. Secondary education was expected to contribute to the enlightenment of the middle class and would improve their relationships with the other classes of society, particularly the lower classes. In 1850 the legislature of Barbados voted funds for the first time to aid the island's two grammar schools on the grounds that it would both ensure a local secondary education of high quality and would improve the attitude of the middle class to other sections of the society. This would result from their experience of mixing in the same schools and in the same classes with a few bright boys from the lower social stratum of society.

When the Queen's Collegiate School (QCS) was established in Trinidad, it was also expected to play an important role in bringing about a degree of social cohesion and common understanding among boys of different social and religious backgrounds. The school was to provide an opportunity for boys of all denominations to meet, with the hope that,

[in the] common pursuits of literature, and the common
development of their faculties, they may be permitted to
learn how possible it is for men to live and act together,
striving to a common end, without dwelling on points of
religious difference, and in the spirit of most cheerful
charity.[9]

3. The decline of the sugar industry meant that a number of middle-class families were finding it difficult to pay the cost of secondary education for their children. The effect of the changing economic conditions on secondary school attendance could be clearly seen in British Guiana during the period 1878-97, when enrollments at the prestigious secondary grammar school, Queen's College, fluctuated because of the changing economic conditions of the colony—as indicated by its per capita expenditure on imports. This can be seen in Figure 20, below.

FIGURE 20

Fluctuations in Attendance at Queen's College and the Prosperity of the Colony as Measured by Imports per Head of Population, 1877-97

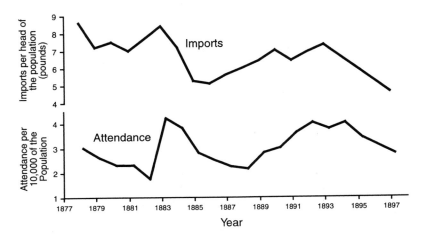

Source: CO 114/78 XC/B/ 8774, Public Records Office, London.

With the colonies' declining economic circumstances it was considered necessary that the middle classes should not lose their chances of securing secondary education for their children. In his dispatch to the colonial secretary in 1877, the governor of Barbados advanced the following case for providing greater assistance for the establishment of schools for these children.

> Your Lordship will not fail to note the very *small number* of boys, [that are involved] bearing in mind the number of upper and middle class in Barbados, who are [now] . . . receiving higher education. This is to be regretted, as it appears to me that the key to the ameliorating of social and other irregularities in Barbados is to be looked for, far more surely in the *enlightenment and culture of its middle class* than in the improved education of the lower, desirable as this, beyond all doubt, is. If juster and more courteous treatment is to be hereafter spontaneously, and as a matter of right feeling, accorded to the labouring population and to the coloured race generally, this must be produced by a more liberal and enlightened training of the boys . . . and by that free intercourse during childhood and youth on a footing of equality as pupils in the same schools, which is likely to be fostered by the bringing up in similar traditions, and under like discipline . . . of white and coloured boys alike as in the case of all these higher schools [emphasis added].[10]

4. Secondary education was to afford some limited opportunities for social mobility for a few children of the more ambitious members of the working class. This was considered useful in containing or cooling off any

dissatisfaction of the masses with the marked inequitable distribution of wealth in these societies. Such education would also contribute to the emergence of an intermediate class which would act as a useful buffer between the higher and the lower classes and would produce greater social stability in these colonies.

5. An education of a higher level than that currently provided in the primary schools for the masses was required to augment the elementary education, while at the same time meeting the emerging need for individuals to fill lower level white-collar occupations. Since the limited educational background of the teachers was a key factor in the poor quality of elementary education, it was necessary to ensure that those who took up teaching had received a higher level of basic education than that provided in the general elementary schools.

The gradual decline in the price of West Indian sugar affected the enrollments, and hence, the economic viability of these secondary schools, since most of them depended on students' fees for their economic survival. Even the more established grammar schools were often in jeopardy because of the decline or marked fluctuations in attendance. In this situation, local legislators and colonial administrators began to seriously consider the role West Indian governments should play in meeting the emerging demand for higher levels of education for middle-class children. The outcome was that they gradually granted subsidies for religious bodies providing secondary education or established government secondary schools.

A commission for Jamaica reflected the changing views about the government's involvement in the provision of such education when it remarked that,

> a majority of us consider that the State has a duty to care for and assist secondary and higher education — a fact recognized in all British countries and . . . increasingly . . . in Great Britain itself. . . . Experience shows that there cannot be efficient, continuous and sufficient provision for secondary education without some assistance from the State.

Nevertheless, the commissioners went on to add that

> It is not meant that the State should meet the entire cost, as in the case of elementary education, but should place [it] within reach of those who need it, and who, either *by private resources can meet the remainder of the cost* or by *exceptional ability can secure scholarships* or *other personal financial assistance* to meet the cost [emphasis added].[11]

Continuing Demand for Secondary Education

The demand for individuals with a higher education continued to rise as lower white-collar positions gradually became open to non-whites. In addition, the local middle-class was also expanding in size, and its members were anxious to provide their children with a better type of education than was available in the ordinary elementary schools. Their ultimate preference was for a secondary grammar school education, and they were usually in a position to meet some of the costs of such education.

But the economic decline in the region also reduced the income levels of members of this group. In British Honduras, for example, it was reported that the upper classes were for the most part struggling to maintain their traditional social distance from the lower orders. They were reduced "to a lower place in society" and some of them even became "indebted to the lower classes and almost dependent upon their will for assistance."[12]

Further, the steady economic decline of these colonies caused whites to migrate from the region in substantial numbers. The openings they left in the occupational structure and vacancies in the more prestigious secondary schools were taken up by the children of the non-whites, whose admission to these schools became more acceptable. This further increased their demand for classical secondary education, especially after the 1870s.

A few missionary bodies encouraged the establishment of secondary schools, since they hoped "to see some of the sable emancipated" West Indian population "respectfully and successfully occupying their station in the pulpit, on the bench and at the bar."[13] They wanted to develop, from among their local congregations, a group of more educated individuals who would eventually play an influential role in the West Indies. Some missionary societies even aimed at providing secondary education opportunities locally for the children of their expatriate staff, partly because it was cheaper than paying for such education abroad. It was also felt that if such an education was available locally, it would be beneficial for the upbringing of these children, who would grow up under the supervision of their own parents.

Jamaica

In Jamaica, very little seems to have been done in the field of secondary education during the first half of the nineteenth century. In 1851 there were, however, "a great number" of schools of "one sort or another," including a school in St. Ann's which afforded a classical education to "between 40 and 50 pupils." As a start in this direction, the government was urged to assume more direct responsibility for the management of the endowments left by various individuals to establish private schools. A special commission appointed to investigate the position of these charities recommended that the endowed schools be thrown open to all sections of the population. Further, it suggested that there should be a "consolidation of the funds of the several charitable establishments," since this would have made it possible for the funds to be used "to establish . . . a school or college in the plan of Eton, Westminster and Winchester," to be "open to all who can afford to board their children in the neighbourhood of the school."[14]

The government dragged its feet over managing these endowments, even though attention was drawn to abuses in the appropriation of the funds, the inefficiency of the governing bodies of some schools, and the misapplication or non-utilization of the money provided for secondary education. In 1852 the governor urged the legislature to take a more active role in the provision of secondary education by assuming responsibility for the management of the various educational endowments. In 1868 two well-endowed schools in Spanish Town which had been "utterly neglected," and their incomes "entirely wasted," were amalgamated into "one good school" under a trained master from England.

In 1869 the inspector of schools called for an early investigation into the state of all the endowed or charity schools on the island. The abuse of these endowments was especially noticeable in connection with the Munro and the Dickenson Charities, whose trustees had departed from the terms of their trust by excluding black children from their school at Potsdam since 1862.

The inspector of schools later noted that the Wolmer's Charity had already been looked into, and preparations were made for its re-establishment upon an improved system. The affairs of three other charities were also under investigation. The proposal was once more put forward that, with the school in St. Ann's as a nucleus, the legislature "might easily construct a large establishment for the whole Island, on a plan somewhat resembling those of the great public schools of England. To this purpose a portion of the funds of the other endowments for education might be made applicable."[15]

In 1865 the government eventually appropriated the monies left in the endowment funds and began to take measures to ensure that they were used for the purposes intended by the donors. Efforts were also made to develop a high-quality secondary educational institution, later known as the Jamaica Free School, which became the best endowed school on the island. In 1879 the Jamaica Schools Commission was established, and the commissioners were given wide powers over existing educational trusts and direct control of the Jamaica Free School.

The foundation provided by Beckford was amalgamated in 1869 with the one that was willed by Francis Smith for the "instruction of the poorer classes of all colour" in the "doctrines of the Church of England," and the "promotion of industry." But the school that was to be developed from this merger was not opened until 1896. However, a classical education was also being provided at the London Missionary Society's institution in Ridgemount for the training of local ministers.

The Jamaica School Commission was "remarkably active and independent" in its outlook on higher education. Most of its achievements were due to the persistence of Bishop Nuttall, who received strong support from the headmaster of the Jamaica Free School. In 1882, this school was reorganized as the Jamaica High School and placed under the control of the Commission. In the same year, the Jamaica scholarship scheme commenced and the Cambridge Local Examinations were held for the first time. By 1885, the school was moved to Hope in St. Andrews, where it became known as Jamaica College. By the mid-1890s, it had a "keen rival" in the Munro School and later in the girls' school at Hampton. By then, Wolmer's boys' and girls' schools were attracting many Kingstonians, and Rusea, Titchfield, Mannings, and Manchester were all well on their way to offering basic secondary education in some rural townships. Incidentally, these were all endowed schools that were reorganized by the Jamaica School Commission immediately after Jamaica College was established and usually offered tuition only up to the Junior Cambridge level.

In 1892 a new Education Act empowered the government, "to declare any important centre of population to be without adequate provision for secondary education and to establish a school there."[16] By this time, the supervision of all developments in the field of post-primary education had been transferred to the Schools Commission, so that some reorganization of the secondary schools had started to take place since the 1880s. In 1895 the establishment of a secondary school at Montego Bay was recommended by the commission, approved by the governor in council, and was in operation the following year. But this was the only additional secondary school that came into existence through the efforts of the commission. However, in a number of private secondary schools in Kingston the quality of work improved, judging by the increased number of students being presented for the Cambridge University secondary school examinations.

In 1864, the Wesleyans had begun to consider the establishment of a secondary school in Jamaica, but nothing was immediately done about it. Later, there was an attempt to develop a classical school in Kingston but this also did not materialize because a suitable schoolmaster could not be found. However, the Methodist Society maintained its interest in the establishment of a secondary school, and by the 1870s, it was again suggested that a high school was indispensable for Wesleyan interests in the region. This was needed to provide an education for the children of their missionaries from overseas and to cater to the sons of "our laity" who might later become "probationers for our Ministry." As the Wesleyan Missionary Society stated, in commenting on the need for secondary schools in the region:

> It is obvious that such schools, to meet the requirements of the children of our Members of the middle and higher ranks of society are necessary, if they are to be kept in connection with our Churches; and further, that it is only from such superior training we can hope to raise up teachers of our schools and probationers for our Ministry.[17]

This concern of the Wesleyans for a secondary school was again mentioned by Stephen Sutton, another Methodist missionary, who in 1879 indicated that,

> what we want is a fairly educated middle class from which we shall get our chief and most efficient supply of leaders and local preachers and stewards thoroughly to do our work and man our societies as our work ought to be done and our societies officered . . . . Many of our local preachers have very poor qualifications to stand before and instruct even our illiterate peasantry.[18]

In the 1870s, the Methodists eventually established the York Castle High School, one of their objectives being to save the expenses involved in sending the sons of their missionaries to England for their education. It was therefore necessary for the society to ensure that the education offered by this school was of a comparably high quality.

Another important concern of the Methodists in providing "higher scholarship" for children from the increasing number of middle-class families was that some of them might eventually fill positions with the society as teachers, catechists, and ministers of the gospel. They also wanted to attract students of various denominational backgrounds to their school, partly to keep enrollment at a level that would make the institution economically viable. The school started out with 39 students, and enrollment reached a peak of 100 before a decline began to take place. These educational concerns of the Wesleyans, as Mavis Burke[19] pointed out, indicated that they were at least becoming interested in recruiting more educated local personnel for their ministry.

A Methodist Girls' Secondary School for Jamaica
As soon as the Methodist boys' high school was established, the pressure for a similar institution for girls began to increase, especially since "the better class of Christian parents" refused to send their girls to co-educational schools, once they had passed the age of nine or ten. In 1877 Sargeant, a Methodist missionary in Jamaica, pointed out that

> for girls of this class especially, we have no suitable schools in the country. The Romanists are the only religious body in the country who have made an effort in the way of higher education for girls, than that of the Common Day School and they have only one school. . . . The consequence is that a vast number of girls, who might, at their parents' expense, have a suitable education to fit them for the position of wives of educated Native teachers, and to become teachers themselves, are obliged to be content with the elementary education which as little children, they obtained in the Day Schools.[20]

As a result, he saw the need to provide an affordable education for girls that would give a "Christian character and tone" to the "domestic life of the country." Therefore, in 1881, a girls' school which offered educational facilities for the daughters of the "Professional and Mercantile classes" of Kingston was started under the principalship of Miss Skinner, who had years of experience in a "first class seminary" for young ladies. The entrance requirements were not high, although the students admitted were able to "read and write" and had a knowledge of the "simple rules of Arithmetic." This school was first intended to meet the needs of Methodists in the West Indies for an institution to which they could send their girls for a sound education. Experiments by the Wesleyans at establishing similar schools were later made in Antigua and British Guiana, but these failed for lack of local support.

Barbados
Overall, Barbados led the way in the provision of secondary education in the West Indies, because its legislature evinced a "very liberal disposition" towards aiding middle-class education. The central schools on the island, originally established for the education of poor whites, later opened their doors to the children of the non-whites. In 1850 Rawle established an intermediate school at St. Marks, to give the children of the more ambitious parents a good English education at a modest cost. In 1852 the government expressed its intention to establish other schools for middle-class children even though the central schools offered some type of

secondary education. Other middle schools geared toward meeting the educational needs of upwardly aspiring members of the working class began to appear on the educational scene. The Pilgrim Place Middle School which opened in 1855 was one such school.

In advocating the expansion of post-primary educational facilities in 1867, the inspector of schools recommended that two small endowed schools, St. Andrews Seminary and Christchurch Middle School, should be granted financial assistance by the government. In 1868 the governor again suggested that greater effort should be made to provide better education for the middle classes. This issue was taken up in 1875 by the Mitchinson Commission, which proposed the establishment and expansion of "second grade" secondary schools, especially for the lower status groups, and the result was the creation of a number of such schools. The Boys' and Girls' Central Schools became the second grade schools of Combermere and Queen's College, respectively. In 1881 Coleridge, Parry, and Alleyne schools were opened and in 1894 Alexandra School, a second grade school for girls, was also established.

The Grammar Schools in Barbados — Codrington Grammar School
The Codrington Grammar School was initially established in 1745 with funds left by Sir Christopher Codrington for the establishment of a post-secondary institution. In the mid-1840s, controversy still prevailed as to whether the Codrington funds should be spent entirely on a college or post-secondary institution as specified by the donor, or continue to support the grammar school. The remainder of the money was to be used to continue providing exhibitions to the best students to pursue further studies abroad in the fields mentioned in the Codrington will.

One of the most vocal supporters for the continuation of the Codrington Grammar School was Chief Justice Bowcher Clarke, an old boy of the school who argued that the island needed a high class grammar school, not a low class college. Rawle, in response, admitted that there was the need for good grammar schools throughout the British West Indies, including Barbados, but suggested that other agencies should provide this type of education from their own resources and not try to appropriate the charitable bequest of the Codrington estate, which was made for a different purpose. He pointed out further that, in the past, the exhibitioners who benefited from studies abroad financed out of the Codrington funds did not even return to serve Barbados or the West Indies.

Rawle eventually succeeded in convincing the Society for the Propagation of the Gospel in Foreign Parts (SPG) that a decision to utilize the funds towards supporting a theological college was the right one, and in the 1850s the controversy over the Codrington bequest was finally resolved in line with the wishes of the benefactor. The Codrington Grammar School was removed to the Chaplain's Lodge, renamed the Lodge Grammar School, and was reorganized into an institution separate from the Codrington Foundation. This school provided a sound English and classical education along the lines of a British grammar school.

During the late 1840s, the two grammar schools in Barbados — the Codrington Grammar School and Harrison College — experienced great financial difficulties due to the economic problems facing the island. Many middle-class parents could no longer afford the cost of providing their children with a classical secondary education, and this resulted in a fall in enrollment. The migration from these colonies of white families, particularly those who might have been able to afford a secondary grammar school education for their children, also contributed to the decline in grammar school enrollment. The situation was made worse by the fact that the number of students from the Windward and Leeward Islands who attended these schools also declined. The lack of funds resulted in the closure of the Codrington school in 1847, but in 1849 the College Council stepped in to make it a junior department of the college. However, the course of instruction still encompassed all the branches of a good English and classical education.

In these difficult circumstances, the Barbados government began to provide some financial assistance for middle-class education. In 1850 a sum of £100 was made available by the board of education to the two main grammar schools on the island. This marked the first involvement by the government in the provision of education specifically for the middle classes. In 1858 the legislature again made a grant of £300 to support the Codrington Grammar School. Later, the school successfully petitioned for a subsidy of £600 over a period of six years, and this was approved on condition that the school should not be a "mere tributary" of a colonial divinity college — the Codrington College — but would become a regular grammar school. The headmaster was also required to be a graduate of an English university. But enrollment at the Codrington Grammar School continued to decline, adding further to the financial difficulties which faced the institution. However, towards the close of 1870, a grant of £600 per year for 10 years was made as an endowment to the school. As well, a sum of £900 was provided for the purchase of a suitable schoolhouse and a further grant of £400 per year was made available for the purpose of securing an adequate salary to pay a first class headmaster.

Harrison College
Harrison College, which was founded with a small endowment in the mid-eighteenth century, had sunk into disrepute. However, after the 1840s, its enrollment rose fairly steadily, even though the school remained small and the quality of its work not very high. In 1845 its enrollment comprised 24 foundationers and eight private students, but by 1850, when the school was officially designated a grammar school, its numbers had increased only slightly to 38 pupils. In that year it received a portion of the government's first grant for secondary education, and in 1857 it again benefited from the decision by the legislature to continue its financial assistance to middle-class education. In 1869, because of the perceived social benefits to the island of a good grammar school in Bridgetown, a further grant of £200 was made to the school out of the £500 provided for the education of the middle classes. It was even hoped that the legislature would continue these grants if the results of the school proved satisfactory.

The sum voted was to provide 20 exhibitions of £10 each for scholars attending the school, and later, an additional £100 was granted for 10 more scholars. This meant that the award covered only two-thirds of the cost of their education, which was £15 per student p.a., with the students' parents or guardians being expected to meet the remaining costs. It was obvious, therefore, that the grant was to help the less affluent middle-class families among whom the desire for a "thoroughly good schooling" for their boys was considered a reasonable ambition. These awards also made it possible for the two major secondary schools on the island to survive. After some reorganization in 1869-70, Harrison also became a first class grammar school, with 67 boys in attendance in 1871.

Subsequently enrollment rose fairly rapidly, reaching 115 in 1874 — an increase of about 72% in these three years. In 1870 the Barbadian legislature decided to increase its financial support for higher schools, since the small endowed and proprietary schools were also faced with economic difficulties and sought aid from public funds. As a consequence, such schools were forced to abandon their policy of discrimination on the grounds of colour.

The appointment of the 1876 Mitchinson Commission, headed by the bishop of Barbados, gave an immediate impetus to the further development of secondary education on the island. The Commission criticized the type of middle-class education offered in many local schools, noting that it was "random in provision" and "too ambitious in aspiration." For children who intended to terminate their schooling at the age of 16, it recommended the establishment of second grade day schools, while the first grade grammar schools were to serve the needs of those middle-class children whose parents intended to keep them in schools until they were at least 18 years of age.

In 1887 there were still only the two first grade schools on the island, with a total enrollment of 188 students. In the following year the girls' secondary school became a first grade school and the average enrollment in the three such schools was 292. By 1895 this figure totalled 322, with about 40% (130) being girls. In addition, there were five second grade schools, with 178 pupils in attendance. With the upgrading of the girls' schools in 1888, there were four second grade schools remaining — Combermere, Coleridge, Alleyne, and Parry — with an average enrollment of about 173. By 1893 this figure reached 201, and the following year, another girls' school, which had an initial enrollment of 32, was added to the list of second grade schools. It was later proposed to establish another first grade secondary school for girls, and in 1883 Queen's College was converted into such an establishment. The college was divided into two sections — one offering preparatory classes and the other offering advanced classes. The overall result of these developments was that Barbados then had some of the best grammar schools in the West Indies and attracted children of the elite throughout the British Caribbean.

Trinidad

Immediately after emancipation, there was an increase in the number of secondary schools in Trinidad as the Roman Catholics began to redirect their attention to this level of education. In 1836 they founded the Ladies of St. Joseph School in Port of Spain which was a classical boarding school. Other private and denominational efforts to establish and operate secondary schools on the island were less successful. In 1846 a secondary school was opened up by Arrowsmith and, in 1849, a grammar school was established by LeMaitre. The Anglican Bishop opened up a "superior school" in Port of Spain that was partly classical and partly commercial. The school was closed in 1857 because it had no "sympathy and support" from the predominantly Roman Catholic population. An Academy was also founded by Professor Marquand from Paris, but it lasted only about 12 years. All these were soon closed because of the lack of local demand for secondary education. Parents who could have afforded such education still sent their children to Europe, North America, and in some cases, to Barbados.

The first government proposal for the provision of secondary education came from Lord Harris, who suggested the establishment of district or second grade secondary schools

> in order that further opportunities for education may be afforded to those children of superior intellect and greater industry . . . [therefore] in each district . . . one or more schools of a superior sort should be established to be called "district schools" to which those who excel might be presented, and where they would receive still further opportunities of improving and distinguishing themselves.[21]

In addition, he proposed that a government high school or college be established in Port of Spain to which students who were doing well in the elementary schools might proceed. This was expected to give "a greater impetus" to "the progress of education throughout the Colony" and this dissemination of a more advanced education was to impart "a higher tone to the moral and social life of the community."[22]

Lord Harris also suggested that this education, which was to combine scientific and agricultural training with a study of the classics, should be provided at a moderate charge so that it could be available to a wide cross-section of society. The school was also to be non-residential, because this would also permit those children whose parents could not afford boarding fees a chance to attend. However, the governor's proposal for a system of state-supported secondary education was temporarily set aside, on account of the economic situation of the island. But in 1852 the government established a Boys' Model School in Port of Spain, where the education provided was clearly designed for pupils of superior intellectual ability.

With the closure of the Anglican Grammar School in 1857, Governor Keate became very concerned about the lack of opportunities for secondary education, especially for the children of the non-Catholic elites. He felt that the government should help to meet this need, even if it meant using some of the funds available for elementary education. Influenced by a fellow Etonian, the attorney-general Charles Warner, Keate pressed the Colonial Office to permit the establishment of a secondary school on the island.

He informed the secretary of state, Labouchère, that with the exception of one or two small and very indifferent private academies, the Roman Catholic College was the only establishment which provided both a classical and a general education for the children of parents in the upper ranks of life. The staff members of this school were often not well qualified and, as a result, many Roman Catholics and Anglicans still sent their children at an early age to Europe for their education. In addition, the sectarian tone of the Roman Catholic College was considered to be very strong, especially under the new Italian Archbishop, Spaccapietra, who even refused to take an oath of allegiance to the British monarch in order to qualify for the state allowance to his salary. With such potential influence, Keate felt that there was every prospect of the Roman Catholic College losing whatever English character it might have acquired, and therefore urged the establishment of a government secondary school.

There were a number of other reasons why Governor Keate wanted a government secondary school established in Trinidad. One of his objectives was to counter the dominant influence of the main Catholic Boys' Secondary School in the colony, which tended to inculcate in its students a positive orientation towards the former colonial power — France. Another was to provide a better calibre and a larger number of fairly well-educated and younger non-Catholics who would eventually enter the civil service. Finally, since the boys who were expected to attend this new school were more likely to be Protestants, this provision was to help counter the hold which the Roman Catholics were said to have had on most of the key posts in the private sector.

In making his proposal to the local legislature, Governor Keate alluded to Lord Harris's suggestion to make secondary education available on the island at a moderate cost. But the views of these two individuals on the role of secondary education in Trinidad were markedly different. While Harris suggested that the school should be open to all on the basis of their ability, Keate proposed a socially exclusive school for children whose parents occupied positions in the higher echelons of society. This was made clear in the governor's communication to the secretary of state in August of 1857, in which he argued that if the children of the middle classes were to maintain "a position in society adequate to their parentage," then they must be able to attain some higher education than that which had so far not been available to them locally.[23]

Charles Warner, the attorney-general of Trinidad, who played a crucial role in the establishment of this school also emphasized that it was not meant for anyone "whose parents worked with their hands."[24] Therefore, even though the fees at QCS were heavily subsidized, they were high enough to exclude the children of the humbler classes. In fact, Governor Keate pointed out that the colony could afford to meet the additional costs of establishing a good secondary school because a considerable portion of the expenditure would be met by fees.

As previously indicated, Harris's plan was to provide further education for the more talented children of the lower orders. But this was almost entirely ignored by Governor Keate, who suggested that "no such desire for extended education has yet been produced as would justify an attempt to establish schools of a higher order for the especial benefit of those who have distinguished themselves in the existing [primary] schools."[25]

Keate also wanted the school to offer a programme of studies which was identical to that provided by the English public schools and preferred "a public school man" to be the headmaster. The school which was originally named Queen's Collegiate School (QCS) was opened in 1859, with an enrollment of 34 pupils.

Catholic Opposition to the Establishment of QCS

While most religious bodies and individuals in Trinidad accepted the proposals for the new government secondary school, there was strong opposition to it from the Roman Catholics, who challenged the value of the education that it provided. In addition, they criticized the social exclusiveness of the school by noting that only nine Roman Catholics as compared to 20 Anglican boys were in attendance, on an island in which the population was predominantly Catholic. But the Catholics' main concern, according to Bhagan,[26] was that QCS was an intrusion by the government into an area of education which was considered to be their preserve. On the other hand, Governor Keate claimed that the Catholic objection to the college stemmed

> entirely from the foreign element of the society of the Island. They were neither numerous nor influential but sought popular support for their objections by giving religion as the reason for what was in fact political objections to the College, thereby attempting to gain popular support for their views. The conflict was really between the Church and the Government and this raised the question whether the Island was to be governed and legislated for by the Governor and Council representing and appointed by Her Majesty or by a faction of the community which sees, with reluctance all attempts to render it in spirit and in principle what it ought to be, a British colony.[27]

In pursuing their objections to QCS, the Roman Catholics petitioned the secretary of state for the colonies to discontinue government assistance to the school. But the governor, in his accompanying letter to the secretary of state, expressed his extreme reluctance to do so, especially since the school was providing "a superior education." He also pointed out that a sectarian school would not have as much influence as a public non-sectarian one in bringing together "in friendly intercourse the different races and faiths" or in diminishing the ethnic and religious divisions which were already quite marked on the island.

To counter the influence of the QCS, the Roman Catholics began to make their own provision for a prestigious boys' secondary school. The Catholic College of St. Marys, which had dwindled in size since it was originally established in 1863 was re-established as the College of Immaculate Conception (CIC) and handed over to the Fathers of the Order of the Holy Ghost. It was well-supported by the influential Catholic community on the island, who were mainly of French origin. Therefore, while QCS was referred to by its critics as the English College, the CIC became known as the French College. The school grew much faster than the government secondary grammar school, and by 1869 its enrollment was 111, nearly twice the number then attending the government institution.

After his initial unsuccessful efforts to get the government to discontinue its support for QCS, the Roman Catholic bishop petitioned the secretary of state in December 1867 for financial assistance for the CIC. He argued that because QCS had failed in its objectives, it was necessary for the Catholics to establish their own college without any government assistance and to accept students from all religious denominations. They requested a modest annual grant and suggested that the needed funds could be raised by reducing the grant to QCS. Further, the Roman Catholic authorities considered that such an acquiescence to the legitimate wishes of the Roman Catholics would be a "most just and most beneficial" act that would help to strengthen the union between the local Catholics and the British government. The request was not granted but, by 1870, under a new governor, assistance was obtained via another route — affiliation of the Catholic college with the government secondary school.

The Emergence of Queen's Royal College (QRC)

Following the criticisms of QCS by the Catholics, and the general controversy which continued over the secular system of state education in Trinidad, the British government appointed Keenan to investigate the overall educational condition of the island. This inspector of schools from Ireland was very critical of the government secondary school and expressed the view that the popularity of the one operated by the Catholics rested on the fact that religion was at the core of its instructional programme. He recommended that the government withdraw its financial support for QCS and that the institution be converted to a proprietary college, aided by the government. He also suggested that comparable financial assistance be made available to the College of Immaculate Conception.

These recommendations found favour with Lord Granville, secretary of state for the colonies, and was in line with the thinking of such individuals at the Colonial Office as Henry Taylor, who had questioned the idea of the state paying for the education of the children of the rich. Therefore, the governor was asked to prepare a scheme for secondary education along the lines suggested by Keenan. But Governor Gordon was very reluctant to change the status of QCS as a government secondary school because of its perceived social benefits to the colony. He pointed out, for example, that such a school was tremendously valuable in preparing boys for entry into the junior clerical positions of the civil service and in bringing about a greater degree of social cohesion between the two dominant religious groups in society.

The persistence of the governor in advocating his point of view finally paid off, and an agreement was reached, whereby QCS was to be reconstituted in 1870 under a new name — Queen's Royal College (QRC) — and with a new constitution that allowed it to accept as "affiliated" institutions, private secondary schools that were providing a sound academic education. Such affiliated schools would then become eligible for financial assistance from the government. This new policy provided the first opportunity for the Catholic secondary school to receive government assistance. The principal of CIC was to be paid by the state and its students were to be allowed to compete for the government of Trinidad university scholarship, previously open only to the students of QCS.

A school for the "education of young ladies" was also opened in 1875 and in 1882 the nuns in San Fernando established a girls' school which was affiliated with St. Joseph's Convent. Another "ladies' academy" was opened up in 1892 in Port of Spain and it attempted to offer a "sound English education."

Other West Indian Colonies

In most of the other West Indian colonies secondary grammar schools had a precarious existence, especially prior to the 1870s. This was partly due to the small population size of these colonies and particularly to the limited number of children of school age who had successfully completed a satisfactory programme of primary education. In addition, many parents were unable to pay the high fees which these schools often charged. The situation was further aggravated by the steady emigration from the region of white middle-class families who were often in a better economic position to pay for their children's attendance at these schools.

In 1847-48 the governor of Tobago reported that he expected to institute a "classical seminary" to provide a "more liberal education" for the upper classes who did not want to incur the expense or the inconvenience of sending their children to England, Barbados, or even to nearby Trinidad. Nothing happened with this venture and nearly a decade later the lieutenant-governor of the island, in a letter to the colonial secretary, commented on the fact that the youths of respectable parents were very much neglected in terms of their ability to obtain a sound secondary education. The absence of a grammar school in Tobago continued to be mentioned regularly. Further, because the cost of boarding a student in England

> is scarcely greater than that in the neighbouring islands [and when] the many advantages of the education in England are considered, no one who has the means of sending a child there [i.e., to England] would entertain the idea of educating him in a Colonial School, however well it may be established and provided with teachers.[28]

In 1883 the island's administrator once more pointed to the need for even a small state-aided second grade school, where the sons of the upper and middle-class might receive a sound grammar school education. But this suggestion was never implemented.

In St. Vincent, the secondary school situation was somewhat similar to that in the other, smaller West Indian islands. In 1845 the island already had two private schools in the capital city of Kingstown. One of these was operated by the Presbyterian Association and the other was a proprietary grammar school that was established by private subscription, under the headship of an Anglican clergyman and "a lady from England." Its enrollment of about 75 pupils in 1847-48 increased to 89 the following year and consisted of the children from the "wealthier class of all colours." From 1851 to 1852, its enrollment fell by about 16%, even though it continued to be reported that the institution was doing well. Yet not very long after this both schools were closed and the island was without a grammar school for a long time afterwards.

In 1865 another school was established for the education of boys of the middle and upper classes, through the efforts of an Anglican clergyman, the Reverend W. H. Laborde. Despite the grant of £50 made to it by the board of education for the salary of the headmaster, the school did not survive for very long. In the years that followed, the island did not attempt to establish or aid any other upper-class school at the secondary level, even though the need for it was very much felt. In 1878 the St. Vincent

Government Grammar School was established in Kingstown, but by 1880, the public seemed to have lost all confidence in the institution, as evidenced by the fact that its total enrollment for that year was only between three and four students.

Due to efforts made to improve the situation, the school enrollment gradually rose to about 13 or 14 pupils in 1881. But a further decline set in, and when Deighton, the headmaster of Harrison College, Barbados, later visited St. Vincent to report on the work of the school, he found only three boys present. During his second visit a few days later, only one boy was in attendance. Therefore, in 1885 a special committee was appointed to investigate the position of the school, which was found to be "deplorably deficient." It therefore concluded that St. Vincent did not have the resources necessary to sustain a good grammar school. Later, there was again a loud, popular outcry for the re-establishment of a grammar school, and to make such a school economically viable it was even proposed that a teachers' training institution might be advantageously opened up as part of the grammar school complex. But there was little immediate progress with this proposal.

Local community members, however, organized themselves in an effort to resuscitate the grammar school, which was re-opened in 1886, as a private school. In 1887 the government made a grant of £50 to the school and later added a girls' department on to it. The inspector of schools was concurrently appointed headmaster of the school. But because it was difficult for one individual to carry out both jobs, in 1891 the government separated the two positions and appointed a new inspector of schools. It nevertheless continued to provide a per capita grant to the grammar school and, in return, it secured the right to nominate two pupils to receive free tuition.

In St. Lucia, following the failure of the island's Protestant grammar school, the need for a school for the education of "boys for the higher pursuits of life" was mentioned in 1846. There were three schools on the island which offered a secondary education, but none of these attempted to teach the "Imperial language." Therefore the need for an English-language secondary school was particularly felt, even by the French Creoles, who recognized the importance of giving their children an education in English rather than sending them to Martinique or even to Paris for their schooling.

In the absence of a classical institution, two or three pupils had been receiving an education in the classics from a Protestant clergyman. Again, in 1856, it was observed that the island was

> in a very anomalous position [with regards to their education] whereas the children of the peasantry have schools within their reach in every part of the island, there is not a single establishment . . . for educating the children of the upper and middle classes; the consequence is that those parents who can afford it are obliged to send their children to Europe to be educated, while those of small means are compelled to witness the sad spectacle of seeing their little ones grow up in ignorance around them.[29]

The lieutenant-governor eventually proposed the establishment of a grammar school in Castries and the recruitment of teachers from England to staff it. But the legislature was unwilling to support the proposal because of its cost. About four years later, the headmaster of a failed normal school attempted to set up a school on the island for boys from economically better-off families but this attempt was also not very successful.

A girls' school for the "upper classes of the community," conducted by the Ladies of the Convent of St. Joseph, was in existence on the island for some years prior to 1870. Its reputation was quite high, and because it was open to both Roman Catholic and Protestant children, it enjoyed a respectable enrollment of 58 in 1870. The government later provided a grant of £50 to the school. Around 1870, a Roman Catholic grammar school for boys was established for the first time on the island with an enrollment of 29 pupils, but by 1874 it was closed.

Nevertheless, in 1889-90, a new grammar school with an enrollment of 40 boys was conducted by Vicar Forain, the head of the local Roman Catholic church. The object of this school was to supply education of a "higher standard" to boys. To achieve this goal, the school was annually examined for the first five years by masters from Harrison College, Barbados. The government's annually renewable contribution of £200 helped to ensure its survival and, in addition, 10 scholarships were provided to enable boys from the primary schools to attend this institution.

In Dominica, a classical seminary was opened in 1845 with an annual grant of £300 from the legislature, even though the governor questioned the suitability of such an institution because of the colony's poor economy. In addition, he did not think that there were enough youths available whose parents could have afforded the cost of such an education. Instead, he suggested that a school of a less pretentious character in which a plain English education was provided would be more suitable. He was obviously correct in his assessment of the situation, because in August 1846 the institution was closed due to low enrollment and limited income which was no longer commensurate with the expenses incurred. In 1847 the school was re-opened for a trial period of six months, but it was observed that the prospect of its survival was rather discouraging.

The government, however, did not give up on the idea of having a local secondary school. Some years later, in 1857, the School Act provided for the appointment of an inspector of schools who was also to be in charge of a classical seminary for the education of the better classes of children, providing there was a demand for such education. By 1862 the desire for higher education by the independent small farmers continued to increase and in 1864 a Bill was proposed to provide a further grant for the establishment of a grammar school. The aim was to permit some boys who had acquired a good primary education to continue their studies at a moderate expense. In 1888, "an admirable school" existed at the Roseau convent in Dominica for the education of "the higher class of young ladies," and in 1890, the Federal Council of the Leeward Islands provided £300 for the establishment of a grammar school on the island. The school was opened around 1892 but lasted only until 1893. After this, the secondary-school situation in Dominica did not substantially change until the twentieth century.

In the late 1840s, St. Kitts had an academy operated by Mr. Wattley, where boys of a higher class in society were being educated. To this school the legislature contributed £40 annually, to assist with the cost of educating six pupils whose families were in distressed circumstances and could not afford the cost of this level of education for their sons. It was hoped that the school would be the nucleus of a grammar school. However, in 1860 an Act was passed formally establishing a grammar school which was opened the following year. A Cambridge graduate was appointed as principal and he "doubled up" as inspector of schools for the industrial classes. Only 16 students were initially registered in the school, a figure which was below the anticipated enrollment. Further, the principal resigned soon after taking office, and the level of enrollment continued to remain low. Despite its earlier difficulties, the grammar school was established on a firm basis by 1865 and was achieving full success. The academic performance of its students who later went from the school to continue their studies in England was of a high standard and the principal also commented favourably on their deportment and behaviour.

But a major problem which plagued the institution — and most other secondary schools in the smaller British West Indian islands — was that of maintaining a reasonable level of enrollment. To help combat this problem, the principal suggested the need for boarding facilities. Boys who had to travel long distances usually failed to do well at school — a factor which no doubt contributed to their early drop-out.

In 1867 the school began with an enrollment of 25 pupils, but the number dwindled to 11 after a fire had damaged the building. It was hoped that there would be a gradual recovery in the enrollment figures, but this did not occur and the school was eventually closed. In 1869, attention was again drawn to the need for a grammar school, and the suggestion was made that, if one was established, parents who could have afforded it might be willing to place their children there as boarders. There seemed to have been a positive response to this proposal because in 1870 a superior grammar school was reported to have been operating in St. Kitts.

Another factor which contributed to the particularly low secondary school enrollment on the island and elsewhere in the region was that children of non-whites, particularly blacks, were often not particularly welcome in these schools. Some were beginning to accept coloured children, but they often did not want to see their numbers rise too high. This was hinted at in the remarks of the principal of the secondary school in St. Kitts, who noted that, "during the present year, two boys have come to the school from the rising portion of the coloured class and from this source I have reason to expect more; to them the gain will be very great, *provided that the staple element of the school should remain as heretofore, white*" [emphasis added].[30]

In 1890 a government grammar school was established so that there were two secondary schools on the island. During the year 1893-94, the post of headmaster of the grammar school was separated from that of the analytical chemist in an effort to give the headmaster enough time to make school a more vibrant institution.

There was a grammar school in St. Johns, Antigua, which never enjoyed "robust vitality." Therefore, when its endowment expired in the early 1850s, it ceased to exist. In 1859 it was suggested that the establishment of a good middle-class school in the capital city would be in the best interest of a "most important part of the population" and "well worthy" of their consideration. Two years later, in 1861, the Lord Bishop established the Antigua Classical School which had an initial enrollment of 25 boys who paid a fee of £12 each p.a. for their education. The Reverend N. E. Page started a school in 1861 — possibly a secondary school — though nothing much was heard of this institution. Around 1883 a grant-in-aid of £200 p.a. for 10 years was made available to the Reverend S. E. Branch, to open a suitable school of a high order for the education of the middle and upper classes. Initially, 30 pupils were enrolled in this institution.

In 1886 the Antigua Girls' High School was started by Mr. and Mrs. Williams, and by 1889 there were reported to have been a few other private schools on the island which also offered secondary education. In that year, 15 candidates entered for the Cambridge Local Examination, and by the following year the number had doubled.

Arrangements were also made for Antigua to be an examinations centre for the University of London examinations, and 56 candidates initially presented themselves for examinations in various subjects. This had the impact of stimulating local demand for more secondary education. Therefore it was later observed that throughout the island there were "distinct and encouraging" signs that the advantages of education were increasingly appreciated by all classes. In view of this growing public interest in secondary education, the government continued its efforts to provide educational opportunities for the middle classes, in order to afford "special facilities" for those who were intending to enter life as "planters or merchants."

In Grenada, a grammar school was established in the capital city around 1858 and operated in conjunction with the normal school, attracting children from mostly middle-class families. It was noted that there was "scarcely a family of respectability in the island having sons to educate, that has not patronized the institution" and that it was "setting a praiseworthy example to those moving in a lower station in life."[31] The school was provided with financial assistance from the government, though the lieutenant-governor was not very supportive of the idea that the legislature should incur expenses to operate a grammar school which, as he saw it, was taking funds from the much-needed educational programs for the masses.

The headmaster also supervised the training of pupil-teachers, an activity which probably contributed to his frequent absence from the secondary school. These absences caused much dissatisfaction among the parents, eventually resulting in a request by the legislature for his dismissal. The institution, with both its grammar and normal school departments, was therefore closed in 1862.

However, due to continuing pressure, largely from middle-class parents, the school was re-opened in 1865, though it still met with little success, with enrollment falling from 30 to 7 by 1866. In that year an Educational Commission concluded that, while it was difficult to identify the precise cause of the decrease, a major factor was probably that the fees were higher than most people in the community could afford, especially with the recent drop in the price of sugar. Another possible cause was the poor quality of the instruction, because it was noted in 1872 that the knowledge of the scholars was very limited and superficial. Many learned merely by rote and were "entirely ignorant" of the meanings of the words they "so glibly read" and repeated.

During the following year, the fees were lowered to boost enrollment, which eventually increased to 20. But these numbers continued to decline and when they reached 15 in 1872, the governor warned that if the situation did not improve the institution would have to be closed. This happened the following year, when the enrollment fell to 11. Another grammar school was established in 1874 and within a year the enrollment had increased to 36. But there was difficulty in finding a suitable candidate for the combined post of the headmaster and inspector of schools for the island. The legislature eventually voted separate funds for these two positions but, nevertheless, the grammar school was closed in 1878.

In addition, there were two girls' schools — St. George's High School and St. Joseph's Convent School — the former having an enrollment of about 30 students. Both schools were opened around 1872. There was also a Central School, and in 1876 the need was expressed for another such school to provide opportunities for advanced primary education for non-whites on the island. This demand for higher level primary education, from the lower middle or the upper working-class groups, continued to increase over the years and, as with most of the other West Indian colonies, developed into a demand for more regular secondary education.

Up to 1866, it was reported that there was no school, public or private, for the education of the middle or upper class in Nevis. However, the president of the colony indicated that he looked forward to the early establishment of a suitable grammar school, which became a reality some years later. In 1890, the secondary school had an enrollment of only 15 pupils. In 1864 a new Education Act in Montserrat provided for the establishment of a grammar school for the upper and middle classes, but not much success was achieved with the proposal until 1890, when a high school was started. Two years later, however, its enrollment was only 26. In the British Virgin Islands, the local resources were considered insufficient to meet the cost of a high class school, and the community was not large enough to provide adequate employment for lads who were highly educated.

In British Guiana, a Church of England grammar school, the Queen's College (QC), was established in 1844 by the Anglican bishop because much was already being done for the education of the lower classes, while correspondingly little attention was paid to the educational needs of the middle classes. Queen's College, which benefited from a government grant, offered a full secondary academic course based on the syllabus of King's College, London, plus a commercial programme to meet the needs of children of local businessmen.

In 1853, a new building was made available for the school and, in 1876-77, the institution was fully taken over by the government. It was considered desirable to make the school a colonial institution because it was to be open to all, irrespective of colour, race, creed, or social position, and the church did not have sufficient additional funds to meet the expected demand. The school enrollment figures ranged from 91 in 1884, to 75 in 1885, 66 in 1887, and 90 in 1890.

In addition, there were a number of private academies, especially in the capital city, which tended to provide an education for younger children somewhat above the level of that offered in the elementary schools. Among these was an excellent girls' school, St. Rose's, operated by nuns from the St. Ursuline Convent. The Smith's Congregational Girls' School was also established and so was the Catholic grammar school. The last named was opened in 1866 but was later closed and re-opened in 1880. This school, along with Queen's College, initially provided an education mainly for the Creole whites, including the Portuguese, and the coloured middle class.

The Saffron School, which also tried to provide a high class education for young ladies, was opened in 1878. In some cases secondary classes were even offered in the better elementary schools, such as Christchurch School in Georgetown, though with the abolition of the Cambridge Local Preliminary Examination this practice virtually came to an end. There were other private schools, such as The Brunswick House School founded by H. J. Cockett in 1879.

Around 1895 the Reverend D. J. Reynolds established two schools on behalf of the Methodists — Kingston High School for boys and Trinity High School for girls. In 1894 a middle school for both boys and girls was started by A. A. Thorne, M.A., which provided an additional opportunity to non-white children of the middle and lower socio-economic groups to get a secondary education. A high school was also opened up in New Amsterdam, the second town in the country, while a Mrs. Vyfhuis, who earlier had been connected with the Saffron School, started a private school in Georgetown — the Minto House School — in 1896.

In British Honduras, the Public Meeting approved an Act in 1845 which converted the free school that had existed for many years into the Honduras Grammar School. The headmaster received the fairly substantial salary of £300 p.a. While the enrollment limit for the school was as high as 175, for a variety of reasons, attendance rarely exceeded 75.

It was intended that the institution should provide both primary education and upper primary, or the beginnings of a secondary education, mainly for middle-class children. The admission age was as low as five years, and the subjects initially taught consisted mainly of the 3Rs and English grammar. This meant that, despite its name, the school was not really a grammar school, since it did not offer classical subjects. By 1848, the number of boys attending the school, which included coloureds and blacks, increased to 110 from 75 in 1846. In the girls' school, which was a distinct part of the same institution, the enrollment was 71. In 1850 the grammar school was renamed the Honduras Free School (which included a Boys' and a Girls' Free School, both housed in the same building) and the focus of the curriculum shifted, somewhat, from academic (classical) to industrial education. However, this school was abandoned in 1856.

Later, a few private secondary schools emerged with little or no aid or control from the government, and by 1866, some facilities existed in Belize for the education of children from the higher grade of society. Mr. Dunbar, who was a master of "good attainments," was in charge of a school which offered Latin as one of the subjects in the curriculum. In 1882 the Wesleyans established a high school but it was discontinued in 1894, due to lack of popular support. In 1896 the St. Johns Berchman College was founded by the

Jesuit Fathers, and in 1883 the St. Catherine's Academy for Girls was established by the Sisters of Mercy from the USA. A Church of England high school was also started.

In the 1890s, provision was made for the award of some scholarships on the basis of a competitive examination. These allowed a few students from the ordinary primary schools to receive a secondary education. By the turn of the century, it was reported that there were eight private secondary schools in operation in British Honduras, though it was only in 1898 that secondary schools that were recognized by the government became subject to annual inspection. Prior to this time they were generally considered to be independent private organizations, although government scholarships were tenable there.

In the Bahamas problems developed over the provision of secondary education and the survival of secondary schools after they were established. One reason for this was the reluctance of the whites to allow coloured and black children to be admitted to the schools which their children attended. Two high schools were opened in the first half of the nineteenth century, but both eventually failed. One of them, a collegiate institution, collapsed because of a conflict over whether admission should be based on race. Therefore, in 1851, educational facilities for those of a higher grade in the society still hardly existed in the colony. In 1854 the Christchurch Grammar School was established by the Anglicans, but it did not last very long either. In 1859 the annual report for the colony noted that no organization yet existed to give a liberal education to the sons of the more affluent members of the society who intended to devote their future to "commercial or professional" activities. This continued to be a matter of some concern, and in that year it was reported that "the sons of our merchants, lawyers and doctors are forced, either to dispense with a liberal education altogether, or go to the United States to complete their studies."[32]

In 1862 it was again observed that while ample provision had been made for the instruction of the children of the lower class, there was not a single educational establishment in the colony in which the children of the more respectable class could receive instruction. In his address to the legislature that year, Governor Bayley reiterated the recommendation he had made the previous year for the establishment of such a school, suggesting that

> among the most striking necessities of the Colony is the one to offer an educational institution of a higher kind. Admirable as are the Government schools which your provident liberality maintains for the humbler classes of society, establishments are still needed for the training of those who are destined for commercial or professional life. The absence of such an endowment is all to be regretted, in as much as the Mother Country is daily extending the opportunities and augmenting the prizes of sound and healthy education. I commend this subject to your discernment and liberality.[33]

A bill embodying the proposal to establish a "higher type" of school was eventually introduced in the legislature, but was rejected mainly for financial reasons. Following this, no further action was taken on the issue for some time.

Efforts were made early in the nineteenth century to establish a classical school for the "better class" whites in Bermuda and, in 1829, a "spacious building" was erected and opened as a "superior classical" boarding school — the Devonshire College. However, student boarders did not come from the West Indies to attend the school as was hoped, forcing the school to close in 1835. Over the next few years, it continued to be noted that there was need for a public secondary institution to educate the children of the higher socio-economic groups on the island. Up to the 1840s, those who received financial aid for their education from the Aaron Dixon Foundation had to attend a private school, where they also were given a classical education.

In 1853 another experiment was made to provide secondary education in the colony, when the Reverend Dowding, an Anglican clergyman, established St. Paul's College. Although the school was initially intended for the children of the coloured population, it was the founder's hope that eventually students of all races would attend it. But, while it flourished for a few years, opposition developed toward its policy of non-discrimination on the basis of race and the institution was soon closed. The upper classes did not particularly want to send their children to the United States for their education and therefore an effort was again made to establish a grammar school on the land endowed to the Devonshire College. However, this plan did not materialize.

In 1876 the governor again pointed out that the social class which was expected to produce the future men of business and landowners of the country, the magistrates, and the members of the assembly, was relatively even worse educated than the class below them. The property of Devonshire College was finally divided between the white and the coloured population, and the Saltus Grammar School for white boys and the Bermuda High School for white girls were opened in 1877 and 1894 respectively. Although the coloured population unsuccessfully petitioned for a racially mixed school in 1889, the American Methodist Episcopal Church (AME) of the USA opened a high school on the island for coloured children only. This school was not granted any aid until it severed its AME connection, and up to 1894 there was only one aided secondary school in Bermuda. The three private secondary schools on the island did not receive any aid.

The Development of Post-secondary Education

In a previous volume entitled *The Utilization, Misuse and Development of Human Resources in the Early West Indian Colonies*, it was noted that while the Spanish colonies and the English settlements in North America developed institutions of higher learning that were essentially replications of similar institutions in the metropole, this did not happen in the British West Indies. A number of factors were responsible for this, including the fact that the whites in these colonies did not see the West Indies as their permanent place of residence. As a result, those who could afford to give their children an education up to the tertiary level wanted them to be educated in the metropole.

Although a few attempts were made to provide higher education in the region, most were not very successful. One of the first of such proposals was put forward by Bishop Berkeley in the first quarter of the eighteenth century. He suggested that an institution offering tertiary education be established in Bermuda to serve all of the British colonies in the region, including those in North America. But, as Braithwaite[34] pointed out, the scheme failed for many reasons, including the proposed location and the limited number of whites in the region who could afford this level of education for their children.

In 1852, through the efforts of Reverend W. C. Dowding, a meeting was held in London to revive Bishop Berkeley's scheme to establish a college of higher education in Bermuda. The new proposal was that a modest start be made by first establishing a grammar school "in a collegiate form," and by organizing simple courses of lectures. St. Paul's College, mentioned above, was therefore opened in 1853 under the principalship of the Reverend Dowding. But he left shortly afterwards, and the college closed its doors in 1856.

In Barbados, Codrington College was established through a bequest of Sir Christopher Codrington to enable students to study "Physic, Chirugery, as well as Divinity." While the institution initially faced many difficulties, it nevertheless matriculated 90 students between 1830 and 1845, 40 of whom were ordained. The education these students received in the classics also prepared them to help staff the local grammar schools, where this subject occupied a prominent place in the curriculum.

The controversy as to whether the foundation funds should be used to support a secondary school and to provide stipends for students pursuing further studies in Britain came to an end in the late 1840s when a firm decision was made to have all the resources of the trust devoted to its work as a theological college.

In 1875 Codrington College was formally affiliated with Durham University in England, and this helped to ensure that its qualifications received a certain amount of recognition, even though it carried the "stigma" of an external degree. However, the pressure throughout the Caribbean was for higher education in the metropole. In Barbados, for example, the more prestigious Island Scholarship was awarded for study at one of the British universities, while the less prestigious one was made tenable at Codrington College.

By the mid-1880s Codrington reached its peak in terms of enrollment, with 26 students. By the end of the nineteenth century, it was proposed to have a principal, a tutor, the chaplain to the Codrington estates, a medical lecturer, and a teacher of Hindi and Urdu appointed to the staff. The student body was to include six foundation scholars, some theological scholars — one for each West Indian Island — who were to be partially supported by the SPCK, four Barbados scholars, "two Leacock [a Barbadian endowment] students, a Rawle Scholarship holder, and Powder students for missionary work."[35] In reviewing the performance of Codrington College during the period from 1830 to 1895, it was observed that the total number of students who passed through the institution was 373. Of these, 135 became assistants and licentiates and a similar number were actually ordained. By then, old Codringtonians were found in most professions in the various West Indian colonies.

For reasons previously indicated, it was difficult for any effective provision to be made locally for a university-type institution. A number of individuals nevertheless continued to be interested in the establishment of at least one regional college to meet the higher educational needs of these colonies. Such interest in higher education was seen, as Braithwaite pointed out, in the July 1838 editorial of the Jamaica *Royal Gazette*, which offered some support for a proposed "Plan for a College in Jamaica." This college would form the apex of the educational system of the colony and would make it unnecessary for youngsters to travel to Britain to obtain their university education. Five professors were to be appointed to the staff, and funding was to be obtained through the consolidation of the existing education trust funds in Jamaica that had been bequeathed by various individuals.

This effort was unsuccessful and led to the desire on the part of the non-conformist missionaries to develop theological seminaries to train their own staff for the West Indies. In 1834 the United Presbyterians established the Theological College in Montego Bay, and the Baptists started one at Calabar. In addition to preparing students to become clergy, these missionary societies were also concerned with providing a body of native teachers to staff their schools. Thus a department that was in essence a normal school was often attached to each of these seminaries.

Efforts continued towards providing university education in the region. Among the advocates of such a facility was the well-known Baptist missionary, the Reverend J. M. Phillippo. Since he was convinced of the intellectual ability of the Africans to benefit from a university education, he wanted some equality in the educational opportunities for them — which a university-type institution was likely to do. He therefore proposed the establishment of a college in Jamaica on the model of the recently established University College of London University. The students and staff were to enjoy "complete liberty of conscience" and there was to be no discrimination on the grounds of religious or political beliefs. The only bases on which the college was to operate were "sound scholarship, good morals, virtuous habits, industry and talent."[36]

The instruction to be provided was to be academic rather than vocational, with the subjects to be offered to include languages (Latin, Greek, Hebrew, French and Spanish), logic, philosophy (including philosophy of the human mind and moral philosophy), politics, the principles of political economy, jurisprudence, and the natural sciences (botany, chemistry and natural history). Some practical courses were also to be offered through a few lectures on the "useful arts, engineering and manufactures." While the main purpose of the institution was "to train young men immediately before entering upon the business of active life in any respectable situation," it was also to be "open to gentlemen of leisure and in the professions to attend occasional lectures."[37] However, nothing came of Phillippo's proposed plan.

Later, Sir Charles Grey, the governor of Jamaica, in a speech to the House Of Assembly in 1850 also mentioned the desirability of providing a higher education institution on the island — one in which professors in the arts and the sciences would give open lectures to students of all denominations. However, he indicated that it would be difficult for the state alone to fund such an institution, and discussions took place with the Church of England authorities, in the hope that they would take the major responsibility for establishing such a college. But nothing came from these efforts either.

Another proposal for a tertiary-level educational institution was made by Lord Harris, the governor of Trinidad, who saw the establishment of a college as being very important for the region. He suggested that such an institution would provide the fitting apex to the educational system he had proposed for the island. Harris further envisaged that the institution would eventually become a university for the entire English-speaking West Indies. But this proposal never got off the ground, despite a reintroduction of some elements of the proposal in 1870 by Keenan.

The idea of a central college for Jamaica continued to be mooted by many voluntary bodies, and the need for it was even drawn to the attention of the Colonial Office. In 1870 the United Presbyterian Mission wrote to the secretary of state for the colonies, indicating that the organization favoured the establishment of such an institution to assist with the education of their teachers and missionaries and enquired whether the British government had any plans for such a project. The governor, Sir Peter Grant, also supported the proposal, pointing out that while adequate educational facilities were being provided for the lower classes, higher education of the middle and upper classes was being neglected.

To meet this need he suggested the "combination of a public central college, where education on the highest order for which a demand can be induced, may be imparted."[38] This centre for higher education, which was to combine some of the features of the old English and Scottish universities, was to be specially adapted to meet local needs and help raise the academic standards of the island's secondary schools. This was considered to be very important since it was realized that, without the support of the local communities, the proposed institution would not be able to survive.

Its focus was to provide a sound liberal education rather than the "compulsory study of dead languages." While it was to provide the educational background for those preparing for the ministry, it was not to be involved in theological training. This was to be imparted by tutors specially appointed by the various denominational bodies themselves. Nevertheless, some professional training in law and medicine was contemplated for a later date. The compulsory subjects were to include history (ancient and modern), geography (political and physical), and English literature. Other subjects to be offered were philosophy (mental and moral), logic or mathematics, and natural science with further options in Greek, Latin, French, Spanish, political economy, geology, and jurisprudence. In 1873, a principal was appointed for this institution — Queen's College — which was opened in Spanish Town in September of the same year. A second master was recruited to teach the classics, mental and moral philosophy, and English literature.

However, the number of applicants for entry was limited, and even these were poorly qualified. For example, only one of the four who applied for entry in the first year passed the entrance examination. The following year, all applications for admission were rejected, partly because of their poor academic background. Some of these students were "unable to read English fluently, or to spell common English words and had an appalling ignorance of history and geography."[39] Even the few who had been accepted by the college were not, in fact, up to matriculation standard and, as a result, it was not possible for the institution to maintain its proposed curriculum. Better qualified individuals, whose parents could afford to give them a "sound secondary education," were still being sent off to Britain for their tertiary education.

It became quite obvious that the demand for post-secondary education on the island had been seriously over-estimated. Further, the secular nature of the institution also presented problems. Therefore, in 1875 when Sir Charles Grey succeeded Sir John Grant as governor, he concluded that the institution could not survive without the support of at least the major Protestant religious groups on the island. In addition, it became increasingly clear that the establishment of the college was premature, especially since the facilities for secondary education in Jamaica were still very limited. In the mid-1870s it was suggested that the college should be transformed into a "truly scientific" institution, but this was ignored. The college was finally closed, after being in existence for only three years.

Another effort at providing university-level education on the island was made in the 1880s, largely through the efforts of Bishop Enos Nuttall, chairman of the Jamaica Schools Commission. Nuttall envisaged an institution that would provide a university education somewhat below the standard of the old English universities, but at a level of the average American or Canadian college, or even another less prestigious British university. He saw Trinity College, the University of Toronto, King's College, London, or Durham University as desirable models for the local institution and therefore sought an affiliation for the college with Durham University. After failing to secure this, he was able to win approval for the students at the college to enter for intermediate and degree-level examinations of the University of London. His hope was that the practice would eventually be established whereby those who completed their studies at the local institution could finish up their education in law, medicine, or divinity in England. The other students were to be in a position to secure jobs locally as teachers in the higher echelons of the civil service.

As King[40] pointed out, Nuttall put much effort and thought into the proposal for the college, and in 1886 he was able to get the idea accepted by the Jamaica Schools Commission. He also secured a grant of £300 p.a. from the government of Jamaica for its operation. The institution was opened in the 1880s and was officially linked to the island's most prestigious secondary school, the Jamaica Free School, which had 50 boarders as compared with the 10 attending the College. It began its activities by preparing students for the B.A and the M.A. degrees and for the first examination in science and medicine of the University of London. It later also took part in the teaching of agricultural science at a higher level. The last-mentioned activity resulted from the proposals that were being made at the time to offer instruction in agriculture in schools and colleges throughout the region.

After 12 years, the outcomes of the college were still very limited. It had only produced five graduates with B.A. degrees, one of whom subsequently obtained the M.A. degree. Several others had passed the intermediate and the matriculation examinations and, of the total of 30 students who went through the college, a considerable number were teaching in the secondary schools of the island. However, before the end of the century, when the government tried to curtail its expenditures, the vote for the institution was reduced from £300 to £50. The Jamaica Schools Commission protested this reduction and argued that the College was an integral part of the larger educational complex. Its funds could therefore not be discontinued without affecting the work of the entire institution. The grant was subsequently restored but, despite this fact, the collegiate division of the institution never flourished again. This was due to the limited supply of students with a sound secondary education who could benefit from the level of instruction offered and the continuing desire of those seeking such university education for their children to send them abroad.

In the southern Caribbean, also, there was an interest in the provision of higher education facilities. In Trinidad, the more well-known proposal was the one put forward by Keenan in 1869. In his report, the author drew attention to the need for the establishment of an institution of higher education for the region — a need which he felt could be met by a single regional university. Therefore, he advocated the establishment of a University of the West Indies and further suggested that it should be a purely examining body, which offered no teaching whatsoever. The provision of instruction was to be the responsibility of fairly autonomous constituent colleges — a structure somewhat akin to the model originally devised for the University of London. Because the university was to have a purely examining function, its cost was expected to be quite modest. Keenan also indicated that the university could be located in any one of the three larger islands — Trinidad, Barbados, or Jamaica — because of the size of the white population in these colonies. This was considered important because it was likely to ensure an adequate supply of students. However, Keenan's suggestion for a university for the region never materialized, partly because West Indians continued to favour university training in Great Britain.

As a result, various governments began to award scholarships tenable overseas, usually based on the results of the Cambridge Overseas Examination. For example, when the government of Barbados made awards available to some students to study at Codrington in 1850, it concurrently introduced the more prestigious Island Scholarship, which was tenable for four years at an English university or an agricultural or technical college in Europe or America. Students also competed, with great success, for the Gilchrist scholarship, tenable at the University of London. Four exhibitions were granted to students in Trinidad in 1870 to study in Great Britain and Ireland. In 1873, two students from that island also secured scholarships to King's College, Cambridge, and another won the Gilchrist scholarship. In 1882 the government of British Guiana, and some years later, the government of Jamaica, also instituted a scholarship scheme for university-level study overseas. This scholarship was open to competition by students from the local secondary schools. Similar steps were taken in some of the other colonies.

Summary and Conclusions

Early attempts were made in most former British West Indian colonies to provide an education at a higher level than that available in the ordinary primary schools. This led to the establishment of (1) central, model, or second grade schools which offered an advanced primary education; and (2) secondary grammar schools which mainly attempted to prepare students for tertiary education.

After emancipation, interest in advanced primary and secondary education increased. But the officials of the Colonial Office and some of the local elites opposed the granting of government subsidies to these schools. They suggested that since such education was meant for the children of the more affluent groups, the parents should be able to afford its full cost. Nevertheless, with an emerging middle class in the region, the demand for a higher level of education continued to increase, and many West Indian legislatures eventually began to make grants to assist with the establishment of secondary grammar schools. The government of Jamaica even established a Secondary Schools Commission to administer the educational endowments on the island and to co-ordinate all secondary and even post-secondary educational efforts. On the other hand, the Crown Colony government of Trinidad decided to establish its own secular secondary grammar school, although after 1870 the denominational secondary schools on the island also became eligible for government subsidies.

The demands for government aid to secondary schools initially met with very little positive response from most local legislatures, primarily because of the colonies' bad economies, especially after the British subsidy for British West Indian sugar ended. Further, the wealthier groups who continued to dominate the local legislatures still sent their own children overseas for their higher education and did not see why they had to subsidize such education for those who wanted it to be provided locally.

In addition, with the termination of the Negro Education Grant in 1845, the West Indian governments were increasingly inundated with requests to provide more funds for education for the children of the ex-slaves. This made it difficult for them to provide financial support for higher education, especially since such education would benefit a small proportion of the population, who were, in any case, among the more affluent sections of these societies.

Therefore, immediately after emancipation, there was very little incentive to establish good secondary schools in the region. But, with the increase in the size of the local middle class, more pressures began to be exerted on the local legislatures to support secondary education, and gradually funds were made available for this purpose, especially from the 1870s. After this time some noticeable progress began to be made in the establishment of secondary schools in the region, particularly in the colonies with a larger population base.

In connection with tertiary-level education, many proposals were made for the establishment of a university in the region during this period. For a number of reasons, however, such plans never came to fruition and those institutions that were started were not very successful. This was due to a number of factors. First, the parents who could afford to give their children a higher education still preferred them to attend a university in the metropole. Most of them intended to return to Britain and they wanted to ensure access to suitable job opportunities and a higher social standing for their children within the metropolitan social structure. This, they felt, could partly be achieved by the children's attendance at a home-based university.

In addition, secondary education facilities were as yet poorly developed in the region, and the number of candidates who were qualified to enter directly into a university degree programme was very limited. But some of those who failed to obtain a university degree often found jobs as teachers in the secondary schools and therefore helped to raise the quality of secondary education in the region. Others continued their education in the local theological seminaries, which provided a number of missionaries to undertake service in the Caribbean and elsewhere.

Notes
1   Gordon, *A Century*, 225-26.
2   Sewell, *The Ordeal of Free Labour in the West Indies*, 68.
3   Ibid.
4   In personal communication with the author.
5   Report of the Government of Grenada, *British Parliamentary Papers*, Vol. 39: *1863* (London: Government of Great Britain), 39.
6   Government of Barbados, "The Report of the Inspector of Schools for 1867" (Bridgetown, Barbados), *British Parliamentary Papers*, Vol. 48: *1867-68* (London: Government of Great Britain), 48.
7   Report of the Government of Barbados, *British Parliamentary Papers*, Vol. 49: *1870* (London: Government of Great Britain), 51.
8   Minutes of the Jamaica Schools Commission, 1889; Mavis Burke, "The History of the Wesleyan-Methodist Contribution to Education in Jamaica in the Nineteenth Century, 1833-1900" (M.A. thesis, Univ. of London, 1965), 226.
9   CO 295/196, Keate to Labouchère, 6 September 1857, no. 91 (London: PRO).
10   Report of the Government of Barbados, *British Parliamentary Papers*, Vol. 59: *1877* (London: Government of Great Britain), 59.
11   Frank Cundall, *Some Notes on The History of Secondary Education in Jamaica* (Kingston: n.d.), 7.
12   Report of the Government of Nevis, *British Parliamentary Papers*, Vol. 34: *1849*(London: Government of Great Britain), 286.
13   Gordon, *A Century*, 225-26.
14   Report of the Government of Jamaica, *British Parliamentary Papers*, Vol. 34: *1849* (London: Government of Great Britain), 98.
15   Ibid., Vol. 31: *1852* , 32.
16   Cundall, *Some Notes*, 6.
17   *Report of the Wesleyan Methodist Missionary*, 1870.
18   Stephen Sutton to Methodist Missionary Society, 6 June 1879.
19   Burke, *History of the Wesleyan Methodist Commission* .
20   Gordon, *A Century*, 248.
21   CO 295/156, Speech by Lord Harris to the Legislative Council, Trinidad, 1 February 1847 (London: PRO).
22   Ibid.
23   CO 295/196, Governor Keate to Secretary of State, 6 August 1857, no. 91 (London: PRO).
24   Brereton, *Race Relations*, 71.
25   CO 295/196, Keate.
26   Bhagan, *A Critical Study*.
27   Gordon, *A Century*, 235-36.

28   Report of the Government of Tobago, *British Parliamentary Papers*, Vol. 64: *1881* (London: Government of Great Britain), 86.

29   Report of the Government of St. Lucia in *British Parliamentary Papers*, Vol. 42: *1856* (London: Government of Great Britain), 110.

30   Report of the Government of St. Kitts, *British Parliamentary Papers*, Vol. 42: *1872* (London: Government of Great Britain), 146.

31   Report of the Government of Grenada, *British Parliamentary Papers*, Vol. 44: *1860* (London: Government of Great Britain), 58.

32   Report of the Government of Bahamas, *British Parliamentary Papers*, Vol. 21: *1859* (London: Government of Great Britain), 51.

33   Ibid., Vol. 36: *1862* , 23.

34   Lloyd Braithwaite, "The Development of Higher Education in the British West Indies," *Social and Economic Studies* 7, 1 (Jamaica: Institute of Social and Economic Research, Univ. of the West Indies, March 1958): 1-64.

35   Ibid., 8-9.

36   Ibid., 14.

37   Ibid.

38   Ibid., 15.

39   Ibid., 17.

40   Ruby King, "The History of the Jamaica Schools Commission and its Role in Education in Jamaica, 1879-1911" (M.A. thesis, Univ. of the West Indies, Mona, Kingston, Jamaica, 1972).

$$C_{HAPTER}\ \textbf{10}$$

SECONDARY SCHOOL CURRICULUM

Introduction

As pointed out earlier, two types of post-primary schools were established in the West Indian colonies during the period under review, each of which had its own curriculum focus and prepared pupils to occupy positions at different levels of the social and occupational hierarchy. The curricula of these institutions, the model and the grammar schools, is discussed below.

The Model Schools

The model or intermediate schools provided a higher level of elementary education mainly for those upper working- and lower middle-class children who aspired to fill such white-collar occupations as teachers, clerks, catechists, or in some cases, even priests. These schools were more suited to meet the educational aspirations and financial resources of children whose parents were among the middling and respectable members of these societies rather than of the lower classes and afforded them "an education that will fit them to fill any position in life short of [those] requiring classical attainments."[1]

The distinctiveness of these schools in comparison with the ordinary primary schools was achieved both by the range of subjects which they offered and the exclusiveness which they maintained, through charging high fees. They were equivalent to the sort of high school which was proposed in the 1834 Colonial Office report and again recommended by the Reverend Sterling and to the second grade schools proposed for Barbados by the Mitchinson Commission in 1876.

The curriculum of most of the model schools extended beyond the 3Rs, with some of them offering, in addition to religious instruction and moral training, such subjects as book-keeping, English, history, and geography with some rudiments of natural history, natural philosophy, and mathematics. Biology was usually taught under the titles "natural history" or "natural philosophy," though other science subjects were given very little or no attention. Generally, the subjects emphasized were considered important for the development of knowledge, skills, attitudes, and values useful to students who were being prepared for lower-level service occupations.

Since most of the students in these schools were expected to become teachers or catechists, considerable emphasis was often placed on developing in them the "moral fitness" necessary for holders of such positions, particularly because it was thought that schools could give a "decided Moral and Religious cultivation," not only to their pupils but also to their communities. Therefore, students who were being prepared by the model schools to become teachers were expected to perform their occupational role effectively and to be aware of their obligations to the community in which they were likely to serve, society at large, the Queen, and the Empire.

In Port of Spain, Trinidad, the Boys' Model School established in 1852 offered, in addition to the 3Rs, the following subjects: geometry, algebra, mensuration, trigonometry, the elements of the "philosophy of the mechanical powers," human anatomy, physiology, optics, and agricultural chemistry. By 1864 the "geography of Europe and other countries" and singing had been added to the curriculum. In his1869 *Report* Keenan noted that the boys attending the model school read and spelt well from the highest books used in the National Schools of Ireland. Those in the upper section of the school could "parse very well," had a good grasp of geography, could do "difficult problems in Arithmetic . . . [and] are grounded well in Grammar." Some of the more advanced students were even reported to have been making "good progress in Euclid, algebra, mensuration and plain trigonometry."[2] The subjects taught at the Girls' Model School and the Borough Council Schools were similar to those mentioned above, except that needlework was offered in the girls' schools.

The programme of instruction in some of these schools was so ambitious that eventually the only difference between their curriculum and that of the secondary grammar schools was the lack of instruction in the classical subjects, i.e., Latin and Greek. A few intermediate schools did attempt to offer introductory courses in the classics. For example, the intermediate school established by Rawle in the early 1850s in St. Marks, Barbados, was to provide instruction in the classical subjects for children whose parents wanted a good English education at a modest cost. In 1867 the inspector of schools for the island also reported that the Christchurch Middle School and the St. Andrews Seminary, both of which were in fact second grade secondary schools, were offering elementary classics and mathematics, in addition to the "ordinary branches of an English Education."

These encroachments on the curriculum of the traditional grammar school led the Mitchinson Commission to conclude that some of the better primary schools in Barbados were attempting to be "first grade" schools in miniature, so that students were being pushed into these higher subjects, irrespective of their likely occupational destination or the amount of time they were expecting to stay on in school.

One might also include under this category of post-primary schools the many private academies throughout the region that tended to provide an education for younger children, at a level somewhat above that offered in the ordinary elementary schools. These schools usually emphasized the development of "social graces," which were considered an important element of character training. For example, at the Brunswick House School in Georgetown, British Guiana, for example, the students were taught "courtesy and chivalry," and it was said that "many a boy took a hiding to save a girl" and that "nobody dared to speak to a lady with his hat on." It was through the dancing lessons that courtesy was chiefly instilled, as boys were taught "good manners in approaching and requesting the lady for a dance and in taking her back to her seat."[3]

The Grammar Schools

The second type of post-primary school was the grammar school, which was probably similar to the school of a "superior order" recommended by C. J. Latrobe after his inspection visit to the region in 1838. The manifest function of these schools was to prepare students for admission into tertiary-level educational institutions in the metropole or for entry into certain higher level white-collar jobs locally. A latent function was to provide an additional means of social differentiation between the upper and middle sections of the population, and the masses, who were increasingly benefiting from a primary and even some post-primary education. For this reason, the inclusion of classical subjects in the curriculum of the grammar schools was considered to be particularly important.

This point was quite vividly stated by the attorney-general of Trinidad when he proposed the bill in the local legislature to establish the Queen's Collegiate School. In his speech he argued that the class distinction between different groups was in danger of being eroded and that the superior classical education that the proposed government grammar school intended to offer would play an important part in helping to maintain the status quo. These schools therefore did not primarily attempt to prepare their students with useful skills for jobs in commerce or agriculture, the main fields of employment in the region. One can get an idea of the dominance of the classics in these schools from an examination of their educational programmes, their students' textbooks, and the system of evaluation that was used.

The Curriculum of the Grammar Schools in the West Indies
Barbados
Students at Harrison studied Latin Grammar, read Ovid's *Metamorphoses* and Justin and were able, with the assistance of a dictionary, to render rapidly into English a lesson in either of these books. They were even able to write Latin correctly, especially in terms of Concord and Grammar. In the upper grades the school offered Greek, Latin, English, French, mathematics, and history (Roman and Greek and scriptural history), along with selections from the Greek Testament. Codrington Grammar School was then devoting more than one-quarter of its total instructional time to the study of the classics. Other subjects were given much less attention, and even science was neglected, with instruction in this subject often consisting only of a weekly lecture. In commenting on the programme of instruction offered at Harrison College Nicholls noted that the principal often ordered for the school such books as "Justin, Ovid Metamorphoses, Phaedrus Fables and Corderius Colloquies."[4]

A secondary school for girls, Queen's College, which later became a "first grade" school, offered the following subjects in 1894: religious knowledge, English, French, German, mathematics, botany, drawing, chemistry, also needlework, writing, singing, and drilling.

Trinidad
The Catholic Grammar School, the College of Immaculate Conception (CIC), operated more on the principle of a comprehensive school, offering a

fairly diversified curriculum to meet the needs of pupils with a wide range of interests and abilities. The school was originally geared not only for students who were destined for the "more learned professions," but also for those who required a thorough, sound, and practical education that was perfectly adapted to the circumstances of the colony. Because of this, it might not have initially offered advanced courses in the classics. In addition to its preparatory programme, which provided basic instruction in the 3Rs, English, French, grammar, history, and geography, the school also offered the following two advanced programmes: *The Commercial Programme*, which offered reading, writing, mathematics, natural sciences, book-keeping, grammar, geography, history and literature; and *The Classical Programme*, which offered such compulsory subjects as Latin and Greek grammar (up to the ancient authors) English and French, plus the optional subjects of German and Spanish. Aesthetic studies, such as drama and vocal music, including instruments of a full orchestra, were also available.

This broader instructional programme of the school was part of the educational philosophy of the headmaster who in 1865 noted that

> I do not consider it the business of a school master so much to make brilliant scholars — that is accidental rather than essential to his work — as to send out each boy entrusted to him, furnished with a stock of elementary knowledge, that self control and regard for the wishes and feelings of others which will enable him, by God's will to do his duty in the struggles and trials of riper years.[5]

The Commercial Programme was offered in an effort to meet the specific needs of the children of the local French elite who were mainly engaged in business.

CIC's more diversified curriculum was commented on positively by Keenan, who observed that

> the character of the instruction is eminently practical. As much Grammar is taught as enables a lad to express himself clearly and succinctly; as much arithmetic as makes him a good calculator and statistician; as much book-keeping as makes him a good clerk or accountant; and as much practice in penmanship as makes him a legible and off-hand writer. The utility of this class is directed mainly to a utilitarian view of instruction.[6]

But this did not mean that the classics were in any way neglected, especially when the school began to present candidates for the University of Cambridge School Certificate Examinations. For example, only 8% of the students were taking commercial subjects, while Latin and Greek were taught every day, from 8.30 to 11.00 a.m., except on Thursdays. Keenan too observed that the boys at the school had a thoroughly excellent knowledge of their Latin and Greek.

It was noted that the college took a heavily moralistic approach to the teaching of the classics and that the curriculum consisted of selections from such works as the *Fables of Phaedrus and Aesop*. This approach was said to have been strongly influenced by the classical education offered in France and Ireland.[7] But by 1870, when CIC began to adopt the curriculum of the government grammar school in order to qualify for government grants, classics came to occupy a dominant, though not an exclusive, place in its curriculum.

In 1887 CIC attempted to reintroduce its commercial or business stream. Most of its pupils "did not go to the length of completing their Classical course," and as a result, it was felt that "they should . . . have special studies that will qualify them for a commercial career."[8] It was re-emphasized that the purpose of the school was not to assemble "the youths of the aristocracy" or even to combine them "with the geniuses of this Island" but to unite all those who aspire to a secondary education. Because of this, it was necessary to introduce into the curriculum both commercial and classical subjects which would "satisfy the aspirations of anyone" who was seeking a higher education.[9]

In Governor Harris's proposal for a government grammar school for Trinidad, he envisaged that the superior programme which was to be offered should include not only the classics, but also such subjects as science and agriculture, which were likely to be more functional to the needs of society. However, his successor, Governor Keate, wanted the instructional programme of the school to differentiate it as an institution intended for the education of the superior social classes, preparing students mainly for the civil service and for further training in one of the learned professions. He therefore did not accept Harris's views as to the type of instructional programme which the school should offer, emphasizing that

> the instruction which is [to be] offered [here] . . . will be that which is generally known as a classical education, founded on the same principles, proposing to itself the same object[ive]s, and attaining those object[ive]s, by the same means as the education which is given at Eton, Harrow and Winchester. This education supposes an early and vigorous but not exclusive, training in Latin and Greek. . . . But, in insisting on the study of Latin and Greek as the basis of instruction, I do not understand that a classical education excludes other branches of learning. The system of the Collegiate School will include mathematics, geography and history, modern languages, and the principles of chemistry [emphasis added].[10]

Keate admitted that a classical education was totally useless to the vast majority of the population, and in no way adapted to their pursuits after they left school. He therefore used this argument to justify the exclusion of boys of "the humbler classes" from the school. From its inception, QCS offered the following subjects: Latin and Greek, French, arithmetic, elementary algebra, dictation, English, history and geography. A class for the study of practical science was also contemplated, and it was hoped that German would be introduced, as soon as the students had acquired some experience with the principles of language.

Overall, the academic performance of the boys came in for much commendation. In mathematics, they were, "in general, quite as proficient as boys of the same age in England." While only one boy had qualified to begin Greek in 1859, it was noted that another four expected to be in a similar position by the following year.

In 1863 the school became the first overseas institution to present students for the secondary school examinations held by the Cambridge University Syndicate. Those who took the first examination offered English, Latin, Greek, French, pure and applied mathematics and Roman history, which was not taught as a separate subject but was taken up as a reading exercise in Latin. Despite the fact that they had a "first class honours scientist" on the staff, no science subject was taken at the external examination by any student.

All seven candidates who entered the Senior Cambridge Examination passed in Latin and five passed in Greek. The examinations held in December 1869 for the senior students included the History of England from 1625-1649, English Literature (Shakespeare's *Merchant of Venice*), Cicero, "Pro Milone," Horace, Thucydides (Book vi, 1-51), Aeschylus "Prometheus Vinctus," Corneille's *Le Cid*, Michelet's *Charles le Temercure*, Epistles Book 1, and mathematics, which included Euclid Book i-vi and K 1 to Proposition 21, algebra, plain trigonometry, and the simple properties of the Conic sections. In addition, the students did translation from English to Latin and also to French.

In his 1863 report on the school, W. Campion, Fellow and Tutor of Queen's College, Cambridge, noted in 1863 that the performance of the boys at QCS in mathematics was "quite equal to that exhibited by boys at good public schools in England." They showed "a sound knowledge of the principles of the subjects in which they were examined" and "they were above the average of boys at good public schools in England." The examiner for Classical Tripos at Corpus Christi College, Cambridge, also remarked that, "your pupils' work [in the three Latin and two Greek papers] contrast most favourably with that of any school in England with which I am acquainted."[11] Other Cambridge University examiners commented very favourably on subsequent occasions on the work of the school, with one of them noting that, in Latin and Greek, students from Liverpool, England, and Trinidad did very good work, while the performance by those from Gravesend and Torquay in England was particularly bad. In fact, it was noted that the method of teaching Latin at QCS was highly intellectual and effective.

A similar comment was made by Keenan in 1869 on the instructional strategy used by one of the masters in the school. He observed that "in class every sentence is analyzed and every word assigned its proper position on the blackboard." He also noted that students' reading of the classics was wide and varied. In Latin, Cicero, Caesar, Sallust, Livy, Juvenal, Virgil, Horace and Ovid, and in Greek, Homer, Herodotus, Xenophor, Demosthenes, Thucydides, and Aeschylus had all been read between 1862 and 1868. This tendency towards parity between Greek and Latin and an emphasis on prose authors followed a pattern that was developing in England, and was strengthened by the dominance of the prose compositions and the absence of any verse, as seen in the homework set for senior boys. Despite his criticisms of certain aspects of the progamme of instruction offered by the school, Keenan was nevertheless impressed with the overall quality of the teaching.

Jamaica

In Jamaica the curriculum of the grammar schools was quite similar to those in Barbados and Trinidad. Later, some newer grammar schools were established, and while still emphasizing the classics, they offered an increasing range of subjects to meet the needs of pupils who were not seeking entrance to a university. For example, in 1880 the York Castle Methodist High School offered Latin, Greek, French, Euclid, algebra, trigonometry, natural philosophy, inorganic chemistry, English language, history, modern geography, and book-keeping. Its sister institution, the Barbican High School for Girls, which opened in 1881, offered "a thorough English Education," which included many subjects of the boys' school, in addition to political economy, geology, calisthenics, music, singing, and drawing.

Other West Indian Colonies

The curriculum of the grammar schools in the other West Indian colonies was similar to those of the schools in Barbados and Trinidad. In British Guiana, by the time Queen's College (QC) was fully taken over by the government in 1876-77, it offered a course of instruction that was "the same as that of a Public School or First Grade Grammar School at home," i.e., England. As the principal explained in 1880,

> Every pupil, from his entrance, is required to study Latin, French and Drawing, besides the usual range of English subjects, and Arithmetic; he has to drill for an hour a week, and when our Science master arrives he will have to attend a class in Elementary Science at least once a week. As he is promoted to the higher Form . . . Latin and French Translation is required as well as Grammar and Exercises; Book-keeping, Geometry and Algebra are introduced, Greek is studied by the Senior Forms, and in future Chemistry will be taken up as a special and more advanced subject in Science, side by side with the Elementary classes in Physics.[12]

Over a quarter of the school's instructional time (28%) in the third, fourth and fifth forms was devoted to Latin alone, and 44% of the time in the sixth form was given to study of the classics. On the occasion of the 1872 Speech Night, the audience was entertained with a whole range of items from the classics, including recitations from Horace's *Ode to Augustus*, a translation from Virgil, parts of *Achilles and Agamemnon* in Homer, Ovid's *Fabiorum Clades*, and *Anchisis Umbrea* and *Aeneas* from Virgil.[13]

Despite the dominant place held by the classics in the instructional programme of QC, "general knowledge and high culture" were, as the principal pointed out, "not altogether neglected."[14] Thus, the norms and behaviours that this school tried to inculcate were those of "English gentlemen." For example, in 1884 the school *Gazette* castigated the boys for their unsportsmanlike behaviour because they booed at an umpire's decision in a game of cricket, noting that this would be "an unheard of occurrence on the part of an English crowd, looking on at a cricket match."[15]

While great attention was devoted to French and Spanish in the instructional programme of the St. Kitts grammar school, the classics were not neglected. Here, too, the curriculum was almost identical to that of grammar schools in England, and in 1867 it was reported that the six boys who had left the school to study in Britain were doing well academically and had no problem coping with the work in their new schools.

In Grenada, the Boys' Grammar School offered Latin, French, English grammar and literature, geography, English composition, history, book-keeping, arithmetic, algebra, Euclid and Greek, which was optional. At the St. George's High School for Girls, political geography, physical geography, English language, arithmetic, elementary mathematics, English literature, French, natural science, history, elementary drawing, singing, and needlework were taught. At the St. Joseph's School, the following subjects were included in the curriculum English grammar and composition, paraphrasing, reading, orthography, penmanship, geography, English and Bible history, arithmetic, algebra, natural history, botany, astronomy, domestic economy, French (reading, grammar exercises and translation), drawing, painting, music (vocal and instrumental), calisthenics, and needlework (plain and ornamental). In St. Lucia, the St. Joseph's School for Girls prepared its students for the College of Preceptors' Examination and offered, in addition to the 3Rs, subjects such as grammar, geography, and plain and fancy needlework.

The Honduras Grammar School provided instruction in the 3Rs and geography in the lower division of the school, while in the upper division, the students were taught the classics and the elementary branches of mathematics. However, by 1855, greater emphasis was placed on industrial education and the board of education had proposed to supply the industrial programme of this school with the "tools, implements, machinery and other objects and materials" that were necessary for "the practical instruction of the pupils." Further, it expected to "engage the services of scientific and practical persons to give lectures or instruction in any branch of Mechanical or Practical Arts." So, in addition to the ordinary branches of instruction, the school was to teach "the elementary principles of practical and mechanical arts and all such industrial pursuits, as may, from time to time be directed by the Board."[16] This school was in fact a grammar school in name only, as the nature of its instructional programme was substantially different from that offered by the traditional grammar schools in the region or in the metropole.

Criticisms of the Curriculum of the Grammar Schools

There were many criticisms of the classical curriculum offered by the grammar schools. The governments of the region, which had begun to make some financial assistance available to these schools, were increasingly anxious to see them provide a broader and more useful education for their pupils. The Barbadian legislature, when voting assistance to the island's two grammar schools in 1870, suggested that they should not only prepare students "who may hereafter be called to the service of the Church" but also those who would proceed "to professional or official work, to the management of estates, or to any other positions of trust or authority." Harrison School was requested to provide opportunities for a "sound and liberal education, embracing, in addition to the Classics, a knowledge of French and German . . . and the Elements of Natural Philosophy."[17] The Codrington Grammar School was to furnish

> a deep and sound education, both religious and secular, as a
> *practical training for business,* and an adequate education
> *for the great competitive examinations,* especially those
> for Woolwich and for all branches of the Indian Civil
> Service, and as a really *scholarly preparation for further
> instruction* at Codrington College or the Universities of the
> United Kingdom [emphasis added].[18]

In Trinidad, the principal critics of the curriculum offered by the
government grammar school (QCS) were the Catholics, who suggested that
a more useful instructional programme would have been one in line with the
occupational needs of the country, rather than being geared toward the
preparation of the sons of civil servants for the types of jobs occupied by
their fathers. Specifically the curriculum was criticized for being ill
adapted to the circumstances of an island where agriculture and commerce
were the principal pursuits of the inhabitants. Further, since religious
instruction was excluded from the curriculum, it was argued that the
education offered by this "godless institution" was incomplete and even
harmful to the students, since it emphasized only one aspect of their
overall development, the intellectual, to the sacrifice of all others,
especially the spiritual.

Keenan too criticized the limited attention paid by the school to some
subjects, as well as the teaching methods used in others. He observed that,
while many arts and science subjects were in the official curriculum, a
number of these, particularly in the science area, were not actually being
taught. These included physics, chemistry, and natural sciences, along with
German. On this point, he noted that the "physico-scientific element" was
kept in the background. There was no laboratory or apparatus for
demonstrations and no museum of geology. The aesthetical element of the
students' education was also "singularly overlooked," since neither music
nor drawing was offered.

In addition, natural history was poorly taught, as evidenced by the
fact that

> the walls [of the schools] are destitute of charts of natural
> history and natural phenomenon. There are no diagrams of
> machinery or illustrations of discoveries. In short an
> English village school would exhibit more of the
> appliances of education than this collegiate institution.[19]

In 1889 the colony's Central Agricultural Board joined in the criticism of
the strong curriculum emphasis on the humanities, pointing out that, while
it was desirable that the inhabitants of the island be afforded the
opportunity to send their sons to study for one of the professions,

> the present system of high class education is producing a
> superabundance of Doctors and Lawyers . . . [while] in an
> essentially agricultural community such as this — in an
> island with thousands of fertile acres waiting to be opened
> up and cultivated, it is not too much to expect that at least
> equal facilities will be given for the education of the youth
> of the Colony in those pursuits which tend to develop the
> resources of the island.[20]

The curriculum of Queen's College (QC) in British Guiana also came in for criticism by some members of the elite who were anxious to see the school's graduates making a more active contribution to the economic life of the country. As Cameron notes, one critic suggested that "too much 'Classicality' and too little learning" took place at QC. He pointed out further that he did not see why the school should "cram into the heads of boys Latin and Greek and the mythology of the old gods and goddesses when there was land surveying to be taught and so many other things to make them useful to the country."[21]

Pressures for Scientific, Agricultural, and Commercial Subjects in the Curriculum

One of the major proposed changes to the grammar school curriculum was the introduction of science, agriculture, and commercial subjects. In 1871 an attempt was made to expand the curriculum of QRC to include subjects such as Spanish, natural science, and Hindustani, which were more likely to be functional to the needs of society. However, not much success resulted from these efforts. When practical chemistry was introduced in 1872, it constituted the total natural science programme of the school. The lack of a laboratory played a part in delaying any improvement in the teaching of the subject, but the general attitude of the school administration to the sciences was also important. The staff considered the classics to be much more important than the sciences in the education of the young.

In 1878 the Trinidad newspaper, *Palladium,* suggested that if the two prestigious grammar schools on the island were to extend their curriculum "so as to embrace Commercial Education" and to include "a class of Agricultural Chemistry," this would allow some students to leave these schools "well trained for a humbler, though not a less useful sphere of life," while others could still pursue their usual course of studies for one of the professions. [22]

The Agricultural Board of Trinidad continued its efforts to bring about these suggested curriculum changes and went on to propose a scheme for the introduction of the study of agriculture at the two secondary grammar schools. The programme consisted of a three-year course of lectures in chemistry, botany, and agriculture, to be supplemented by visits to the botanical gardens and the government stock farm. The introduction of this programme required a substantial modification of the curriculum of these secondary schools.

The establishment of a Model Farm School was also proposed, where selected students could pursue an advanced course of practical agricultural training, botany, chemistry, horticulture, physiology, veterinary anatomy, book-keeping, and mechanics and where experiments in crop cultivation might be carried out. It was even suggested that two of the five university scholarships awarded by the government should be in the field of agriculture.

To motivate students to enter the modern, or commercial, stream it was also proposed that two of the four university scholarships should be awarded on a competitive basis to students who had successfully completed this programme, which was to include such compulsory subjects as book-keeping, commercial arithmetic, English, and history. Optional subjects would include mathematics, chemistry, physics, botany, zoology, mechanics, political economy, and mercantile law.

It was also proposed that those students completing the intermediate and modern courses might also be instructed in the theory and practice of teaching, so as to qualify them to teach in the elementary schools. The motivation behind this proposal was to improve the quality of instruction in these schools, which could later introduce science and 'industrial education' subjects.

In 1891 the government of Barbados put forward proposals to strengthen and develop the scientific and agricultural education of the senior boys attending grammar schools. At the Harrison College attempts were made to provide instruction in one or more of the branches of the natural sciences. However, it was pointed out that classroom space could not be found for the teaching of such additional subjects and particularly for a science laboratory, which would have been needed for the "practicals."

Later, the establishment of a Department of Agriculture and Science was proposed, the objectives of which were (1) to give instruction in science and particularly agricultural science in the first and second grade secondary schools; and (2) to provide for the formation of a Science College offering instruction in natural science to those attending secondary schools on the island.

In connection with these aims, the government laboratory, which was established within the precincts of Harrison College, was to provide a two-year advanced course in natural science and mathematics (including geometry, algebra, trigonometry, mechanics, and hydrostatics). In addition, students were to take modern languages, with French being compulsory and German optional. All students attending first and second grade secondary schools who were at least 15 years of age and had passed an examination in elementary classics, mathematics, English, and a modern language, were to be eligible for admission into the science programme.

In 1890 the leading local newspaper in British Guiana, the *Daily Chronicle*, commenting on the absence of science in the curriculum of QC, observed that

> What we want in this Colony are men who received a scientific education. . . . At present, the majority of these have to be imported at high salaries. . . . The alumni of Queen's College will make very nice gentlemanly clerks in government offices, but they are not turned out to the battle of life, equipped with weapons of modern precision.[23]

Other Efforts at Reforming the Secondary Curriculum

As a result of these proposals and criticisms, various efforts were made to reform the grammar school curriculum in the West Indies. The Catholics who had strongly criticized the curriculum of the government grammar school in Trinidad (QCS) set about preparing plans for the conversion of the St. Mary's College into the College of Immaculate Conception (CIC), in 1863. From its inception CIC offered both commercial and classical subjects and gave prominence to French in its instructional programme and its ceremonials.

But one outcome of its later affiliation with the government grammar school was a gradual reduction of the French and a corresponding increase in the English influence in the curriculum. Keenan had suggested a movement toward "the suppression of the French element" at CIC, but went on to add that, "at the same time, I think that, without being made less French, the college could be made more English than it is." He also noted that, "the professors are themselves of this opinion, and have expressed their readiness to act upon it."[24] By 1874 the *Star of the West* was able to observe that

> the education of our youth has become English . . . and the heads of the College and Convent (though French themselves) are more than ever convinced of the importance of cultivating the English element in those useful institutions. Whether boys are intended for commercial or professional life, or for the Government service, or the services of the Church it is alike important that their English education should be as complete and thorough as possible.[25]

In 1892 a Committee of the Council of CIC was appointed to consider the introduction of mercantile and agricultural education in the school curriculum. In its *Report,* the Committee went even further, recommending the development of a broader modern course to include book-keeping, commercial arithmetic, Euclid, history, geography with special reference to the West Indies, modern languages, and one other subject from the following list — natural science, political economy, or mercantile law. In 1890 a two-person committee was appointed to consider curriculum changes at the secondary level, with special emphasis on mercantile and agricultural education. It recommended that during the first three years of the secondary-school course, students should not be required to study the classics, but undertake instead an intermediate course which would give them time to master English before they attempted Latin or Greek. At the time this was a revolutionary idea.

On completing this course, the students were to be divided into two streams, the classical or the modern, with the aim of the latter being to make secondary-schooling more "utilitarian." As Governor Broomes suggested, those secondary school students in Trinidad who did not intend to enter a learned profession needed to be given an opportunity to learn practical subjects,

Most students in the West Indies who won the university scholarships went on to study law or medicine, a practice which was sometimes condemned, especially because, as Governor Robinson pointed out for Trinidad, these fields were already overstocked. To encourage the Island Scholarship winners to pursue careers in the field of the applied sciences, the local board of education introduced an ordinance in 1886 that widened the definition of university to include any recognized scientific institution.

In British Guiana, succumbing to public pressure, Governor James Longden indicated in 1875 that science teaching was to be given greater attention at Queen's College, although the institutional focus was still to prepare students for admission to British universities.

The Mitchinson Report for Barbados

The most comprehensive plan for reforming secondary education emanated from the efforts of the Mitchinson Commission that was appointed in Barbados 1875. The Commission was highly critical of the attempts of so many schools on the island to offer a secondary education in which the study of the classics dominated the curriculum. It noted that even some of the better primary or intermediate schools were pushing their students to take up the higher subjects, including the classics, irrespective of their ability, the length of time they had planned to remain in school, or the occupations they would likely occupy after leaving school. The Commission held that a classical education was unsuitable for most of the students to whom it was being offered and even suggested that one evil of the system of education in Barbados was that boys "not destined for a profession, nor showing capacity for high intellectual culture"[26] were allowed to remain at school for far too long. It therefore proposed that secondary schools should be classified into first grade (grammar schools) and second grade schools and that each should focus on providing a different type of secondary education.

The programme of instruction to be offered in the second grade schools was to build on the educational foundations already laid in the primary schools. But while the objective of the elementary school was to develop in the students "memory, attention and intelligence," the second grade schools were to train them in the "power of analysis, in accuracy," in skillful command of language and how to make use of their reasoning powers and their faculties of observation.

The Commission recognized the pressure exerted by parents for classical education and therefore suggested that the study of the classics not be excluded altogether from the curriculum of second grade schools, but only given less prominence than in the grammar schools. Therefore, in addition to religious instruction, the second grade schools were to offer (1) arithmetic, geometry and elementary mathematics — to develop accuracy and reasoning power; (2) Latin, studied as a language, rather than as literature; (3) English, to develop analytical power and a command of language as well as thought and expression; (4) one of the natural sciences, to foster the powers of observation; (5) if possible, a living modern language such as French, in order to give to the students a more intelligent grasp of English and an appreciation of its structure and idioms; and (6) finally, such aesthetic subjects as vocal music and drawing were considered desirable adjuncts to this course of study, since they would help the cultivation of taste among the students.

In order to meet the growing demand for secondary education, the Commission recommended the establishment of a number of second grade schools to satisfy the legitimate craving among the emergent middle class for a higher level but truly useful education. These schools were also to meet the educational needs of the sprinkling of children from the higher class living in the rural areas who might reasonably desire a first grade education but whose parents could not afford to meet the boarding costs for them to attend a grammar school.

In order for the second grade schools to flourish and to continue to meet the educational aspirations of their pupils, especially in areas where no first grade secondary school was available, it was recommended that these schools be entitled to operate an Upper Department that could offer, for higher fees, instruction in Greek, higher mathematics, and advanced Latin. This additional education was to be for boys whose social position and destination in life would normally require a first grade education. The Upper Departments of the second grade schools were not to become the "essential feature" of these schools, however, and were "never (to) be allowed to determine the whole structure of their curriculum,"[27] which would distort the main purpose of providing a sound but more useful education to those destined for the lower level white-collar occupations.

The first grade, or grammar, schools were to be geared toward educating "the boy's tastes, to inform his mind, to create a desire for further information and to impart to him that indescribable something which we call 'culture' through the study of classical or modern subjects." These schools were to provide for all their students a "General Preliminary Training" which would involve the teaching of such subjects as "Grammar, Arithmetic and General Knowledge, i.e. History and Geography and the like." In addition, the students were to be well drilled in Latin and Greek grammar, with construing exercises; they were to be provided with a sound foundation in arithmetic and the elements of geometry, and would acquire at least a rudimentary acquaintance with the French language. Finally, "if they can also have rationally mastered the rudiments of one of the less abstruse Sciences of Observation, say Botany or Zoology, so much the better for the after superstructure."[28] This "General Preliminary Training" was to be given to the students regardless of the "whims or fancies" of their parents.

By the time the students had completed this training the school would be in a position to identify the "bias of the boy's mind" and place him in (1) a Classical or (2) a modern course, partly depending on the profession which his parents had selected for him.

1. In the classical programme students were to undertake a careful study of the "copious literature of Greece and Rome." Accuracy and thoroughness were to be ensured by a deeper insight into grammar and philology, while the child's cultural development was to be fostered by a mastery of the two classical languages. This was to be supplemented by "a modicum" of mathematics and a modern language training.

2. In the modern programme, Greek was to be dropped; Latin, "merely kept up . . . and anything like Composition [except in the field of English] abandoned." The backbone of the work was to be mathematics. "Accuracy and Observation as well as the Inductive Faculty" were to be "trained by [the study of] one or more branches of the Natural Sciences such as Chemistry, Physics and the like," while "taste" was to be cultivated by a critical study of some works of English literature and French or German or both, "not only for the languages' sake, but also for their literature."[29]

The first grade or grammar school education that was to be provided at Harrison College and Lodge School was meant for boys who were not planning to terminate their formal education until they were at least 18 years of age. It was suggested that a modern programme could also be developed at Harrison College, without superseding its work in the classics. This could give a distinctive character to the school, and would provide a choice for those parents who had tended either to undervalue a classical education, or had considered that a modern education was more likely to advance their sons' interests in life.

It was also suggested that the evaluation of the work of the first grade schools would best be done by bringing down annually an examiner of academic eminence from England. It was even hinted that such a practice might also be followed with advantage for the second grade schools. In addition, it was proposed that students in the higher forms should write the overseas Joint Oxford and Cambridge examinations (later, the University of Cambridge School Certificate Examinations) since this would enable the schools to compare the intellectual growth of their students with that of English boys in attendance at the best schools "which England possesses."

The introduction of agricultural science as a subject in the secondary schools was also recommended because it was considered essential to the future planters and attorneys. A number of island professorships were to be created in such fields as French, German, drawing, and chemistry, with prospective candidates for this last-named position having a "collateral interest" in agriculture. In addition, there was to be a professor in one of the "sciences of observation," such as geology, botany or zoology. It was thought that the individuals appointed to these positions would play a valuable role in the development of the intellectual culture among the young men engaged in business and in agriculture and among students in the secondary schools.

The Commission observed that there was no adequate provision for the education of girls and recommended the establishment of a girls' secondary school, the curriculum of which was to include the following subjects: divinity, English language, composition and literature, history, geography, arithmetic, French, class singing, and one of the branches of science. In addition, the following optional subjects were proposed, for which extra fees were to be charged: music (theory and practice), drawing, and singing.

Resistance to Changes in the Classical Curriculum

As noted above there were many criticisms levelled at the grammar schools for their continued focus on a classical education. In an attempt to respond, the managers of the Codrington Grammar School permitted instruction in the classics only to those boys who were "discovered" to have a "mark of genius" or on the request of parents. In 1847 Rawle reported that the greater number of boys in that school were instructed only in writing, arithmetic, and English grammar and other subjects that were considered most useful to them in their likely fields of employment. Only those intending to take up divinity, medicine, or law were instructed in Latin and Greek.

In July 1859 the headmaster of QCS reported that Latin was only taught in the second and upper classes (grades). In the social studies area, he noted that, "we have spent a good deal of time and trouble over History [English mainly] and Geography, but in this branch of culture we have found the soil most wretchedly barren in most instances."[30] French was taught, though the scarcity of books presented a problem, and German was still to be introduced. In addition, it was also hoped that the school would introduce a class in practical science.

But these curriculum changes occurred at an extremely slow pace, with the result that the traditional classical subjects continued to dominate the instruction offered by the grammar schools in the region. In 1878 the *Palladium*, a Trinidad newspaper, admitted that the Cambridge examiner's report on the quality of the secondary education on the island was generally satisfactory, but nevertheless raised the issue again as to whether

> the education given at our Collegiate Institutions is the one most suited to the wants of the great majority of those for whose benefit the Colleges were founded [i.e. the children of the upper and middle classes]. . . . Throughout the year the energies of both professors and pupils [at the Royal College and the College of Immaculate Conception] are devoted to one object — preparing [students] for the Cambridge Examin-ation. . . . The ordinary curriculum consists of Latin, Greek, French, Geography, Roman and Grecian History, English Grammar and Analysis, Arithmetic, Algebra and Euclid; in fact the ordinary course pursued at the great English Schools such as Eton, Rugby, Harrow and Westminster. There can be no question that this is a high class of education and for those whose means or influence enable them to look forward to the learned professions as the future of their sons, nothing could be more desired. But what of those, and they are, and always will be the great majority, who do not obtain the Scholarships, or who even if they do, cannot take advantage of them? . . . Without in any way seeking to depreciate the value of a classical education, we would ask of what advantage is it to a boy who, when leaving school, must at once begin to earn his living . . . as an overseer on an estate or a junior clerk in a mercantile establishment, to be able to translate Sophocles or to quote fluently, line after line, of the Georgics of Virgil? [31]

The article continued by noting that this was a matter which deserved serious attention because it affected the very future of the colony. It was suggested that

> by extending the curriculum so as to embrace a Commercial education, and by establishing a class of Agricultural Chemistry, the youth of Trinidad will be enabled to pursue such a course of studies as is required for those professions for which . . . many of them have shown themselves pre-eminently fitted . . . [while others who lack the] ability or . . . the mate-rial means by which that ability can be turned to use [should be educated] to leave the College well trained for the humbler, though not less useful sphere of life. [32]

The focus on a classical education continued, however, because of some other developments taking place in the region. For example, the establishment of the Codrington Theological College offered an opportunity for higher education to be pursued in the Caribbean, especially after the institution became affiliated with the University of Durham. This motivated some students to try and secure their university matriculation, which required a knowledge of the classics.

In addition, the awarding of scholarships tenable at British and other recognized universities and in the case of Barbados also at the Codrington College helped to strengthen the place of the classics in the curriculum of the secondary grammar schools, since a knowledge of these subjects was usually required for university studies in Britain or for theological training at Codrington. The local grammar schools that continued to emphasize the teaching of the classics were also strongly influenced by their English counterparts. Further, as the principal of Harrison College observed, most parents wanted instruction in the classical subjects for their children because of the "polish" which such education was supposed to impart.

The study of Greek was also still being defended on the grounds that it could provide invaluable lessons, especially for West Indians. In 1891 the *Agricultural Reporter* commented on this issue, noting that

> from the point of view of its peculiar value to the few out of every hundred boys at school who are capable of receiving intellectual cultivation, it is of advantage to West Indian communities [for the boys to study Greek]. Into their hands will the higher life, the real progress of the communities, pass in due course. And it is in the educating of those who have guided the real progress of the world, that Greek has played and still plays, so important, so essential a part. . . . Above all, nowhere have the political questions of small communities [and the West Indies were characterized by such communities] been more thoroughly threshed out to their logical conclusions than in the Greek states.[33]

The importance of the classics, even for science students, continued to be emphasized by the fact that entry to the advanced course in science depended on students having completed a sound course of instruction in elementary classics.

The Effect of External Examinations on the Curriculum of the Grammar Schools

Another factor responsible for the resistance to any major changes in the curriculum of the West Indian grammar schools was the influence of the external examinations conducted by British universities. There were a number of reasons why these grammar schools felt it necessary to enter their students for such examinations.

First, the examinations helped to give credibility to their work, since their students were able to compare their performance with that of the pupils attending similar schools in the metropole. Preparation for these external examinations was also made easier because the teachers in the local grammar schools, having usually been recruited from Britain, were very familiar with them. Second, West Indians welcomed a copy, even a pale copy, of the education provided by schools in the Mother Country often as a means of showing that they were on an equal intellectual footing with their colonizers. Later, the tertiary-education scholarships provided by the West Indian governments on the basis of the results of these examinations added to their importance.

The Barbados Board of Education, which had always expressed an interest in reforming secondary education on the island, still continued to view the chief purpose of the grammar schools as preparing students for scholarship examinations tenable at an English university. The Gilchrist scholarship, which also became available to students in the West Indies in the early 1870s, was awarded on the basis of students' performance at the University of London examination for secondary schools, in which the classics occupied a prominent position. The value of the award was fairly substantial, making it quite popular in the region. Commenting on its effect on the curriculum of Harrison College, Nicholls suggested, "it is more than a coincidence that the classical books read in Form VI were those prescribed by the Gilchrist Scholarship in January 1875."[34] These scholarships not only provided an opportunity for students to obtain a free university education, but the runners-up at these examinations were also able to secure excellent positions in the civil service or in teaching.

The Catholics who had sharply criticized the government secondary school in Trinidad for the inappropriateness of its curriculum tried to offer in their own school both an academic and an industrial education programme, which included commercial or business courses. But, after CIC became formally affiliated with this school (QRC), the amount of grants it received depended on the academic performance of its students at the Cambridge Syndicate examinations. Further, these students also became eligible to compete for the university exhibitions offered by the government of Trinidad. As a result, CIC also began to concentrate its programme of studies on the prescribed syllabus for these external examinations. In the process, it de-emphasized its non-academic courses, and concentrated on those which could earn the school maximum financial assistance.

CIC also discarded those elements of its classics programme which had been heavily influenced by the teaching of the subject in France and Ireland in favour of the approach suggested by these English universities' secondary school examinations. As a result of these changes the Cambridge University examinations came to dominate the work of CIC almost completely as it did Queen's Royal College. In 1878 the *Palladium* observed that in the two prestigious secondary schools on the island, the "energies of both professors and pupils were devoted to one object," i.e., the preparation of their students for the Cambridge examinations.[35]

By the end of the century, when entry into the public service was based increasingly on the results of the Cambridge examinations, their influence on the work of the local grammar schools increased. Latin was an important subject in the civil service examination instituted by the government of Trinidad. Therefore, students who had been prepared for the Cambridge examinations also had a better chance of acquiring entry to public service occupations. This new development meant that "young men of industry and ability [had] an additional incentive to work" more diligently at school or college since they were "offered an early opportunity of obtaining their livelihood by their own exertion."[36]

These examinations also influenced the instructional strategies that were used in these schools. It was suggested that the teachers often focussed their efforts on the brightest students, the "show boys," while the educational needs of the less talented were often neglected. In denying this charge as it applied to the York Castle High School in Jamaica, the school authorities pointed out that the students whom they presented for the Cambridge examination were "not the forced blossoms of a sickly nursing, but the inflorescences of a healthy and vigorous plant." However, it was admitted that there were other schools on the island in which the show boys received all the attention.[37]

There were two examinations taken by secondary school students — the Senior Cambridge and the Junior Cambridge examination. However, despite the influence that the former exerted on the work of the grammar school, most students terminated their education after taking the Junior Cambridge examination. In 1890 about 62% of the candidates who entered for the Cambridge examinations took the Junior Cambridge examination, and nine years later this percentage had only risen to about 66%. This meant that a relatively small percentage of these students were actually preparing themselves for matriculation into a British university.

However, these external examinations were increasingly affecting the work of the secondary schools in these colonies. This can be seen from the figures in Table 2, which show a substantial increase — about 160% — in the number of West Indian students who were entering for them between 1890 and 1899.

TABLE 2
Number of Candidates Who Took the Cambridge Examination in Various West Indian Colonies, 1880-99

Year	Dominica	St. Lucia	Trinidad	Antigua	Barbados	British Guiana	Jamaica	Total
1880	—	—	11	—	—	—	11	22
1890	—	—	22	22	8	17	35	104
1899	2	5	42	3	53	23	142	270

Source: *Annual Reports of the Colonies.*

These external examinations nevertheless had some positive influence on the work of the schools, particularly in motivating teachers and their students to work hard. Commenting on this point as it related to the work of the QCS, the principal noted in 1863 that

> to the boys it gives an energy and an interest in their work, such as it would be almost impossible to inspire by any other means; the honour of obtaining a certificate is one of which any boy may be proud; and for which most boys will be eager to contend. To the masters on the other hand it is of great use in showing them to what points they should direct their teaching, and in bringing under their notice weak points which even the most careful are apt to overlook, if left to their own unaided judgment.[38]

Keenan made a similar observation a few years later, noting that even though the "preparation for the [external] examination" was the "predominant characteristic of the course of studies" pursued at QCS, the "masters and pupils alike seem to be animated by an enthusiastic determination to exercise all their energies and employ all their resources to produce creditable results at the[se] examinations."[39] But while he was impressed with their influence in stimulating the efforts of teachers and pupils, he felt it necessary to advise against the policy of concentrating upon them because they were an "enterprise of limited scope and dimension" which already absorbed too much of the energy of the institution.

There was also a tremendous sense of local pride in the students' performance at these examinations. A local Trinidad newspaper reported in 1867 that two boys from the College had beaten all the English students in Latin and Greek and all but one in French, with one of the boys coming second among all the students who took the Cambridge School Certificate examinations.

Judging by examination results and the reports of the examiners, there was some substance to the general observation that the quality of the education offered by the grammar schools was enhanced by the external examinations. In commenting on the work done by the pupils at the two grammar schools of Trinidad in 1882, the examiner of the Cambridge Syndicate noted that it was a reflection of the fact that, "the teachers of each college must be zealous and capable, and I should say that the Island enjoys great educational advantages in possessing two schools in such good working order."[40]

Summary and Conclusions

The two types of schools in the British West Indies that provided some form of post-primary education often maintained a somewhat separate focus in their educational programmes. The curriculum of the model schools was really geared toward providing an advanced primary education for students who were likely to occupy lower level white-collar jobs, mainly as elementary school teachers. The secondary grammar schools tried to give their students an education that would help them to secure admission to a tertiary-level educational institution, usually a university in the metropole, or into a middle-level white-collar job locally.

Some of the teachers in the model schools became so ambitious for their pupils that they offered them a wide range of subjects, following the pattern of those available in the grammar schools. In some cases the only difference between the two types of schools was that the grammar schools offered instruction in the classical subjects, while the model schools did not, although in a few cases even this distinction was blurred, with some model or intermediate schools also offering instruction in elementary classics.

In addition, most grammar schools focussed their instructional programme on the academic preparation of those relatively few students who were likely to proceed to do further studies abroad. Many criticisms were levelled at their failure to diversify their curriculum and provide a more useful or practical education, especially for those who were likely to go into business or to work in a supervisory capacity in agriculture on the sugar plantations. The importance of a secondary education programme which took into consideration the needs of less academically inclined students was also mentioned by the Mitchinson Commission of Barbados, which proposed that secondary schools be classified as first grade or second grade schools. The former were to concentrate heavily on the more academic programmes, especially the classical subjects, while the latter were to provide a broader but more practical and hence more immediately useful education. Pressure continued to be exerted in most of the secondary schools for the inclusion of the sciences in their curriculum, especially those subjects which had direct relevance to agriculture. These demands became stronger as the schools began to receive subsidies from public funds.

But while some progress was gradually made in this direction, the classics continued to dominate the curriculum of grammar schools for most of the period covered by this study. This was particularly noticeable in the main secondary schools in Barbados, Trinidad, Jamaica, British Guiana, and most other British Caribbean colonies — with the exception of British Honduras, where the so-called Honduras Grammar School was attempting to develop a strong emphasis on industrial education.

As these schools entered more of their students for the overseas external examination of the British universities, they gave up most of their autonomy in determining their own curriculum. This meant that the nature and content of the subjects which they offered were increasingly similar to those of the English grammar schools. As a result, criticisms of the grammar schools for their failure to adapt their programme of instruction to the realities of West Indian life continued. The curriculum debate still focussed on whether these schools should continue their traditional practice of providing a classical education or whether they should offer modern subjects, such as commerce, science, and agriculture, which would be more useful to many of the students and would contribute more to the economic development of the region. The conflict persisted between those who held the view that the grammar schools should mainly prepare their students for entry into tertiary-level educational institutions abroad and those who felt that they should provide their students with skills that would be useful in the jobs which most of them would fill after leaving school.

In addition to the virtual absence of science and commercial subjects from the curriculum of the grammar schools, the instructional strategies which they used also came in for some negative comments. Their teaching methods were usually described as essentially "bookish and verbal," and this characterized the teaching even of practical subjects, when these were offered. In addition, teachers' efforts often remained focussed on the brighter students.

But the grammar schools in the West Indies continued to focus their efforts on preparing their students for the external examinations set by the British universities. This focus was based on the rather dubious assumption that it was the best preparation for all their students, even those who had no prospect of pursuing further studies. For example, up to 1925, Wynn Williams, an H.M.I. (Her Majesty's Inspector) from the United Kingdom and a member of the 1925 Commission on Education in British Guiana, was still pointing out that, in connection with the need for curriculum change at Queen's College,

The time has come when the object and purpose of this school should be considered in light of modern requirements. The main objective is to train boys for the professions and the university. The course of prescribed studies is severely and exclusively academic and in this respect a little behind the times . . . the inappropriateness of the syllabus for the purposes of the majority at the school may be seen at a glance: they may be suitable for certain types of secondary schools in England but they certainly do appear to be in the highest degree artificial, especially as regards the teaching of science for secondary schools in the Tropics. It is almost a scandal that manual work should be entirely neglected in the principal school of the Colony where so much depends on the industrial life of the community, upon the introduction of a highly skilled element in agriculture and upon applied sciences generally. . . . No serious attempt is made to arouse and cultivate in the children an abiding interest in their surroundings, no effort is made to penetrate the secrets of scientific husbandry and to interest the children in the countless wonders of nature in which the Tropics abound, and the attraction of biology, geology, and entomology, are passed up in favour of the Anarchy of "Stephen's Reign" or the "Religious Difficulties of Queen Elizabeth." [41]

However, the academic performance of those who went on to achieve a higher level of secondary education was considered to be of a high standard, since the students fared quite well in comparison with those attending similar types of schools in England. A latent outcome of the work of the grammar schools was therefore to differentiate socially between individuals who received this type of education and those who had benefited only from some other type of post-primary training in these societies.

Notes

1   Gordon, *A Century*.
2   CO295/232.
3   George D. Bailey, *A Précis of the History of Elementary Education in British Guiana* (Georgetown, British Guiana: Argosy, 1907).
4   C. Nicholls, "The Development of Classical Education in Barbados and Trinidad" (Ph.D. diss., Univ. of Exeter, 1965), 8.
5   CO 295/232, no. 137, *Report of the Principal, Queen's Collegiate School*, 8 May 1865 (London: PRO).
6   *Keenan Report*, 21.
7   Nicholls, "The Development of Classical Education."
8   *Keenan Report*, 21.
9   Ibid.
10   CO 295/196, Governor Keate to Secretary of State, 6 August 1857, no. 91 (London: PRO).
11   Report by W. Campion on Queen's Collegiate School, 27 February 1863, *British Parliamentary Papers*, Vol. 40: *1864* (London: Government of Great Britain), 35.
12   *Report of the Principal, Queen's College*, 12 January 1880 (Port-of-Spain, Trinidad), 3.
13   The Government of British Guiana, N. E. Cameron, *150 Years of Education in Guyana* (Georgetown, Guyana, 1968), 26.
14   *Report of the Principal, Queen's College*, 12 January 1880.

15   *The Queen's College Gazette*, 4, 13 (March 1884).
16   CO 123/70, Honduras, 1845, Vol. 2.
17   Report of the Government of Barbados, *British Parliamentary Papers*, Vol. 48: *1873* (London: Government of Great Britain), 117-18.
18   Ibid.
19   *Keenan Report*, 55.
20   *Report of the Central Agricultural Board, 1889*; Gordon, *A Century*, 256.
21   N. E. Cameron, *A History of the Queen's College of British Guiana* (Georgetown, Guyana: A. Persick, 1951), 8.
22   *Palladium* [Trinidad], 13 July 1878.
23   *The Daily Chronicle*, 7 March 1870.
24   *Keenan Report*, 60.
25   *The Star of the West* [Trinidad], 30 July 1874.
26   *Mitchinson Report*, 7.
27   Ibid.
28   Ibid.
29   Ibid.
30   *Report of the Principal, Queen's Collegiate School*, 30 July 1859; Gordon, *A Century*, 236.
31   *Palladium* [Trinidad], 13 July 1878; Gordon, *A Century*, 254.
32   Ibid.
33   *The Agricultural Reporter* [Barbados], 15 September 1891; Gordon, *A Century*, 266.
34   Nicholls, "The Development of Classical Education," 64.
35   *Palladium* [Trinidad], 13 July 1878.
36   CO 295/397, no.149, *Governor of Trinidad to Secretary of State*, 25 May 1896 (London: PRO).
37   C. Murray, *Governor of York Castle High School, to the Methodist Missionary Society*, 14 June 1884; Gordon, *A Century*, 260.
38   *Report by Deighton, Principal, Queen's Collegiate School, on the 1863 Examinations*; Gordon, *A Century*, 252.
39   Nicholls, "The Development of Classical Education."
40   *Report of the Cambridge Syndicate Examinations on Queen's Royal College and the College of Immaculate Conception* (Port-of-Spain, Trinidad: 1872).
41   Government of British Guiana, *Report of the Educational Commission, 1925* (Georgetown, British Guiana, 1925), 10 and Appendix D, p. ix.

CHAPTER *11*

SECONDARY EDUCATION AND
UPWARD SOCIAL MOBILITY

School Enrollment and Social Stratification

The type of school that children in the West Indies attended depended very much on the socio-economic background of their parents. For example, in Trinidad, Brereton observed that

> Government and assisted schools in the rural districts were attended by children of labourers, artisans and peasant farmers who were both black and coloured. Upper and middle class parents in the country would not send their children to these schools because they thought it undesirable for them to mix with lower class pupils. They would be sent to private schools in the towns. . . . Upper class white children would go to private elitist schools.[1]

This fairly rigid socio-economic stratification of the school system was a characteristic of most other West Indian colonies at the time. But the situation gradually changed as the number of non-whites who belonged to the middle-class in these societies began to increase.

Increasing Middle-class Demand for Higher Education

By 1870, in many of the West Indian colonies there was a steady increase in the number of non-whites, particularly of coloureds, who were engaged in work other than manual labour on the sugar estates or in the cultivation of other crops. Davy, writing in 1854, commented on this rising middle class and the "industrious peasantry" which were to be found in the region.[2]

Hall[3] also noted that in the 1860s blacks and coloureds in Jamaica had attained positions of prominence not only as merchants and the owners of landed property, but also as members of the legislative assembly, magistrates, barristers, school-teachers, newspaper editors, clergymen, and the occupants of important public offices. For example, in 1866, the headmaster of Wolmer's Free School — one of the two main primary schools in Kingston, with an enrollment of 500 pupils — was Robert Gordon, a black man and a clergy of the Church of England. Later, in 1877, a well-known Methodist missionary observed that the island continued to have "a largely increasing middle class black and coloured population."[4]

In Trinidad it was noted that "a middle class of intelligence," was emerging, especially during the latter part of the nineteenth century. This group comprised very industrious individuals who were "destined" to become an "important element" in the future prosperity of the colony. In British Guiana, the first generation of educated blacks "secured for themselves positions as teachers and public servants," thereby laying "the groundwork for the formation of a social class distinct from the estate labourers, draycart men and unskilled labourers." However, for black

Guyanese, "the post of head teacher or rural postmaster was as high on the social ladder as they could normally hope to aspire."[5] A newspaper correspondent for the *Argosy* also drew attention, in December 1880, to the "several indications of the growth of a middle proprietary class" and described this phenomenon as "a thing greatly to be desired."[6] Rodney noted that, because the members of this new class were "rising above the mass . . . [they] were not nameless or faceless" but were "outstanding persons in the community."[7]

In Dominica, "a class . . . composed of the purchasers and cultivators of small portions of land" was "growing rapidly into existence," and from "their advance in intelligence," they were "becoming more alive to the benefits of education."[8] In 1856 the lieutenant-governor of Tobago observed that "the black and coloured classes" had acquired "a considerable amount of property." Many had raised themselves "to the position of lessees of sugar estates," and among them, "a spirit of emulation seems to be on the increase."[9]

In 1861 Sewell observed that the middle class in Barbados, comprising small landed proprietors, businessmen, clerks in public and private establish-ments, editors, tradesmen and mechanics, was already very large and that their numbers were increasing, especially since membership in these groups did not always have to depend on the sponsorship of the whites for their mobility.

Anthony Trollope had made a similar observation in the late 1850s about the enlargement of the black and coloured middle class when he noted that "at present when the old planter sits on a magisterial bench, a coloured man sits beside him; one probably on each side of him." Coloured men often outvoted him and the situation became "worse and worse." Not only did "coloured men get into office, but black men also [did]. . . . At the present day the coloured people do stand on strong ground, and they do not stand with the good will of the old aristocracy of the country. They have forced their way up."[10]

A number of social and economic factors contributed to the increasing size of the coloured and black middle-class population. The colour bar that prevented the admission of non-white children to some of the better schools was becoming less rigid in some colonies. Many of those who received an education for any reasonable period of time were able to move into lower level white-collar jobs. The administrative and spiritual authorities in these colonies become increasingly critical of racially segregated schools, especially those aided by public funds, and advocated an end to such practice. For example, Bishop Parry of Jamaica argued against having separate schools for whites and non-whites. In 1847 he made a frontal attack on the issue by informing the secretary of the SPG that he intended to throw open all Anglican educational institutions to anyone, irrespective of colour. Again, in 1852, he continued to suggest to all groups providing education in the region that

> the principle of providing a *separate* education for the free coloured population of the West Indies . . . [is] a very objectionable one, as is teaching to perpetrate the antipathy of race, which is the primary objective with us to eradicate.[11]

In Barbados, Governor Reed also criticized the practice of racial discrimination by some school authorities and argued that the "qualities of the mind" rather than the colour of one's skin should be the basis on which individuals were admitted to educational institutions. Rawle, too, strongly opposed racial discrimination in schools and suggested that a man's colour had no more to do with his character or his intellect than the colour of his eyes. In 1850 he successfully persuaded the directors of the central schools in Barbados to convert their schools into teacher-training institutions and to open them on an equal basis to non-whites. This policy resulted in a marked increase in the enrollment figures at the central school, especially from the mid-1840s to the mid-1850s. It also led to a decline in the number of whites at these schools, though this was alleged to be due to class rather than colour differences.

By the late 1840s, children of all races were also being admitted to the Codrington Grammar School and to the Codrington College, where young men, especially those of African descent, were being trained to carry out missionary activities in Africa. The first non-white to win the Barbados Island Scholarship in the early 1850s was therefore allowed to study at Codrington. Around the same time, the Society for the Education of the Poor in the Principles of the Established Church also recommended that schools on the island be open to all without distinction of race or complexion.

This opening of the better educational institutions to blacks and coloureds helped to improve access for them into the more desired white-collar jobs. The Methodists drew attention to the fact that they were producing a large number of leaders and Sunday school teachers from the "common scholars," some of whom were eventually being accepted for training as teachers. In 1860 a rural school in Jamaica was reported to have produced the village teacher, the sergeant of police, the manager of the local post-office, and a number of Sunday school teachers. In commenting on this role of education in facilitating social mobility among the lower classes, the governor of Jamaica reported in 1874 that

> numerous instances have of late come to our notice of youths leaving our elementary schools, getting into respectable situations in counting houses, stores and even Government offices . . . where they are . . . in receipt of very fair pay . . . such as they could never have dreamt of but for the education they had received.[12]

For many black and coloured working-class boys, primary school teaching often represented the first step up the occupational ladder. It was noted that any individual who had completed primary school

> was qualified to become a pupil teacher and to proceed upward through several "certificated" grades. When young scholars completed this phase, they were immediately appointed headmasters of primary schools. Such an appointment lifted the individual out of the working class. The position of headmaster of a primary school must [therefore] be viewed as constituting the cornerstone of the black and brown middle class. Biographical data on a number of prominent lawyers show that they filled the posts of headmasters as a first step in a professional

career. . . . Alternatively, when a headmaster remained on
the job for many years, he became an active force within
the middle class responsible for the training and shaping of
many others who would become professionals.[13]

While the above statement referred specifically to the teaching
profession in British Guiana, the observations were applicable to most
other West Indian colonies.

As education steadily developed into an instrument of occupational and
social mobility for blacks and coloureds they acquired a real interest in it,
especially beyond the basic primary level. In addition, the emergent
middle classes were in a better position to afford the cost of such education
for their children. In Jamaica, this growing demand for education by the
coloureds and blacks resulted in the recommendation by the Methodist
missionary, Sergeant, for the establishment of a Methodist secondary
school for middle-class girls.

These efforts of parents to secure more and better schooling for their
children were also manifested in the *type* and *level* of education that they
sought. Some parents even wanted a higher education for their children to
help them maintain the social distance that had developed between
themselves and the lowest status groups. As a result, in some of the larger
colonies, the demand for such education reached a point where it could
sustain an increased number of post-primary institutions, including grammar
schools.

In some cases, the local governing authorities and the missionaries
tried to encourage this desire for education among the coloureds and black
sections of the population. For example, the president of the Turks and
Caicos Islands decided to recommend "one of the brightest lads to become a
pupil-teacher at the principal school in the colony." He took this step in
order to "encourage others to imitate" the example set by this young black
man. It was hoped that it would "lead parents to discover that other roads
to preferment . . . [were] open to their children than the now apparent acme
of their ambition," which was "to own an acre of salt pond or keep a petty
shop."[14] Similarly, when the black son of a "Negro" elementary school
teacher appeared to be doing very well at the York Castle High School,
the governor of the institution wrote to the Methodist Society to point out
that this student, though black, had "an intellect and smartness" which
could be equated to the whites and indicated that he would be delighted if
the youngster were to win the Jamaican Scholarship because of the benefits
it would bring to the students and to society as a whole.

The overall outcome was that many West Indian parents who could
afford it tried to give their children a higher level education than that
available in the ordinary primary schools. Over a period of time, more of
them were able to meet the costs involved, especially with the
development of non-traditional crops for export. This also resulted in the
increased demand for private schools. For example, in Barbados in 1848,
36.6% of the children attending schools were enrolled in private
institutions, but by 1860 the figure had increased to 50%. In the two central
schools, enrollment also rose by about 76% between 1846 and 1854, mainly
due to an increase in the number of coloured and black students.

Another factor that raised the demand for higher education among the non-whites was the growing acceptance of the idea that children with exceptional talent deserved more than a basic primary school education. This led to a willingness by some legislators to assist such children from poor but ambitious families to obtain a higher level of education. They perceived that the social benefits likely to accrue from such a measure would be great and that society could not afford the loss of such potential talent. Further, such a measure was considered useful in strengthening the belief in the openness of these societies and thereby enhancing the legitimacy of the state in the eyes of the masses. The outcome was likely to be greater social stability in the region.

This growing demand for higher education in the West Indies also resulted from the relative diminution of such ascriptive criteria as race and class in determining social status, allowing a number of educated coloureds and blacks to move into lower status white-collar jobs, and further strengthening the desire among non-whites to demand a better education for their children. For example, William Conrad Reeves of Barbados, whose mother was black, was made the island's attorney-general in 1882, its Chief Justice two years later, and was knighted in 1889. Because of his colour, he had been denied admission to Harrison College in the 1830s, but he was able to secure a secondary education at one of the less prestigious secondary schools. Reeve's rise to such an exalted position and the appointment of blacks to other white-collar jobs, even those much lower down on the social scale, made non-whites feel that social ascent through education was possible for them also.

The ruling groups argued that such occupational mobility was evidence that colonial society provided opportunities for blacks with talent who were willing to work hard. The Chief Justice of British Guiana drew attention to a black man of limited circumstances in that colony who was able to gain sufficient knowledge at the local grammar school (QCS) to be "sent home" (to Britain), where he was studying to be a Minister of Religion. He suggested that others of an equally low status be given the same educational opportunity that would raise them to the position of judges and legislators.[15]

Some of these observations about the increasing openness of these societies were undoubtedly exaggerated. Status distinctions based on shades of colour continued to persist in the Caribbean, especially in those colonies with a high percentage of resident whites. Even the missionaries indicated their acceptance of these rigid status distinctions in these societies by providing their churches with pews for rental by the coloureds and with benches for the poor blacks.

Some planters and other members of the elite groups were still unhappy about the aspirations to upward mobility that the better elementary schools encouraged. They felt that this was giving too great a boost to the desire for occupational mobility, particularly among the black populations, whom they considered destined to work as agricultural labourers, and that this was creating a shortage of labour on the sugar estates. For example, in 1856 President Seymour of Nevis purposely absented himself from the island's annual exhibitions and distribution of prizes by schools because he felt that on such occasions "everything . . . [was] done to unsettle the minds of the children and unfit them for manfully and honestly earning their bread by *humble* and steady exertion."[16]

As a result, many legislators were often unwilling to increase the funds voted for education, particularly higher education for blacks. Therefore, in the majority of primary schools in the region the instruction provided was not expected to be of an "ambitious character," children were taught by female teachers who were satisfied with a "very moderate remuneration," and "direct religious teaching" formed an essential part of the instructional programme. These schools, intended for children "in their humble sphere of action," were considered to be doing a worthwhile job if they simply produced individuals who would continue to form the pool of workers from which the estate labour force could be drawn.

Problems Faced by Non-whites in Obtaining a Higher Education

While a higher education was gradually becoming a means of upward mobility for the coloured and the black population, counterstrategies were being developed by the whites to maintain their dominance of these societies. Recognizing that an education beyond the basic level offered by most primary schools was likely to be an instrument by which blacks could obtain better jobs and improved social status, the dominant white groups often placed restrictions on the chances of non-whites acquiring such an education.

There was a growing fear among members of the traditional white middle class that their "proper" place in society was likely to be threatened by the advancing blacks and coloureds who were acquiring a higher education. The economic difficulties faced by the whites added to their concern. As was noted in British Honduras, poor economic conditions were putting them in a position of "becoming indebted to the lower classes and almost dependent on their will for assistance. . . . In many cases they [the whites] have been compelled, from want of means, to relinquish the education of their children and thus more lasting evil is done"[17] to their position in society.

As noted earlier, many local legislators were in the earlier years quite reluctant to provide public funds to support secondary education. This often resulted in the fee structure of these schools remaining at a level that most black parents could not afford. With the declining number of the white middle-class families in these societies, some private secondary schools were prepared to admit a few non-white children. However, they often set their fees at a level that only the wealthier black and coloured parents could afford. Commenting on this development, R. N. Murray[18] noted that the private schools raised their fees beyond the capacity of any but the "well-to-do," thereby erecting another barrier against the admission of black children. In Trinidad, even the government secondary school charged high fees, that, as Keenan noted, were beyond the financial ability of most parents, especially blacks at the lower levels of the social and economic hierarchy.

Another strategy used to maintain the social exclusiveness of the secondary schools was to refuse admission to all illegitimate children. This measure automatically denied a chance for a grammar school education to about 75% of the children of the non-white population. The principal of

Lodge School, the Reverend Prideaux, argued the case for excluding illegitimate children, irrespective of the level of their ability, from the more prestigious secondary schools in Barbados. He even suggested to the Education Committee that illegitimate children be disqualified from competing for the exhibitions awarded by the government to such schools since these "were intended not only as a reward for deserving boys, but as an assistance to honest and respectable parents" who wanted to obtain a secondary education for their children. His point was that "unless a line be drawn between legitimacy and illegitimacy in the admission of candidates for the Exhibitions," the question to be considered would come to be ,"at what point in the social scale would they [the Committee members] fix the lower limit of the respectable middle class for whose benefit the Exhibitions were designed?"[19]

This refusal to admit illegitimate children was practised by most secondary schools in the region, although this policy was often publicly challenged by the non-whites. In June 1859, the *Trinidad Press* noted, somewhat sarcastically, that "our honest Government says that the youth of the present generation, the unfortunate offspring of a hell born system, shall not receive the advantage of a superior education, but shall, regardless of their natural capabilities . . . be forced back . . . to use the hoe or axe." The newspaper then went on to ask "will the bone and sinew of the land be suffered to soften and contract, because the lungs of a few of the would-be aristocracy are too tender to inhale the atmosphere in close proximity to those, the union of whose parents has not been blessed by the Church?"[20]

The Wesleyans in Jamaica faced a controversy over the education of illegitimate children when the headmaster of the York Castle School expelled two illegitimate brothers from the school. The local Jamaican Methodist ministers argued in favour of retaining the boys in the school, and the General Committee decided to readmit them, even passing a resolution that, in future, if the parents of a child were living together but not married this would not, by itself, debar the child from admission to the school.[21] It was pointed out that, in addition, individuals of illegitimate birth were in the ranks of the Ministry and were also local preachers, custodes, magistrates, landowners, and merchants. But the admission of illegitimate children by the better secondary schools was not adopted throughout the region. For example, Murray drew attention to the fact that in Jamaica the Wolmer's School underwent changes in the opposite direction, some years after emancipation, when an attempt was made to reduce the access of non-whites to the school.

Further, the instruction provided in the ordinary primary schools was poor, making it difficult for their pupils to pass the scholarship examination that would have provided them with an exhibition at one of the local grammar schools. For example, in 1889 in Trinidad, only nine free places out of the 24 that were made available were taken, up because enough students did not pass the entrance examination to the secondary schools.

In addition to these efforts to restrict the entry of non-whites into the higher educational institutions, other steps were taken to limit the access of blacks to positions of power and to political decision-making roles. One indication of this was the very restrictive franchise of these colonies. In Jamaica, for example, the income qualification for voters in Jamaica was raised by about 300% in 1838. On this point, Ryall noted that between 1834 and 1865, the pattern of legislation enacted on that island reflected an attempt to maintain the supremacy of the old planter class.[22] In 1866 it was also observed that social and occupational mobility was impeded by the general course of the island's legislation which, rather than attempting to encourage the industry and enterprise of the peasantry, was tending to repress and check it. In British Guiana also, the franchise was made so exclusive in 1850 that there were only 916 voters in a population of 128,000. The electorate then probably "consisted almost exclusively of the adult male population of the European race, which formed 11% of the total male population of the colony."[23]

Finally, some coloureds and blacks, especially those who had climbed the social ladder, saw nothing basically wrong with the efforts of the white elites to maintain the existing system of stratification, provided that they were included among those who enjoyed its privileges. Therefore, their major concern was to make themselves acceptable in every way possible to the whites. Two steps taken in this direction were to reject their affinity with their "sable brethren" and to acquire as much as possible of the culture, values, and behaviours of the white population. Some of them therefore offered little assistance to the efforts of blacks.

Secondary Education as Status Confirmation

The role of secondary education as an instrument of social reproduction was quite clearly demonstrated in Trinidad. In 1869, after reviewing various aspects of the work of Queens Collegiate School, Keenan commented on the social composition of the student body, noting that the school admission policy was far removed from the hopes of Lord Harris. This former governor of Trinidad had wanted to give encouragement to boys of ability and determination, "however humble their birth," by providing them with a chance of securing a "superior" education. Instead, with the current policy, Keenan noted that, "no such encouragement" was being "afforded to the poor" to enter Queen's Collegiate School, "for the high rate of fees effectually bars the door against them."[24] Thus, while it was being stated that the school was intended to provide an education for the "youth of the colony," in reality this meant the "youth of the wealthy classes" because the fees were as high as £15 per year — the entire annual salary of some teachers in the West Indies. As Keenan pointed out, the fees were far from "moderate, even for the more wealthy families. [But] in the case of the poor man who is father of a youth desirous of a classical education, the term 'moderate charge'. . . is certainly misapplied."[25]

The elitist nature of the institution was further brought home by the fact that while in 1857 Trinidad was spending £3,450 on the education of about 2,000 pupils in its 26 ward schools, its budget for operating QCS, with its enrollment of 34 pupils, all of whom were children of the more affluent members of the society, was about £3,000 p.a. This meant that the per pupil expenditure at this government secondary school was about 50 times greater than for the primary schools. As Furlonge noted, Governor Keate wanted to emphasize the exclusive nature of the education provided by the schools and therefore, "displayed a disproportionately greater attention to the education of a select few, thus minimizing the resources which might have been available for a more efficient system of elementary schools."[26]

The aim of Queen's Collegiate School was to provide a classical education mainly for the children of the "higher orders" of society, particularly those of the British administrative elite. When it was first opened there were no scholarships that would have allowed bright but impecunious boys from the primary schools to gain access to this institution. Though the school admitted 206 pupils during the first 10 years of its existence, less than a fifth of the students were coloured, none was black, and none was of East Indian parentage.[27] Out of the 68 pupils enrolled in 1870, only 17 (25%) were Catholics in an island which was predominantly Catholic. Moreover, 28 were sons of civil servants who, despite their better economic circumstances, were able to receive this heavily subsidized education. Incidentally, 8 of these students were sons of deceased civil servants and were educated free of charge. Like most other prestigious secondary schools in the region, QCS also excluded illegitimate children.

While it was suggested that one of the aims of this school was to produce greater social cohesion and common understanding among boys of different social and religious backgrounds, the governor was mainly concerned with the bringing together of boys from the different elite groups in the society and not with providing an opportunity for those of different social and economic levels mixing with one another. Therefore, when the governor received a petition from 350 rural farmers and proprietors criticizing various aspects of the proposal for the school, he dismissed it as coming from those occupying a "rank of life" below that for which the college was intended.

Although it was a highly subsidized public institution, the socio-economic background of the students at QCS was not very different from that of the students in the other prestigious secondary school on the island — the Catholic College of Immaculate Conception. There, the full boarding fees were £40 per year (£22.10s for half boarding fees), and the fact that there were no scholarships and free places available for bright boys from poorer families effectively excluded all but the children of the very wealthy. On this point, the Catholics pleaded that without state aid they were not able to provide subsidies or scholarships for students from the lower socio-economic groups. This meant that the lower classes were virtually unrepresented in these schools. So, while the whites made up only about 8-10% of the total population on the island, the number of their children enrolled in these two secondary schools (QCS & CIC) was nearly four times as great as the number of non-whites. The occupational background of parents, which is indicated in Table 3 below, bears out this assessment of the higher social status of the student bodies at these schools.

After Trinidad became the first overseas centre for the Cambridge Junior and Senior Certificate Examinations, students' performance at these examinations became the basis on which the more prestigious jobs, especially those in the civil service, were awarded. This helped to perpetuate the dominance of the wealthier groups in the higher level occupations, since it was only their children who could have afforded to attend better secondary schools and to remain there long enough to prepare themselves for these external examinations.

When some blacks began to move into senior civil service positions, as a result of their performance at these examinations, this method of recruitment came to be regarded as a "dangerous experiment" and was suspended. The whites, who traditionally monopolized the senior civil service posts, "preferred the governor to have absolute discretion in appointments, undeterred by blacks and coloureds waving certificates."[28]

In Barbados, also, the great majority of the boys attending secondary schools were recruited from the "middle classes." This can be seen in Table 4, which indicates the occupational background of the students who attended the two more prestigious schools on the island, Harrison College and Lodge Grammar School.

The secondary education provided at the time in government or government-aided schools was virtually a gift from the poor to the comparatively well-off groups. Because of their hard work and their numbers, the poor made a substantial contribution to the revenues of these colonies, especially through indirect taxation. However, it was the children of the more advantaged groups who mainly enjoyed the benefits of a state-subsidized secondary education.

TABLE 3

Occupational Background of Students Attending the Elite Secondary Schools in Trinidad (QCS and CIC) , 1869

Parents' Occupation	QCS	CIC
Merchants, proprietors, and planters	27 (39.7%)	82 (73.8%)
Public servants	28 (41.1%)	6 (5.4%)
Professionals – lawyers, doctors, accountants, rectors etc.	13 (19.1%)	16 (14.4%)
Other persons	0 (0%)	7 (6.3%)

Source: *Annual Reports of the Colonies.*

TABLE 4

Occupational Background of Students Attending Elite Secondary Schools in Barbados (Lodge Grammar School and Harrison College), 1875-76

Parents' Occupation	No. / Percent	
Planters, proprietors, merchants, and managers	16	(27%)
Schoolmasters (secondary) and other government staff	29	(49%)
Lower level white-collar workers, e.g. clerks, booksellers, storekeepers, etc.	13	(22%)
Widow	1	(2%)
Total	59	(100%)

Source: *Annual Reports of the Colonies.*

However, as indicated earlier, the colour bar, which often prevented many non-whites from receiving a secondary education, gradually became less rigid. Despite the difficulties which these groups faced in their efforts to improve their economic and social status, they continued to see such education as an important means of occupational and social mobility — even though they often recognized that schooling by itself could not overcome all the existing barriers that prevented their access to better jobs. This partly explains their unflagging desire for advanced primary or secondary education and their willingness to make the sacrifices necessary for their children to receive such education. As this desire grew, entrance to the better elementary or the grammar schools became highly sought after, and competition increased between the local whites on one hand and the coloureds and blacks on the other for admission into these institutions. For example, the central schools in Barbados, which were originally established to provide education for poor whites, later began admitting coloured and black children to the point where they represented a greater percentage of the student population than white children. Similarly, at Wolmer's School in Jamaica, the enrollment of non-white children had substantially overtaken that of whites by 1837.

State Scholarships for Post-secondary Education

Although access to higher education by non-whites steadily increased, it was obvious that most of them, particularly blacks, continued to find it difficult to gain admission to the more prestigious secondary schools. However, their situation gradually improved with the assistance of the governments in the region, which often provided secondary-school scholarships or exhibitions for some primary-school children to attend secondary schools (although this took place only in 1892). In a few cases, such as Trinidad, government secondary schools were established where the full costs of the education of "deserving" students were met by the state.

The elite groups were anxious to create in the population a sense that economic and social improvement was attainable through ability and hard work. Therefore, many West Indian governments began to allow a few students of working-class origin to secure an education at one of the more prestigious secondary schools on the basis of their performance in the regular elementary schools. For example, following the criticisms made by Keenan about the social exclusivity of QCS, the government of Trinidad decided to make provision in its 1870 Education Ordinance for six awards to pupils from the primary (ward) schools to be tenable at the Queen's Royal College. These were available on the basis of open competitive examinations. The editor of the *Public Opinion*, a Trinidad newspaper, noted that in 1876 the money voted for exhibitions was £176, but in 1886 and 1887, the amount was increased to £1,800 annually "a more than tenfold increase" in 10 years. During the 11 years from 1876-87, the total amount spent on exhibitions was £12,187.[29]

In Barbados, also, the legislature voted funds for scholarships to allow a few students from the primary schools to attend the local grammar schools. Grants were first given in 1850 to the two local grammar schools, and with their endowments they were able to provide assistance to a number of "foundationers" who were in attendance alongside the private scholars. But such funds were initially granted to children of the respectable though impecunious middle class. The government later granted financial support for a number of exhibitioners, specifically from among those students who were attending the ordinary primary schools. In

Jamaica, the Act of 1892 which provided for the establishment of secondary schools also allowed the granting of scholarships to the most promising students from the elementary schools to further their education at the secondary-level.

The government of St. Lucia was not only making an annual contribution to the local grammar school, but also provided 10 scholarships to enable boys from the primary schools on the island to study there. It was noted that in some cases awards were available to a few pupils to upgrade their primary education so that they might effectively compete for these scholarships. In Grenada, six scholarships tenable for five years at the secondary school were provided for boys from the local primary schools. In British Guiana, some scholarships to secondary schools were made available through the generosity of various bodies, such as the De Saffron and the Mitchell endowments. As well, in 1895 the government made six secondary-school scholarships available on the basis of a competitive examination to four boys and two girls attending primary schools. British Honduras also later introduced regulations to provide scholarships for a few primary-school students to attend local secondary schools.

While most of these awards were at first won by the children of the whites and the coloureds, the black population later also benefited from them. This provided some hope for upward mobility among children of the labouring classes. In fact, when signs of social instability began to develop, as they increasingly did among workers in these colonies, an increase in the number of these secondary-school awards was usually considered as one of the measures that might be taken to defuse the situation.

But, as previously indicated, the elites were anxious to ensure that the numbers from the lower class who would rise up the social ladder by means of acquiring a good secondary education were very restricted. The idea was to create a semblance of openness to talent in the occupational and social structure of these societies rather than to make a real move toward equalizing opportunities among the races on the basis of ability. For example, although a proposal was made for 10 exhibitions to Queen's College in British Guiana to assist those students whose parents could not afford the full cost of such an education, the legislature refused to approve the necessary funds. In 1880 a Mr. Exley Percival failed in this attempt to convince the legislature to award scholarships to the best students from the primary schools to enter QC. He then offered three such scholarships from his own resources, and in the following year, another private award was provided by a Major Turner.

As a result of such increasing public pressure on the government, the legislature began to provide primary-school scholarships tenable at QC in 1894. A year later, another scholarship was also awarded based on the results on the Cambridge Local Preliminary Examination for which some of the better primary schools provided instruction. But there was still resistance among the elites to providing this level of education for the children of the lower classes. For example, when Queen's College was initially made a government grammar school, many members of the elite regarded the provision of higher education for the middle classes as a step in the right direction, especially since so much had been done for the lower classes. But when enrollments at the school reached 60, the elite groups became alarmed and requested that a limit be placed on the number of admissions to QC. Possibly as a result of these pressures, the governor announced that there would be no more free places to the school.

Not only were awards offered for boys to enter the grammar schools, but some colonies also began to make scholarships available to outstanding students from the grammar schools to pursue further studies in a British university or other institution of higher learning. The Trinidad scholarship scheme was initiated in 1862 to allow the two candidates with the best results at the Cambridge Senior School Certificate Examination to pursue university studies in the United Kingdom. In 1864 four such scholarships were awarded to boys at QCS who had obtained first or second class honours at the examination. In 1866 the principal of CIC petitioned for the right of his students to enter for the Trinidad Scholarship Examination on the grounds that they were the sons of "Englishmen by birth." This request was later granted when CIC became an affiliated institution to QRC and its students began to compete for these university scholarships. In addition, another scholarship was made available to a deserving boy in the middle form to help him complete his secondary education.

In 1878, the governor of Jamaica proposed that a Jamaica Scholarship be made available to secondary-school graduates for studies overseas. He pointed out that this, more than "any other single step," would help to "stimulate the energies" of pupils and teachers alike and thus improve "the standards and general character" of the better middle-class schools in Kingston and elsewhere in the colony. Further, it would "bestow advantages of incalculable value" on those students who had won the scholarships and even on those "who have striven all but successfully" for them because they would

> have had their standards of education permanently raised, and would have gained for themselves an amount of discipline, training and culture . . . of which nothing can subsequently deprive them. I think the importance can scarcely be over-rated of thus diffusing a keener appreciation of the advantages of study throughout large sections of the community. [30]

Barbados, too, provided some awards for the best students from the secondary schools to pursue further education and training, both in the United Kingdom and at the Codrington College. In 1879 Mitchinson strongly influenced the decision of the government to establish the Barbados scholarship for overseas studies in a British university by financing a scholarship from his own funds for a boy from the island to study at Pembroke College, Oxford.

In 1883 the government of British Guiana introduced the Guiana scholarship, which provided for the student who performed best at the final Secondary School Certificate Examination to proceed to a British university or an institution of similar rank. This measure was hailed as indicative of the liberal views of the government in helping working-class children to improve their opportunities for occupational and social advancement. As the 1895 *Annual Report* noted, these scholarships would enable a boy to proceed directly from a primary school to "an approved higher grade school," where he would "eventually be able to compete for the Colonial scholarship which will take him home" to pursue further studies and "give him a profession."[31] When two young Creoles won scholarships in 1895 to pursue studies in medicine and law, it was suggested that these gentlemen were setting "wholesome examples to their race" and showed "a small link in the chain of possibilities of the Creoles of this Colony."[32]

In addition, the Gilchrist scholarship, which became open to West Indians in the early 1870s, also helped to raise educational and mobility aspirations among students of modest means. In Jamaica, it was said to have been "productive of good" and had the effect of stimulating "the cause of educa-tion . . . by inducing young men of ability in the island to strive for higher degrees of attainment in their studies." This helped to encourage and develop "native talent," and the successful candidates were "enabled, by further culture in the Universities of England to attain to positions of eminence and usefulness."[33]

Because of its value, the Gilchrist scholarship became a much sought-after award, and keen competition for it developed among the various colonies. Between 1871 and 1884, it was won eight times by students from Barbados, six of whom passed the examination with honours and two in the first division. Therefore, the withdrawal of the award in 1884 was seen as a great loss, since the success of the educational systems in these colonies was attributed partly to the availability of these exhibitions. The awards which were placed within reach of all boys in the secondary schools and made it possible for them to move from the lowest to the highest levels of the educational ladder acted as an important motivating factor among them. Therefore, "the great goal of the curriculum" of the secondary schools became "the Scholarship at an English University." The effect of a scholarship such as the Gilchrist was therefore said to have been "incalculable and its withdrawal would be most deplorable."[34]

What was important to the dominant groups was not so much to increase the number of children from the lower classes who were able to secure a secondary education, as it was to create the *belief* among their parents and the population in general that there was an openness in these societies. The ultimate aim was to help pacify the masses by convincing them that chances for educational and occupational mobility were open to their children. When the Mitchinson Commission advanced the case for increased provision of post-primary education in Barbados, it did so partly on the grounds that such a step would provide a limited opportunity for advancement among the masses which in turn would help to ensure the stability of society. The Commission recommended that more facilities be provided for higher education among the lower classes despite the chairman's limited faith in the intellectual capability of the coloured and black population. He had even suggested that the experience of his diocese "has taught us to be mistrustful of the intellectual gifts in the coloured race, for they do not seem generally to connote sterling worth and fitness for the Christian ministry."[35] However, in putting forward its views on this point, the Commission which he chaired suggested that

> it is not only desirable that the best stratum in each
> primary school should gravitate upwards, i.e. should

> struggle into a more advantageous position, socially
> speaking; it will always conduce to the interests of the
> community and the *stability* of its institutions, if the very
> best units in the best stratum be placed, through means of
> access to our highest type of education, within reach of the
> best social and professional positions attainable in the
> Colony. . . . There will probably be but *very few* who are
> worth this exceptional treatment, and even of these some
> will turn out failures, after promise. It is however, an
> *experiment worth trying,* and the existence of even *one* such
> exhibition per annum from primary to first grade schools,
> will have a wholesomely stimulating effect on primary
> education generally [emphasis added].[36]

Fostering the belief that someone from the lowest socio-economic background could rise up the occupational ladder through education was important in deterring many socially aspiring blacks from criticizing the rigidity of the existing structure of these societies. In Barbados, as in other West Indian colonies, the government often boasted that the educational system was open enough to allow anyone, whatever his financial circumstance, to move right up the educational ladder — from a primary school to a university. This was considered by some to be a tremendous achievement for these societies. The inspector of schools in Trinidad also pointed out in 1872 that

> the advantages now offered in Trinidad to an industrious
> lad can hardly be surpassed. Any boy, whatever his origin,
> may attend gratuitously any Government primary School;
> he may become a Candidate for and gain free admission to
> the Queen's Royal College where a liberal endowment of
> four annual exhibitions of £150 a year is open to enable him
> to proceed to an English University and once there he will
> again find scholarships and prizes open to him.[37]

The major objective in providing a limited number of government scholarships for some students of poorer socio-economic circumstances to attend the secondary schools was not to change radically the existing system of social stratification in these societies which was based largely on race and class, but to create what was essentially a myth, that on the basis of his ability, any boy could rise up the occupational and social ladder, irrespective of his social class origin.

Secondary Schools and the Perpetuation of Class Distinction
Despite this semblance of openness in these societies which the scholarship system helped to create, steps were taken to ensure that opportunities for upward mobility through education were restricted. The grammar schools continued to recruit their students mainly from the higher classes in these societies. In Trinidad, for example, it was noted that girls' secondary schools, even more than those for boys, "remained closed to all but the upper and upper middle classes."[38] The number of scholarships available was very limited, and in some cases, the examination standards for entry into the secondary schools were too high for students from the ordinary primary schools. For example, in Trinidad, there were six awards

available for boys to enter QRC annually, but at the first examination held in 1872, only three candidates of the twelve who entered were successful — one from a ward school and two from the Boys' Model School. Sixteen candidates wrote the next examination, and again, only three were successful, two of them being students from the Boys' Model School.

Children from the lower socio-economic groups and those in the rural areas were particularly handicapped. For example, in 1889 the principal of QRC still noted that provision of secondary education existed only for the "children of professional men, Government officers, Ministers of religion and business people" in Port of Spain. It was mainly their children who were able to get "a fairly good Grammar School education at a comparatively cheap rate."[39] The principal, however, considered the existing provisions of secondary education as adequate since, as he argued, the demand for such education in the colony was limited.

The social exclusivity of the more prestigious secondary schools was also maintained, partly because of their selection process. These schools often had two departments — their regular secondary departments and preparatory departments or "feeder" schools which were linked to and provided students for the secondary departments. Many middle-class parents did not want their children to mix with the children of the rank and file in the regular primary schools and were therefore willing to pay the fees so that their children could attend these more exclusive preparatory departments or feeder schools. At Harrison College, for example, it was noted that the existence of a preparatory form made it possible for children to begin their preparation for secondary school at an early age, an opportunity which was increasingly being appreciated by their parents. The preparatory department of the government secondary school in Trinidad provided elementary instruction in the 3Rs, in addition to grammar and geography. In drawing attention to the provision of primary and secondary courses at this school, the governor noted that it was

> open to very young boys and offers them careful elementary instruction .... Indeed a boy may enter the school, knowing little or nothing, and pursue his studies there . . . until he has obtained proficiency, either as a classical scholar or a mathematician which will ensure him a good position at Oxford or Cambridge.[40]

The students in the preparatory departments obviously had first priority in admission to the secondary department of these schools and often in the available awards or exhibitions. This helped to maintain the schools' social exclusiveness and "perpetuated class snobbery" that "tended to take deeper roots over time."[41] As a result, a great gulf continued to exist between the beneficiaries of primary and secondary education. This was one reason why the term secondary schools was sometimes used synonymously with middle-class schools during this period.

Since a grammar school education was to serve as a mechanism of social differentiation, by helping to secure for its recipients admission into the higher echelons of society, these schools maintained certain features which made it possible for them to confer this higher prestige on their graduates. These features included (1) their social exclusivity and (2) the nature of the instructional programmes which they offered.

1. Reference was made above to the exclusivity that was maintained by the level of fees that was charged. The fees at two grammar schools in Trinidad were more than five times higher than those at the model schools on the island. In 1871 when the governor proposed a reduction in the fees charged at QRC so as to allow for an increased entry into this excellent grammar school, his concern was to attract more sons of senior civil servants and members of the learned professions, merchants, managers of estates, and others who could not afford to send their children to England for an education. He realized that even with his proposed fee reduction the social composition of the student body was not likely to change to include children of lower classes.

Further, when scholarships to secondary schools were initially provided by the governments of some of these colonies, they were not always awarded on an open competitive basis. For example, in Barbados, the selection procedure for these awards was initially carried out through nomination by members of the boards of the grammar schools. Nepotism was the apparent result of this system, judging from the allegations that were often publicly made. There tended to be a prejudice in the selection of these exhibitioners against children from the lower socio-economic groups, particularly from black or even coloured families. The exhibitions were initially awarded mainly to children of eminent public officers — including in one case the son of the inspector of schools and in another the son of a judge — all of whom were in a position to afford the fees without government assistance.

These charges of discrimination in the selection of scholarship holders were not denied and were even defended on the grounds that the practice helped to ensure that the awards were not given to students who were likely to be considered undesirable for these middle-class schools. A local Barbadian newspaper commented that these awards were "frequently conferred upon the sons of men with large incomes." The newspaper, after naming individuals whose children were awarded these scholarships, expressed surprise "to find gentlemen of such calibre lending themselves to the perpetration of such jobbery."[42] The accusation was made that even when formal examination tests were used and non-white students were selected by this means the results were altered and these students rejected.

Rawson, the inspector of schools for Barbados, saw nothing wrong with this selection process, which he considered to be an excellent means of extending the foundation of middle-class education to those children whose parents, though of a respectable social background, were unable to afford the cost of such education. He also argued that it was the mode of selection which he found in place when he assumed his duties and that it had seemed to work well in the past. There were others who also supported this method of selecting exhibitioners, and they argued that it was bound "to protect the schools against the admission of such boys as Exhibitioners as would be obnoxious to the sons of gentlemen who attend the schools as paying pupils; otherwise the Committee will wreck the vessels which the State has entrusted them to steer."[43]

As a related concern of the Committee was to exclude illegitimate children, it suggested that this could be achieved only on the basis of sponsorship, rather than performance on examinations. Up to 1871, the exhibitioners at St. Andrews Middle School were largely children from a middle-class background. Three of those awarded exhibitions were sons of managers of sugar estates, two were the children of civil servants, including a magistrate's clerk, one was the son of a shopkeeper, and one "the dependent nephew of Mr. Fletcher, a potter."

In Jamaica, however, because the government's involvement in secondary education began later, some emphasis was placed on making this type of education available to the new coloured and black middle class rather than to the whites only. But in some cases, scholarship holders from the primary schools who were mainly black or coloured were still discriminated against in the prestigious schools.

In Trinidad, it was reported that these students were often refused books and were not examined in their lessons for days. Sometimes they received no direct teaching at all. At QRC, one of the principals, William Niles, did not put any of these boys in his own class, thereby making it impossible for them to compete for the Island scholarship and the opportunity to receive a university education in the metropole.

2. The second distinguishing feature of the grammar schools was the particular instructional programme which they offered. This included classical subjects, which were not ordinarily taught in the senior elementary schools. This difference was important because, at the time, a classical education conferred much prestige on the learner. This point was made by the inspector of schools in Trinidad when, in his 1861 report, he attempted to justify the establishment in that colony of the Queen's Collegiate School (QCS) as a classical grammar school. He noted that with an increasing number from the labouring classes receiving a primary education, there was a "morbid sensitiveness" about and a "lack of sympathy" for "over-educating the minds of persons in the humbler walks of life, [those] whose careers . . . had better be confined to mechanical and manual occupations, [rather] than those requiring an exercise of the more elevated powers of the mind.[44]

He therefore went on to suggest that

> A distinction will always, however, be maintained in the social scale by means of the superior classical education afforded at the Queen's Collegiate School. And had it not been for the establishment of this important institution, there seemed a likelihood of the "toe of the peasant coming so near the heel of the courtier as to gall his kibe," for those born in the higher positions of life may have had to give way in point of intellectual culture to the pupils of popular education.[45]

The Occupational Destination of Secondary-school Graduates

Those who obtained their advanced primary education from the model, intermediate, or even second grade schools often filled positions at a lower level of the occupational hierarchy, while the boys who attended the grammar schools moved into more prestigious jobs. In addition to working as skilled craftsmen, some of the pupils who attended the model or better primary schools later went into commerce as tavern keepers and higglers. Some had stalls in the market as fruiterers, fishmongers, or petty hucksters, while others kept retail shops. Many, including the non-whites, also found employment as general and accounting clerks in offices since, as Mrs. Carmichael[46] observed earlier during her visit to a number of these colonies, the coloured males were "excellent accountants" and could "write well." Several were also engaged as clerks, either in the stores of merchants or as copying clerks to lawyers, while others found employment as regular clerks in offices.

As early as 1837, Thome and Kimball[47] had noted that there was hardly a respectable house operated by white merchants in which some important office, often that of the head clerk, was not filled by a person of colour who, no doubt, had some form of higher education. In the Bahamas, those who left the better schools were sought after to hold important positions such as teachers and clerks in stores, while others were learning useful trades. In British Guiana and probably elsewhere in the Caribbean, those who had acquired a primary education also became rural postmasters and dispensers on the sugar estates.

Only a limited number of individuals who attended grammar schools were able to pursue further studies overseas. The vast majority of them had no prospect of further education beyond the secondary school. In fact, about two-thirds of the students in the grammar schools never proceeded to study for the examination which would have qualified them for entry into a British university. Those who completed their grammar school education usually had no problem in finding suitable employment and were usually employed as clerks in government or commercial offices.

Passes at the Cambridge Secondary Examination increasingly became a passport to the more respectable white-collar jobs. The civil service examinations in Trinidad opened up another avenue of employment, and many ex-students of QCS tended, like their parents, to join the Trinidad civil service. In fact, one of the expressed expectations of that school was to prepare middle-class boys for the civil service examination. The chief justice also indicated that the education and hard work of the boys at this school would be rewarded with a certain and easy livelihood and the position of a gentleman because the highest posts in the civil service would be open to them. As a result they would have a "marked influence" on the "destiny of the Colony." When the proposal was made for a discontinuation of QCS as a government college, Governor Gordon strongly opposed such a measure. As he pointed out, the school was of "incalculable advantage" to the government and to the colony since it helped to provide recruits to the "junior departments of the Civil Service." Further, since selection of such candidates was based on the objective criterion of examination results, rather than by patronage, the school was playing a crucial role in preparing these students to help operate an efficient public service.

The students attending the CIC were predominantly from a French middle-class background, and therefore, once they had completed their schooling, they were likely to be employed in the more remunerative and influential positions, especially in the private sector of the local economy. In his address at the school's prize giving in the 1840s, the Bishop of

Roseau noted that many young men who had completed three or four years in the school

> are now filling very honourable and respectable situations
> with satisfaction to their employers and great advantage
> to themselves and their families, to whom they have
> given a speedy return for the trifle of money expended on
> their education. . . . I do not of course allude to those who
> are destined for the more learned professions . . . but I speak
> of those — and they are the greatest part — which are to
> become planters, clerks or accountants . . . with regard to
> them it may be safely said that they can obtain here . . . a
> more practical education, and one far better suited to their
> future avocations in life than [an education obtained] in
> Europe.[48]

It was estimated that between 1863 and 1882 St. Mary's College (CIC) had produced "60 civil servants, including doctors, engineers and surveyors [working for the Government], three priests, eleven lawyers, nine doctors in private practice and one hundred and ten merchants and planters."[49]

In the Crown colony of Trinidad, secondary education was seen by some of the local French elite as a "training ground for political action," while in other colonies it was said to be preparing individuals for the struggle to retain their elected systems of government.

In Jamaica, the headmaster of Wolmer's Boys' School mentioned that his ex-students went into "various mechanic trades," to counting houses, attorneys' offices, and as clerks to planting attorneys, while others become planters. Most of these were probably children of whites, others were coloureds, while there was also a small but growing number of blacks. The 1880 *Report of the York Castle High School* also noted that the "products" of the school had taken up "respectable callings," with two having become junior members of the school staff. Girls from the Barbican School who did well at the Cambridge Local Examinations went on to occupy positions of "usefulness" and "responsibility" in the colony. Some girls from the Wolmer's School became "seamstresses, mantuamakers and a considerable proportion tailoresses in Kingston and throughout Jamaica as situations offer."[50]

By 1870 most of the British West Indian colonies had their constitutional status changed to that of Crown colonies. This meant that the opportunity for the public to have some influence in the selection of political figures to help manage the state was not available, and as result, black or coloured individuals had little chance to hold high positions in public life. Those who could afford it therefore sought advancement via the two independent professions of law and medicine, particularly the former, as legal training was less costly. A few senior public service positions were made open to West Indians, and the island scholarships which were provided by some colonial governments allowed a few more to qualify for the older professions.

Summary

In review, it can be seen that there were two opposing views about the role of secondary education in the West Indies — whether it should be an instrument for socially reproducing the higher and the middle classes in these societies or whether it should provide an opportunity for poorer boys to rise up the social ladder. In Trinidad, for example, the latter view was held to some extent by Lord Harris, while the former was shared by Governor Keate. Out of these conflicting views emerged a compromise which generally favoured the use of higher education as an instrument of social reproduction while still permitting some limited opportunities for children from the lower socio-economic groups to rise up the social ladder by filling certain white-collar jobs such as teaching.

During this period and particularly after the 1870s, there was an increasing demand for advanced primary and secondary grammar school education in the Caribbean. As this happened, public funds were gradually provided to support this level of education, despite the initial objection to such a step by some key individuals in the Colonial Office. A number of awards were made available by the local legislatures for students to study at both the secondary and the post-secondary levels. The scholarships provided by some governments in the region allowed some primary-school students to obtain a secondary-school education locally and the best secondary-school graduates to secure a tertiary-level education in the United Kingdom at government expense.

The increased availability of such education to the local population was also seen as an important factor contributing to the stability of these societies. It gave working-class families some hope that through their children's academic success they might be able to improve their social and economic position. This helped to defuse somewhat the increasing resentment among the masses against the ruling groups in some of these colonies. The importance of higher educational opportunities for the social stability of these societies was recognized by the Mitchinson Commission which recommended the provision of two types of higher education for Barbados. It suggested that if the community were to prosper and remain stable, a few members of the lower class should be allowed to achieve these higher education goals. While their numbers were to be very limited, the commission felt that the example that they would provide would have a stabilizing effect on society. Parents would know that such opportunities did exist and would direct their efforts toward their children's educational advancement rather than focussing their frustrations on criticizing the elites in these societies.

This provision of secondary educational opportunities by the government was often supported by some members of the local elite because of the effect it had on the behaviour and outlook of the students. As the principal of the St. Kitts Grammar School noted, no doubt with some degree of satisfaction,

> a more docile, well conducted boy than has uniformly come under my notice here, I could not wish to find; it is an extremely rare exception for a boy, after his first few days at school, to show the slightest symptom of recalcitrance, impertinence, sulkiness of obstinacy, or give me any cause to complain of want of industry during school hours.[51]

This was like music to the ears of the ruling groups, since such behaviours were seen as likely to prevent the emergence of social discontent and foster social stability and economic progress in these societies. The *Mitchinson Report* also drew attention to somewhat similar benefits that were likely to accrue from those children who were given some post-primary education, because even though

> their school learning may, probably will, soon be forgot-ten . . . the habit of obedience, order, punctuality, honesty and the like, which a child ought insensibly to acquire in his progress, be it ever so slow, through a well disciplined school, are likely to stick to him all through life, and make him a better labourer than he would have been without that training.[52]

Notes

1 Brereton, *Race Relations.*
2 Davy, *The West Indies,* 104.
3 Douglas Hall, *Free Jamica, 1838-1865,* reprint ed. (Kingston, Jamaica:, Caribbean Universities Press, 1959).
4 *Sargeant to Punshon,* 9 June 1877.
5 Latin America Bureau, *Guyana* (London, 1984), 19.
6 *The Argosy,* 4 December 1880.
7 Rodney, *A History of the Guyanese Working People,* 105.
8 Report of the Government of Dominica, *British Parliamentary Papers,* Vol. 36: *1862* (London: Government of Great Britain), 103.
9 Report of the Government of Tobago, *British Parliamentary Papers,* Vol. 10: *1857* (London: Government of Great Britain), 126.
10 Anthony Trollope, *The West Indies and the Spanish Main* (London: Frank Cass, 1859), 95-96.
11 Bishop Parry to SPG, 14 April 1852.
12 Report of the Government of Jamaica, *British Parliamentary Papers,* Vol. 44: *1874* (London: Government of Great Britain), 5.
13 Rodney, *History of the Guyanese Working People,* 115.
14 Report of the Government of the Turks and Caicos Islands, *British Parliamentary Papers,* Vol. 49: *1866* (London: Government of Great Britain), 69.
15 Cameron, *A History of the Queen's College,.*
16 Report of the Government of Nevis, *British Parliamentary Papers,* Vol. 10: *1857* (London: Government of Great Britain), 208.
17 Report of the Government of British Honduras, *British Parliamentary Papers,* Vol. 34: *1849* (London: Government of Great Britain), 286.
18 Reginald N. Murray, "The Education of Jamaica: Its Historical Background and Possible Future Developments" (M.A. thesis, Univ. of London, 1947).
19 Reverend W. Prideaux to Education Committee, 16 February 1873; Gordon, *A Century,* 250.
20 *Trinidad Press,* 4 June 1858; Gordon, *A Century,* 237.
21 See *Minutes of the York Castle High School Management Committee,* 1898-1900; Burke, "The History of the Wesleyan Methodist Contribution," 195.
22 Ryall, "The Organization of Missionary Societies."
23 Sir Cecil Clementi, *A Constitutional History of British Guiana* (London: Macmillan, 1937), 366.
24 *Keenan Report,* 62.
25 Ibid., 50.
26 Furlonge, "The Development of Secondary Education," 50.
27 Eric Williams, *History of the People of Trinidad & Tobago* (London: Andre Deutsch, 1964), 203.
28 Carl Campbell, *The Young Colonials* , 124 (in Press).
29 Philip Rostant, *Speech at the St. Mary's Past Students' Union Dinner,* January 1887; Gordon, *A Century,* 265.
30 Governor Musgrave to Secretary of State, 1 March 1878; Gordon, *A Century,* 264.

31   Report of the Government of British Guiana, *British Parliamentary Papers*, Vol. 99 :1895 (London: Government of Great Britain), 13.
32   *Annual Report of the Congregational Union* (Georgetown, British Guiana, 1895); Rodney, *A History of the Guyanese*, 116.
33   Gordon, *A Century*, 263.
34   Ibid.
35   *West Indian*, 6 September 1878.
36   *Mitchinson Report*, 7.
37   Government of Trinidad, *Report of the Inspector of Schools for the Year 1872* (Port-of-Spain, Trinidad).
38   Brereton, *Race Relations*, 74.
39   Gordon, *A Century*, 245.
40   Report of the Government of Trinidad, *British Parliamentary Papers*, Vol. 40: *1857-58* (London: Government of Great Britain), 74.
41   Murray, "The Education of Jamaica," 34.
42   Gordon, *A Century*, 246.
43   Letter to the Editor from "E", *Agricultural Reporter*, 28 March 1873; Gordon, *A Century*, 246-47.
44   CO 299/12.
45   *Report of the Inspector of Schools for Trinidad, 1861.*
46   Mrs. Carmichael, *Domestic Manners and Social Conditions of the Whites Coloured, and Negro Population in the West Indies* (London: Whittaker, 1833).
47   J. A. Thome and J. H. Kimball, *Emancipation in the West Indies* (New York: n.p., 1838).
48   Bishop of Roseau, *Address at the Prize Giving 24 Dec. 1842*; Gordon, *A Century*, 231.
49   Brereton, *Race Relations*, 74.
50   Thome and Kimball, *Emancipation*, 87.
51   Report of the Government of St. Kitts, *British Parliamentary Papers*, Vol. 42: *1872* (London: Government of Great Britain), 145.
52   *Mitchinson Report*, 6.

CHAPTER 12

ANALYSIS AND INTERPRETATION

Introduction

Before attempting to put forward a theoretical explanation of the educational developments in the British West Indies during the latter half of the nineteenth century, it is necessary to emphasize that there were many groups and institutions interested in, or directly involved with, the provision of popular education in the region. These included the British government, the local West Indian legislatures, and various denominational bodies with their missionaries and teachers, and the parents who, in some colonies, even helped to build schools.

The facilities that were provided and the programmes that were implemented did not arise simply out of supply forces responding to demand for school places. The former initially stimulated the latter, which eventually took on its own momentum. In addition, there was little consensus among the various groups providing educational services in the region about the type of education that was likely to make a significant contribution to the development of these societies. These groups usually had divergent world views of the future of post-emancipation West Indian societies which they wanted to help create through the education that they were providing and different amounts of power to translate their visions into reality.

It also became apparent that success with the introduction of any educational programme was not likely to be achieved simply by the most powerful group working alone. This required the co-operation of all the actors on the educational scene in the region. Therefore, while the planters had the greatest influence on the machinery of the state, the views of other important groups could not have been entirely ignored, with the result that the educational policies and programmes which finally emerged did not exclusively represent the views of the ruling class.

The Major Actors on the Educational Scene

Some of the major actors on the educational scene in the Caribbean included:

The State in the West Indian Colonies

During the period under review the United Kingdom government began to take more direct responsibility for the administration of its colonies. Attempts were made by the colonizing power to remove authority from individuals, organized groups, or even companies to which Royal Charters had been originally granted, and relocate it within the metropolitan political power structure. Accordingly, the machinery established in each colony to assist with its administration was placed under an appointed governor, who was directly accountable to the Colonial Office for his actions. In his role as chief policy-maker, the governor was usually assisted by members of a predominantly nominated legislative council. This development marked the emergence of a political state in the various West Indian colonies which gradually tried to assume a monopoly over the use of physical force. But these efforts were not always without opposition, as the Morant Bay Rebellion of 1865 clearly indicated.

This change in British colonial policy became manifest not simply in the expulsion of pirates from the region, as is indicated in the motto of the Bahamian coat-of-arms — *Piratis Expulsis: Restituo Commercia* (Pirates Expelled: Commerce Restored) — but in the constitutional development that occurred in these colonies which resulted in their movement from representative governments to full Crown colonies. Under the former system, the planters were able to direct most local affairs in accordance with their own interests, especially since the franchise was based on the ownership of a substantial amount of property and/or high incomes. For example, in 1850 the 26 members of the Grenadian Assembly were selected from a total electorate of 99 persons — a fact which suggested that the early West Indian state virtually functioned as the executive committee of the ruling class. With the new Crown colony status, the state was expected to become more benevolently paternalistic, assuming a greater interest in the welfare of the masses and ensuring a more even-handed allocation of rewards and sanctions to all sections of the population.

The Plantocracy

Nevertheless, the planters who controlled virtually all local economic institutions were able to continue their domination of these societies by ensuring that state policies served, or were compatible with, their own interests. They were therefore able to continue their domination of these societies. Further, close links had always existed between the officials of the metropolitan government and the West Indian planters. Estate-owning families like the Quintin Hoggs, the Gladstones (William Gladstone was the father of the British prime minister), and others were well connected with the British ruling class. Later, key British commercial establishments, including some London financial houses which had investments in the sugar industry, established direct links with British parliamentarians who also had or acquired an economic interest in the West Indian sugar industry. Even when this relationship became attenuated somewhat by the Reform Act of 1832 and the Second Reform Act of 1856, the influence which the sugar planters continued to exert on the British government's policies toward the West Indies remained considerable.

Sometimes there were differences in the points of view between the officials of the Colonial Office and the local planters over such issues as the provision of education in the region. One source of disagreement emerged from the fact that the plantocracy tended to have a shorter time perspective than the officials of the Colonial Office for the recovery of the sugar industry. Many of them were anxious to extract as much immediate return as possible from their investment and to ensure that the expenditures made by the state were primarily in their economic interest. This was why the funds spent by the governments of Trinidad and British Guiana on the importation of indentured labourers outstripped that amount available for education. Another reason for this was that most planters, including those who continued to reside in the region, still looked to Britain as the place where they could send their children for an education.

The Colonial Office, on the other hand, was more interested in the long-term prosperity of these colonies, since this was considered the best way to ensure the continued profitable exploitation of the region. Nevertheless, both the imperial government and the local planters shared an overriding congruence of interest in their desire to develop the most cost-effective system of exploiting the physical and the human resources in the region and maintaining social stability.

One of the strategies adopted by the planters in pursuit of their goal of profit maximization was to create a reserve pool of cheap, usually "unfree" labour from which the sugar plantations could draw workers. For this purpose, some colonies, with the support of the British government, imported indentured labourers. The influx of such cheap labour reduced the power of black workers to secure wage increases, a result which often led to antagonism between them and the new immigrant workers.

Another strategy used to reduce labour costs was to increase the workers' dependency on the plantation. For this, the planters adopted such measures as charging high rents for housing if the occupants did not work for the estates. The planters also considered that wages could be kept as low as possible if the labourers remained uneducated.

But some members of the Colonial Office and the plantocracy sensed a need for the "moral rehabilitation" of the "Negro population," a goal which they considered could be achieved by providing them with a "suitable" education. This is partly why the United Kingdom government was prepared to meet the expenses involved in laying the foundation for a system of popular education even before the local legislatures agreed to vote funds to support this activity.

Mannoni[1] has argued that there was usually a marked difference in the attitude toward the colonized between the "mediocre European colonial" resident in the colonies and the "best representatives of the European civilization" who tended to remain in the metropole. This observation was sometimes used to account for the seemingly more liberal attitude to popular education in the metropole than prevailed among local planters. However, both groups were essentially interested in pursuing a common objective — the successful exploitation of the colonized — and saw the maintenance of the dominant/submissive relationship between the colonizers and the colonized as necessary for the achievement of this goal. But while many local planters considered that education might disturb this relationship, officials at the Colonial Office thought that the right type of education could help to strengthen it.

Other Influential Groups

Other groups involved in providing popular education in the region were the missionaries, teachers, and parents, all of whom had some degree of influence on the nature of the education that was offered in the schools.

The *missionaries,* who were responsible for establishing most of the local schools, had a vested interest in the nature of the education provided for their students. They therefore wanted to ensure that their rights were protected in any new educational policy that was introduced in these colonies. The members of the Established Church, i.e., the Anglicans, enjoyed the support of some of the more influential groups both in the West Indies and the metropole, including members of the British Parliament, the colonial governors, the civil service, and the local legislators. Other missionary groups, such as the Baptists, were sometimes looked upon with suspicion by the elites, although they enjoyed much popularity among the masses. The Roman Catholics were initially seen as having a loyalty to other European powers, especially France and Spain. But all these denominational bodies had a fairly common concern with maintaining their control of the local school systems and the content of the education that was offered.

To cite one example of the influence of these missionary bodies, in 1850 an Education Commission for British Guiana had recommended the establishment of a government-sponsored system of secular education. But although this recommendation was approved by the local legislature, it was eventually rejected by the Colonial Office because of the opposition "from members of the Church of England, from the Ministers of the Wesleyans, and from the Presbytery of Demerara, all in a genuine spirit of bigotry."[2] The ability of these church groups to successfully derail efforts by a government to gain some control over education demonstrates the power enjoyed by these sectional interest groups at the time.

The activities of the *teachers* were rigidly monitored by the missionaries who usually served as school managers and tried to ensure that the content of the lessons which they taught was acceptable to the respective ecclesiastical authorities. Nevertheless, many teachers had a substantial influence on the communities in which their schools were located, and they often became role models and formed a very important reference group for the children of the upwardly mobile blacks and coloureds. In addition, they tried to stimulate the mobility aspirations of their students by encouraging the brighter ones to continue their schooling to a level that would have qualified them for lower level white-collar jobs. Some of them also extended the instructional programmes of their schools beyond the 3Rs, which were the only subjects they were often expected or sometimes allowed to teach. Further, since their incomes depended on the level of attendance at their schools, they tried to raise the level of popular demand for education by encouraging youngsters to attend school regularly and remain there to complete their programme of elementary education.

While *parents* were allowed little direct participation in any major educational decisions, they had some impact on the amount and type of education that their children received. If they were not satisfied with the educational programme offered, or the level of school fees charged, they would often withdraw their children from school. This was a factor which the missionaries and teachers were obliged to take into account, since the amount of financial assistance that schools received was usually dependent on their enrollment. In addition, it was the parents' objection to the introduction of industrial education which partly prevented the subject from being effectively introduced in the elementary schools in the West Indies at this time.

But while all these groups had an influence in determining the amount and type of primary education that was offered, the colonial state and those who influenced its administration increasingly played the dominant role in determining local developments in education. And, as previously suggested, of all the groups involved in providing education, the planters exerted the strongest pressure on the formulation of the state's educational policies. This situation slightly changed over time, though the dominant role of the planters in these colonies continued. For example, prior to the abolition of slavery, the planters had almost absolute power over the lives of the black population. With emancipation, their power, though still formidable, was legally modified, and as a result, the state could no longer be as openly oppressive against the black population as during the days of slavery. Increasingly, the concerns of the colonized groups had to be taken into consideration if any new measure that would affect their lives was to be successfully introduced in these societies.

Reasons for Increasing State Involvement in Education

A question which arises is, "Why did the colonial legislatures, which still largely represented the interests of the planter class, decide to provide more financial aid for the education of the black population and to assume an even larger role in administering and controlling the educational systems of these colonies?" Further, it needs to be asked why these events took place at a time when the region was experiencing substantial economic difficulties, and many planters remained doubtful about the economic and social benefits of formal schooling for the masses.

Two supplementary concerns also need to be addressed. The first concerns the intended role and the unintended consequences of the education that was provided during this period. The second relates to the gradual acceptance by the elites of the view that the state should help to finance higher education when initially they believed that those who wanted such education for their children should meet its full cost.

Among the factors that were taken into consideration by the West Indian states in providing more financial support for education were the following: (1) technical or efficiency considerations, aimed at ensuring that the funds which these legislatures were called upon to provide for education were efficiently utilized; and (2) considerations related to the role of education in helping to improve the economy and enhancing the legitimacy of the state.

Technical or Efficiency Concerns

The local legislatures were saddled with the financial responsibility of funding elementary education after the imperial government discontinued its Negro Education Grant. It therefore became necessary to reduce the administrative inefficiency of these educational systems which resulted from the absence of some national co-ordinating agency for education. The governor of Antigua pointed out that to improve the administration of education on the island there was need for a central authority to manage all the schools. In 1850 the president administering the government of Tobago also observed that the "whole progress of education [in Tobago] has been materially impeded by the fact that there were three different bodies conducting schools on the Island."[3] In Grenada, it was reported that, in addition to the language issue, the other major obstacle to the improvement of the educational system was the number of religious sects conducting schools.

Mr. Castello, editor of the *Falmouth Post* of Jamaica, commented in January 1850 on the pitfalls of having an educational system divided on the basis of denominational interests. He noted that the value of the contribution from the church bodies was reduced because of lack of co-operation among them and argued that

> so long as the education of the poor depended on the efforts
> of rival and contending parties, . . . in competition for the
> largest share in the education of the children . . . the
> education will not be governed by a regard to that which is
> absolutely best, but to that which is conducive to the ends
> of the party which directs it.[4]

The development of unco-ordinated educational systems in the region also left the denominational bodies free to establish schools wherever they saw fit. This resulted in educational expansion taking place largely as a result of inter-denominational competition for converts rather than from the educational needs of the population. The outcome was often an over-supply of schools in some areas, while other areas remained under-serviced. West Indian governments therefore considered it necessary to develop a mechanism which would help to overcome this unequal geographical distribution of schools. In 1867 the lieutenant-governor of Dominica pointed out that the island faced many problems in education due to the absence of a central body to plan and co-ordinate current efforts. There, also, "education never spread itself over the country, but centralized and confined itself; favouring some districts and parishes and leaving others wholly unhelped and excluded."[5]

This unco-ordinated educational expansion also increased the financial pressure faced by these colonial governments, since it resulted in demands for more financial support. The governments had little or no influence on the decisions made about the numbers of schools that were being established or their location, despite the fact that they were expected to contribute to the cost of their operation. The tight financial situation which increasingly faced these colonies therefore became another compelling reason for West Indian governments to become more involved in monitoring and even regulating the establishment of schools in the region.

In addition, quantitative expansion of education usually took precedence over its qualitative improvement. In some of the cheaper private schools such as those in Bermuda, this meant that the instruction given, in too many cases, scarcely deserved the name of education. While these colonial governments often expressed an interest in improving the quality of education, it was obvious that they could only do this if they had in place some mechanism to regulate public expenditures on education, control the expansion and location of schools, and exercise some influence over their curriculum and the training of teachers.

The substantial differences in the religious, linguistic, and ethnic or racial background of the West Indian population, further heightened by the importation of indentured labourers from India and China, created a need for social cohesion and the reduction of the possibility of social conflict among these groups. This was another reason advanced for the involvement of government in education. For example, the multi-ethnic composition of the society in British Guiana led the 1850 Commission on Education to suggest that the state should be more actively involved in the administration of the educational services of the country. This Commission even recommended the introduction of a government-controlled secular system of education. It was the hope that a policy of open access to all primary schools, irrespective of the colour or the religious affiliation of the students, might eventually help to reduce inter-ethnic and religious conflicts in the society. As it argued, with "the variety composing the population, and the diversity among them of language and creed . . . it becomes then, [a matter] of the utmost importance that such a system [of education] be adopted."[6]

A need was also seen for the residents in the colonies more recently acquired by Britain to develop a greater degree of loyalty to the British monarch. While in the Leeward Islands the fervent loyalty and attachment to British institutions for which the West Indian colonists were noted continued unabated, the situation was quite different in the newer colonies and among recent arrivals to the region. In Trinidad, Governors McLeod and Harris stressed the need for more state involvement in education to help achieve the dual goals of greater social integration among the various ethnic groups and a stronger sense of loyalty to the British Crown in the society. The alternative, of simply letting the absence of some government control of education perpetuate sectional rivalries, jealousies, and conflicts, was to them not an acceptable one. Harris argued that

> there is perhaps no British Colony, where, from the mixed nature of its inhabitants . . . the necessity of some general plan of Education is more required than in Trinidad. The number of Immigrants we are receiving renders the demand of an extension of the means of Education of greater consequence every day. . . . The differences of language and religion make it more imperative that the system to be adopted should be one, under the control of the Government not only with a view to make it accessible to all parties and creeds, but to cause the language spoken to be that of the Country to which this Colony belongs.[7]

These proposals were an indication of the changing attitudes among some members of the elite about the need for the state to play a more active role in the field of education. The ruling groups also recognized the contribution which education could make toward the political socialization of the young. But this required the government of these colonies to be in a position to influence the curriculum used in schools.

Because of these social benefits that were likely to accrue from education, many legislators increasingly felt that it should be a matter of national rather than denominational concern. Boards of education were therefore established to help with the administration of grants allocated to schools, and inspectors of schools were appointed to monitor the instructional strategies and the curriculum content offered by teachers.

These efforts increasingly received the support of a number of influential groups. A few planters even felt that if the state took some control of education it could curb the efforts of some missionaries to use education to empower the masses, since this was likely to produce popular confrontation with the authoritarian West Indian states.

The Colonial Office, in its persistence to ensure that the educational welfare of the black population was not unduly neglected, tried to bring pressure on the local legislatures to become more involved in the provision of educational facilities and to improve the relevance of the instructional programmes that were being offered. The more rapid expansion of education in the region after the 1870s was therefore partly due to the fact that, with these colonies now under Crown colony government, more attention had to be paid to the views of the officials of the Colonial Office regarding the need to expand and monitor the educational services.

Concern with Capital Accumulation and the Establishment of the Legitimacy of the State

Every state which is concerned with helping to improve the living standards among its population must try to balance the two sometimes contradictory functions of (1) fostering capital accumulation for further economic growth; and (2) strengthening and consolidating its legitimacy in the eyes of its citizenry.

The relationship between these two functions is usually a dialectical one. For example, societal disruption is more likely to occur when the legitimacy of the state is being questioned by the population, and this can result in the need for increased expenditures to maintain law and order. In such an instance, the process of economic growth and capital accumulation would be impeded and the amount of governmental revenues collected would decline. This would result in a reduction of the state's financial ability to provide the facilities which were being demanded by the citizens and which, if supplied, might contribute to the enhancement of the legitimacy of the state. As a study by Bornischier[8] indicates, economic success is more likely to occur in states which have succeeded in reconciling the profit logic with the claims of legitimacy. Lipset, in his analysis of the early development of the USA, also observes that "all claims to a legitimate title to rule must ultimately win acceptance through demonstrating effectiveness. . . . particularly in the economic sphere."[9]

A nation's educational system tends to reflect these concerns, since schools serve as both economic and political instruments of the state to help it achieve these goals. Therefore, any meaningful study of the educational system of a society must include an analysis of the purposes and the functioning of the state,[10] especially since a theory of the state is also often considered a theory of society and of the distribution of power. A fuller understanding of the direction of a society's development must therefore entail a grasp of who controls and directs the state and the goals which are important to them.

An analysis will now be made of the two most important concerns of the state in West Indian society in the post-1845 period — stimulating economic growth and strengthening or establishing, in the eyes of the recently emancipated population, of its legitimacy and the "right" of the ruling groups to their positions of power and control.

The Role of Education in Economic Rehabilitation and Capital Accumulation

Emphasis was placed on the role of education in helping to enhance economic growth and capital accumulation as a means of raising the standard of living of the population. An important goal of colonial education was "to improve the value of colonial production"[11] by providing the labouring class with those skills, knowledge, and attitudes that would make them reliable workers. An additional aim was to educate a comprador elite group whose members would bridge the communication gap between the colonizer and the colonized. This group was also expected to fill, at a lower cost, those jobs which had previously been held by whites possessing a minimum level of education.

In India, such individuals were required to be proficient in English and were to act as "teachers, translators, and compilers of useful works for the masses of the people."[12] As Homi Bhabba pointed out "the exercise of colonialist authority . . . requires the production of differentiations, individuations, and identity effects through which discriminatory practices can map subject populations that are tarred with the visible and transparent mark of power."[13]

A general consensus obtained among the ruling elites as to the importance of preparing youths for their future role as agricultural workers on the sugar estates. A programme of industrial education, such as the one proposed by Kay Shuttleworth, was therefore considered to be crucial for the economic and social development of these colonies. However, while this plan was quite comprehensive, there were many reasons why no real attempt was made to introduce it in its entirety. The high cost, along with the general opposition of the planters to an education geared toward producing small independent peasant farmers, were formidable obstacles to its implementation. The planters wished that the schools would produce individuals with the attitudes and outlook required of productive estate labourers. For this, a simple education with a practical bias that emphasized the development of moral values was all that was considered necessary. It was felt that with such an educational focus the youths could be taught to behave properly and to accept their "divinely ordained" occupational positions.

The planters were also concerned about what they considered to be the declining work ethic among West Indian youths who had not been exposed to the "discipline of slavery." In British Guiana, according to the governor, there existed "among the rising generation a vast amount of idleness and a lamentable disinclination to do anything for themselves,"[14] while in Trinidad, Keenan reported that "laziness is a chronic disorder of the lower classes" of the island — a point of view which no doubt was generally shared by most West Indian elites. But due to the high cost of fully implementing the Kay Shuttleworth proposal, the secretary of state urged that modified versions of the plan should be adopted instead. However, even these efforts were not very successful, largely because of the strong parental opposition to any form of practical training in schools, especially one that focussed on agriculture.

The need for a more scientific approach to farming, including sugar cane farming, led some individuals, such as Governor Harris of Trinidad, to propose that the pupils at school should be provided with some elementary knowledge of science as it related to agriculture. But this suggestion did not take off. However, of these two concerns — the inculcation of certain *moral qualities* and *desirable attitudes* to practical work and the development of some useful *practical skills* — the former acquired precedence over the latter. However, at the turn of the century, there was a tremendous push to introduce science in West Indian schools, especially agricultural science. This had become a matter of such great concern to the Colonial Office, particularly to the Colonial Secretary, Joseph Chamberlain, that it dominated the focus of primary, and to some extent, even secondary and tertiary education in the region during most of the first half of the twentieth century.

The Legitimacy Function of Education

The planters' aim was to incorporate the ex-slaves into post-emancipation West Indian society, while severely limiting their chances of upward social mobility and without giving them any political rights or privileges. In other words they did not want to secure the legitimacy of the state among the masses by introducing democratic reforms through allowing them to participate in the political decision-making process. Rather, those who favoured popular education wished it to be used to engender support for the state by a process of proper political socialization or political indoctrination. The school was therefore viewed as part of the state-supported ideological apparatus for stabilizing the existing and emerging social order.

Originally, the source of legitimacy of the West Indian state was derived from the act of conquest. This right to ownership to lands was eventually transferred to the sugar planters by the British government. Therefore, any threat to the authority of the state, such as external invasion or slave uprising, was usually resisted jointly by the metropolitan and the colonial state. But after the dismantling of the legal structure which supported slavery, the use of physical force alone could no longer be depended on by the state to maintain its authority over the masses. Efforts therefore had to be made to obtain the moral support of the population, partly through the education which they received.

The particular interpretation of social reality transmitted to the students through the formal and informal curriculum was seen to be the primary means of achieving this goal. The mobility opportunities which were to be provided for a few educated lower class individuals were to supplement this process. But the aim of pacifying the masses was not entirely achieved by education, and there continued to be a tension between the two goals of maintaining the dominance and almost total control of the state by the planters on the one hand, and deterring the masses from taking action to protest the marked economic, political, and social inequalities in these societies on the other.

The major function of elementary education among the black population was therefore to attempt to legitimize the highly unequal social and economic structures of these colonies, largely by teaching the black masses to accept them as given and even to see their own place and role in society as divinely sanctioned. This also involved teaching the pupils those values, attitudes, and beliefs which were to make them hard-working and responsible "hewers of wood" and drawers of water. Although many planters were doubtful about the returns from popular education, they continued to hold the view that the recently emancipated black population needed to be instilled with a world view that would develop in them a voluntary subservience to the white ruling groups and a willingness to continue occupying their positions on the lowest rungs of the occupational and social ladder. As in any colonial society, this required "the internalization and acceptance of the total superiority of European culture" rather than through the use of "force alone."[15] Reliance on education as a means of developing in the colonized a sense of psychological subordination to the dominant white group therefore tended to increase.

A number of quite effective strategies were developed to ensure that the education that was being provided was likely to contribute to the legitimacy of the ruling groups in the eyes of the black majority. As suggested above, the most important of these were the instructional programmes and teaching strategies used in schools. The missionaries, as Burke pointed out, were strongly of the view that "if the work of education . . . is neglected," then hopes for the spiritual freedom and moral regeneration of the Negro population "will be both dim and distant."[16]

Religious education was therefore considered to have a crucial role to play in this proper education of the young, and it came to occupy a prominent place in the curriculum of all schools, both as a subject in its own right and as one that was integrated into nearly all others on the timetable. Even in Trinidad, where the teaching of religion was legally forbidden in the government ward schools during the regular school hours, it was found that, in practice, the exclusion of the subject was never total and that most primary school children were receiving some form of religious education as part of their ordinary programme of instruction.

The spiritual and moral instruction which the students would receive as part of a religious education were expected to help ensure that they would abandon their primitive beliefs and behaviours and live according to the tenets of the white man's religion, Christianity. Another expected outcome was a reduction in the rising crime rates in these societies and the elimination of the increasing amount of unruly behaviours which were said to have been noticeable among the youths who had not been exposed to slavery. Incidentally, even the definition of crime had a socially constructed definition to represent all acts against the interests of the planter class. It was a crime, for example, for workers to organize in an attempt to seek better wages, and in Barbados, one Samuel Carrington was found guilty in 1877 of the crime of "entering into a conspiracy to raise the rate of wages on a sugar plantation."[17]

Other arguments were advanced for maintaining religious education as the focus of the primary school curriculum in the West Indies. The ruling groups generally assumed that blacks were ill-equipped for their role as parents and therefore needed the support of the educational system to help with the proper upbringing of their children. The young were to be provided with this sound Christian education in their infant schools so that they could rise above the degraded social and moral environment that was said to be characteristic of life on the plantations. One piece of evidence of the marked degree of moral laxity in the adult population was said to have been the high percentage of illegitimate births in these colonies.

The importance attached to Christianity also reaffirmed the alleged moral superiority of the colonizers and strengthened their claims to dominance in these societies. Commenting on this phenomenon as it was experienced in India, Homi Bhabba refers to the organization of a group of Indians "united to acknowledge the superiority of the doctrine of the Holy Book [the Bible] to everything which they [had] hitherto heard or known."[18] Bhabba observes that this "miraculous authority of Colonial Christianity . . . lies precisely in its being both English and universal, empirical and uncanny."[19]

In addition, it was also suggested that the arrival of new, non-Christian immigrants from Asia was exacerbating the moral problems which some colonies faced, and to overcome this, a Christian education was necessary for their children also. This was to help rid them of the less desirable or even barbarous influences which their parents were said to have introduced into the West Indies.

Another problem arose from the steady emigration of whites who were considered to be on a higher level of civilization. To the elites, this departure of the whites meant that the blacks were losing important role models. Further, white emigration meant that some blacks and coloureds would soon be charged with the responsibility of undertaking more important political and social functions in these societies. In view of these circumstances, the development of moral competence through a programme of religious education was felt to be required for the blacks and coloureds, to prepare them to carry out their new responsibilities in an acceptable manner.

Finally, religious education was considered to have an important cooling-off effect on the aspirations of the young black population, by helping them to set more realistic goals for themselves and to accept their positions of subservience as inevitable. As one West Indian colonial governor suggested, a Christian education would help to equip the upcoming generation, both in mind and character, to cheerfully and satisfactorily perform their unavoidable duties as labourers on the sugar estates.

In addition to religious education, the content of the materials which appeared in the English readers used by the students and the programme of social studies to which they were exposed also helped to develop attitudes of dependency, docility, and subordinacy among the black and coloured population. The students were expected to conduct themselves in a manner that was acceptable to the dominant groups, showing, as one schoolmaster noted, little "recalcitrance, impertinence, sulkiness or obstinacy, nor [giving] me any cause to complain."[20] In 1847 the governor of Antigua commented on the continued absence of "all crimes of an exaggerated character" on the island which, by itself, was "remarkable." He also drew attention to the "peaceful and orderly demeanour of the rural peasantry and their general propriety of conduct," as evidenced by their adherence to the law. These behaviours which "entitle[d] them [the population] to high commendation" were seen as an outcome of the elementary education which they received in the public schools.[21] The Mitchinson Commission saw somewhat similar social benefits accruing from education to the lower orders because "the habits of obedience, order, punctuality and honesty . . . which a child ought to acquire in his progress . . . through well disciplined schools are likely to stick to him all through his life and make him a better labourer than he would have been without that training."[22]

The instruction given to the students was therefore thought to be making a particularly important contribution towards their character formation, producing the type of person who would more readily accept the existing order, rather than try to advocate or implement any radical changes in these societies. In addition, the teaching strategies used in schools resulted in students becoming almost entirely dependent on the structure of knowledge and the interpretation of reality that was presented to them by the teachers and the missionaries. The teachers were the main formal agents of cultural transmission and generally had showed no desire to encourage their students to be creative, to show initiative, or to assume responsibility beyond carrying out orders. The expected outcomes, in terms of students' behaviours, were, as previously indicated, docility, humility, and obedience, and a display of these qualities was usually regarded as a sign that the students' education had been effective. Good discipline was considered a more important outcome of schooling than scholastic progress, and schools were viewed primarily as institutions where habits of diligence, contentment, and stability were induced. It was therefore not surprising that the teaching strategies in schools lacked creativity and that *répétez sans cesse* (constant repetition) remained the most popular means of instruction.

Through the education they received, blacks were also made to think that the white ruling groups possessed a superior level of technical competence which made them equipped to govern. The development of this view of the colonizer was reinforced by the fact that most of the instructional materials used in the children's education were from the metropole. They were foreign to the life experiences of the children, especially since they were often used without modification, thereby reinforcing the belief that all real knowledge emanated from the metropole.

Therefore, the curriculum offered in West Indian schools was not simply the result of a natural process of cultural diffusion, as Blouet[23] suggested, but was an act of cultural imperialism, meant to convey to the colonized the view that the colonizer was intellectually superior and technically better prepared to administer the affairs of the state. The knowledge that the colonizer possessed and his knowledge-producing and knowledge-transmitting institutions were regarded as evidence of his cultural and intellectual superiority.

This point was made very forcefully by Charles Warner, the attorney-general of Trinidad, when he advocated legislative support for the establishment of the island's first government grammar school. In suggesting that the institution be modelled after the English public schools, Warner aimed to impress the locals with the superiority of the English classical education which was provided for the British upper and middle classes. As he observed when introducing the bill to establish this institution,

> There is, I believe, no training equal to that of the great English schools. . . . It may be that Providence has seen fit to make us Englishmen with such a breadth of pelvis, physical and intellectual, that the love of freedom is a law of our being. Be that as it may, there can be no doubt that Eton, and so in their order, the other public schools . . . does produce the men who whether in the State, or at the Bar, or in the field, in the House of Commons, or in Westminster Hall, or in the Crimea, are the leaders in the world.[24]

Further, the fact that the recognized preparation for any of the learned professions in these colonies could only be obtained from a metropolitan institution of higher learning helped to add to the colonizers' claim to technical and intellectual superiority.

The more ambitious blacks and coloureds were very keen to adopt much of the cultural values and beliefs of the white population because they were seen as a prerequisite for upward social mobility and overall status improvement in West Indian societies. Their assimilation into European culture was made easier by the fact that, with the prior enslavement of the Africans, much of their culture had been either destroyed or negated by the colonizers.

In the colonies that had more recently been under French rule, the population spoke French, were familiar with French culture, and had their spiritual needs met by French Roman Catholic priests. However, with the accession of British rule, every attempt was made to ignore or even remove the French fact from these islands. In most of them, particularly in Trinidad, the government launched a programme of Anglicization in the attempt to get rid of the French elements of their culture, including their French patois. An important contribution to these efforts was made by the local schools, in which English became the only medium of instruction. This was a requirement for any schools seeking government aid, even though most of their pupils did not know a word of English.

The aim to produce a culturally and linguistically homogeneous British West Indies was reflected in a similar disregard for other languages and cultures. For example, the cultural heritage of the East Indians, who made up a large percentage of the population in Trinidad and British Guiana, was often officially denounced and not given any recognition in schools. Instead, the education of these children was to be an act of Christianization which would cause them to forget their own cultural and religious roots. Attempts were also made to de-emphasize the educational efforts of the Roman Catholics, whose source of support came initially from rival European powers, mainly France and sometimes Spain. Therefore, their schools were initially given no government support. The education vote was often allocated solely to those schools operated by the Church of England and later by other denominational bodies such as the Wesleyans.

The Roman Catholics were almost invariably the last to benefit from these subsidies.

Commenting on the socialization of the West Indian black, Frantz Fanon noted that he had so completely adopted the metropolitan culture that, even as late as the 1930s, he was still not considered to be an African, but a quasi-metropolitan, a European. While Fanon's observations referred more specifically to the educated elite in the French West Indies, they were equally applicable to the comparable groups in the British West Indies. Gordon Lewis, in commenting on the same point, also noted that "by seeking through education to convert the West Indian person into a coloured English gentleman," the colonizer produced the spectacle of a West Indian who was "culturally disinherited."[25] Homi Bhabba describes this process as "colonial mimicry."

These efforts in colonial societies to establish the pre-eminence of the culture of the colonizer was a pattern followed by other colonizing powers. For example, it was noted that in the French African colonies "cultural depersonalization" among the colonized was a key element in the education policy of the metropole. The locals who were to fill lower level jobs within the administration were given "a purely French training" which was to convince them of the superiority of the French, their language, and their culture. In return for this, it was expected that the beneficiaries of such education should pledge "respect, gratitude and above all, obedience" to their colonizer. Further, "while they were allowed to reveal the distance separating them from the common masses, they were carefully invited not to forget the distance separating them from their European masters." The local culture was largely ignored, and the education provided "proceeded from the only culture considered to be of any value — that of the colonizer."[26] This was part of the process of cultural depersonalization and a further attempt to develop and strengthen the belief among the locals in the superiority of the colonizer, thereby enhancing his claim to rule.

The Expansion of Education as a Legitimating Device

Opportunities for occupational mobility through education created the sense that West Indian societies were becoming more meritocratic — more open to achievement. This increased the legitimacy of the state and contributed to a growing demand among the masses for education.

By the time the Negro Education Grant was terminated in 1845, the idea of popular education had become generally accepted in the region. As Shirley Gordon noted, "no responsible person queried whether schools should be maintained, after the grant was finally withdrawn by the British Government."[27] The local legislatures were therefore faced with a dilemma. They could either provide some financial assistance to the missionaries and the Mico Trust to continue their work in education or they could refuse to do so, thereby running the risk of public outcry and a further challenge to their legitimacy as the educational programmes in the region were phased out.

Therefore Governor Grey of Barbados argued that education was so important an activity that it should become a state responsibility. He even proposed the introduction of a secular system of instruction, but this was turned down by the secretary of state for the colonies because it represented too much of a departure from the practice then current in England. Proposals were also made in Antigua, Grenada, St. Kitts, British Guiana, and Trinidad for the state to take over full control of the local educational systems. Although the colonial legislatures (with the exception of Trinidad) often failed in this effort due to the objections raised by the various denominational bodies, most West Indian governments did provide increasing levels of financial assistance for the provision of elementary education.

Another of these developments was the change in admission policy for publicly funded educational institutions. At the primary level, access to the government-aided schools was becoming open to all, regardless of the colour of their skin. This change came partly in response to criticisms from prominent individuals in the region concerning the discriminatory nature of the initial policy. In Barbados, for example, the practice of separating primary school pupils on the basis of their skin colour was attacked, even from Bishop Parry, who was "notoriously hostile to the intellectual progress of the masses," having little faith in their intellectual capacity.[28] Nevertheless, in 1852 he raised objections to the "principle of providing a separate education for the free coloured population of the West Indies," suggesting that this practice was an inappropriate one which the Church was committed to eradicate.[29] Therefore, by 1878, an Act was introduced in the Barbadian legislature which forbade the granting of public funds to any school which admitted only children of a particular colour or complexion. This policy was also adopted by other British Caribbean colonies.

With the segmented occupational and social structure of the West Indies still based primarily on colour and ethnicity, it was sometimes argued that the provision of advanced educational opportunities for the black and coloured populations would contribute to their dissatisfaction with the highly unequal distribution of rewards in these societies, possibly leading to social unrest and disruption. Because of this, the voluntary agencies which were establishing schools initially provided only elementary education for the children of the non-white population and elementary and secondary education for the children of the whites. But tensions later developed as a result of this practice, and efforts were made, through more fluid school admission policies, to provide some safety valves to prevent open social conflict from developing over this issue.

Therefore, in the years immediately after emancipation, some opportunities for higher education were made available to the non-whites, through the model, intermediate, or second grade schools. Such opportunities enabled a few blacks to move into lower level white-collar positions as teachers, catechists, and later as messengers and other junior functionaries in the public service. As a result, Brereton noted for Trinidad that, "education was . . . the crucial factor in the gradual emergence of a coloured and black middle class."[30] This was also the case in the other West Indian colonies.

As coloureds and blacks became more politically restless and opposed to the state financing of any institution from which their children were excluded, the economically better-off parents from these groups sought access to the government-sponsored grammar schools for their children.

These schools, which began to be established in the region especially after the 1870s, provided the type of academic preparation required for higher status white-collar positions in these societies. The ruling groups recognized that unless the grammar schools were open to all races, an increase in popular social discontent and instability could result. Therefore, this type of education also gradually became more available to children of non-white parents who could afford to pay the necessary school fees. This was facilitated by the steady emigration of white families from the region, who left some vacant places in the schools which coloureds and black pupils were allowed to fill.

Later, many West Indian governments responded to the pressure for higher education, which also began to be exerted by lower class blacks, by providing a limited number of scholarships for children from the elementary schools to enter the grammar schools. In Barbados these exhibitions were initially made on the basis of sponsorship, but this was changed and throughout the region they became subject to open competition. These awards made it possible for a few primary school pupils, some of whom were from black families of fairly modest means, to attend the relatively prestigious secondary schools. This further stimulated the interest of other working-class parents in elementary education.

In addition to these secondary school scholarships, West Indian governments provided university awards annually or every two years, based on the results of the Cambridge University Secondary School Leaving Examination. Technically, this made it possible for a student without any economic resources to reach the pinnacle of the educational system — a university in the metropole — on the basis of ability.

Even though the Bishop of Barbados, who served as the Chairman of the Mitchinson Commission of 1875, was mistrustful of the intellectual ability of non-whites, his Commission recommended that the best primary school students on the island should have an opportunity to move up the occupational and social ladder through education. The Commission suggested that if a few lower class individuals were allowed to secure a higher level of education, it would have a stabilizing effect on the society, partly because many parents would remain satisfied to direct their energies toward helping their children to achieve this goal.

However, the total number of secondary school scholarships was extremely small, and most of them were won by children of the elites. Only rarely did black or coloured boys from poor homes win one of these awards. This resulted in some parents becoming more anxious to see an improvement in the quality of primary education in order to increase their children's chances of winning one of the government scholarships to a local secondary grammar school.

In addition, entrance to the civil service increasingly became more open to individuals on the basis of their education and less dependent on patronage. Some colonies even introduced a special competitive examination for entry into the lower ranks of the public service, as Jamaica did in 1885 and Trinidad, a few years later. In other colonies individuals had to pass one of the Cambridge University Examinations in order to qualify for a civil service position. This changing basis of recruitment, from ascription to achievement, opened up a few of the better paying government jobs to blacks and coloureds and helped to confirm the belief that West Indian societies were becoming meritocratic. These minor adjustments in the educational system therefore gave some credence to the myth about the increasing openness of these societies. They provided the masses with some hope that through their children's academic success they might be able to improve their own social and economic position.

The ruling groups therefore gave considerable publicity to these limited opportunities for a boy of a humble origin to rise up the educational ladder and even attend a prestigious British university. For example, even though on average less than three scholarships per year were awarded to primary school students to attend Queen's Royal College in Trinidad between 1871 and 1876, the inspector of schools suggested that the educational advantages open to industrious boys from poor families on the island could "hardly be surpassed." These measures functioned to defuse somewhat the resentment that was building among the black population toward the privileges that were enjoyed by the whites in West Indian societies.

The award of these open scholarships to local secondary schools and universities overseas also marked a formal increase in the efforts by the colonial rulers to create a comprador elite group who, in return for their own chances of upward social mobility, were expected to internalize and even espouse the view of the total superiority of the British, and especially the English culture, and to give full support to the ruling groups when appointed to positions of administrative responsibility. For example, in Barbados, it was observed that when "coloured inhabitants" were "entrusted with authority the zeal they have manifested in support of the laws, and for the preservation of peace and order, have been highly creditable to them."[31] This was also observed in the other British West Indian colonies. These comprador elites, like their Indian counterparts described by Macaulay, became "English in tastes, in opinions in morals and intellect." This was expected to provide additional evidence of the pre-eminence of the technical skills and knowledge and the superiority of the culture of the colonizer, thus adding to the legitimacy of his claims to rule.

But, with the growing appearance of openness in these societies, those who were already positioned on the higher rungs of the social ladder began to express concern about their relative place in the social hierarchy, which they viewed as being threatened by the increasing upward mobility, through education, of the children of the lower classes. They tried to maintain a comfortable social distance between themselves and the masses, using a number of mechanisms to help achieve this goal. For example, in British Guiana, some plantation owners discontinued the practice of hiring young coloured overseers, an occupation which defined the estate hierarchy as the "unquestioned preserve" of "expatriate appointees, and creole whites." A somewhat similar policy was in existence in the civil service where blacks and coloureds were not usually employed in positions above a certain grade and, up to the end of the century, "the Governor [of British Guiana] still operated on the presumption that educated blacks could make good rural postmasters but nothing more."[32] For example, in 1890 he refused to appoint Dr. Rohlehr as a medical officer because he was black and only relented in response to public pressure.

In Trinidad, when blacks began to be appointed to some of the senior civil service positions on the basis of their examination results, this method of recruitment began to be seen as a dangerous experiment and was suspended. As Campbell noted, the whites, who traditionally monopolized the senior civil service posts, strongly preferred the governor to have total discretion in making appointments. They felt that he was likely to select white in preference to black candidates and they did not want his decisions to be affected by the fact that the black candidates, might have been academically better qualified for these jobs.[33] The principal of QRC even suggested that the number of free places to the secondary schools should be reduced from the eight which were then available to two. The sharp racial demarcation in the membership of the local social clubs was also often invariably maintained.

Another mechanism which the whites used to help keep their social distance from the blacks was to provide, or get the government to help provide, better educational opportunities for their own children. Many influential individuals began to support the idea that the local legislatures should give financial aid to this type of education, and the inspector of schools for Trinidad even suggested that, unless children of these higher social classes, particularly the whites, were provided with a somewhat superior education to the classes below them, then their position in the social hierarchy might be adversely affected, with the "toe of the peasant" increasingly coming "so near the heel of the courtier as to gall his kibe."

These whites, therefore, exerted pressures on the ruling authorities to provide a level and type of education for their children which was of a quality superior to the education available to the masses. It was for this reason that the local legislatures began to take a more active role in helping to establish fee-paying classical grammar schools throughout the region. This represented a change in their position on this issue. Up to the 1850s, the members of the House of Assembly objected to the proposal that state funds should be spent on secondary education for the children of the middle class. But, by the 1870s, largely in response to the changing relationships between the white middle class and the upwardly mobile non-whites in these societies, the legislators had reversed their view on this issue. As a result, a number of private or Church schools offering a classical education were established, usually with the financial assistance of the government, though some colonies even opened their own grammar schools.

Initially, attempts were made to ignore the rights of the blacks to this higher level of education. For example, when Queen's Collegiate School (QCS) was to be established in Trinidad, Governor Keate promised to make one or more free places available to the children attending primary schools. This was to be in accordance with Lord Harris's original proposal that such education should be open to the brightest students in the colony, irrespective of their background. However, for a long time Keate did nothing about this issue. Similarly, when the board of education passed a resolution in 1858 to admit a few free pupils from the Boys' Model School to QCS, no action was taken on the matter because it was considered likely to interfere with the policy of maintaining the social exclusiveness of the school. Even when the fees were eventually lowered by 37.5%, following Keenan's criticism that they were too high for parents with moderate incomes, the new level of fees was still beyond the resources of parents from the labouring classes. Those who were most likely to benefit from the reduced fees were, as the governor himself admitted, the sons of members of the civil service, the learned professions, merchants and managers of estates, not the children of black labourers. This policy of restricting the numbers admitted to the grammar schools, often through the introduction of relatively high school fees, therefore remained fairly firm. But over time, some members of the emerging coloured and black middle class began to accumulate wealth and were able to pay for their children to attend these schools, thereby intruding into the domains which were formerly exclusive to the white oligarchies in these colonies.[34]

Another attempt to limit quite severely the access of non-whites to the more prestigious grammar schools was seen in the fact that most scholarships provided for primary school students to attend these schools usually required the family to meet part of the costs involved. This meant that the poorest parents were often unable to take advantage of these awards. Entry to the grammar schools was also denied to illegitimate children because it was realized that such a step would effectively exclude most black children, as possibly over 75% of them were illegitimate.

Despite the apparent mobility which some blacks and coloureds experienced as a result of their education, the system of social stratification of these societies remained fairly rigid, partly because the non-whites who moved up the social ladder were not particularly interested in bringing about any radical changes in the existing reward structures. For example, those who were newly enfranchised initially often voted for white rather than black or coloured representatives.

William Conrad Reeves, a mulatto from Barbados, was a case in point. Having earlier been denied admission to Harrison College, Reeves nevertheless rose to the distinguished position of attorney-general and later chief justice of the island. Yet he showed little interest in helping other non-whites overcome some of the barriers which impeded their chances of upward mobility. In fact, he was said to have "kicked down the ladder" by which he had ascended, a pattern of behaviour which was not uncommon among coloureds and blacks who considered themselves to have arrived. The social distance he kept from the coloured and black population was probably one reason why the Colonial Office felt it safe to appoint him to these prestigious positions and recommend him for a knighthood.

The few individuals who had succeeded in breaking through the educational and occupational barriers were used as evidence that non-whites were increasingly able to secure higher status jobs in these societies, based on ability and performance. In addition, aspiring coloureds and blacks used individuals such as Reeves as role models, often following their patterns of behaviour if they were successful in securing higher status positions.

These strategies, which helped to pacify the white middle-class parents and satisfy the aspiring coloureds and blacks, sometimes made it more difficult for others on the lowest rung of the socio-economic ladder to

318 Education as and for Legitimacy

challenge the existing social structure. Many parents directed their efforts at encouraging their children to take advantage of the limited educational opportunities available rather than attempt to challenge the highly inequitable system. This was particularly obvious among the emerging coloured and black middle class.

But the opportunities for social mobility through education were available only to a limited number of non-whites and left the great majority of blacks, who constituted the poorest sections of these societies, with virtually no real possibility for social and economic advancement. In addition, they were denied any political power through which they might have brought about some change in the existing social order. Therefore, with the general decline in the economy, they experienced a deterioration of their standard of living through low wages and high rates of unemployment.

So while education did provide limited opportunities for upward social mobility among some blacks it was still essentially an instrument for reproducing the existing social order. The tension between these two functions of social reproduction and social change continued to be present in these societies, with the former being ascendant over the latter throughout the period under review. It seemed that, while the whites were willing to tolerate the few educated coloureds and blacks who were rising up the social ladder, they were quite adamant about preventing an invasion from the upwardly aspiring lower class blacks.

This resulted in the relationships between the blacks and the ruling whites becoming even more strained. Commenting on this situation in Jamaica around the 1860s, the missionary Underhill observed a growing "antagonism of interests" between the two groups which was characterized "by hauteur, by peremptoriness, by indifference and not seldom by contempt" on the part of the whites. As a result the "distrust of the fairness and impartiality of the whites" by the blacks was "almost universally present."[35] Another outcome was "a gradual shifting away of the black population from the European clergy and ministers to the Ministry of men of their own colour."[36] This contributed to the popularity of such religious groups as the Baptists in Jamaica and the rise of other non-traditional religious sects in the West Indies.

The frustrations which these marginalized groups experienced also erupted in a number of social disturbances throughout the period. These included the Angel Gabriel Riots in 1857, the Toll Bar Riots in 1859, the Morant Bay Riots in 1865, the 1876 disturbances in Barbados in which 40 people were killed, and the Muharram massacre in Trinidad in 1884. While each of these had its own proximate causes, they were all indications of something "rotten in the state of Denmark."

Under these circumstances, it was no wonder that many planters remained unconvinced by the argument that an increased amount of education among the masses would reduce the possibility of social disturbances in these societies. As Green suggested, while "Christian education had been advanced as a means of achieving individual enlightenment as well as social control," by the 1860s there was every reason to suspect that it "had failed on both counts."[37] As a result, the planters did not shift their faith in the importance of the repressive state apparatus in maintaining social order to a belief that education could become an effective alternative instrument of social control, as was sometimes being suggested. This fact was partly reflected in government budgetary allocations for education, as compared to that for the repressive state apparatus in a number of these colonies. The following graphs, comparing expenditures on education and the RSA in Jamaica, Montserrat, St. Vincent, St. Lucia and Trinidad, bear out this point. From these graphs (Figures 21 A-E) it is clear that, while there was a tendency for educational expenditures to rise, there was no marked reduction in the funds allocated to the repressive state apparatus during this period. This was typical of the expenditure pattern of nearly all the West Indian colonies.

Summary

In review, the opportunities for higher education being made available to a few black children helped to inculcate in them the belief that social and occupational advancement in these societies was becoming less dependent on such ascriptive features as skin colour and more on merit. The ultimate hope of the ruling class was that this would contribute to a reduction of any popular discontent with, and resentment toward, the existing economic and social reward structures of these societies. It was also expected that the few educational changes that were being made would inculcate in the masses a greater acceptance of, and a more positive attitude toward, their societies with their fairly rigid hierarchical systems of social and economic differentiation. This was partly why the local legislatures, under the control of the planters, became steadily more involved in financing primary and later, even secondary, education. While the latter was originally meant only for the local whites, it slowly became available to the children of the coloured and black population.

The ruling groups recognized that it would be more effective and economical in the long run to foster the development of a degree of voluntaristic support among the masses for the colonial governments, and education became one of the means by which such support was to be achieved. Through it, the young were to be properly socialized to accept the legitimacy of the state and of those who, by virtue of their economic and political power, effectively controlled it or at least had a dominant influence over its decision-making machinery.

The process of socialization through formal education was seen as important in helping to create social stability by reducing discontent among the population. Therefore, despite the many problems which these colonies faced in financing education, due to the decline of the sugar industry and the termination of the Negro Education Grant, the ruling authorities made considerable efforts to provide greater access to education for the masses, especially after the 1870s.

But the planters still attached much importance to the repressive apparatus of the state in ultimately preventing disturbances which might threaten their position of dominance in these societies. Therefore, they did not reduce to any extent their expenditure on the state mechanisms of physical control. This, no doubt, was partly why Nicole claimed that political progress in the region was never the result of a gift from the white elites to the black masses, but was usually achieved through violence.

The deteriorating economic and social conditions in these colonies eventually led to the appointment of the West Indian Royal Commission in 1897 to investigate and put forward recommendations for the economic rehabilitation of the region. The moribund state of these economies, rather than such features as the gross inequalities in the distribution of power and other resources, continued to be seen by most members of the ruling elite as the root cause of the problems which these societies faced.

But the crux of the issue stemmed largely from the virtual impossibility of developing among the general population, by a process of education or indoctrination, an acceptance of the legitimacy of a highly unequal social order, especially in a situation in which adversity among the masses was increasing. Commenting on social change in situations of marked social inequality, Moore pointed out that it appears impossible that

> any mode of rewarding positions unequally and any mode of determining access to those positions would be so firmly institutionalized that those persons most injured would accept the justice of their fate. . . .The rules governing assignments to positions and their unequal rewards and the values that "justify" these rules will not be accepted as totally valid by those who are thereby excluded.[38]

This, in essence, summarizes the dilemma which faced Caribbean societies during this period under review, despite the steps that were often taken to increase and improve educational opportunities for the masses.

FIGURE 21 (A)
Comparing Expenditures on RSAs and on Education for Montserrat, 1867-79

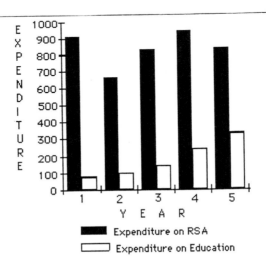

KEY: 1= 1867; 2 = 1870; 3 = 1873; 4 = 1876; 5 = 1879;
Source: *Annual Reports of Montserrat.*

FIGURE 21 (B)
Comparing Expenditures on RSAs and on Education for St. Vincent, 1867-81

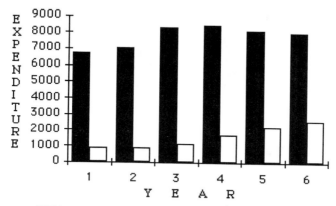

KEY: 1= 1867; 2= 1870; 3 = 1873; 4 = 1876; 5 = 1879; 6 = 1881.
Source: *Annual Reports of St. Vincent.*

FIGURE 21 (C)
Comparing Expenditures on RSAs and on Education for St. Lucia, 1867-81

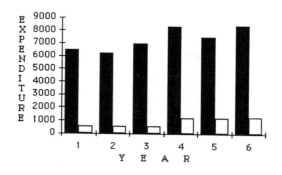

■ Expenditure on RSA

□ Expenditure on Education

KEY: 1= 1867; 2 = 1870; 3 = 1873 4 = 1876; 5 = 1879; 6 = 1881.
Source: *Annual Reports of St. Lucia.*

FIGURE 21 (D)
Comparing Expenditures on RSAs and on Education for Trinidad, 1885-95

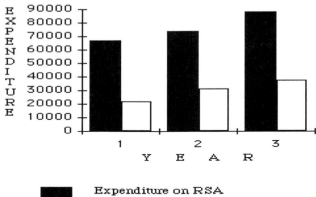

KEY: 1 = 1885; 2 = 1890; 3 = 1895 (Year 3 includes Trinidad and Tobago).
Source: *Annual Reports of Trinidad.*

FIGURE 21 (E)
Comparing Expenditures on RSAs and on Education for Jamaica, 1858-86

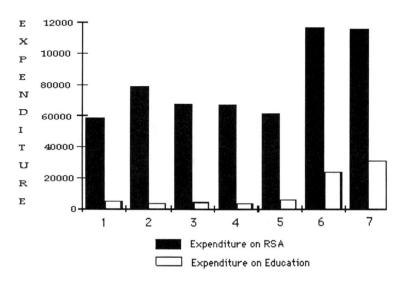

KEY: 1= 1858; 2= 1865-66; 3 = 1866-67; 4= 1867-68;
5= 1868-69; 6 = 1881; 7 = 1885-86.
Source: *Annual Reports of Jamaica.*

Notes

1   O. Mannoni, *Prospero and Caliban: The Psychology of Colonization* (New York: Frederick A. Praeger, 1956).

2   British Guiana, *The Colonist*, 16 June 1851.

3   Report of the Government of Tobago, *British Parliamentary Papers*, Vol. 36: *1850* (London, Government of Great Britain), 22.

4   *Falmouth Post*, 4 January 1850.

5   *Lieutenant Governor of Dominica to Secretary of State*, 26 December 1867. Cited in Gordon, *A Century*, 55.

6   British Guiana, *The Colonist*, 16 June 1851.

7   *Lieutenant Governor of Trinidad to Secretary of State*, 13 October 1842. Cited in Gordon, *A Century*, 47.

8   Volker Bornischier, "Legitimacy and Comparative Economic Success at the Core of the World System," *European Sociological Review* 5, 3 (December 1989): 215-30.

9   Seymour Martin Lipset, *The First New Nation* (London: Heinemann, 1963), 45.

10   M. Carnoy, and H. Levin, *Schooling and Work in the Democratic State*. (Stanford: Stanford University Press, 1985).

11   See Jean Suret-Canale (*French Colonialism in Tropical Africa* [New York: Pica Press, 1971], 380-81) for statement by Albert Sarraut, French Minister for the Colonies.

12   Thomas B. Macaulay, "Minute on Education." See E. H. Cutts, The Background of Macaulay's Minute," *American Historical Review* 58 (July 1953), 839.

13   Homi K. Bhabba, "Signs Taken for Wonders: Questions of Ambivalency and Authority under a Tree Outside Delhi, May 1817." In *"Race," Writing and Difference*, edited by Henry Louis Gates, Jr. 172 (Chicago: University of Chicago Press, 1985).

14   Report of the Government of British Guiana, *British Parliamentary Papers*, Vol. 42: *1872* (London: Government of Great Britain), 46.

15   Peter Worsley, The *Third World* (London: Weidenfeld and Nicholson, 1964), 29.

16   Burke, "History of the Wesleyan Methodist Contribution," 146.

17   B. Hamilton, *Barbados and the Confederation Question, 1871-1885* (London: Crown Agents for Overseas Governments and Administrations on Behalf of the Government of Barbados, 1956), 3-4.

18   Homi K. Bhabba, "Signs taken for Wonders," 164-72.

19   Ibid., 178.

20   Report of the Government of St. Kitts in *British Parliamentary Papers*, Vol. 42: *1872* (London: Government of Great Britain), 145.

21   Report of the Government of Antigua in *British Parliamentary Papers*, Vol. 37: *1847* (London: Government of Great Britain), 48.

22   *Mitchinson Report*, 6.

23   Mary Olwyn Blouet, "Education and Emancipation in Barbados, 1833-1846," *Ethnic and Racial Studies* 4, 2 (1981).

24   Government of Trinidad, *Report of the Legislative Council of Trinidad*, 2 Sept. 1857 (Port-of-Spain, Trinidad).

25   Gordon Lewis, *The Growth of the Modern West Indies* (New York: Monthly Review Press, 1968), 28

26   Suret-Canal, *French Colonialism* , 371.

27   Gordon, *A Century*, 43.

28   *Barbados Times*, 16 February 1870.

29   Gordon, *A Century*, 230.

30   Brereton, *Race Relations*, 85.

31   Report of the Government of Barbados, *British Parliamentary Papers*, Vol. 36: *1850* (London: Government of Great Britain), 10.

32   Rodney, *History of the Guyanese Working People*, 117.

33   Campbell, *The Young Colonials* .

34   D.A.G. Waddell, *The West Indies and the Guianas* (New Jersey: Prentice-Hall,1967), 99.

35   Edward Bean Underhill, *The West Indies* (London: Jackson, Walford and Hodder, 1862), 192.

36   Ibid.

37   Green, *British Slave Emancipation*, 350.

38   Wilbert E. Moore, *Social Change* (Englewood Cliffs, New Jersey: Prentice-Hall, 1963), 83.

Books and Periodicals

Adamson, Alan H. *Sugar Without Slaves*. New Haven: Yale University Press, 1972.

Ayearst, Morley. *The British West Indies*. London, Ruskin House: George Allen and Unwin, Ltd.,1960.

Bacchus, M. Kazim. *Education for Development or Underdevelopment*. Waterloo, Ontario, Canada: Wilfrid Laurier University Press, 1980.

————. *The Utilization, Misuse and Development of Human Resources in the Early West Indian Colonies*. Waterloo, Ontario, Canada: Wilfrid Laurier University Press, 1990.

Bailey, George D. *A Précis of the History of Elementary Education in British Guiana*. Georgetown, British Guiana: Argosy Co. Printers, 1907.

Beckford, George L. *Persistent Poverty*. New York: Oxford University Press, 1972.

Bhabba, Homi K. "Signs Taken for Wonders: Questions of Ambivalency and Authority under a Tree Outside Delhi, May 1817." In *"Race," Writing and Difference*. Edited by Henry Louis Gates, Jr. Chicago: University of Chicago Press, 1985.

Bhagan, C. "A Critical Study of the Development of Education in Trinidad." M.A. thesis, Univ. of London, 1964.

Blouet, Mary Olwyn. "Education and Emancipation in Barbados, 1833-1846." *Ethnic and Racial Studies* 4, 2 (April 1981).

Bornischier, Volker. "Legitimacy and Comparative Economic Success at the Core of the World System." *European Sociological Review* 5, 3 (Dec. 1989).

Braithwaite, Lloyd. "The Development of Higher Education in the British West Indies." *Social and Economic Studiesn* 7, 1 (March 1958).

Brereton, B. *Race Relations in Colonial Trinidad, 1870-1900*. Cambridge: Cambridge University Press, 1979.

Brizan, George. *Grenada, Island of Conflict, From Amerindians to People's Revolution 1498-1979*. London: Zed Books Ltd., 1984.

Burke, Mavis. "The History of the Wesleyan-Methodist Contribution to Education in Jamaica in the Nineteenth Century, 1833-1900." M.A. thesis, Univ. of London, 1965.

Burn, W. L. *The British West Indies*. London: Hutchinson's University Press, 1951.

Cameron, N. E. *150 Years of Education in Guyana*. Georgetown, Guyana, 1968.

————. *A History of the Queen's College of British Guiana*. Georgetown, Guyana: A. Persick Ltd. Publishers, 1951.

————. *The Evolution of the Negro*. Georgetown, British Guiana: Argosy Co., 1934.

Campbell, Carl. "The Development of Education in Trinidad 1834-1870." Ph.D. diss., Univ. of the West Indies, Mona, Kingston, Jamaica, 1973.

————. "The Development of Primary Education in Jamaica, 1835-1865." M.A. thesis, Univ. of London, 1963.

————. *The Young Colonials: A Social History of Education in Trinidad and Tobago, 1834-1939.* In press.

Carmichael, Mrs. *Domestic Manners and Social Conditions of the Whites, Coloured, and Negro Population in the West Indies.* London: Whittaker and Co., 1833.

Carnoy, M., and H. Levin. *Schooling and Work in the Democratic State.* California: Stanford University Press, 1985.

Clementi, Sir Cecil. *A Constitutional History of British Guiana.* London: Macmillan and Co. Ltd., 1937.

Comins, D. W. *Note on Emigration to Trinidad.* Trinidad, 1893.

Cork, Josiah. *Six Essays on the Best Mode of Establishing and Conducting Industrial Schools.* London: 1845.

Craton, M. *A History of the Bahamas.* London: Collins, 1968.

Cundall, Frank. *Some Notes on The History of Secondary Education in Jamaica.* Kingston: n.d.

Curtin, Philip D. *Two Jamaicas: The Role of Ideas in a Tropical Colony, 1830-1865.* New York: Atheneum, 1975.

Daly, Vera, T. *A Short History of the Guyanese People.* Georgetown, Guyana: The Daily Chronicle Ltd., 1966.

Davy, J. *The West Indies Before and Since Slave Emancipation.* London: W. & F. G. Cash, 1854.

De Verteuill, A. A. *Trinidad, Its Geography, Natural Resources, Administration, Present Conditions and Prospects.* London: Ward and Lock, 1850.

Dookhan, I. *A Post-Emancipation History of the West Indies.* Great Britain: Collins, 1985.

Furlonge, Errol A. "The Development of Secondary Education in Trinidad and Tobago." Ph.D. diss., Univ. of Sheffield, 1968.

Goodridge, R. V. *The Development of Education in Barbados , 1818-1866.* M.Ed. thesis, Univ. of Leeds, 1966.

Gordon, Shirley. *A Century of West Indian Education: A Source Book.* London: Longmans, Green and Co., 1963.

Government of Antigua. *Historical Notes on Education in Antigua, 1834-1984.* Antigua: Antigua Printing and Publishing Company Ltd., 1985.

Green, William A. *British Slave Emancipation: The Sugar Colonies and the Great Experiment, 1830 – 65.* Oxford: Clarendon Press, 1976.

Grey, Earl. *The Colonial Policy of Lord Russell's Administration, vol. 1* [of 2 volumes]. London: Richard Bentley, 1853.

Hall, Douglas. *Free Jamaica, 1838-1865.* [Reprinted in] Kingston, Jamaica: Caribbean Universities Press, 1959.

Hamilton, B. *Barbados and the Confederation Question, 1871-1885.* London: Crown Agents for Overseas Governments and Administrations on behalf of the Government of Barbados, 1956.

Hamshere, Cyril, *The British in the Caribbean.* London: Weidenfeld and Nicholson, 1972.

Hans, Nicholas. "The Anglican Tradition in Education." *Yearbook of Education, 1938.* London: Evans Bros.Ltd., 1938.

Harvey, Thomas, and William Brewin. *Jamaica in 1866.* London: A.W. Bennett.

Henriques, F. M. *Family and Colour in Jamaica.* London: Eyre and Spottiswoode, 1953.

Huitt, Homer Carroll. "The British West Indies in Eclipse 1838-1902." Ph.D. diss., Univ. of Missouri, 1937.

Johnston, F. A. J. "Education in Jamaica and Trinidad in the Generation After Emancipation." Ph.D. diss., Univ. of Oxford, 1971.

King, Ruby. "The History of the Jamaica Schools Commission and its Role in Education in Jamaica, 1879-1911." M.A. thesis, Univ. of the West Indies, 1972.

Laurence, K. O. *Immigration into the West Indies in the Nineteenth Century.* Kingston, Jamaica: Caribbean Universities Press, 1976.

Lewis, Gordon. *The Growth of the Modern West Indies.* New York: Monthly Review Press, 1968.

Lipset, Seymour Martin. *The First New Nation.* London: Heinemann Educational Books Ltd., 1963.

Mannoni, O. *Prospero and Caliban: The Psychology of Colonization.* New York: Frederick A. Praeger. Inc., 1956.

Marable, Manning. *African and Caribbean Politics.* Norfolk, U.K.: Verso Publishers, 1987.

Maxwell, James. *Remarks on the Present State of Jamaica.* London: Smith Elder and Co., 1848.

McBean-Hartley, Dorothy. "The Jamaican Educational System and the Maintenance of Existing Class Boundaries." Ph.D. diss., State Univ. of New York at Buffalo, 1964.

Monteith, Kathleen. "The Victoria Jubilee Celebrations of 1887 in Jamaica." *Jamaica Journal* 20, 4 (Nov. 1987–Jan. 1988). Kingston: Institute of Jamaica.

Moore, Wilbert, E. *Social Change.* Englewood Cliffs, New Jersey: Prentice-Hall Inc., 1963.

Moxly, Reverend J. H. Sutton. *An Account of a West Indian Sanatorium and a Guide to Barbados.* London: Sampson Low, Marston, Searle and Rivington, 1886.

Murray, Reginald N. "The Education of Jamaica - Its Historical Background and Possible Future Developments." M.A. thesis, Univ. of London, 1947.

Nicholls, C. "The Development of Classical Education in Barbados and Trinidad." Ph.D. diss., Univ. of Exeter, 1965.

Nicole, C. *The West Indies: Their People and History.* London: Hutchinson & Co. Ltd., 1965.

Quarterly Publications of the American Statistical Association 4, New Series 30 (Jan. 1895). Boston: American Statistical Association, 1895.

Read, Margaret. "Educational Problems in Non-Autonomous Territories." In Principles and Methods of Colonial Administration. Edited by C.M. MacInnes. London, 1950.

Rodney, Walter. *A History of the Guyanese Working People, 1881-1905.* London: Heinemann Educational Books, Ltd., 1981.

Root, J. W. *The British West Indies and The Sugar Industry.* Liverpool: J. W. Root, 1899.

Ryall, Dorothy Ann. "The Organization of Missionary Societies and the Recruitment of Missionaries in Britain and the Role of the Missionaries in the Diffusion of British Culture in Jamaica, During the Period 1834-1865." Ph.D. diss., Univ. of London, 1959.

Schomburgk, Sir Robert. *The History of Barbados.* London: Longman, 1848.

Sewell, Wm. G. *The Ordeal of Free Labour in the West Indies.* New York: Harper and Bros., Publishers, 1861.

Sheperd, Verene. *The Education of East Indian Children in Jamaica, 1879-1949.* Library of the University of the West Indies: Mona Jamaica, 1983.

Smith, M. G. *The Plural Society in the British West Indies.* Berkeley and Los Angeles: University of California Press, 1959.

Stark, J. H. *Stark's History and Guide to Barbados and the Caribee Islands.* Boston, Massachusetts, 1893.

Suret-Canale, Jean. *French Colonialism in Tropical Africa.* New York: Pica Press, 1971.

The Queen's College Gazette 4. New Series. 13 March 1884.

Thomas, C. Y. *The Rise of the Authoritarian State in Peripheral Societies.* New York: Monthly Review Press, Heinemann, 1984.

Thome, J. A., and J. H. Kimball. *Emancipation in the West Indies.* New York: n.p., 1838.

Thorne, A. A. "Education in British Guiana." *Timehri*, 18, 1.

Trollope, Anthony. *The West Indies and the Spanish Main.* London: Frank Cass and Co., 1859.

Underhill, Edward Bean. *The West Indies.* London: Jackson, Walford and Hodder, 1862.

Waddell, D. A. G. *The West Indies and the Guianas.* New Jersey: Prentice-Hall, Inc., 1967.

Will, H. A. *Constitutional Change in the British West Indies 1880-1903.* Oxford: Clarendon Press, 1970.

Williams, A. G. "The Development of Education in Barbados With Special Reference to the Social and Economic Conditions, 1834-1958." M.A. thesis, Univ. of London, 1964.

Williams, Eric. *From Columbus to Castro, The History of the Caribbean, 1492-1969.* London: Andre Deutsch, 1970.

————. *History of the People of Trinidad & Tobago.* London: Andre Deutsch, 1964.

Wood, Donald. *Trinidad in Transition: The Year after Slavery.* London: Oxford University Press, 1986.

Worsley, Peter. *The Third World.* London: Weidenfeld and Nicholson, 1964.

Reports from Missionary Societies and Other Organizations

Annual Report of the Congregational Union. Georgetown, British Guiana, 1895.

Bishop of Roseau. *Address at the Prize Giving 24 Dec. 1842.*

Cox, James. *Letter of 1 June 1848.*

Dyett, Isidore L. to the President of Nevis, 14 May 1857.

Gregory, Robert. *Report of the Scottish Missionary Society, 1846.*

McLean, D. *Letter to Edinburgh University's Student Missionary Society.* U. P. Miss. R., 1860.

Memorial of the Clergy and Laity of the Church of England, 1851.

Memorial of the Presbytery of Demerara and Essequibo, 1851.

Minutes of the York Castle High School Management Committee, 1898-1900.

Murray, W. C. *Governor of York Castle High School to the Methodist Missionary Society,* 14 June 1884.

Parry, Bishop. *Letter to S. P. G.,* 14 April 1852.

Prideaux, Reverend W. *Letter to Education Committee,* 16 Feb. 1873.

Rawle, R. *Printed Papers.*

Report of the Wesleyan Methodist Missionary, 1870.

Rostant, Philip. *Speech at the St. Marys Past Students' Union Dinner,* January 1887.

Sargeant to Punshon, 9 June 1877.

Stanley, Earl. *Letter of 26 January 1847*. Collection of the Colonial
    Department, Vol. 3, 1841-47.
Sutton, Stephen. *Report to Methodist Missionary Society*, 6 June 1879.
Thomas, Hon. G. E. Address as President of the Agricultural Society of
    Barbados,1856.

Newspapers

Barbadian. 21 July 1849.
Barbados Times. 16 Feb. 1870.
Falmouth Post. 4 Jan. 1850.
Chronicle, 12 March 1874.
Guyana [London]. Latin America Bureau. 1984.
Kingston Chronicle and City Advertizer [Jamaica]. 3 Nov. 1835.
Morning Journal. 13 Dec. 1864.
Palladium [Trinidad]. 13 July 1878.
Port of Spain Gazette [Trinidad]. 2 Feb. 1847.
Port-of-Spain Gazette [Trinidad]. 1850.
Port of Spain Gazette, 5 December, 1885.
Royal Gazette [Trinidad]. 8 Oct. 1851.
The Agricultural Reporter [Barbados]. 15 Sept. 1891.
The Agricultural Reporter. Letter to the Editor. 28 March 1873.
The Argosy. 4 Dec. 1880.
The Barbadian. 6 May 1856.
The Colonial Standard. 9 June 1887.
The Colonist [British Guiana]. 16 June 1851.
The Colonist. 6 July 1881.
The Daily Chronicle [British Guiana]. 7 March 1870.
The Liberal. 18 April 1846.
The Queen's College Gazette, Vol. 4, New Series, 13 March 1884.
The Star of the West [Trinidad]. 30 July 1874.
The Times [London]. 17 Jan. 1848.
Trinidad Press. 4 June 1858.
Trinidad Spectator. 10 Dec. 1895.
West Indian. 6 Sept. 1878.

Government Reports and Despatches

Reports on Schools by Inspectors of Schools, etc.

*Report of the Cambridge Syndicate Examinations on Queen's Royal College
    and the College of Immaculate Conception*. Port-of-Spain, Trinidad:
    1872.
Report of the Central Agricultural Board,Trinidad 1889.
*Report of the Commission on Education in Barbados (The Mitchinson
    Report), 1875-76*. Bridgetown, Barbados: Barclay and Fraser, Printers to
    the Legislature, 1876.
*Report of the Inspector of Schools and Principal of St. Kitts Grammar
    School, 1871*. St. Kitts.
Report of the Inspector of Schools for Antigua for 1875. St. Johns, Antigua.
Report of the Inspector of Schools for Barbados for 1867. Bridgetown,
    Barbados.

Report of the Inspector of Schools for British Guiana for 1847. 20 October 1848. Georgetown, British Guiana.

Report of the Inspector of Schools for British Guiana for 1893-94. Georgetown, British Guiana.

Report of the Inspector of Schools for British Guiana for the Year 1896–97, no. 997. Georgetown, British Guiana: 1897.

Report of the Inspector of Schools for Dominica for 1887. Dominica.

Report of the Inspector of Schools for Grenada for 1855. 22 April 1856. St. George's, Grenada.

Report of the Inspector of Schools for Jamaica, 14 December 1863.

Report of the Inspector of Schools for Jamaica for 1881. Kingston, Jamaica: 1882.

Report of the Inspector of Schools for the Bahamas, 1856. Nassau, Bahamas.

Report of the Inspector of Schools for the Bahamas, 1871. Nassau, Bahamas.

Report of the Inspector of Schools for Trinidad, 1861 Port-of-Spain, Trinidad.

Report of the Inspector of Schools for Trinidad for 1868. 2 February 1869. Port of Spain, Trinidad.

Report of the Inspector of Schools for Trinidad for 1872. Port-of-Spain, Trinidad.

Report of the Inspector of Schools for Trinidad for 1874. Port-of Spain, Trinidad.

Report of the Inspector of Schools for Trinidad for the Year 1852. Port-of-Spain, Trinidad.

Report of the Inspector of Schools for Trinidad for the Year 1854. Port-of-Spain, Trinidad.

Report of the Inspector of Schools for Trinidad for the Year 1860. 1 March 1861. Port-of-Spain, Trinidad.

Report of the Inspector of Schools for Trinidad for the Year 1861. 1 March 1862. Port-of Spain, Trinidad.

Report of the Inspector of Schools for Trinidad, 1862. Port-of Spain, Trinidad.

Report of the Inspector of Schools for Trinidad, 1864. Port-of-Spain, Trinidad.

Report of the Principal, Queen's College. 12 January 1880. Port-of-Spain, Trinidad.

Report of the Principal, Queen's College. 12 January 1880. Georgetown, British Guiana.

Report of the Principal, Queen's Collegiate School. 8 May 1865. Port-of-Spain, Trinidad.

Report of the Principal, Queen's Collegiate School. 30 July 1859. Georgetown, British Guiana.

Report of the Royal Commission appointed December 1882. *Memo from J. Fadelle, Provost Marshall, Dominica.* 10 April 1883. London.

Report on Queen's Collegiate School, by W. Campion, Cambridge University. 27 February 1863. Trinidad.

Report on the 1863 Examinations, by Deighton, Principal of Queen's Collegiate School. Trinidad: 1864.

Report of the Government of Antigua. *Historical Notes on Education in Antigua, 1834-1984* St. Johns, Antigua: Government of Antigua, 1984.

Report of the Government of Barbados. *British Parliamentary Papers,* Vol 36: *1850.* London : Government of Great Britain, 10.

The Board of Education. *Special Reports on Education Subjects.* Vol. 4, col. 416. London: HMSO, 1901.
Report Upon the State of Education in the Island of Trinidad by Patrick Joseph Keenan (*The Keenan Report*). *British Parliamentary Papers,* Vol. 50: *1870* London: Government of Great Britain.

British Parliamentary Reports

British Parliamentary Papers, Vol. 29: 1846. London: Government of Great Britain.
British Parliamentary Papers, Vol. 37: 1847. London: Government of Great Britain.
British Parliamentary Papers, Vol. 46: 1847-48. London: Government of Great Britain.
British Parliamentary Papers, Vol. 34: 1849. London: Government of Great Britain.
British Parliamentary Papers, Vol. 36: 1850. London: Government of Great Britain.
British Parliamentary Papers, Vol. 34: 1851. London: Government of Great Britain.
British Parliamentary Papers, Vol. 31:, 1852. London: Government of Great Britain.
British Parliamentary Papers, Vol. 62: 1852-53. London: Government of Great Britain.
British Parliamentary Papers, Vol. 42: 1856. London: Government of Great Britain.
British Parliamentary Papers, Vol. 10: 1857. London: Government of Great Britain.
British Parliamentary Papers, Vol. 40: 1857-58. London: Government of Great Britain.
British Parliamentary Papers, Vol. 21: 1859. London: Government of Great Britain.
British Parliamentary Papers, Vol. 44: 1860. London: Government of Great Britain.
British Parliamentary Papers, Vol. 40: 1861. London: Government of Great Britain.
British Parliamentary Papers, Vol. 36: 1862. London: Government of Great Britain.
British Parliamentary Papers, Vol. 39: 1863. London: Government of Great Britain.
British Parliamentary Papers, Vol. 40: 1864. London: Government of Great Britain.
British Parliamentary Papers, Vol. 37: 1865. London: Government of Great Britain.
British Parliamentary Papers, Vol. 49: 1866. London: Government of Great Britain.
British Parliamentary Papers, Vol. 48: 1867. London: Government of Great Britain.
British Parliamentary Papers, Vol. 48: 1867-68. London: Government of Great Britain.
British Parliamentary Papers, Vol. 49: 1870. London: Government of Great Britain.

British Parliamentary Papers, Vol. 47: 1871. London: Government of Great Britain.

British Parliamentary Papers, Vol. 42: 1872. London: Government of Great Britain.

British Parliamentary Papers, Vol. 48: 1873. London: Government of Great Britain.

British Parliamentary Papers, Vol. 44: 1874. London: Government of Great Britain.

British Parliamentary Papers, Vol. 51: 1875. London: Government of Great Britain.

British Parliamentary Papers, Vol. 51: 1876. London: Government of Great Britain.

British Parliamentary Papers, Vol. 59: 1877. London: Government of Great Britain.

British Parliamentary Papers, Vol. 55: 1878. London: Government of Great Britain.

British Parliamentary Papers, Vol. 50: 1878-79. London: Government of Great Britain.

British Parliamentary Papers, Vol. 48: 1880. London: Government of Great Britain.

British Parliamentary Papers, Vol. 44: 1881. London: Government of Great Britain.

British Parliamentary Papers, Vol. 44: 1882. London: Government of Great Britain.

British Parliamentary Papers, Vol. 45: 1883. London: Government of Great Britain.

British Parliamentary Papers, Vol. 54: 1884. London: Government of Great Britain.

British Parliamentary Papers, Vol. 54: 1889. London: Government of Great Britain.

British Parliamentary Papers, Vol. 52: 1884-85. London: Government of Great Britain.

British Parliamentary Papers, Vol. 57: 1887. London: Government of Great Britain.

British Parliamentary Papers, Vol. 72: 1888. London: Government of Great Britain.

British Parliamentary Papers, Vol. 55: 1892. London: Government of Great Britain.

British Parliamentary Papers, Vol. 60: 1893-94. London: Government of Great Britain.

British Parliamentary Papers, Vol. 59: 1893-94. London: Goverment of Great Britain.

British Parliamentary Papers, Vol. 69: 1895. London: Government of Great Britain.

Other Government Reports and Documents

Circular Despatch to West Indian Governors, October 1838. London: Colonial Office, Government of Great Britain.

Circular Letter from the Colonial Secretary to West Indian Governors. 10 Oct. 1845.

Governor Lord Elgin, *Confidential Despatch to the Secretary of State, 5 August 1845.*

Lord Elgin, Despatch with the Blue Book, 7 May 1845; Gordon 59.

CO 31/56. Circular Dispatch by Secretary of State to Governor Reid and other West Indian Governors, 29 Sept. 1847.

CO 31/56. Governor Reid's Address to the Legislature, 29 Dec. 1847.

CO 31/56. Papers of Earl Grey Presented to the Legislature, 25 Jan. 1848.

CO 111/259. *Report of The Inspector of Schools for British Guiana, The State of Public Schools in the Colony*, 20 Oct. 1848, [by John McSwiney]. London: PRO, 1848.

CO 111/406. Governor Longden to the Secretary of State, 27 Nov. 1875.

CO 111/410. Longden to Secretary of State for the Colonies, 1874.

CO 123/70. Honduras, 1845, Vol 2.

CO 137/323. Barclay to Newcastle, 26 May 1854, no. 75.

CO 137/353. The Third Annual Report of the K& A's Reformatory and Indust-rial Association for Girls, 19 Oct. 1857.

CO 137/390. Reverend J.Campbell to the Bishop of Jamaica April 1865.

CO 137/390. Reverend Magnan and W. M. Anderson to the Bishop of Jamaica, 1865.

CO 259/181. Enclosure in Papers and Reports on Secular Education 1853.

CO 295/134. McLeod to Secretary of State for the Colonies, 13 Oct. 1841.

CO 295/151. C. F. Stollemeyer in Enclosure from Harris to Secretary of State, 31 July 1846, no. 35.

CO 295/156. Speech by Lord Harris to the Legislative Council, Trinidad, 1 Feb. 1847.

CO 295/160. Harris to Grey, 21 Feb. 1848. London: PRO.

CO 295/181. Harris to Secretary of State, 20 June 1853, no. 76.

CO 295/193. Keate to Labouchère, 6 July 1857, no. 54. London: PRO.

CO 295/196. Governor Keate to Secretary of State, 6 Aug. 1857, no. 91.

CO 295/196. Keate to Labouchère, 6 Sept. 1857, no. 91. London: PRO.

CO 295/197. Letter by the Bishop of Barbados to Governor Keate, 8 Sept. 1857.

CO 295/208. Governor to Secretary of State, 30 March 1860, no. 43. PRO.

CO 295/232. Report of the Inspector of Schools for Trinidad 1860, Port-of Spain, Trinidad.

CO 295/232. *Report of the Principal, Queen's Collegiate School*, 8 May 1865, no. 137. London: PRO.

CO 295/397. Governor of Trinidad to Secretary of State, 25 May 1896, no.149.

CO 299/10. *Report of the Inspector of Schools for Trinidad, 1860*. Government of Trinidad.

CO 299/11. Government of Trinidad, *Report of the Inspector of Schools for the Year 1860*, 1 March 1861. Trinidad: the Royal Gazette.

CO 299/12. *Report of the Inspector of Schools for Trinidad for the Year 1861*, 1 March 1862. Port-of Spain, Trinidad.

CO-300/72 , Government of Trinidad, *Report of the Inspector of Schools for the Year 1862*. PRO.

CO 299/19. Government of Trinidad. *Report of the Inspector of Schools for Trinidad for the Year 1868*, Vol. 37, no. 16. Port-of-Spain, Trinidad, 2 February 1869; London: PRO.

CO 318/138. *The Kay Shuttleworth Report*, 1947.

Despatch from Earl Grey to Governor Reid, 27 Aug. 1847.

Despatch from Earl Grey. Collection of the Colonial Department 1841-47, 26 Jan. 1847, Vol. 3.

Despatch from Governor Harris to Earl Grey, 19 June 1848, no. 71. London: PRO.

Despatch from Governor Higginson to Earl Grey, 17 April 1847

Despatch from Governor Hincks to Rt. Hon. H. Labouchère, 22 May 22 1856.

Despatch from Governor Musgrave to Secretary of State, 1 March 1878.

Despatch from Lieutenant Governor Blackwell to Governor in Chief, Leeward Islands, 12 April 1856.

Despatch from Lieutenant Governor of Dominica to Secretary of State, 26 Dec. 1867.

Despatch from Lieutenant Governor of Trinidad to Secretary of State, 13 Oct. 1842.

Despatch from R.G. Rice to the Colonial Secretary, 16 July 1855.

Despatch to West Indian Governors from Colonial Office Oct. l838.

Government of Barbados. *Blue Book for 1865*. Bridgetown, Barbados.

Government of Barbados. Response of Legislature to Opening Address by the Governor on the 1851 Education Act, 27 May 1851.

Government of Great Britain. *West Indian Royal Commission on Public Expenditure Report*, 1885. London: HMSO.

Government of Jamaica. *1883 Report on the Blue Book*. Kingston, Jamaica.

Government of Jamaica. *Government Regulations With Regard to Grants in Aid of Elementary Schools*. Spanish Town, Jamaica: Government Printer, 1867.

Government of Jamaica. *Minutes of the Jamaica Schools Commission*, 1889.

Government of Trinidad. *Report of the Legislative Council of Trinidad*, 2 Sept. 1857. Port-of-Spain.